RESTAURANTS AND CLOUDBREAK, MAMANUCAS, FIJI

BERNARD TESTEMALE

THE **STORMRIDER** SURF GUIDE
TROPICAL ISLANDS

LOW PRESSURE

THE **STORMRIDER** SURF GUIDE **TROPICAL ISLANDS**

First published in 2013 by LOW PRESSURE LTD©
Tel/Fax +33 (0)5 58 77 76 85   enquiries@lowpressure.co.uk

Worldwide Surfspots 2.0 database, YEP©
Compilation of all weather and swell data using Visual
Passage Planner software, creation of all zone maps
YEP/Low Pressure Ltd 2013©

Creation of all other maps, graphic arrangement,
pictograms, text and index Low Pressure Ltd 2013©

A catalogue reference for this book can be obtained from the
British Library. ISBN Softback: 978-1-908520-33-3

Printed by Hong Kong Graphics and Printing using 100% chlorine-
free paper stock from managed forests.

Ducking transparent lips and diving as shallow as
possible are handy skills to have when surfing this
fickle Rarotonga right in the Cook Islands.

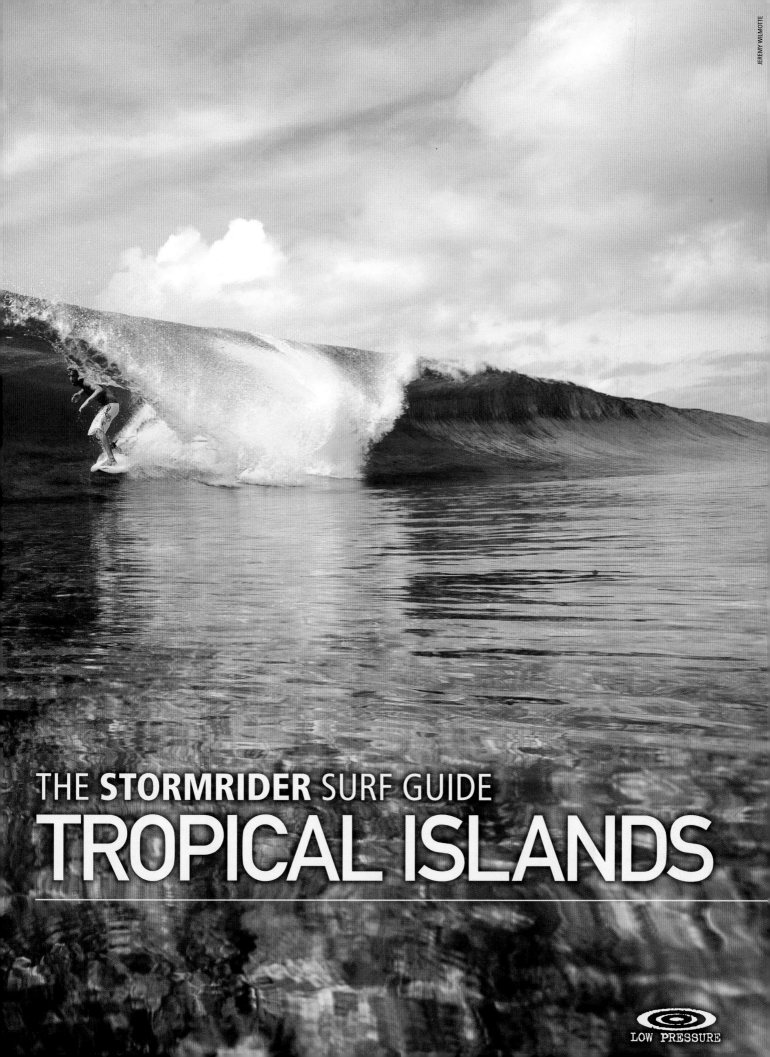

THE **STORMRIDER** SURF GUIDE
TROPICAL ISLANDS

LOW PRESSURE

FOREWORD

Tropical islands have been the preferred travel destination for surfers worldwide since the dawn of modern surfing a hundred years ago. The first tropical island destination to attract surfers was of course Oahu, Hawaii. Jack London, one of the widest-read writers in America at the time, gave a glowing account of surfing at Waikiki in his 1911 memoir, *The Cruise of the Snark*, describing surfing at Waikiki as "the royal sport for the natural kings of the earth". The 1912 Olympic swimming gold medallist, Duke Kahanamoku, travelled the world, evangelizing about surfing in the Hawaiian Islands and by the 1930s surfers from California were spending months surfing in Waikiki and Makaha on the west side. Surfing's popularity grew through the 1950s and '60s and with the smaller and lighter boards of the Shortboard Revolution and airplanes like the massive Boeing 747, many more surfers were travelling by the 1970s. Australians were travelling north to the great archipelago of Indonesia and surfing some of the world's best tropical waves at Uluwatu in Bali and G-land in Java. Getting shipwrecked in the Maldives in 1973 turned out to be a good move for Hinde and Scanlon as their nemesis became their playground. Meanwhile, French surfers had already discovered the perfect waves of Tamarin Bay, Mauritius and dipped into other French territories like Reunion, Guadeloupe and Martinique. More tropical island discoveries followed into the 1980's, principally in Indonesia and the South Pacific. From Timor to Nias, good waves kept appearing, until the world's ultimate tropical surfing area was unveiled in the Mentawai Islands, serviced by live-aboard boats, freeing surfers from the necessity of land-based accommodations. USA Peace Corps volunteers and other surf travellers accessed south Pacific island groups like Fiji, Tahiti, Tonga and Samoa, revealing new and unridden tropical waves. Tavarua Island in Fiji established and expanded on a new travel concept, the purpose-built "surf resort", using their sublime location and exclusivity to world-class reef waves at Cloudbreak and Restaurants to deliver a luxury tropical surfing experience to their paying customers. So the bulk of the tropical belt had been opened up by the '90s, yet literally tens-of-thousands of the 45,000 tropical islands on the planet remained a mystery to the surf world.

In the past fifteen years, we at SurfEXPLORE have pioneered a number of these undocumented tropical island surf locations, sometimes as the first surfers ever seen in the area. One of our earliest projects of this type was to access the Andaman Islands of India by boat from Phuket in Thailand. As many of the digital research tools available now did not exist, it was an analogue research effort with British Admiralty nautical charts and the NE monsoon weather records proving invaluable. After the hellishly long, rough crossing of the Andaman Sea by boat and assorted dramas in Port Blair with the Indian authorities, waves were found — some very good waves, which had undoubtedly never been surfed before. Many projects have followed, in locations from New Caledonia to The Philippines to the mysterious Comoros Islands off the coast of east Africa. The Comoros are not easy to reach in any case and the farcical, dysfunctional government ensures getting visas, clearing customs and all the red tape is never an easy or cheap task. Money often speeds up the process and smoothed our bumpy passage to the waves of Anjouan, which ended up being worth all the hassle and effort. Another tropical African island destination that sees very few surfers in a calendar year is the former Portuguese colony of São Tomé in the Gulf of Guinea. The small islet of Rolas sits bang on the equator, where we surfed some great new waves and master shaper

Randy Rarick built a board of local wood for the village kids. One of the best waves was at "Radiation Point", a great righthander in front of the Voice of America transmission station. The manager told us not to surf when the power was on as the signal is strong enough to reach from Cairo to Cape Town and we could be rendered sterile for life!

Anyone who thinks organising this kind of exploratory trip is easy had better think again. Months of research go into each project, with more than one person scouring nautical charts, weather records, photo libraries like flickr and Getty Images and more recently, the trove of worldwide satellite imagery available on that indispensable tool for surf exploration - Google Earth. Governments, wars, travel restrictions and natural disasters can sometimes destroy months of planning. Illnesses like yellow fever, dengue, TB, leprosy or the dreaded malaria are constant worries. Then there are all the logistics that can go wrong from lost passports, boards, luggage, connections, skin or weight, to lost in the jungle, lost at sea or simply a loss of sanity or will to go on.

So why do it? Why risk life and limb to be the first? Why not hit the resorts and relax, getting fed and ferried to the line-up? Is it just for the bragging rights and the brief job description of being a pioneering adventurer? More likely the true motivations are buried in the belief that a chance to surf a new break with good swell, offshore winds, clean, warm water, no wetsuit, no crowds and just a few mates is the ultimate reward in modern surfing. And the good news is there are literally thousands of surf spots out there, just waiting to be uncovered.

John Callahan – SurfEXPLORE

It takes dedication, determination and a lot of hard work to strike out into the unknown, but the rewards are eureka moments and unsullied visions of purity like this Pacific Indonesia four-pack.

CONTRIBUTORS

Publishing Directors
Ollie Fitzjones Bruce Sutherland Dan Haylock

Editor Bruce Sutherland

Design and Production Dan Haylock

Advertising and Distribution Ollie Fitzjones

Accounts Andrea Fitzjones

Original Zone Material
Antony 'YEP' Colas
Olivier Servaire Bruno Morand Jérôme Laigneau
Julia Rastimandesy Mireille Lahiholle

Special Thanks
Tiki Yates Camilo Gallardo Marc Hare
Kore Antonsen Neil Stuart Patagonia
Jo Finn Maisie Sandy Sue and John Haylock
Andrea Dillon Ty Ryder Sheila Jake Shani Marla Fitzjones
Louise Aedan Anna Ella Jamie Millais

Photographic Contributors
Joel Agostino Aura Surf Resort Balicamp Luis Blanco Chris Burkard Stuart Butler
John Callahan Guillaume Capette Matt Cardinal Tom Carey Sylvain Cazenave
Pierre de Champs David Charbonnel Jason Childs Antony 'YEP' Colas Sean Davey
Alex Dick-Read Jason Feast Juan Fernandez Steve Fitpatrick Ollie Fitzjones Ronan Gladu
Dan Haylock Heri Bryan Jackson Paul Kennedy Michael Kew Obdulio Luna
Jody Macdonald Al Mackinnon Baby Marmotte Brad Masters Laurent Masurel
Russel Mccarthy Twysden Moore Kieran Nash Laurent Nevarez Rammohan Paranjape
Celso Pereira Photogerson Damien Poullenot David Pu'u Jason Reposar Stéphane Robin
Antoine le Roux Roger Sharp Andrew Shield David Sparkes Surf Banyak Bernard Testemale
Henner Thies Ben Thouard Alan Van Gysen Frederic Verger Waidroka Surf Camp
Jeremy Wilmotte Peter 'Joli' Wilson Scott Winer

Editorial Contributors
Joel Agostino Teiki Ballian Jim Banks Valérie Basset Klaus Baumgaerner Jerôme Blanco
Steve Bridge Steve Burling Stuart Butler Danny Butt John Callahan Guillaume Capette
Paul Clark Cookie and Tod from Indo Jiwa Alexis Deforges Alex Dick-Reid Jason Feast
Steve Fitzpatrick Mark "Rock" Flint Ray Guinn Jr Rudolf Hajek Lawrence Harmer
Stuart Horstmans Simon James Curt Johnson Harley Jones Paul Kennedy Mike Kew
Nicolas Labat Carlo Lacovino Florian Lang Mark Loughran Ed Lovell Marcus (Take Off)
Andy Morrell Ian Muller Tama Pacomme Rob Parker Pohnpei Surf Club John Spicer
Niki's Surfshop Dr. Colin Sutherland Fanny Terrer Dan Thorn Hiroshi Yonekawa Nik Zanella

Boats of all shapes and sizes provide the most important means of transport and access throughout the tropical islands belt. Mystery Mentawai maw.

CONTENTS

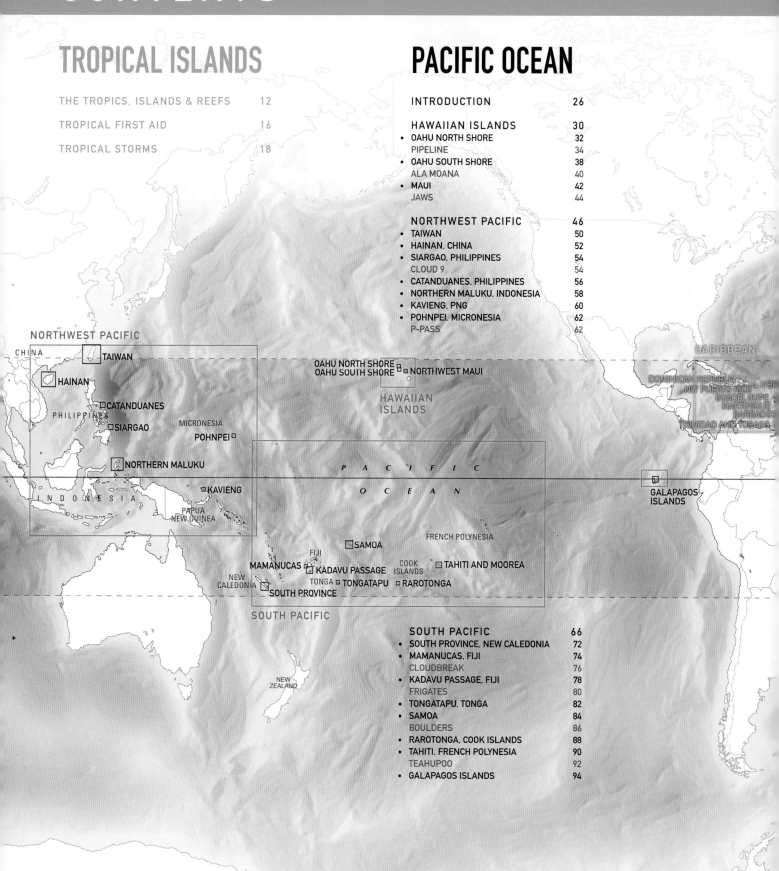

TROPICAL ISLANDS

PACIFIC OCEAN

ATLANTIC OCEAN

INDIAN OCEAN

ISLANDS

SAL

CAPE VERDE

SAO TOMÉ

FERNANDO DE NORONHA

ATLANTIC

OCEAN

MALDIVES

NORTH MALÉ

THAA AND LAAMU

HUVADHOO

ANDAMAN ISLANDS

SE SRI LANKA

SW SRI LANKA

SIMEULUE, BANYAKS

NIAS & HINAKOS

MENTAWAI ISLANDS

BAY OF BENGAL

INDONESIA

INDIAN

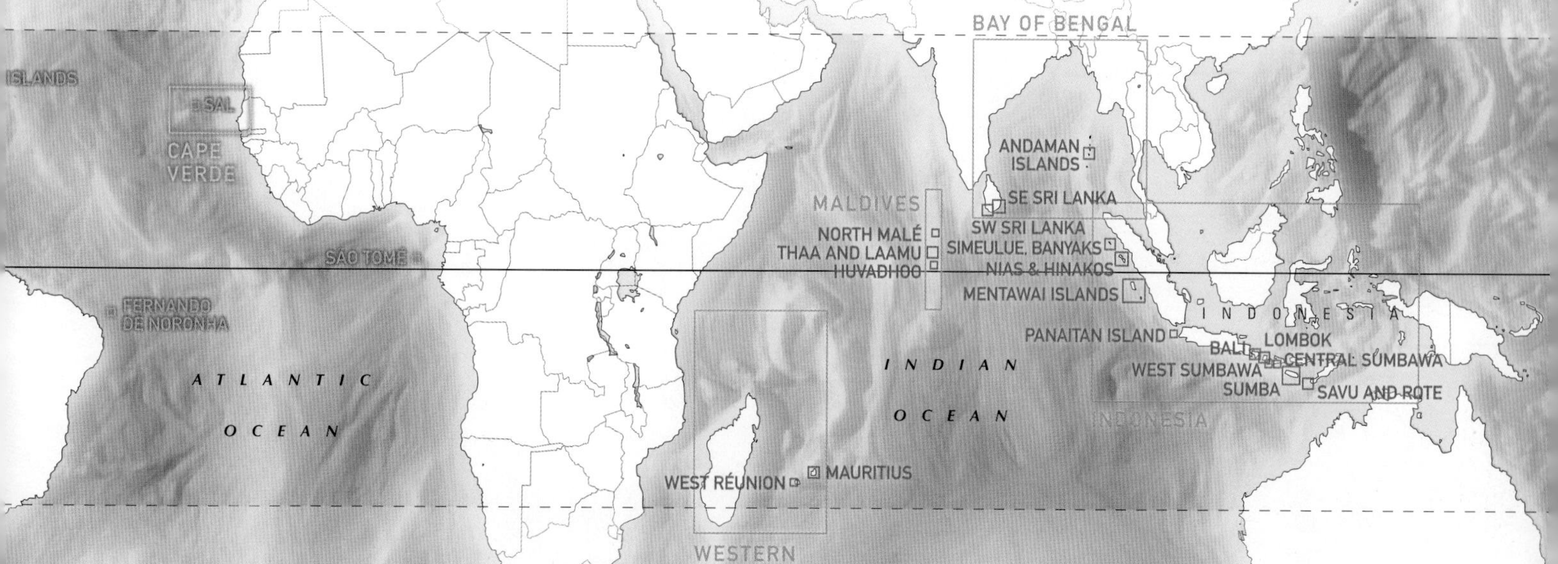

OCEAN

PANAITAN ISLAND

BALI

LOMBOK

WEST SUMBAWA

CENTRAL SUMBAWA

SUMBA

SAVU AND ROTE

WEST RÉUNION

MAURITIUS

WESTERN
INDIAN
OCEAN

TROPICAL

ALIBABA, SAL, CAPE VERDE

Not all tropical islands
are clothed in palms or
rainforest, yet they all share
a fiery, volcanic birth from
molten magma, bubbling up
through the Earth's mantle.

ISLANDS

THE TROPICS, ISLANDS AND REEFS

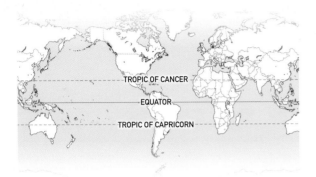

Planet Earth is accurately encircled by concentric lines of latitude and the tropical islands in this book are delineated and divided by three of the most prominent parallels of latitude. The Tropic of Cancer forms the northern limit of the tropics, where the sun will appear directly overhead for the June or Northern solstice, somewhere around the 23.5° N line of latitude. As the Earth's slightly tilted orbit around the sun continues, the Equator is next to line up in the same plane with the sun, causing the bi-annual occurrence best described as the September equinox and March equinox. The southern border of the tropics is denoted by the Tropic of Capricorn, which mirrors its northern cousin by aligning with the sun at an almost identical latitude for the Southern solstice in December. Islands which are located between these two great lines cast on the surface of the earth by the sun are included, with the exception of large, multi zone islands (Papua New Guinea, Madagascar Sumatra, Java), any continental land masses (Australia, Central America, India) and islands that receive little in the way of regular surf.

TROPICAL FACTS
- When the Tropics of Cancer and Capricorn were named 2000 years ago, the sun was rising in those two star constellations.
- Other northern hemisphere-centric names for September equinox include autumnal, southward and fall, while the March equinox is also referred to as vernal, northward and spring.
- The exact position of the tropics fluctuates as the Earth's axial tilt slowly changes meaning the tropical area is shrinking by 1100km² as it loses almost half a second (0.47°) of latitude per year.
- In 1917, both tropics sat at exactly 23° 27', but now lie at 23° 26°15.143°N and 23° 26' 14.908"S respectively.
- Equinox comes from Latin for 'equal night' and occurs when day and night are roughly the same length at most points across the planet.
- The equator is known as the 'great circle' since it is the longest of the parallels, is always the straightest line between two points on it and is centered on the centre of the earth, rather than on the earth's axis.

"An island is a naturally formed area of land, surrounded by water, which is above water at high tide." UNITED NATIONS CONVENTION ON THE LAW OF THE SEA

ISLAND FORMATION

Most islands are formed by some sort of volcanic activity and are most often found along the margins of the Earth's tectonic plates, 15 or so great slabs that form the planet's crust or lithosphere. These plates move by either crashing into one another (convergent), pulling apart (divergent) or moving sideways in relation to each other (transform).

Converging ocean plates will create deep trenches through subduction, where one plate dives beneath another, melts and is then spewed out through volcanoes formed on the uplifted plate.This is referred to as a volcanic island arc and typical examples from the three oceans are the Philippines, the Lesser Antilles and the Mentawai Islands which are all found next to deep trenches.

Divergent plates create mid-ocean ridges where lava rises to fill the gaps. These volcanic islands created by oceanic rift are often where three plates meet (Iceland) and definitions can be blurred with hotspots. The Galapagos Triple Junction is where the Pacific, Cocos and Nazca Plates meet.

Volcanic island chains are produced when a tectonic plate drifts over a stationary hot spot where molten magma rises from the Earth's interior. Huge conical mountains soar from the ocean floor and break through the waves, bringing volcanic activity to the surface. As the plate moves off the hotspot, the growth is halted and the island will start a process of erosion. Hawaii, the Cape Verde Islands and Reunion, are all thought to be created by hot spots.

Volcanoes have nothing to do with continental islands, which are pieces of continental crust that broke off long ago from a continent and drifted out to sea. Changes in sea level and deposition of sediment can also form barrier islands on continental shelves. New Caledonia, Cuba and Sri Lanka are examples of this island type.

EARTH FACTS
- Tectonic plates make up the Earth's outer shell or crust, called the lithosphere.
- Continental lithosphere floats higher on Earth's molten interior than oceanic crust, which is denser.
- There are at least 45 hotspots on Earth, but only 10 appear on continental land masses.
- Occasionally, plate tectonics can force the ocean floor above the surface without volcanism as seen at the St Peter and St Paul Archipelago off Brazil.
- The global mid-ocean ridge is the longest mountain range in the world at 64,370km (40,389mi), dwarfing the land-based Andes range that measures only 7,000km (4,350mi).

ISLAND AND REEF EVOLUTION

Charles Darwin formed his theory on how islands were formed during his Beagle expedition and said "Volcanoes have grown into mountains, have been degraded and sunk beneath the ocean". This is a simplified description of how once an oceanic island is formed and the volcanic magma stops flowing, all islands begin to erode and slump back towards the ocean floor. This provides a time line for both the type of island and the type of reef that encircles the land. A young volcanic island (fig 1), will have **lava reefs**, before the **fringing coral reef** (fig 2) can establish a foothold. As geological time progresses, the central landmass compacts and a gap appears between the

BARRIER REEF, TAHITI

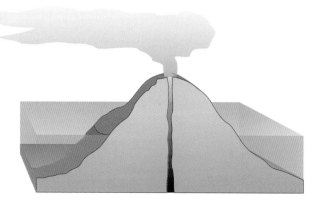

FIG 1. Lava reefs are a feature of younger volcanic islands, created by lava flows into the sea or sea level change. Molten basaltic rock is more fluid and will create gently sloping sides into the ocean, while a higher silica content magma will be more viscous, resulting in blocky, steeper sided volcanoes.

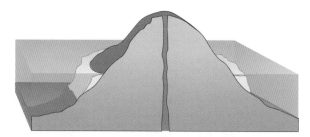

FIG 2. Fringing reefs grow on or near the coastline around islands or continents and have a steep seaward edge. They usually have an uneven tabletop appearance that is exposed at low tide and can be separated from the shore by a narrow, shallow lagoon. Fringing reefs are the most common type of tropical island reef.

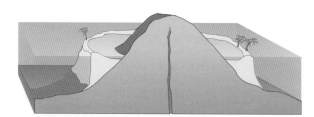

FIG 3. Barrier reefs form a long, narrow ridge of coral, parallel to the coastline and separated by a deeper, wider lagoon. Barrier reefs rarely form an unbroken line with breaks along their length caused by storms and erosion.

FIG 4. Atolls are roughly circular rings of oceanic coral reef, formed around a central lagoon. The island land mass has eroded, subsided or been inundated by rising sea levels and only the reef remains above the surface.

barrier reef (fig 3) and the island. Eventually, the tip of the conical volcano slips below water level leaving a ring of reef surrounding a lagoon known as an **atoll** (fig4). Further erosion will reduce atolls to reefs, shallow banks, shoals and eventually seamounts (submerged mountains) or guyots (flat-topped seamounts). These island chains perfectly illustrate the effects of erosion over time, with the oldest and furthest from the hotspot eventually disappearing beneath the waves.

OCEAN FACTS

- There are approximately 45,000 tropical islands on Earth and anything from 15,000 to 100,000 seamounts.
- The oceans contain 97% of all water, polar caps and glaciers account for almost 3%, of which less than 0.1% is in rivers, lakes, groundwater, clouds and rain.
- Dense cold and warm water, currents and gravitational forces from rock masses far beneath the ocean create mounds and troughs at sea level from 3-100m.
- Sunlight only penetrates the open ocean down to 200m and the water temperature drops to an un-tropical 10°C.

ATOLL, TUAMOTU ARCHIPELAGO

FORMATION OF CORAL REEFS

Tropical oceans suffer from a lack of surface nutrients, blocked by the thermocline, which is a layer separating the deep cold from the sun-warmed surface. No nutrients means no phytoplankton, followed by no zooplankton and on up the marine food chain to the biggest fish, leaving much of the open ocean a desert (unless there is upwelling). Fortunately, coral is nature's answer to this dilemma, and providing there is some light, a symbiotic relationship occurs between the coral animal or polyp and zooxanthellae, a microscopic, photosynthesizing 'plant-like' organism that swaps some of the food it produces in exchange for the nutrients contained within the polyps excrement. The polyps form a hard, circular 'corallite' or exoskeleton secreted as calcium carbonate and feed from within its strong walls. Coral reproductive methods vary from hermaphrodites producing both sperm and eggs to single sex gonochoric species that only produce sperm in their colony while a neighboring colony only produces eggs. Fertilization takes place either inside an adult polyp or outside on the reef during a synchronized mass coral spawning event. The resulting planula larva then sink, attach themselves to a hard structure, metamorphasize into a coral polyp and then produce exact genetic copies by splitting and cloning itself. As generations die, the corallite builds up in either a mound or branching shape. Coral heads can exist for thousands of years and provide solid foundations for upward growth as the reef is built on layers of limestone corallite skeletons, plus other materials like spines, shells, seaweed, sponges, molluscs and sediment that is all cemented together by coralline algae.

CORAL POLYP FACTS

- Invertebrate polyps are related to anemones and jellyfish and come in all sizes from pinhead tiny up to a 30cm in diameter.
- Zooxanthellae give many corals their colour and if they leave, the polyps can become bleached and die.
- Tropical reef building corals would starve without the zooxanthellae, who provide 80% of the polyps food requirements in the form of simple sugar molecules.
- Hard corals are known as hermatypes, while soft corals (ahermatypes) don't need zooxanthellae or shallow tropical water to thrive.
- Coral polyps are usually nocturnal, catching prey in the stinging tentacles surrounding their mouths.
- Coral reef colonies often spawn on the same night of the year, synchronizing the release of pink balls from their mouths, containing eggs and/or sperm.

CORAL REEF DISTRIBUTION

Shallow water, tropical coral reefs barely cover 0.1% of the oceans' surface area and are mostly found on latitudes between the two Tropics. The bulk are found in the Indo-Pacific region, while the west coasts of continental Africa and South America are virtually devoid of coral, thanks to nutrient rich upwelling and cold currents. The Great

THREATS TO CORAL REEFS

Coral reefs are an extremely complex and delicately balanced habitat, requiring a large number of specific environmental conditions in order to survive and flourish. Consequently, there are a correspondingly large number of external forces that can upset the equilibrium required for stable, long-term growth. The following is a brief summary from The Coral Reef Alliance.

OCEAN ACIDIFICATION

Scientists have known for decades that high carbon dioxide (CO2) emissions from fossil fuel burning are increasing the levels of carbonic acid in the world's oceans, leading to increased acidity. Atmospheric concentration of CO2 is now higher than experienced on Earth for at least the last 800,000 years and probably over 20 million years and the ocean is absorbing one-third of these emissions. The resultant lowering of the pH in surface waters has a weakening effect on calcifying organisms such as corals, shellfish and plankton to form their shells or exoskeletons, making them more vulnerable to damage from waves, careless tourists, and destructive fishers.

OCEAN WARMING AND CORAL BLEACHING

As the planet warms due to excess carbon dioxide and other gasses trapped inside the atmosphere, many scientists believe that this is also causing sea surface temperatures to rise. Ocean warming is extremely dangerous to temperature sensitive coral organisms and can cause mass coral bleaching. Heat stressed coral polyps will expel the zooxanthellae algae that normally provide the coral with its colour

and up to 80% of its energy, so unless temperatures quickly return to normal, the bleached coral colonies will die. During El Nino years of higher water temperatures, severe bleaching lowers the corals' reproductive output and a slow recovery is never guaranteed. Increased levels of ultraviolet radiation also damage coral in shallow areas thanks to ozone layer depletion.

WATER POLLUTION

Pollution is one of the leading causes of coral reef degradation. Oil, gas and pesticides contaminate and poison corals and marine life. Human sewage, animal waste and fertilizer all increase nitrogen levels, causing an overgrowth of sunlight-smothering algae. Floating trash can also block light and plastic bags, mistaken for jellyfish, kill many animals that eat them. Lost or discarded fishing nets can snag on reefs and ensnare thousands of fish, sea turtles and marine mammals over time.

SEDIMENTATION

Coral reefs are being smothered by increasing amounts of sediment arising from coastal and inshore construction, mining, logging and farming along coastal rivers. Mangrove trees and seagrasses, which normally act as filters for sediment, are also being rapidly destroyed, which exacerbates coastal erosion.

COASTAL DEVELOPMENT

Coastal populations have risen, increasing the pressures on coastal resources. In many areas,

developers have constructed piers and other structures directly on top of coral reefs. Big cities such as Hong Kong, Singapore, Manila and Honolulu have all destroyed thriving coral reefs and the trend is growing in many coastal communities.

DESTRUCTIVE FISHING PRACTICES

These include cyanide fishing, overfishing and blast fishing. Cyanide fishing involves squirting a cloud of poison into crevices in the reef, killing the polyps and stunning fish for easy capture and export to tropical aquarium tanks or Asian fresh fish restaurants. Overfishing is another leading cause for coral reef degradation, causing species crashes and unbalancing the fine equilibrium between the reef and its resident animals. Banging on the reef with sticks (muro-ami), along with blast fishing techniques using explosives literally tears the reef apart and destroys the fish habitat.

CORAL MINING

Mining destroys coral, which is extracted in large quantities for use as bricks, road-fill or limestone for cement. Souvenirs and jewellery made from coral are often sold to tourists and exporters in the markets of developing countries.

CARELESS TOURISM

Careless boating, diving, snorkeling and fishing can also damage coral reefs. Dropping anchors, walking on, touching or removing coral and stirring up sediment all have negative impacts on the reef ecosystem.

TEAVAITI, TAHITI, FRENCH POLYNESIA

BERNARD TESTEMALE

Millions of tiny animals and plant-like organisms coalesce to build the world's largest living structures, yet their very existence is threatened by destructive human behavior.

Barrier Reef off Australia's east coast forms the longest and largest collection of reefs (2,900), including 900 islands. Both coral reefs and surfers seem to thrive in water temperatures between 21–29°C (70–85°F) , although extremes as low as 13°C (55°F) and high as 38°C (100°F) have been recorded in the Persian Gulf. Water temperature, oxygen level, amount of turbulence, and availability of food all affect growth rate. Some species are better adapted to the reef face where waves will quickly erode and smash the more elegant branch structures of staghorn and spiral corals, but the solid brain and plate corals will fare much better. Coral also has a rough surface to help create turbulence and separate passing nutrients from the protective boundary layer of water, aiding growth efficiency and deterring larger animal contact, like surfers!

CORAL REEF FACTS
- Most coral reefs are less than 10,000 years old, but their ancestors formed at least 240 million years ago.
- Coral reefs have great bio-diversity, providing habitat for 25% of ocean species.
- Western Pacific reefs near Australia average over 300 species of coral, while the Caribbean averages only 25.
- Ideal temperature for fast coral growth is around 26-27°C (80°F) in clear, sunny, shallow water above a depth of 50m.
- Maximum annual growth rates are up to 3cm outwards and 25cm upwards, but many large species only manage a few millimeters per year.
- Freshwater kills coral so rivermouths create a pass in the reef, often aiding good wave creation.
- All reefs are unique and may grow to be any shape that will constantly change over time.

REEF PROTECTION

IN THE WATER SNORKELING & SCUBA DIVING
- Never touch corals; even a slight contact can harm them and some corals can sting or cut you.
- Carefully select points of entry and exit to avoid walking on corals.
- Make sure all your equipment is well secured.
- Make sure you are neutrally buoyant at all times.
- Maintain a comfortable distance and avoid all contact with the reef.
- Practice good finning and body control to avoid accidental contact with the reef or stirring up the sediment.
- Stay off the bottom and never stand or rest on corals.
- Avoid using gloves and kneepads in coral environments.
- Stay horizontal in the water while swimming above the reef.
- Take nothing living or dead out of the water, except recent garbage.
- Do not chase, harass or try to ride marine life.
- Do not touch, handle or feed marine life except under expert guidance and following established guidelines.

ABOVE THE WATER - SURFING AND SWIMMING
- Carefully select points of entry and exit to avoid walking on corals.
- Access reefs from a boat where possible.
- Always use keyholes, jump rocks and channels.
- If walking on reef is unavoidable, use your board to support weight.
- Begin paddling as soon as possible with fins flipped up if necessary.
- When duck-diving, push down on deck to avoid knuckle dragging on the reef, then grab the rail on the way up.
- Wearing booties will provide some protection for your feet and some cushioning for the coral.
- Avoid diving off board or ejecting off the back of the wave and try to stay flat on the surface when bailing.
- Use waterproof sunscreens that are designed not to wash off and allow plenty of time to absorb into skin.

TROPICAL FIRST AID

Exposure to excessive sun and contracting some form of infection are the two most common health risks likely to afflict surfers in the tropics. Early identification and appropriate treatment are crucial for a rapid, full recovery, but as always, prevention is better than the cure.

MALARIA

Widespread across the tropics, malaria parasites (*Plasmodium*) are transmitted by the Anopheles mosquito. Six *Plasmodium* species usually infect humans and the main killers are P. falciparum and *P. vivax*. Drug resistant strains exist and the risk varies regionally so consult a doctor before travelling. High-risk islands include eastern Indonesia, Solomons, Vanuatu, Hispaniola and Sao Tomé. Prevention is paramount by avoiding bites (mosquito nets, long clothing, repellent) and oral medication (prophylaxis).
Symptoms: May include fever, sweats, chills, convulsions, joint or back pain, headaches, dry cough, enlarged spleen, nausea or vomiting and can take anything from 8-40 days to appear (longer if taking prophylaxis). Many other conditions can present the same symptoms, so expert diagnosis (blood test) is crucial. *P. falciparum* can cause confusion, neurologic focal signs, respiratory difficulties and coma.

Treatment: Reliable prophylaxis is provided by mefloquine (Lariam), doxycycline (generic), and atovaquone-proguanil (Malarone), which is now coming off patent and expected to fall significantly in price. Side effects limit the usefulness of Larium in certain people. Fake malaria drugs are common in Asia and Africa, so source drugs before you travel. Effective treatment for malaria requires expert knowledge of drugs and correct dosage.

SUNBURN

Covering skin with high SPF waterproof sunscreen is the simplest preventative measure, however using SPF-rated lycra, a surf hat and avoiding midday exposure is more effective. The lips, ears, lower back, thighs, calves and behind the knees are problem areas requiring added attention.

Treatment: for sunburn and possible heat exhaustion includes slow rehydration with water or sports drinks to replace electrolytes, whether feeling thirsty or not. Cool showers, moisturizing creams and taking ibuprofen can lessen the severity of the symptoms. Do not peel, pick or burst blisters and seek medical attention if more than 20% of body is burned and symptoms like headache, dizziness, sleepiness, fevers or chills persist.

INFECTION

Tropical waters carry higher levels of bacteria than cooler water. This means that infections can occur very rapidly, even on the smallest of wounds. They should be treated immediately and constantly monitored for signs of infection, which include swelling, bruising, extreme pain, increasing redness, tenderness, warmth or drainage around the wound. Also, any flu-like symptoms, such as fever, exhaustion, and swollen glands could be signs of infection or a disease. If these are present, consult a doctor immediately. Keeping the wound covered and clean will ensure that it heals quickly and effectively.

Treatment: If infection is present, scrub the wound using gauze dipped in antiseptic. Once all the yellow pus is removed, re-apply antiseptic and dress appropriately.

Malaria Information Courtesy of London School of Hygiene & Tropical Medicine

Sun protection is paramount in the tropics, coupled with adequate hydration to avoid sunburn and sunstroke.

CUTS
CORAL CUTS
Usually consist of an inflamed, swollen, red, tender wound that may develop into a sore or ulcer with infectious drainage. Redness around the skin of the wounded area suggests infection and requires immediate medical attention.

Treatment: Scrub with soap and water, then flush with fresh water. If the wound stings, rinse it with acetic acid (vinegar) or isopropyl alcohol. Flush the wound with a mixture of half water and half hydrogen peroxide to remove coral dust, then flush with fresh water. Rinse daily and apply an antibiotic ointment 3-4 times per day.

FIRE CORAL CUTS
Fire coral has a bright yellow-green and brown skeletal covering and are widely found in tropical and subtropical waters.
Symptoms: Within 5-30 minutes following skin contact with fire coral, a burning sensation or a stinging pain develops. A red rash with raised wheals or vesicles appears, and itching develops. Lymph glands may swell over time.

Treatment: Rinse with seawater. Avoid fresh water because it will increase pain. Apply topical acetic acid (vinegar) or isopropyl alcohol. Remove tentacles with tweezers. Immobilize the affected area because movement may cause the venom to spread. Apply hydrocortisone cream 2-3 times daily as needed for itching. Discontinue immediately if any signs of infection appear.

TUESDAY ROCK, SIARGAO

JS CALLAHAN/SURFEXPLORE

REEF CUTS

Rocky volcanic reefs carry many bacteria and cuts from them pose a high risk for infection.

Treatment: Scrub the wound to remove all debris and apply lime juice (this helps to stop the bleeding in a short amount of time) while scrubbing. Apply an antiseptic. Apply povidone-iodine solution (ie; betadine) twice a day to help keep the wound clean.

BITES AND STINGS

For all types of bites and stings: DO NOT attempt to suck out the venom with your mouth, apply a tourniquet, place ice directly on the bite or sting, administer alcohol, stimulants or aspirin.

BLUE BOTTLE / PORTUGUESE MAN OF WAR STING

The tentacles of these jellyfish will cause a sharp, painful sting. Do not rub sting area with towel or wet sand to rub tentacles off – this may make the pain worse.

Treatment: Prevent further stings. Using a stick or gloved fingers, carefully remove tentacles. Rinse the affected area with seawater. Do NOT use fresh water or vinegar, as these may cause the stinging cells to sting all at once! Do not scrub the affected area. Apply ice to reduce pain and swelling.

SEA URCHIN PUNCTURE, STONEFISH, SCORPIONFISH, OR LIONFISH STINGS.

The spines from any of these sea creatures can cause redness, swelling, or numbness around the area. This may lead to severe pain or infection. Tissue shredding may occur. Throbbing pain may peak in 1-2hrs and last 12hrs. Seek immediate medical attention for stonefish, scorpionfish, or lionfish envenomation as anti-venom is needed. Death may occur.

Treatment: Immerse the affected area for 30-90 minutes in water as hot as the injured person can tolerate. Repeat as necessary to control pain. Use tweezers to remove any large spines, but don't dig around wound. If black markings are present after 48 to 72 hours, seek medical attention, as spines may have been left in the wound. Remove sea urchin spines (the claw-shaped pedicellaria) by applying shaving cream and gently scraping with a razor, or use tweezers. Scrub wound with soap and water followed by extensive flushing with fresh water. Do not close the wound with tape or glue skin.

SHARK BITES

Provide emergency care immediately. A medical healthcare provider should evaluate all shark bite victims. Control any bleeding by applying direct pressure to bite area. Keep the victim calm and warm. If only a minor wound is present, consider washing the wound with soap and water and cover it with a clean dressing until medical care arrives. If the wound appears serious, do not attempt to clean it yourself. If swelling, bruising, extreme pain, increasing redness (sometimes seen as streaks), tenderness, warmth or drainage around the bite area and any flu-like symptoms occur then seek medical help immediately.

CUTS, SCRAPES, WOUNDS

The faster you can treat and manage your wounds effectively, the less chance for infection you will have. Use the following guidelines to treat most minor cuts, scrapes, or wounds.

1. STOP THE BLEEDING

Before you clean the wound, try to the stop the bleeding. Put on medical gloves before applying direct pressure to the wound. In case

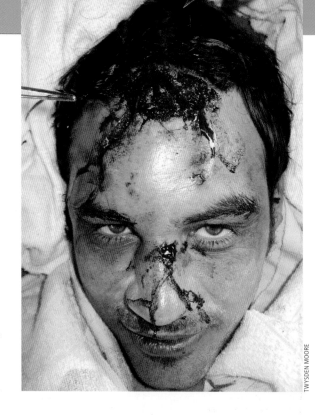

Major coral or reef cuts present a high probability of infection if not carefully cleaned, treated and dressed.

TWYSDEN MOORE

of swelling, remove any clothing or jewelry from around the wound. Use a sterile gauze pad or other clean piece of cloth to place over the wound. Apply direct pressure on the wound for a full 15 minutes. Resist the temptation to check to see if the bleeding has stopped.

2. CLEAN THE WOUND

Wash hands thoroughly. Use medical gloves when cleaning the wound. Remove large pieces of dirt or other debris from the wound with sterilized tweezers. Do not dig tweezers deeply into the wound. Wash the wound under clean, fresh water (lots of it) to remove all the dirt, debris, and bacteria from the wound. Lukewarm water and mild soap are the best. Gently scrub with a washcloth or gauze pad. (Moderate scrubbing may be needed if the wound is very dirty.) Hard scrubbing may actually cause more damage to the tissue and increase the chance of infection. Scrubbing the wound will probably hurt and may increase bleeding, but it is necessary to clean the wound thoroughly. If some dirt or other debris remains in the wound, repeat the cleaning. Apply antiseptic to further aid in cleansing before bandaging.

3. BANDAGE THE WOUND

Most wounds heal better with less scaring if they are kept covered. Use an antibiotic ointment and non-stick dressing before applying a clean bandage to the wound. If a bandage is stuck to a scab, soak it in warm water to soften the scab and make the bandage easier to remove. Use adhesive steri-strips (butterfly stitches) to hold the edges of the wound together. Take the dressing off and leave it off whenever you are sure the wound will not become irritated or dirty. Stitches are only an option within a few hours of injury, as the risk of enclosing an infection becomes too great. A quick test to determine whether you need stitches is to stop the bleeding and wash the wound well, then pinch the sides of the wound together. If the edges of the wound come together and it looks better, you may want to consider getting stitches. If stitches may be needed, avoid using an antiseptic or antibiotic ointment until after a health professional has examined the wound.

Most of the information here has been provided with the help and permission of Global Odyssi Surfers First Aid Kits – The only specialist in surfer specific first aid kits. To read more from their First Aid handbook or buy the kits – www.GlobalOdyssi.com

TROPICAL STORMS

A tropical cyclone is the generic term for a non-frontal synoptic scale low-pressure system over tropical or sub-tropical waters with organized convection (i.e. thunderstorm activity) and definite cyclonic surface wind circulation. (Holland 1993)

Cyclone, hurricane or typhoon are all geographically specific names for these strong tropical depressions, so choosing the correct name depends on where they form. **Cyclone** is the generic term used in the Indian Ocean and the Southwest Pacific Ocean (west of 160ºE). **Hurricane** is the Atlantic word, plus it is used for any storm that appears in the Northeast Pacific (east of dateline or 160ºE), while **Typhoon** and Super-Typhoon are reserved for the Northwest Pacific Ocean west of the dateline. There are also many different scales of measurement for tropical cyclones used by Regional Specialized Meteorological Centres and so the categories don't always match up and some measure winds at different heights, for different lengths of time, arriving at different averages. The Saffir–Simpson Hurricane Scale is used for hurricanes only and the winds must reach 119km/h (33 m/s, 64 kt, 74 mph) in order for the storm to be officially named as a Category 1 hurricane. However this is equal to Cat 3 on the Australian scale (see table). Tropical storm and Tropical depression are further terms used at the lower end of the scale.

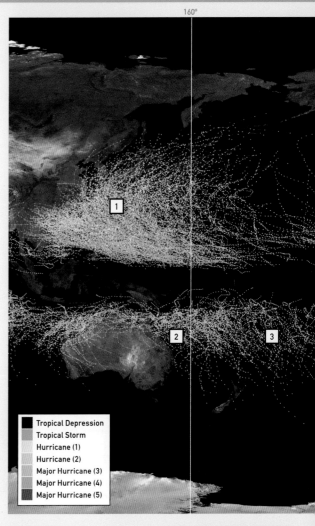

160º

- ■ Tropical Depression
- ■ Tropical Storm
- Hurricane (1)
- Hurricane (2)
- Major Hurricane (3)
- Major Hurricane (4)
- Major Hurricane (5)

TROPICAL CYCLONE CLASSIFICATIONS

10-MIN SUSTAINED WIND			BEAU-FORT SCALE	[1] NW PACIFIC (JAPAN)	[1] NW PACIFIC (US)	[2] SW PACIFIC	[3] AUSTRALIA	[4] NE PACIFIC	[5] N ATLANTIC	[6] SW INDIAN OCEAN	[7] N INDIAN OCEAN
KNOTS	KMPH	MPH									
<28	<52	<32	0-6	Tropical Depression	Tropical Depression	Tropical Depression	Tropical Low	Tropical Depression	Tropical Depression	Tropical Disturbance	Depression
28-29	52-56	32-35	7							Tropical Depression	Deep Depression
30-33	56-63	35-39									
34-47	63-89	39-55	8-9	Tropical Storm	Tropical Storm	Tropical Cyclone (1)	Tropical Cyclone (1)	Tropical Storm	Tropical Storm	Moderate Tropical Storm	Cyclonic Storm
48-55	89-104	55-64	10	Severe Tropical Storm		Tropical Cyclone (2)	Tropical Cyclone (2)			Severe Tropical Storm	Severe Cyclonic Storm
56-63	104-119	64-74	11								
64-72	19-135	74-84	12	Typhoon	Typhoon	Severe Tropical Cyclone (3)	Severe Tropical Cyclone (3)	Hurricane (1)	Hurricane (1)	Tropical Cyclone	Very Severe Cyclonic Storm
73-85	135-159	84-99	13					Hurricane (2)	Hurricane (2)		
86-89	159-167	99-104	14			Severe Tropical Cyclone (4)	Severe Tropical Cyclone (4)	Hurricane (3)	Hurricane (3)		
90-99	167-185	104-115	15							Intense Tropical Cyclone	
100-106	185-198	115-123	16					Major Hurricane (4)	Major Hurricane (4)		
107-114	198-213	123-132									
115-119	213-222	132-138	17		Super Typhoon	Severe Tropical Cyclone (5)	Severe Tropical Cyclone (5)			Very Intense Tropical Cyclone	Super Cyclonic Storm
>120	>222	>138						Major Hurricane (5)	Major Hurricane (5)		

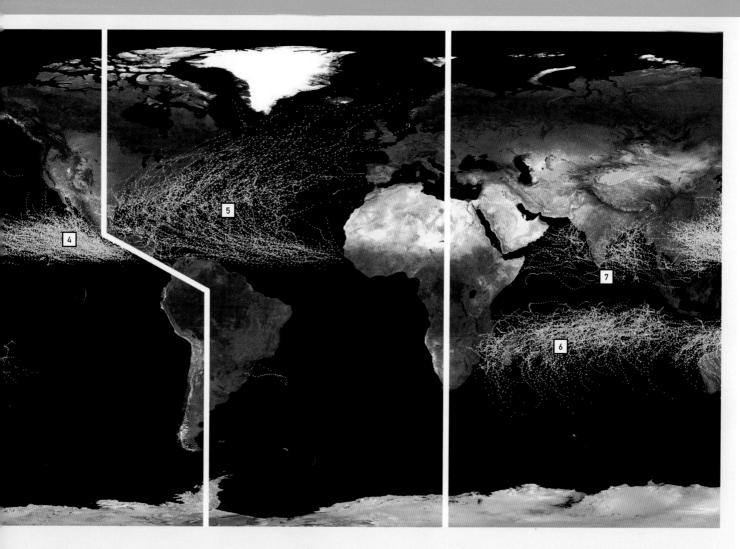

THE MAGNIFICENT SEVEN

1. NORTHWEST PACIFIC (APR – JAN)

This region holds the record for tropical storms, spinning up the biggest, fastest and highest number of typhoons every year. Their tracks cover a vast area of ocean so a lot of countries are in the firing line. Micronesia, Philippines, Taiwan, China, Japan and then a second blast for those mid-Pacific islands if the storm throws a curve-ball and heads back east. June – Sept will be the heart of the typhoon season, which extends for 10 months, appreciably longer than any other region.

2. AUSTRALIA & 3. SOUTHWEST PACIFIC (NOV – APR)

These storms are harder to predict as historical data shows some fairly random tracks, with loops, stalls and sudden direction changes a common occurrence. Cyclones can also traverse the top of Australia, effectively linking the Pacific and Indian oceans. The Solomon's, New Hebrides, New Caledonia, Fiji, Tonga and Samoa can all take direct hits, but it is really Australia and even New Zealand that benefit the most from the west and south tracking storms while the South Pacific Islands further east are more likely to experience the lower category 1 and 2 storms. Whole seasons can pass without anything over category 3, so there's no banking on a cyclone swell in the temperamental SW Pacific.

4. NORTHEAST PACIFIC (MAY – NOV)

These are the hurricanes that form off the coast of Mexico and Central America, then head in a west to north arc, bringing shorter, stronger swell events to these countries, plus longer distance waves to California and the West Coast USA, as well as the southeast exposed shores of Hawaii, thousands of miles away. Both coasts of North America experience their highest water temperatures in late August early September, so this usually coincides with prime hurricane time.

5. NORTH ATLANTIC HURRICANES (JUNE – NOV)

Forming around disturbances off the coast of West Africa, the storms have a fairly straight run down 'Hurricane Alley', a swathe of warm water that leads all the way to the east coast of Central America. That means there's a lot of good surfing real estate affected, either side of the alley including all the countries bordering the Caribbean, East Coast USA, the Gulf of Mexico coast and NE South America. Don't forget the chance of a hurricane re-energizing as it heads polewards and joining the procession of lows heading west to Europe. The South Atlantic isn't completely devoid of hurricanes (Catarina, Brazil, Cat2, 2004), but water temps and wind shear are usually against tropical storm formation.

6. SOUTHERN INDIAN (NOV – APR)

Madagascar and the Mascarenes are in the favoured path of these cyclones that start off heading west before a short parabola to the south snuffs them out in the cooler waters. These inconsistent storms, which like the other Southern Hemisphere cyclones off both coasts of Australia, are generally less intense, shorter-lived and harder to track than their Northern Hemisphere cousins. Few of the bigger systems make landfall on Africa, while Madagascar bears the brunt and Western Australia is also prone to some cat 3 direct hits to the northwest coast.

7. NORTHERN INDIAN (APR – DEC)

The Bay of Bengal witnessed the most deadly cyclone ever, when Bhola surged ashore in Bangladesh, 1970. More recently, Nargis killed hundreds of thousands in Myanmar proving this basin may not be the most active, but it is certainly capable of occasionally producing powerful cyclones. Waves can result in India, Sri Lanka, Thailand, Andaman Islands and Sumatra, but high season is short from May-June. Across the Sub-Continent in the Arabian Sea is even less storm activity and little cyclone swell for established surf nations like the Maldives, which sit in the equatorial doldrums and experience too much decay in the swells from both the north and the south.

FORMATION

For all cyclones, hurricanes or typhoons to form, a handful of weather conditions must first combine.

- Surface water temps have to be above 26.5°C/80°F.
- Atmospheric instability – basically it is thunderstorm activity that allows the heat stored in the ocean waters to be liberated for the tropical cyclone development through fast cooling and moist convection.
- High humidity and relatively moist layers near the mid-troposphere 5km (3mi) up. Moisture is required for continuing development of widespread thunderstorm activity.
- Enough Coriolis force to get a low pressure centre spinning. That's why cyclones cannot form within 500km (300mi) of the equator.
- A pre-existing, near-surface disturbance with sizable spin and low-level inflow. Tropical cyclones cannot be generated spontaneously; they need some kind of spinning weather system to get started.
- Low vertical wind shear refers to the magnitude of wind change between the surface and the upper troposphere. Large values of vertical wind shear disrupt or destroy the tropical cyclone. Low values of less than about 37km/h (10m/s, 20kts, 23mph) of vertical wind shear are ideal.

NAMING

Tropical cyclones have been given names since the practice was popularised by US Army Air Corp and Navy meteorologists, who were monitoring tropical cyclones over the Pacific during WWII. They chose girlfriends or wives' names, unlike the Australian forecaster that had

HURRICANE FRAN, FLORIDA 1996

Hurricanes that traverse the Caribbean or Gulf of Mexico can produce awesome waves on coasts that normally lie dormant.

dubbed them as political figures whom he disliked, years earlier. In 1945, the armed services publicly adopted a name list of typhoons of the western Pacific and in 1953 the US Weather Bureau switched to women's names until 1979 when men's names were included. Other regions followed this pattern until January 2000, whereby tropical cyclones in the Northwest Pacific basin are now given Asian names including flowers, animals, birds, trees, or even foods, etc, while some are simply descriptive adjectives. The Australian and South Pacific region started giving women's names to the storms in 1964

and both men's and women's names in 1974/1975. The Southwest Indian Ocean tropical cyclones were first named during the 1960/1961 season. The North Indian Ocean region tropical cyclones were slow on the name game and only started in 2006. Storm names are allocated alphabetically through any one season and traditionally provide surfers with a reference point, giving the storm a personality and allowing a deeper, more memorable interaction with the waves that are produced.

TROPICAL STORM TRACKING

Forecasts for individual storms and their impacts are provided by NOAA's National Hurricane Center, which continuously monitors the tropics for storm development and tracking throughout the season using an array of tools including satellites, hurricane hunter aircraft, radars, buoys and advance computer modeling. Two of these hi-tech programs include the Hurricane Weather Research and Forecasting (HWRF) and the Geophysical Fluid Dynamics Laboratory (GFDL) models, boasting a vast improvement in forecasting a storm's track and intensity, which should save some lives. The Regional Specialized Meteorological Centres are strung across the 7 major tropical cyclone basins, sited in Florida, Hawaii, Japan, India, Reunion, Australia and Fiji, plus a handful of regional offices, all working together as part of the World Weather Watch. From all these agencies, global trends and facts emerge like; annual average = 86 tropical cyclones (tropical storm intensity), 47 reach hurricane/typhoon strength and 20 become powerful tropical cyclones (Category 3+, severe, intense, super, major). The major surf forecasting websites often provide cyclone, hurricane and typhoon tracking tools that are specifically designed to help surfers with where, when and how big?

TROPICAL STORM SURF CREATION

There are a few notable differences between the swell and waves produced by a cyclone, hurricane or typhoon and the surf produced by a normal (mid-latitude or extra-tropical) low pressure. They both create waves in exactly the same way by winds blowing across the surface of the ocean, but cyclones are usually much smaller in diameter with far less fetch than a sprawling winter, mid-latitude low that will produce greater wave height. These fetch-limited tropical storms can move extremely quickly and often change direction suddenly, which doesn't allow enough time for a good swell to spawn from a single direction. This can translate to really short swell events that decay rapidly over the open ocean, further limited by the small seasonal window that tropical storms are active in. Conversely, a storm that stalls or travels slowly in a straight line can make the surf pump for days on end and send out swell in many directions. Other factors to consider are how the bulk of the swell propagates out from the storm in the direction of travel, with the right side of the storm (regardless of hemisphere) always containing more energy,

Sailors soon learned that the leading right quadrant of any tropical storm will bring more wind, swell and rain to anything in its path.

so the leading quadrant on the right should create more swell. Examples include strong SE swell for the US East Coast as a hurricane approaches on a direct E to W path towards the Caribbean and ideal NE swell for the East Coast of Australia as a cyclone heads south from New Guinea through the Coral Sea. Sailors dubbed the right half of the cyclone the dangerous semicircle since the heaviest rain, strongest winds and biggest seas were located in this half of the storm. Some storms can wind-up, make landfall, lose intensity and fizzle out or else head back out to sea and re-energize, even combining with the mid-latitude depressions and become an extra-tropical cyclone bringing swell to west-facing shores like Europe in the late summer. Knowing when a storm swell may arrive by calculating speed is fraught with variables, but if you know the swell period or the size of the storm then a few guess-timations can be made. Lower scale storms outputting swell periods of 10-12secs will travel about 650km (400mi) per 24hrs. Moderate scale with around 14secs period should cover 800km (500mi) while the big Cat 4 and 5 storms will see 16+sec period swells march over almost 1000kms (620mi) of open ocean if

JS CALLAHAN/SURFEXPLORE

WEST COAST TAIWAN

the storm track is heading your way. Anecdotal evidence suggests there is something about cyclone swells, which ramps up the power and also the number of waves in a set, as typhoon surfers often report sets of 12-15 waves compared to the average 4-6. No matter which ocean you are in, there is always a fine line between chasing down some tropical storm swell and getting caught in the storm itself, which brings strong winds, heavy rain and storm surges to low-lying areas. Storm surges are responsible for 90% of tropical storm deaths.

TROPICAL STORM FACTS

HURRICANES
NAME: From *Huracan* – West Indian god of storms
HIGHEST RECORDED WIND SPEED
Hurricane Gilbert, 1998 = 320km/h (200mph);
HIGHEST DEATH TOLL
The Great Hurricane, Martinique, Barbados, 1780 = 22,000
HIGHEST COST
Hurricane Katrina = $81 billion USD

TYPHOONS
NAME: From Chinese *dàfēng* great wind, altered by association with Greek *tȳphôn* violent wind)
HIGHEST RECORDED WIND SPEED Typhoon Ida 1958 and Typhoon Nancy 1961, 346 km/h (215mph)
HIGHEST DEATH TOLL
Typhoon Nina, China 1975 = 171,000
(62 collapsed dams & disease epidemic)
LOWEST PRESSURE
Typhoon Tip, Guam, 1979 = 870 mbar (25.69 inHg) and record diameter of 2,220km (1,380 mi)

CYCLONES
NAME: From Greek *kyklôn* revolving
HIGHEST RECORDED WIND SPEED - Cyclone Olivia, Barrow Island, Australia, 1996 = 408 km/h (253 mph)
HIGHEST DEATH TOLL
Cyclone Bhola, Bangladesh 1970 = 300,000 – 1,000,000 est. (deadliest recorded tropical storm)
LARGEST DIAMETER
Cyclone Yasi, Queensland, 2011 - 1,450km (900mi)

Otto Flores adding to his tube time at home in Puerto Rico. MONCHO DAPENA

Check out the entire range of Patagonia wetsuits and FCD surfboards at **PATAGONIASURFEUROPE.COM**

BUILT FOR _Gettin' Barreled._

patagonia®

PACIFIC

TEAHUPOO, TAHITI, FRENCH POLYNESIA

The place they call "the end of the road"
is also the end of the rainbow for fearless
riders, looking for liquid gold.

OCEAN

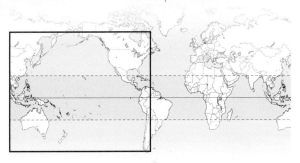

Everything about the Pacific Ocean is big! Dwarfing the Atlantic with a surface area twice the size, the Pacific covers a third of the globe and is by far the Earth's biggest single feature. It is also the deepest ocean, holds the tallest mountains and the largest coral reef, but even more importantly, it is home to the planet's biggest surf! Booming winter Aleutian swells saturate the North Pacific, while southern hemisphere lines roar out of the forties latitudes almost year-round, peppering the South Pacific and beyond. The Pacific is encircled by The Ring of Fire, where cracks and faults in the earth's crust help the formation of 452 volcanoes that extend from New Zealand to Japan, across Alaska to the West coast of the Americas and all the way down to the Nazca plate off Chile. Sitting majestically at the centre of this enormous lava-fed halo is Hawaii, which fittingly represents both the centre of The Ring of Fire and the centre of the surfing universe.

SWELL

With no less than five groundswell-producing sources, the Pacific is constantly agitated by mid-latitude depressions in the north and the endlessly circling low pressures that ply the landless waters of the great Southern Ocean. Alongside these two main supply lines, there's always a chance of cyclones, hurricanes or typhoons, which are geographically specific names for strong tropical depressions. So centrally located islands like Hawaii, Tahiti or Samoa are fortunately exposed to wave energy from far off storms in both hemispheres while the western rim of the Pacific basin in Asia have to wait for typhoons or monsoons to generate most of its waves, especially in the China Sea (which is the largest sea in the world). Trade winds provide the final source of swell, blowing in NE, E or SE lines, depending on which hemisphere you are in.

The North Pacific storms are more seasonal and more extreme than their southern counterparts. In winter, the ocean comes alive from October to March, pounding the northerly coasts of Hawaii, including the legendary North Shore of Oahu with the world's biggest waves. The Aleutian low pressures usually start winding up in the Russian Kuril and blast across the North Pacific to Alaska. The strongest North Pacific storms in the Aleutians will bring smaller, clean lines to the north coasts of many South Pacific islands, particularly French

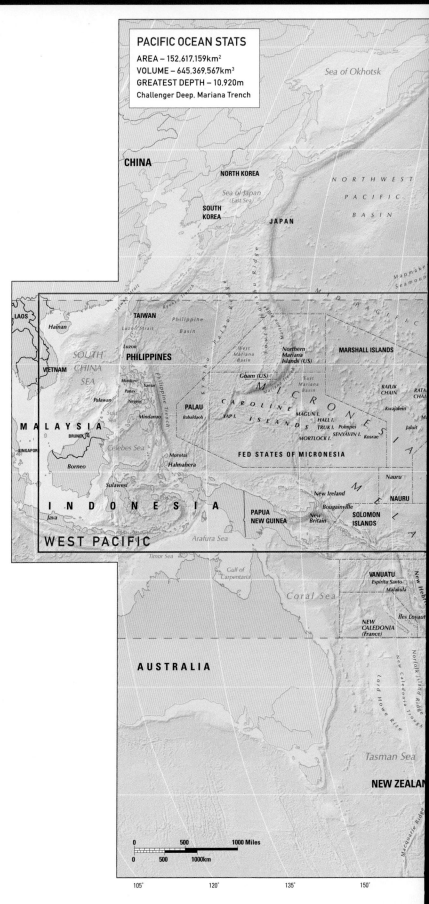

PACIFIC OCEAN STATS
AREA – 152,617,159km²
VOLUME – 645,369,567km³
GREATEST DEPTH – 10,920m
Challenger Deep, Mariana Trench

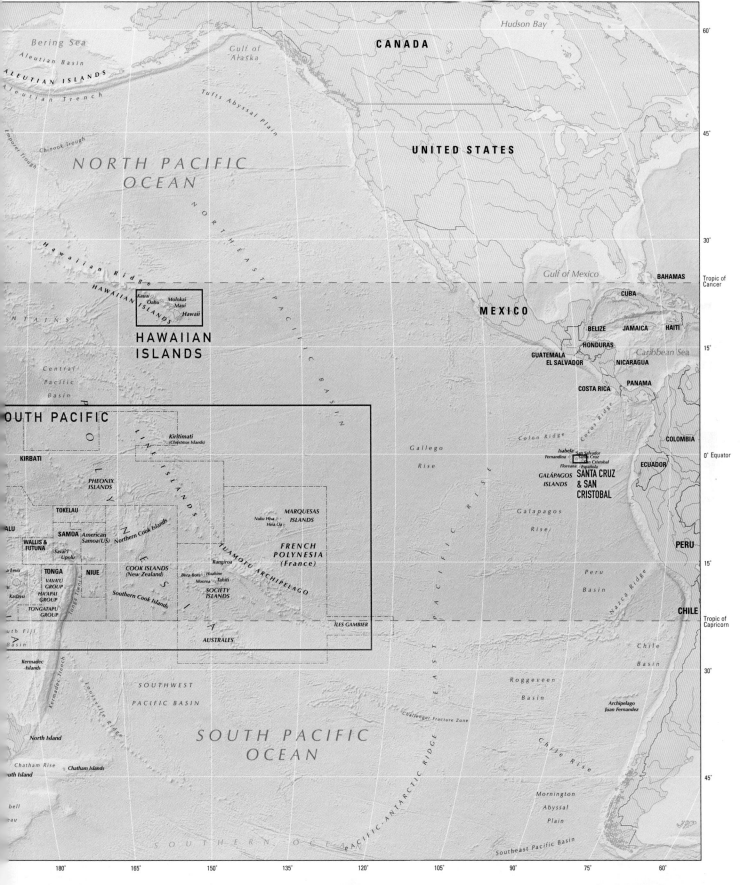

NORTH PACIFIC
OCEAN

Bering Sea

Aleutian Basin

ALEUTIAN ISLANDS

Aleutian Trench

Emperor Trough

Chinook Trough

Gulf of Alaska

Tufts Abyssal Plain

CANADA

Hudson Bay

UNITED STATES

NORTHEAST PACIFIC BASIN

Gulf of Mexico

Tropic of
Cancer

BAHAMAS

CUBA

MEXICO

BELIZE   JAMAICA   HAITI

HONDURAS

GUATEMALA   *Caribbean Sea*
EL SALVADOR   NICARAGUA

COSTA RICA   PANAMA

Cocos Ridge

Colon Ridge

COLOMBIA

Hawaiian Ridge

HAWAIIAN ISLANDS

Kauai *Molokai*
Oahu *Maui*
Hawaii

HAWAIIAN
ISLANDS

MOUNTAINS

*Central
Pacific
Basin*

SOUTH PACIFIC

POLYNESIA

KIRBATI

*Kiritimati
(Christmas Islands)*

LINE ISLANDS

PHEONIX
ISLANDS

TOKELAU

ALU

SAMOA   *American
Samoa(US)*

WALLIS &   *Savai'i*
FUTUNA   *Upolu*

Northern Cook Islands

a Levu

TONGA
*VAVA'U
GROUP*
Kadavu   *HA'APAI
GROUP*
*TONGATAPU
GROUP*

NIUE

COOK ISLANDS
(New Zealand)

Southern Cook Islands

NEW ZEALAND

Rangiroa

Bora-Bora *Huahine*
Moorea *Tahiti*

SOCIETY
ISLANDS

Nuku Hiva
Hiva Oa

MARQUESAS
ISLANDS

FRENCH
POLYNESIA
(France)

TUAMOTU ARCHIPELAGO

ÎLES GAMBIER

AUSTRALES

*Gallego
Rise*

*Galapagos
Rise*

EAST PACIFIC RISE

Isabela *San Salvador*
Fernandina *Santa Cruz*
Floreana *San Cristobal*
Española

GALÁPAGOS   SANTA CRUZ
ISLANDS   & SAN
CRISTOBAL

0° Equator

ECUADOR

PERU

*Peru
Basin*

Nazca Ridge

CHILE

Tropic of
Capricorn

Tonga Trench

*Kermadec
Islands*

*South Fiji
Basin*

Louisville Ridge

SOUTHWEST
PACIFIC BASIN

North Island

Chatham Rise   *Chatham Islands*

South Island

bell

eau

SOUTH PACIFIC
OCEAN

Challenger Fracture Zone

PACIFIC-ANTARCTIC RIDGE

SOUTHERN   OCEAN

*Roggeveen
Basin*

*Chile
Basin*

Chile Rise

*Archipelago
Juan Fernandez*

*Mornington
Abyssal
Plain*

Southeast Pacific Basin

60°
45°
30°
15°
0°
15°
30°
45°

180°   165°   150°   135°   120°   105°   90°   75°   60°

Polynesia and the far flung eastern outposts of Rapa Nui and the Galapagos as the bulk of the swell propagates eastwards.

South Pacific lows are the source of most groundswells, which travel from Australia towards South America, at latitudes between 35°and 60°S. Statistics show a slightly less intense pattern than the Indian Ocean Roaring Forties or the North Pacific, but it is still a major swell producer. Polynesia gets sprayed from April to September and the SW swells only fade slightly in the southern hemisphere summer. Many of the South Pacific islands suffer from the swell shadow cast by New Zealand, including New Caledonia, Fiji, Tonga and Samoa. This shadow doesn't stop all the SW swell and once the lows move further east, the S and SE swells will hit these Polynesian shores unhindered. Swell direction will often be an important factor at some reef passes, so waiting for the low pressures to enter the ideal window is crucial.

Asia's Pacific side relies on typhoons and monsoon windswells, so consistency is much lower than the rest of the Pacific. The primary season for surf in the Philippines is June-November, when an estimated 25 typhoons or tropical storms roll west towards the China Sea. The western Pacific experiences the strongest cyclonic activity in the world but nevertheless, typhoons are far less reliable sources of waves than groundswells. August-September is a fairly consistent time to score these magic typhoon swells, which tend to cram in 8-10 waves per set and sometimes as many as 12-15, compared to the more normal 4-6 that groundswells produce. The track of these typhoons, as with all tropical storms, is hard to predict. Most commonly, they will form in the open ocean over Micronesia

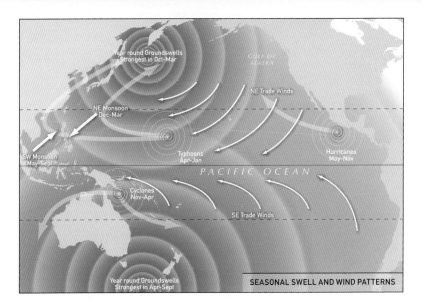

SEASONAL SWELL AND WIND PATTERNS

The North Shore of Oahu is a serendipitous example of ideal North Pacific winter groundswell exposure and reliable offshore trade winds.

and head due west towards the Philippines, before starting to arc northwards in the direction of Japan. It is this arc that produces NE swell for the Philippine spots and possibly some W-NW swells for Micronesia. The Philippines benefit from a deep ocean trench that is 10km (6mi) deep and does a great job of attracting and amplifying marginal swells for Siargao and the SE region. The winter months will

PIPELINE

see some NE groundswell being sent down off the back of the big lows that spin across the North Pacific, but most of the size is heading in the opposite direction. When these short-lived swells do occur they mainly affect the more NE exposed parts of the Philippines. The NE monsoon from mid-December to March can be responsible for a bit of windswell in the South China Sea, producing rideable waves in Vietnam, Taiwan and West Luzon, as well as creating the best chance of favourable conditions for Indonesia's Pacific coastline around Maluku. Papua New Guinea relies on windswell kicked up by the NW monsoon between Nov and April. Offshore mornings followed by the onshore trades and generally smaller swells are the staple diet in this diverse Melanesian outpost.

The Southwest Pacific cyclone activity off the east coast of Australia is the least predictable of the world's tropical storm zones so swell forecasting is more luck than good planning. Generally, cyclones form between 10° and 20°S, just off the end of New Guinea or Queensland and then head south in an arc towards New Zealand. If the storm stays far enough away from any of the neighbouring islands, then extremely good surf conditions will probably result, avoiding the major devastation that will definitely result if the cyclone makes landfall!

WIND

The tropics belt is combed by dependable, often forceful easterly trade winds, quadrant opposed in each hemisphere by the Coriolis effect, which bends the winds towards the equator as the earth spins through it's daily rotation. This is graphically illustrated by NE winds in the Northern Hemisphere islands of Hawaii and Micronesia to a decidedly SE dominance in all the South Pacific nations. Variations are rare, with a bit of wavering to the E, but it categorically means that west-facing spots are ideal for most Pacific islands while the windward east coasts get blown out. Over in the western Pacific, the Asian monsoonal influence will see F3-F4 SW winds sweep the region throughout the middle of the year, bookended by the aforementioned NE monsoon flow, which generally heralds the best surf season in the Philippines, South China Sea, Maluku and PNG.

TIDES, CURRENTS AND TEMPERATURES

Tidal ranges across the Pacific are small <6ft (<2m), but they usually matter on shallow reefbreaks, especially when the surf is smaller. As size increases, the waves often start breaking on a deeper part of the reef (eg Pipeline), yet this doesn't mean that it gets any safer. In the Philippines, range increases on some islands and many reefs are

CLOUD 9, SIARGAO

Typhoons are a major swell producer for the West Pacific and plenty of countries rely on them to produce surf on many coastlines that would otherwise remain flat.

only rideable from mid to high, while over in the South China Sea, the average 3ft (1m) range is rarely exceeded except on Hainan. The offshore islands of New Ireland, PNG see the biggest daily change of up to 12ft (4m), often flooding the reef and making surfers wait for low to mid tide. Semi-diurnal even (two daily tides, same range) covers most of Polynesia and eastern Micronesia. Semi-diurnal odd (two daily tides, different range) describes the tides found across Hawaii, Melanesia, most of the Solomon's, PNG, the bulk of the Philippines, Taiwan and Hainan. The western Solomon Islands experiences mixed tides, meaning sometimes one tide a day and sometimes two.

The two main circulations of Pacific currents are made up of a few sub-currents. The South Pacific sends cold water from the West Wind Drift into the Peru (or Humboldt) current then up into the westwards flow of the South Equatorial Current. The North Pacific gyre spins in the opposite direction whereby the North Equatorial Current, sweeps past Japan (Kuroshio Current), into the North Pacific Current and finally into the California Current. There is an Alaskan and Aleutian offshoot plus a weird Equatorial Counter Current, which flows at odds to the other two Pacific Equatorial Currents. The powerful El Niño/Southern Oscillation (ENSO) occurs when the E equatorial trade winds slacken, which cause changes in circulation and sea surface temperatures (SST), allowing warmer than normal water (+ 2-4°C) to cross the Pacific from the date line to Ecuador and Peru. This anomaly can affect world weather patterns and happens every 2-7 years, before reverting back to normal, cooler SST's known as the La Niña phase.

Ocean surface temperatures in the Pacific fluctuate noticeably depending on the El Nino/La Nina cycle, but one certainty is the warmest ocean water on the planet is found in the western Pacific. The Indo-Pacific warm pool (IPWP) is the largest body of warm water in the world and has a major effect on global climate as it contracts and expands in size and varies in temperature over decades. Within the Pacific tropical zone, expect maximums around the Solomons to exceed 30°C (86°F) and minimums down to 20°C (68°F) in the Galapagos, thanks to nutrient rich upwelling from the depths.

PAPUA NEW GUINEA

Two tides a day with different heights is a widespread pattern from China's Hainan right across the North Pacific to Hawaii. Southern PNG has the biggest range.

The spiritual home of surfing and the modern birthplace for all sorts of wave riding, Hawaii is and always has been the centre of the surfing universe. Here, on one of the remotest island chains on the planet, waves have been arriving from all the points of the compass and pounding the lava, coral and sand for eons. These waves have been shaping Hawaii and the Polynesian people, whose ancestors "fished up" the islands, while exploring the vast unknown regions of the Pacific in the 12th century AD. The "Sport of Kings" owes much to the Hawaiian royalty who enshrined the art of surfing into many aspects of day-to-day life, encouraging all levels of society to frolic in the waves.

CANOES

JS CALLAHAN/SURFEXPLORE

OAHU

Oahu is Hawaii to the rest of the world – Waikiki, hula girls and Hawaii-5-0, the long-running cop show whose opening shot tantalizingly offered up a perfect vision of an empty grinding left thought to be Ala Moana Bowl (or Rockpile or Sunset reversed!). But it is really the "7 Mile Miracle" otherwise known as **THE NORTH SHORE** where the modern heart of Hawaiian surfing resides. Pipe, Sunset, Waimea – a truly terrifying triumvirate of Pacific wave-power, ably supported by a glut of equally forceful and photogenic breaks,

spooned onto the coastline like thick cream. This in turn attracts the cream of the crop from across the surfing world, focused on rising to the challenge these awesome waves throw down. West of Haleiwa, through Mokuleia, a few spots are ridden when the wind dies or goes some flavour of S, otherwise it is a bit of mess in NE-E trades. These cross-shore winds attract the wind/kite crew, but it is generally low crowds and hassle, offering intermediates some respite from the intensity of the North Shore proper. The reefs can be sharp and shallow at low tide and the outside nature of some of the breaks mean sightings of tiger and hammerhead sharks are way too common. Lefts and rights near the Pu'uiki Beach Park will run off way outside, depending on swell angle and kind winds. Mokuleia Beach Park is an easy check from the campground when N-NE pulses make the right hold up enough to connect between the rolling outside wall and the inside racetrack section over the coral. A mile west and there are more similar corners at Army Beach, which will conjure some lefts in NW swell under 8ft and hopefully S winds, otherwise the windy rigs will be flying all over the place. From here out to Kaena Point is hiking territory with trails into the Waianae Mountains and a taste of Hawaii au natural!

The **SOUTH SHORE** cityscape of Honolulu and Diamond Head provide the perfect backdrop for a gentle surf among the tourist throngs of what has always been referred to as 'Town'. The trampled sands of downtown Waikiki are home to the unique cadre of legendary Beach Boys that have taught generations of Hawaiians and introduced hundreds of thousands of tourists to the full gamut of waveriding options, gently infused with plenty of aloha spirit. Incredibly, surfing on Oahu is not just about Town and there is a lot more Country than just the North Shore. The leeward Westside breaks from Barbers Point on the SW tip of the island up past majestic Makaha to Kaena Point, are where constant offshores meet both summer and winter swells, giving the tight-knit community plenty of opportunity to impart their wave-riding knowledge and traditions. The windward East coast, passes the body-bashing shoredumpers of Sandy Beach and Makapu'u up to Kailua on a coast just waiting for Kona winds to airbrush the constant E trade wind swell into something sweet.

MAUI

Out of all the Hawaiian Islands, Maui suffers the most swell shadowing from neighboring islands and therefore some coastlines are not worth checking in certain swell patterns. The busy Kihei stretch encompasses many of the tourist resorts and hotels on the island and is usually either flat or small, which is perfect for visiting non-surfers to hit the many surf schools and catch some perfect beginner waves. The Cove is the most popular spot, working best on W or S swells, with sandy peaks at the northern end of Kalama Park or a rocky left at the southern end. Makena State Park offers the occasional ride at Little Beach and Big Beach but it's rarely any good and better suited to bodyboard/bash. Super fast, bordering on the close-out and super shallow, bordering on the insane can be applied to both Dumps and La Perouse, lefts over nasty, coral-studded lava on the SW corner of the island. Picks up all S swell and is usually offshore all day, yet is pretty fickle and hard to read. Surf is at a premium from here all the way to Hana on the NE coast thanks to sheer cliffs, crazy volcanic rock formations and swell shadowing from the Big Island. Hana Bay is typical windward surf with some longer lefts sweeping towards the rivermouth with big N or E swell and kona winds. Round the corner back on the NE-facing coast are a couple of waves like Keanae, which gets some trade wind protection from the eastern headland and gives intermediates a chance to get some waves without much crowd pressure. Similar story at the deeply indented Honomanu Bay where there can be some good lefts on the exposed side in light or kona winds.

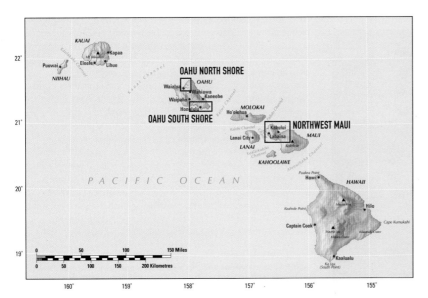

OTHER ISLANDS TO CONSIDER

HANALEI BAY

For more information, check these other Stormrider Surf Guides and/or eBooks.

SYLVAIN CAZENAVE

KAUAI

Known as the "The Garden Island", Kauai is an ancient and deeply eroded extinct volcano, rising 5000m (15,250ft) above the sea floor. Separated from Oahu by the angry, open ocean of the Kauai Channel, it was the only island that repelled King Kamehameha's efforts to unite Hawaii and remained self-governing until the 1820's. Kauai regulations state that no building may exceed the height of a coconut tree, preventing development from scarring the breathtaking scenery. There are more sandy beaches than many other islands and nearly 45% of its coastline is virtually deserted. Despite having over 300 surf spots,

+ YEAR-ROUND SWELLS
+ HAWAIIAN POWER
+ SUPER-SCENIC ISLAND
+ VARIETY OF COASTLINE
+ HAWAIIAN SURF CULTURE

– MOSTLY "EXPERTS ONLY" SURF
– PROTECTIVE LOCALS
– HIGH LOCAL PRICES
– RAINY AND WINDY
– SHARKS

underwater topography is, allegedly, not as ideal as Oahu. High volcanic cliffs line the North Shore, reducing options, plus the inaccessibility of the Na Pali coast makes it very dangerous to find and ride the few spots that face the brunt of the winter swells.

+ EXPOSED TO MOST SWELLS
+ KONA SPOT DENSITY
+ REMOTE, UNCROWDED WAVES
+ TROPICAL SNOW SPORTS

– NW SWELL SHADOW
– STEEP CLIFFS, TRICKY ACCESS
– SUPER-RAINY EAST COAST
– LOCALISED URBAN SPOTS
– 4WD REQUIRED FOR REMOTE SPOTS

HAWAII (BIG ISLAND)

While Oahu and Kauai are known for their north/south shore divide, the Big Island is an east/west side story. The youngest island in the chain, Hawaii is known as the Big Island, due to its size, which is nearly double that of the others combined and being a live volcano, continues to grow. Lava flowing from Kilauea is continually shaping a new landscape on its way to the sea where it can both create future surf breaks or destroy existing ones. Whilst Oahu usually grabs the surf history limelight, Polynesian immigrants probably initiated surfing at Kealakekua Bay centuries ago, making the Big Island the birthplace of surfing and the aloha spirit. Crowds and localism do exist, but remote spots requiring long hikes or 4WD access will be empty and conditions will be less competitive than most Hawaiian line-ups.

ANDREW SHIELD

KONA COAST

OAHU – NORTH SHORE

+ THE PROVING GROUND
+ SEVEN MILE MIRACLE
+ MYTHICAL SURF CULTURE
+ GREAT SPECTATOR ARENA

− DANGEROUS SURFING CONDITIONS
− AMAZING CROWD PRESSURES
− NOT SUITABLE FOR BEGINNERS
− EXPENSIVE

There is no denying that the North Shore of Oahu is surfing's Mecca. Its undisputed attractions challenge every surfer on the planet to find out if they have got what it takes. Conquering the fear of dropping into a bomb at Pipe, or paddling over the edge of a Waimea cliff represent the zenith of the surfing experience. Thousands make the pilgrimage every year to the Hawaiian Islands, which are tips of volcanic mountains, that rise precipitously from the ocean floor. There's no continental shelf or barrier reef to dampen the force of the powerful swells that come thundering out of the North Pacific and slam into the world's most famous surf zone on Oahu's beautiful North Shore. Reverentially dubbed 'The Seven Mile Miracle' this short, savage coastline between Haleiwa and Velzyland has it all from kiddies reforms to tow-in monsters of the deep, often displayed tantalizingly close to shore. The North Shore coast faces due northwest, and early season W swells tend to break cleaner at many spots than N or NE swells, plus they also do a good job of scouring away the summer sand build-up so the reefs are exposed and the beach angle backwash is reduced. Whatever the swell direction, the surf here can jump from 2ft to 15ft (0.6-5m) within a few hours and sneaker sets are common. On smaller swells, most spots break on lava reef close to golden sand beaches with deep channels, which make paddling out easier but also create some strong rips in larger surf. From mid Nov-Jan, all the professional surfers in the world flock to Hawaii, and it becomes a major achievement to snag a wave off the hungry pack.

and gusty NE trades. After slamming the exposed outside point, swells filter into a shelf that sucks hard and barrels before letting up and drifting into the deep channel. NW swell and mid tide is best for the dominant right while lefts appear when the swell is more W. The rip can be nasty and sharks patrol the harbour entrance. All the information you need is in the name. **AVALANCHE** is a proper bombproof bombora, rearing up from the depths to rumble left into a death or occasional glory end shack section. Best watched from the safety of Haleiwa unless packing jet propulsion or equipment and attitude to handle the power rips, random set shifts and limitless size range. Big wave junkies only. **LANIAKEA** is a rare righthander that can be perfect when a N swell meets a light E wind at mid tide. When it finally fires, surfers descend, looking for their share of one of the North Shore's best rights, as it combines down-the-line speed with cylindrical beauty, especially on the inside wedge sections. Some lefts in W swells as the line-up breaks up, but going against the grain will involve some punishment over a reef prone to baring it's teeth above water-level. Way offshore from Lani's, a predominant left peak entices the self assured to take on this scary, shifting monster called **HIMALAYAS**. W-NW swells will wall lengthy lefts, while N will see rights off the peak, throwing up wildly fluctuating wave-heights and only those with a ski will avoid some deep water tumbling under the maverick sets. Only experienced watermen will handle the rips and clean-ups. **JOCKO'S** (named after '60s switchfoot tuberider, Jock Sutherland) is a sucky, Pipe-esque affair when a W-NW swell unfurls over coral heads and a gruesome, lava rock strewn reef. Both the

LANIAKEA

LAURENT MASUREL

The town of **HALEIWA** provides a variety of facilities and amenities and is the commercial centre of the North Shore as well as being the breeding ground for many of the best Hawaiian talents, both past and present. Pulling up at the Ali'i Beach Park on a small day may be deceptive as broken peaks look easy, but when an overhead W-NW swell hits, a challenging, powerful right jumps the reef, outputting lightning fast walls and hollow hooks through to a shallow, inside shutdown section called the Toilet Bowl. Crazy crowds are guaranteed as is getting plenty of sets on the head trying to fight the ever-present rip. Experts only at size while beginners can ride the shorebreak reforms. The rights of **PUAENA POINT** (Puni's) break into the Haleiwa boat channel, offering protection from unruly N swells

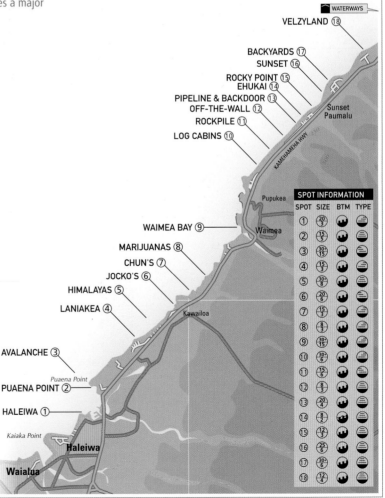

WATERWAYS

VELZYLAND ⑱

BACKYARDS ⑰
SUNSET ⑯
ROCKY POINT ⑮
EHUKAI ⑭
PIPELINE & BACKDOOR ⑬
OFF-THE-WALL ⑫
ROCKPILE ⑪
LOG CABINS ⑩

Sunset
Paumalu

KAMEHAMEHA HWY

Pupukea

WAIMEA BAY ⑨
Waimea

MARIJUANAS ⑧
CHUN'S ⑦
JOCKO'S ⑥
HIMALAYAS ⑤
LANIAKEA ④
Kawailoa

AVALANCHE ③
Puaena Point
PUAENA POINT ②

HALEIWA ①
Kaiaka Point
Haleiwa

Waialua

SPOT	SIZE	BTM	TYPE
①	20/5		
②	15/3		
③	30/15		
④	15/3		
⑤	30/8		
⑥	20/3		
⑦	15/3		
⑧	8/3		
⑨	30/15		
⑩	30/6		
⑪	15/6		
⑫	8/3		
⑬	20/4		
⑭	8/3		
⑮	12/2		
⑯	25/6		
⑰	30/6		
⑱	12/4		

WAIMEA

LAT: 21.643213° LONG: -158.066465°

The benchmark, big-wave forum of Hawaii's North Shore. Although somewhat eclipsed by outer reef tow-in breaks, mere mortals will find the 20-25ft (6-8m) swells that Waimea can provide more than enough of a challenge. Deep water swells arrive suddenly, tripping on a lava shelf sitting a good 100m+ out from the northern headland. This creates a wave that lurches violently up, then out, resulting in the famous Waimea air drop take-off, followed by an endless plunge over boils, chops and gutters to the trough, then a race to the channel, chased by hundreds of tons of water. Strong trades, funneling down Waimea Valley are far from ideal, getting under the nose of your gun and holding you in a lip that's renowned for thick, high psi power, so light ESE wind is best, mid tide and a long period NW swell. On smaller days below 15ft (5m), when The Bay proper isn't working, a sandbar and boulder section called Pinballs can reel off some juicy little pockets right along the lava rock point. Waimea's shorebreak is a gnarly mix of crashing lips and powerful death-pits; once avoided, today it's packed with suicidal bodyboarders and even a few stand-up surfers. Getting in and out of the water requires timing through the shorebreak in the northern corner, while the overpowering current drags victims down to the jump rock. Crowds are thick, especially at the starting size around 15ft and sharing a set is common practice although flying boards and bodies heighten the risks. Specialist equipment, big wave experience and total commitment required. Parking is a nightmare when the swell jumps with the Kam choked by stationary cars looking for somewhere to stop and watch the show from. Walk in from further afield.

take-off peaks are steep and rapid, leading to mist exhaling tubes or wailing speed walls to another inside bowl section before the safety of the deep channel. Bonus right off outside suck leads to a rocky minefield. Handles plenty of size until the channel closes out to Chun's and the really strong out-going rip makes getting back to the beach an effort. Often crowded, but more chance of scoring a memorable pit to yourself than up the coast. One of the more improver-friendly spots on the North Shore, CHUN'S welcomes any swell onto 3 sections

of righthand reef. The outside, middle and bowl all feature nice roll-ins, shredable walls and some inviting tubes in places. Best on small NW swells with any trade wind direction and even handles a bit of S wind. There's a bonus left off the middle section, but the paddle back out is no fun. Absolutely always crowded since it's in full view of the Kam Highway, plus it's an easy, yet long paddle using the rip to the left. There are easier rolling waves to the north at Rightovers and Leftovers, plus some suckier action at Alligator Rock (not to be confused with Alligators outside tow-in reef). Tricky, rock-hopping entry and exit keeps the crowds manageable. You would expect **MARIJUANAS** to be a mellow spot and compared to the smoking bombs further north it is, yet it can still spin off a speedy, walled right across a shallow-ish reef offering cover-ups and lip-bashing potential. Waist high to overhead NW swells and a bit of protection from the NE trades make it a tasty little number away from the crush. Halfway up the North Shore, the Kam Highway swings wide around a bay called **WAIMEA** – the spot that has set the standard for big wave surfing for over 40 years. **LOG CABINS** is an underrated right that shifts around a lot over an ill-defined reef, relying on peaky N swells to prevent it from shutting down violently. It breaks over a treacherous lava bottom that has sharp, upthrusting fingers and sand fills the gaps in places. From shoulder to overhead it is accessible to experienced riders, but as the size rises, it becomes increasingly malevolent and twisted. Way outside is Outer Log Cabins, a notorious tow-in reef that has held some of the biggest waves ever ridden. A good distance offshore lies a series of reefy protuberances that catch a NW swell and conduct it back towards Off-The-Wall in the shape of a meaty and often sketchy left. Heavily reliant on sand deposition, **ROCKPILES** is notorious for lava fingers popping up when surfing it small, or when getting a

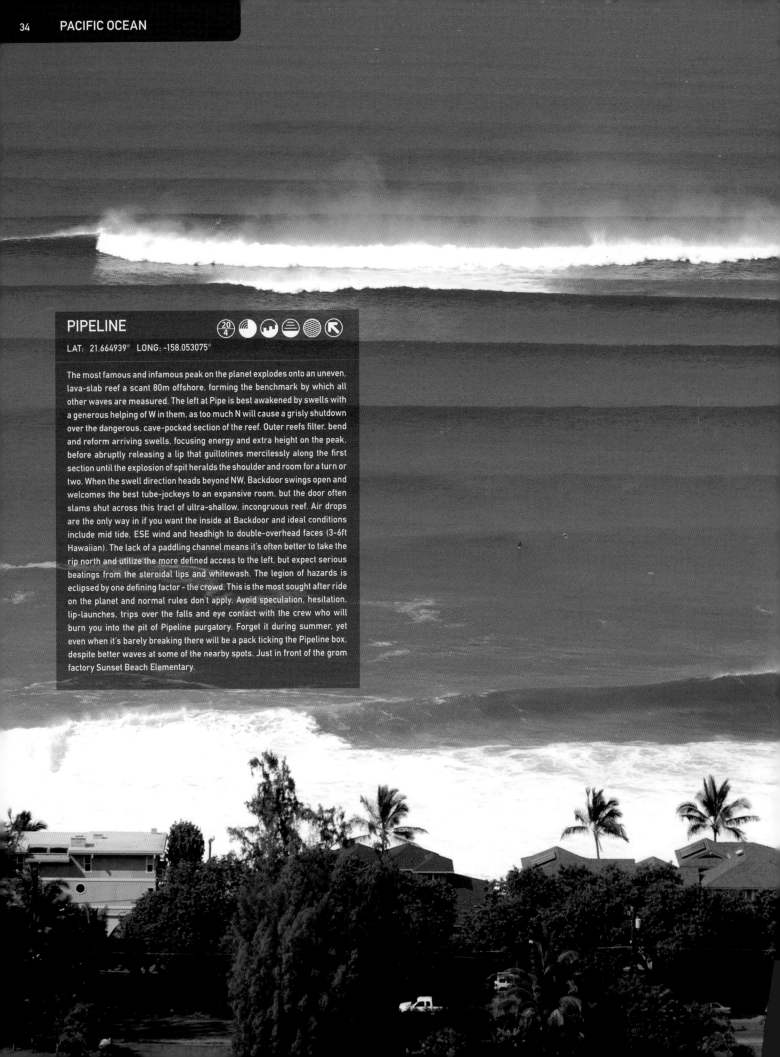

PIPELINE

LAT: 21.664939°   LONG: -158.053075°

The most famous and infamous peak on the planet explodes onto an uneven, lava-slab reef a scant 80m offshore, forming the benchmark by which all other waves are measured. The left at Pipe is best awakened by swells with a generous helping of W in them, as too much N will cause a grisly shutdown over the dangerous, cave-pocked section of the reef. Outer reefs filter, bend and reform arriving swells, focusing energy and extra height on the peak, before abruptly releasing a lip that guillotines mercilessly along the first section until the explosion of spit heralds the shoulder and room for a turn or two. When the swell direction heads beyond NW, Backdoor swings open and welcomes the best tube-jockeys to an expansive room, but the door often slams shut across this tract of ultra-shallow, incongruous reef. Air drops are the only way in if you want the inside at Backdoor and ideal conditions include mid tide, ESE wind and headhigh to double-overhead faces (3-6ft Hawaiian). The lack of a paddling channel means it's often better to take the rip north and utilize the more defined access to the left, but expect serious beatings from the steroidal lips and whitewash. The legion of hazards is eclipsed by one defining factor - the crowd. This is the most sought after ride on the planet and normal rules don't apply. Avoid speculation, hesitation, lip-launches, trips over the falls and eye contact with the crew who will burn you into the pit of Pipeline purgatory. Forget it during summer, yet even when it's barely breaking there will be a pack ticking the Pipeline box, despite better waves at some of the nearby spots. Just in front of the grom factory Sunset Beach Elementary.

SUNSET BEACH

JOLI

beating paddling out. Therefore it's safer from mid and works in all N swell directions above headhigh and E-SE trades. There are some rights that head over towards Log Cabins, but the risk versus reward balance is all wrong. Crowds are lighter than Pipe, especially at size, but some say the consequences are heavier - be very sure of your ability. **OFF-THE-WALL** (a.k.a Kodak Reef) is the classic, high quality, super-crowded, right sprint that's been a favourite with photographers since the '70s. Separated from Pipe by a short channel, swells need to arrive with N in them to get the rights opening up over what is essentially a straight bit of reef. Smaller, less perfect lefts peel back towards Backdoor and may offer visitors more of a chance of actually catching a wave, because the crowds can be very intense. Shallow and unforgiving, but barrels guaranteed at mid-tide on an overhead NW swell. **PIPELINE & BACKDOOR** form the most famous peak in the world. Backdoors' racing rights and Pipe's cylindrical, spitting lefts explode on a jagged lava reef. No other spot on earth quite matches the full Pipeline experience - the power, the barrels ,the crowds, the glory, the humility......this is quintessential North Shore. Small day reef peaks at **EHUKAI** offer some respite from the

power of adrenaline-pumping surrounding waves, but not necessarily from the incessant crowds. Lefts and rights over the wildly uneven lava shelf can be hollow and epic when the sand has built up just right, giving less confident surfers a forum for turns, airs and barrels, when peaky headhigh N swells bounce around this Pupukea stretch that also includes the shallow spitting pits of Gas Chambers. All amenities at the Ehukai Beach Park area. The modest lava jut of **ROCKY POINT** is a swell magnet and a jam-packed theatre of progressive school surfing, logged by the ever-present surf photographers lining the beach. The rights reel off in N swells while the handful of speedy lefts prefer more W-NW. It's very consistent in all small to moderate swells and the curve of reef allows for some wind variation from NE-S depending on what section you are riding. Access path from the giant wood statue on Kamehameha Hwy. Past Kammieland, a fun near-shore peak opposite Kammies Market, the famous **SUNSET BEACH** starts it's curve northwards. Incorporating Vals, Inside Bowl, West Peak, Middles and Sunset Point on the inside, this break has more personalities than reality TV. Under headhigh, NE windswell will still break at The Point, then overhead, W-NW swells start popping up over the fingers of reef at Middles, before double-overhead awakens Inside Bowl and maybe West Peak on a long period W-NW swell. Sunset's default mode is unpredictable as N swells will break up along the ragged hem of reef, while W will launch threatening slabs from wide, punishing the reckless in the turbulent inside. When the long, roller-coaster rights lead into the hollow Inside Bowl, board, leash and body snapping power is apparent, with many shutdowns and unmakeable sections before the wave fattens out into the channel. The real difficulty is trying to get a bomb set off the entrenched local crew on large boards who dominate, leaving mere mortals to dodge the bullets on the inside. 15ft Hawaiian for upper size limit when Outside Backyards sets start to wash through. Rips, phantom sets and the wide playing field help dismantle the pack. Shallow when small at The Point, but it is rare to bounce at size when depth increases and hold-downs are long rag-doll affairs in mid water at the West Bowl. Scattergun peaks stalk the exposed, wide reef flanking Sunset, providing a crowd-free option for those willing to take the inevitable beating **BACKYARDS** is famous for. Extremely hard for paddle surfers to manage, it has become the domain of wind, kite and tow surfers when the swell jumps up. Outside Backyards will suck in more ocean swell than Waimea and 50ft + faces are on the cards.

BERNARD TESTEMALE

ROCKPILES

Shallow, urchin-covered reef adds to the heaviness. Almost a mile north of Sunset is **VELZYLAND**, perhaps the most localised and intensely crowded spot on the strip. Outer reefs like Phantoms filter the swell size before it reforms and lurches onto a sharp lava reef, spinning fast right bowls and shreddable walls before hitting a positively square inside barrel section. Less competitive, shorter lefts can be had, but there's no paddle channel to get back out. Mid tide, light SE and small to medium NW swell best. Experts or pros only and intermediates will be better off at Freddyland across the channel.

OFF-THE-WALL

ROGER SHARP

WIND AND SWELL

The winter season can extend as far as from Oct to May, but January holds the aces in the historical stats. Average swell height is 12ft, average period is 12secs and there are virtually no flat days! Peaks hit 27ft and 18secs respectively and the dominant E wind hits 20mph (32kmh) every 1 day in 3 (30% of the time). November, December and February figures are very similar, just a little less swell consistency and a bit more NE wind, so don't discount early or late season, which can pump without so many pros and journeymen in town. From April to September, the North Shore is generally flat, but other sides of the island see frequent 3-8ft (1-2.6m) NE windswell and 2-8ft (0.6-2.6m) SE-SW summer groundswell. The more NE in the wind, the more sideshore it will be at many North Shore spots, so if it gets too strong, it will mess up the waves. South to westerly winds (referred to as kona winds) occur periodically in winter when a large frontal system associated with a deep low pressure appears to the W or NW of Hawaii. This can bring large swells, accompanied by wind and rain for a day or two before returning to trade winds from the opposite direction. While the max tidal range at Haleiwa never exceeds 2ft (0.6m), it is enough to cause real changes at many breaks. ●

SURF STATS		J F	M A	M J	J A	S O	N D
SWELL	Dominant swell	◉	◉	◉	◉	◉	◉
	Size (m)	8-9	6-7	3-4	1-2	4-5	7-8
	Consistency (%)	90	70	40	30	60	80
WIND	Dominant wind	◔	◔	◔	◔	◔	◔
	Average force	F4	F4	F4	F4	F4	F4
	Consistency (%)	63	66	76	88	77	77
TEMP.	Wetsuit	🏄	🏄	🏄	🏄	🏄	🏄
	Water temp.	24	24	25	26	27	25

TRAVEL INFORMATION

LOCAL POPULATION	COASTLINE – 204km (128mi)
Oahu - 953.207	TIME ZONE – GMT -10hr

GETTING THERE – Once you land in Honolulu (HNL - see Oahu South Shore), there are limited options to get to the North Shore. Shuttles from the airport to Turtle Bay at the far end of the North Shore will cost around $90 for the first person and $9 for each additional person. Otherwise it's rental car to drive the 30mins to Haleiwa or hour to Turtle Bay in light traffic periods.

GETTING AROUND – Most people rent a car and the airport rental choice is large. Hawaii Car Rentals offer economy vehicles from $135/wk, but added charges, insurance and taxes will inflate that figure. Fuel is 25% more than the US mainland. Parking on big swell days is a nightmare at Waimea and Sunset which makes a scooter or moped rental a bit more attractive (fr. $35/d). The Oahu bus system, officially called TheBus (thebus.org), runs between most towns, 24/7. TheBus circuits the north and east coasts (Route 55, 88A). Fare for any trip on TheBus is US$2.50 for adults, exact change is compulsory. Bodyboards, skateboards and bikes are OK - no surfboards! Cycling the 7 mile miracle is easy with some bike paths and many rentals offering a board rack (from $10/d for longer rentals).

LODGING AND FOOD – The only North Shore hotel is Turtle Bay Hilton (from $199/n - 5th night free). Most people stay at Backpackers Vacation Inn and Plantation Village near Waimea (dorm bed from $27/n; private dbl rooms $62-$85/n; studio $120-$145/n; Cabins sleep 4-8p $160-$290; 10% off weekly rates.), B&B's in Haleiwa (fr $37/d) or rent a flat (from $600/w for 4 people). Winter is high season. Food is not cheap: $20 for a basic meal or buy it at Foodland, one of the most expensive supermarkets in the US.

WEATHER – The stability of the air temperature is amazing. Between day and night, winter and summer, temps vary little from a near perfect 25°C (77°F). It's the same story in the sea surface water temps, which hover between 25-29°C (77-84°F), but during the winter surf season rainy periods from Kona fronts and a bit of upwelling from the strong offshore trades will see lows of 24°C (75°F) at times. When NE-E trades blow, skies are usually clear. The west shore is much drier than the easterly windward coast.

WEATHER	J/F	M/A	M/J	J/A	S/O	N/D
Total Rainfall (mm)	90	55	17	18	35	65
Consistency (d/m)	8	7	5	6	6	9
Temperature min. (°C)	19	19	21	23	22	20
Temperature max. (°C)	26	27	29	29	30	27

NATURE AND CULTURE – Hike to Kaena Point or hit the Kahuku Sugarmill disco. Historic train tours through the Dole plantation outside of Haleiwa. The Hele Huli Adventure Center at Turtle Bay does surfing, stand up paddle boarding, golf, tennis, helicopter tours, horse riding, hiking, biking, fishing, glass bottom kayaking, whale watching and more. Check out the Polynesian Cultural Center, Oahu's biggest cultural attraction over on the windward side and take your board in case the lefts are firing.

HAZARDS AND HASSLES – Drowning, collisions with the reef, heavy rips, flying boards and angry locals will all keep you on your toes! Minimize the risks by surfing the low-key spots or by surfing very early and being patient and cautious in the line-up. Car rip-offs are common so leave nothing in it and leave it unlocked.

HANDY HINTS – The yellow pages of the phone book are loaded with surf shops, both in Town and out in the Country (North Shore). Haleiwa has the biggest concentration, where picking up a board designed for the local waves is a good idea, rather than paddling-out under-gunned, which is a bad idea.

OAHU — SOUTH SHORE

+ CONSISTENT ALL SEASON SWELLS
+ WORLD'S SURFING HERITAGE
+ BEGINNER-FRIENDLY WAIKIKI REEFS
+ BIG CITY ENTERTAINMENT
+ PERFECT WEATHER, UNIQUE SCENERY

– MESSY WINDSWELLS
– INTENSE CROWDS & LOCALS
– SOME POLLUTION & SHARKS
– LONG-HAUL PACIFIC FLIGHT
– EXPENSIVE US DESTINATION

Although Oahu is only the third-largest island in the Hawaiian chain, it houses 70% of the state's population, mostly in the ever-growing city and county of Honolulu that has nearly hit 1m residents. Oahu is thought of as paradise, with it's mix of spectacular, exotic scenery and the fantastic weather. Waikiki means "spouting waters", is the state's tourism mecca and the place where Duke Kahanamoku helped to relaunch surfing a century ago. During summer (June-Sept), swells vary in height from 2-8ft (0.6-2.5m) and on very rare occasions, can get huge like in 1917, when Duke caught a 35ft (11+m) wave for a distance of 1.25 miles (2 km). Stretching from Duke Beach near the Hilton Hawaiian Village to the Duke statue on Kuhio Beach, hundreds if not thousands of all kinds of waveriders are in the surf almost every day of the year, enjoying the fun, user-friendly conditions. Further afield there are some really good waves on the windward coast and a growing number of spots from Ewa Beach down south to the wild west coast where Makaha has already forged a famous reputation for everything from beginner curls to monstrous swells.

Arguably Oahu's best bodysurf/bodyboard spot **MAKAPU'U BEACH** has long trundling lefts ending in a huge shorebreak barrel that works best in winter with E swell and opposing winds. Really strong currents preside, keeping the lifeguards busy, who police the no surfboards policy at the Beach Park, but allow stand-ups to take on the heavy barreling right over the lava shelf at Makapu'u Point, in front of Sea Life Park. It's also worth being curious about Rabbit Island in bigger NE swells. Similar conditions at **SANDY BEACH**, a neck-breaking shorebreak for crazy, talented lids and fins on any E to S swell. Boards can head outside for the shallow left reef, which is usually blown to pieces by the trades. Always crowded when it's on. Among the mansions of Portlock, Koko Kai Park allows access to China Walls, an unusual left that hugs the rock platform and spins down the point for a long way in big swells. Near Kawaiku'i Beach Park, check the uncrowded offshore reefs of **SECRETS** long rights & good shortboard lefts on high tide, plus **TOES** longboard peak when winds are calm or N. More spots along this line of reef including Pillars, Boneyards and Wailupes, which are all long paddle outs. Below the Diamond Head Rd lookouts, **CLIFFS** is a scattering of 5-6 reefs and channels with consistently long walls that absorb the crowds of surfers and kites. Picks up S and E swell, so it's messy in trades, but it can be classic on N or glassy days and is often the biggest South shore spot. Long, ripable walls for improvers plus, with less crowds at the mushier breaks off the side of the main peak. Closer to Waikiki, Lighthouse is hollow, fast and usually oversubscribed. The lefts at **TONGGS** are improver-friendly with the odd hollow section as it doubles-up over the uneven coral. The right is faster before closing-

WAIKIKI

ANDREW SHIELD

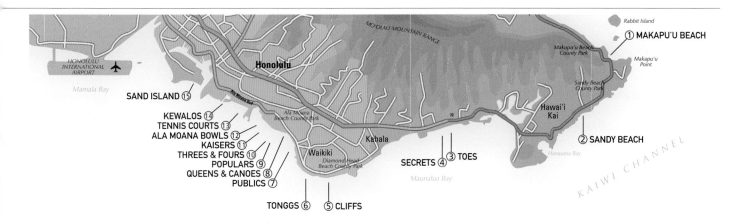

Rabbit Island
① MAKAPU'U BEACH
Makapu'u Beach County Park
Makapu'u Point
Sandy Beach County Park
HONOLULU INTERNATIONAL AIRPORT
MO'OLAU MOUNTAIN RANGE
Honolulu
Mamala Bay
Hawai'i Kai
SAND ISLAND ⑮
KEWALOS ⑭
TENNIS COURTS ⑬
ALA MOANA BOWLS ⑫
KAISERS ⑪
THREES & FOURS ⑩
POPULARS ⑨
QUEENS & CANOES ⑧
PUBLICS ⑦
Kahala
Waikiki
Diamond Head Beach County Park
Ala Moana Beach County Park
② SANDY BEACH
SECRETS ④ ③ TOES
Maunalua Bay
Hanauma Bay
TONGGS ⑥ ⑤ CLIFFS
KAIWI CHANNEL

out, while the left fades out in a deeper channel. Further east are the dangerous sounding lefts at Graveyards and Suicides, which is more of a fun wall, as long as the tide is not super-low. Across the channel from Tonggs left is Rice Bowl, a sucky, spinning right/left combo that offers tube time and coping in equal measure, but is rare, sought after and capable of dishing out some punishment on the shallow shelf. All the breaks around Tonggs handle NE trades much better than Cliffs. Paddle out from the tiny beach off of Kalakaua. Named after a long gone public baths, **PUBLICS** are the easy to spot left lines hugging the fringe of reef on the east flank of Waikiki. Often looks uncrowded and seductive, thanks to handfuls of coral fingers, reaching out to grab the unwary, especially at lower tides. Not for the unskilled, unlike further up the reef where the coral shelf relents, creating a deeper, small swell spot called Old Mans, which gives you a hint about the mellow crowd on all craft. **QUEENS & CANOES** are fabled fun Waikiki reefs packed with all kinds of surf crafts. Queen's rights offer ripable walls up to 6ft over forgiving reef, while Canoes can handle bigger, mushier waves for longboarders and learners. No danger from the reef but getting mowed down by anything from a soft top to an outrigger is real and present. Neither like big swell or wind and it is fair to say this could be the most crowded line-up on the planet most days. Further outside check **POPULARS** slightly less crowded and less localised rights that run down the reef nicely in SE-S swells. There's a paddling channel to the right of the break and some shorter soft lefts. When Pops gets overhead and pumping on a big S swell, loads of shredders appear to destroy the waves and the usual mellow vibe. **THREES** and **FOURS** are a fair way from the beach, but this does little to dampen the crowd that rate Threes as one of the go to spots in a good S swell. Speed runs into some hollow sections end in a defined channel and then it's an easy paddle back out. Fours is more sectiony, with some easier lefts heading towards Kaisers. Experienced surfers only. When a channel was blown in the coral reef for boat access, **KAISERS** superb right was created for tube-junkies not fazed by shallow coral, shipwrecks and a carpet of urchins. The lefts are less intense but still worthy and more peaks comb the coral all the way down through Inbetweens and Rockpile to the Bowl. Confident and patient surfers with a low profile may just have a chance of snagging a wave at the infamous **ALA MOANA BOWLS**. Across the channel and off the tip of Magic Island is Bomboras, a rolling wall that shows in sizable S swells, plus further in is Little Haleiwa, a rare right breaking back towards the island. Various other named spots line the reef here like Big Lefts, Big Rights and Concession, but the main break in the middle is **TENNIS COURTS**. Courts is a fun-filled, hot-dogging righthander that may start off a little slower for the longboard crew, but is soon racing and barreling over the inside double-up section. Likes S to W overhead swell, N winds and lower tides, while a SE swell will make the short, shouldering lefts a bit more interesting, but no competition for the rights. If you manage to find a parking space in the Ala

SPOT INFORMATION			
SPOT	SIZE	BTM	TYPE
①			
②			
③			
④			
⑤			
⑥			
⑦			
⑧			
⑨			
⑩			
⑪			
⑫			
⑬			
⑭			
⑮			

Moana Park area and paddle out from the tennis courts, keep to the right of the three rocks where there is a deeper paddling channel over the sharp, shallow reef. Crowds are thick in all conditions so improvers only on small days. **KEWALOS** is super-consistent, dragging in swell toward the deep Kewalo Basin channel before unleashing a hollow, bad-tempered left that barrels, sections and shuts down with unpredictable regularity, shifting around the line-up and keeping the throng on their toes. The rights can also barrel, but quickly lead to shallow close-outs. Picks up all S and likes the angle from the E quadrant. Sharks are often spotted, lots of fishing boat traffic, some pollution and really nasty coral heads by the rip torn channel. There's no beach, so paddle out from the wall. Point Panic is across the channel, a mesmerizing, metronomic right tube that is reserved for the speedo and fin set, seen skillfully pirouetting and planing close to the rock seawall, as seen in the seminal bodysurf film *Come Hell or High Water*. Screened by the hulking warehouses and shipyards on the industrialised **SAND ISLAND**, this State Recreation Area and it's brilliant white ribbon of sand holds a mish-mash of reefy peaks. Mainly surfed at the east end near the tower where waves can break outside and reform nicely, so something for all abilities. Camping, showers and laid-back uncrowded feel. Sewer outfall offshore so avoid onshores and a reputation for big sharks (but no attacks). Spooky outside reefs toward the airport require a boat.

LAURENT MASUREL

SANDY BEACH

ALA MOANA

LAT: 21.280296°   LONG: -157.844067°

Long, shacking lefts peel down a shallow reef outside the Ala Wai Harbor. The wave was created by dredging a deepwater channel for boats to access the harbour and S swell will refract out of the channel and wedge up along the reef. Think big, round curves as it bowls over sections of reef, shoulders off, then gathers up another barrel section on the shallow inside. One of the best waves on Oahu, attracting many of the best surfers in Town, who don't often feel the need to share. Try the lesser rights or further down the reef at Rockpiles or Inbetweens in smaller swells. Paddle out from Magic Island when it's big or straight into the channel when small. Lower tides, not too much E in the swell and any wind with a sniff of N in it, although E is still OK. Can be consistent in summer, sometimes breaking every day for a month, but winter can be very patchy. This break ticks all the hazard boxes. Currents sweep the channel, as do large sharks and vessels, while the ugly sharp coral reef, urchins and maybe even the rusty remnants of the navigation pole all conspire to take their pound of flesh. Then there's the expensive parking, long paddle, locals, etc, etc!

SWELL AND WIND

Between the prime South Shore months of April and October, South Pacific swells travel great distances with very long 14-22 sec wave periods, but small wave heights (1-4 ft/0.3-1.2m). These groundswells are far from reliable and usually only last a couple of days, before the constant ENE trade wind swell returns to dominance. Wave height ranges from 4-12ft (1.2-4m) with short 5-8 sec periods. This will show up on the windward coast all the way round to Diamond Head, plus the Kaena Pt to Mokuleia stretch. North Pacific swells deliver the highest waves (8-20ft/2.5-6m) with mid-to-long 10-18 second wave periods mostly from Oct - May. W-N direction will hit the leeward coast (although Kuaui does filter some swell) and spots like Makaha get famously big. This side of the island breaks year-round since it also picks up summer S swells. Waves from winter kona storms associated with fronts passing just north of Hawaii are very steep with moderate heights (10-15ft/3-5m) and short to medium 8-10 sec periods. Kona storm waves have the greatest impact on south and west-facing coasts, but the associated winds mean it's prime time for the windward coasts. Waves from hurricanes and tropical storms (June-November) can reach extreme heights (10-35ft/3-8m) and occur

JS CALLAHAN/SURFEXPLORE

mostly on east, south and west-facing shores. The metronomic ENE trade winds rarely falter, gathering pace in summer and bending down the backside of Diamond Head, fanning Waikiki and the west coast with virtually permanent offshores. The micro tides make quite a difference to a select few South Shore breaks, but most spots are considered all tides, with high being a little mushier in most cases. ●

SURF STATS

SURF STATS	J	F	M	A	M	J	J	A	S	O	N	D
SWELL Dominant swell												
Size (m)	5-6		4-5		2-3		4-5		5		5-6	
Consistency (%)	95		85		75		80		85		90	
WIND Dominant wind												
Average force	F4		F4		F4		F4		F4		F4	
Consistency (%)	51		66		76		88		77		65	
TEMP. Wetsuit												
Water temp.	24		24		25		26		27		25	

TRAVEL INFORMATION

LOCAL POPULATION	COASTLINE – 204km (128mi)
Oahu - 953,207	TIME ZONE – GMT -10h

GETTING THERE – Visitors visas have been waived for Australian, British, Canadian and most EU passport holders. However, you must be carrying a biometric passport (kids too), with at least 90 days before expiry, otherwise a visitor visa must be obtained before travel. Honolulu (HNL) is the major Pacific hub with daily flights from North America, Kiritimati, Tahiti, American Samoa, Samoa, Fiji, Sydney, Brisbane, Auckland, Manila, Seoul and Japan. Most major airlines travelling to Oahu charge each way per surfboard. The best include the weight in your allowance, the worst charge more than a wounded bull! Hawaiian Airlines have loads of small print. Pay $35 inter-island and $100 to/from USA per double bag (max 50lbs/23kg) each way. Choose your airline carefully, or rent your boards.

GETTING AROUND – TheBus is Honolulu's public bus network ($2.50/trip - no surfboards). Most car rental agencies require a minimum age of 25. Headline prices might be as low as $18 per day but with tax, fees and insurance it costs more like $30 for an economy or compact car. Getting longboards inside a small rental can be problematic - take soft racks/ straps. Gas is about 25% more expensive than the US mainland. Traffic can be intense on weekends and parking around Waikiki is both a nightmare and expensive. This makes mopeds, bicycles and even skateboards an attractive option in downtown areas as the city of Honolulu implements it's plan to make the county extremely bike friendly with dedicated cycle lanes and racks on the back of The Bus.

LODGING AND FOOD – Anything from historic hotels and condominiums, landscaped resorts and boutique hotels, familiar brands and trend-setting chic addresses. Prices vary with the view: Diamond Head, ocean or Ko'olau mountain views are at a premium. The Aloha Surf is a 3-star hotel: fr $130/nt dbl. Surfcondos $1440/wk for 4 pax. At camping. honolulu.gov you can reserve a campsite up to 2 weeks in advance (3d/$37, 5d/$57). No camping is allowed on either Wednesday or Thursday so 3-5 day max stay applies. Largest concentration of fancy restaurants and fast food in the state.

WEATHER – Waikiki features a marine, tropical climate thanks to its isolated position in the middle of the Pacific Ocean. It is situated on a narrow plain between the ocean and the Ko'olau mountain range that serves to block trade wind moisture, resulting in a drier climate. The area enjoys warm, balmy weather year-round with temps ranging from 19-27°C (66-80°F) in winter and between 21-30°C (70-86°F) in summer. From October to April, the kona (SW-W) wind brings hot, sticky air and thunderstorm activity, often with gusty winds and days of rain. An average year may see 3 or 4 kona storms. Occasionally, slack winds see morning offshores descending from the interior mountains, making all coasts clean before the cooling, year-round, NE-E trade winds arrive, blowing hardest during the summer months. Average annual rainfall is 900mm (36in), mostly from November through March. Boardshorts, year-round.

WEATHER	J/F	M/A	M/J	J/A	S/O	N/D
Total Rainfall (mm)	104	86	43	43	65	108
Consistency (d/m)	10	9	8	8	9	11
Temperature min. (°C)	19	19	21	23	22	20
Temperature max. (°C)	25	27	29	29	30	28

NATURE AND CULTURE – Being a prime honeymoon trip, Waikiki provides big-city amenities, shopping, culture and night-time entertainment. Honolulu was recently ranked first among America's largest cities for having the cleanest air and water, and the lowest crime rate. Visit the Bishop Museum for it's archive of historical surf artifacts.

HAZARDS AND HASSLES – Sharp coral reefs and unpredictable shorebreaks have caused many serious neck and spinal injuries to all kinds of surfers. Strong currents frequently accompany big surf and rapid tide changes can also cause problems. Theft from cars is common at many of the bigger parking lots in and out of town. While Oahu's north and west sides are more notorious for localism, it also exists on the south shore. Tread carefully.

HANDY HINTS – One of the first things you will learn about Hawaii is the influence of pidgin, a kind of slang that you will find on most Polynesian islands. World famous Waikiki Beach Boys offer daily surf lessons & outrigger canoe rides. Low rental rates from a large number of rental outfits; Standard NSP board ($40 for first 2 days then $10/day). Surftech Performance rental ($65/2 days then $10/day). SUP from $90/2 days then $20 a day. Delivery and pick up from anywhere on the island.

NORTHWEST MAUI

+ WORLD-CLASS SPOTS
+ THINNER CROWDS THAN OAHU
+ WIND AND KITESURFING HEAVEN
+ AMAZING VOLCANIC SCENERY

– SWELL SHADOWS
– STRONG TRADE WINDS
– DIFFICULT ACCESS TO SOME SPOTS
– HIGH PRICES

While Oahu's North Shore has dominated media coverage of Hawaiian surf, each island in the chain gets its share of waves and Maui has some of the best, if not the most. The legendary rights of Honolua and Maalaea are part of surfing's heritage and now Jaws, the biggest name of all can be added to Maui's list of insane waves. It's an island of contrasts, where lush green valleys give way to arid coastline, tropical fruits and flowers meet barren lava and cactus, beneath the towering peaks that dominate the landscape. The shroud of islands that include Molokai, Lanai and Kahoolawe block out some swell directions and there is an element of real luck and timing to score the big names, but there is a back-up cast of consistent, quality waves just waiting to keep the locals and visitors stoked.

WINDMILLS

One of Hawai'is most famous summer spots is **MAALAEA**, where a harbour breakwall has created a righthand wave that's considered to be the fastest in the world, but it needs a huge S-SW swell to break and is notoriously fickle. Use an F1 fast board to make the drop, bottom turn and pump into a racetrack so crowded that there will probably be someone dropping in with that chandelier section up ahead. In May 2012, local activists and environmental groups finally won a 23yr battle and successfully blocked the proposed extensions of the Ma'alaea jetty, which would have destroyed this world-class gem. There's more inclusive, fun peaks around on smaller S swells and a rocky right down the coast road. Lahaina breaks all suffer from the split swell window so **SHARK PIT**'s shallow, slabbing lefts like the S-SW swells more and the less hectic rights prefer the N swells. Low tide is sketchy. There are more waves to the south. Named for a reason - be vigilant. **LAHAINA BREAKWALL** is an excellent, swell-sucking reef that squeezes the best from a S-SW pulse and conjures up snappy left walls and tubes out in front of the harbour wall. Winter N can penetrate the narrow gap between Maui and Molokai, producing high performance rights running the other way and the E trades groom both line-ups. The crowd is as consistent as the wave and lesser surfers should look towards the easier peaks to the south. The summer SW swells hit at the perfect angle for rapid lefthand walls at **LAHAINA HARBOUR** provided the tide

is on the high side of mid, covering the ugly coral and urchin carpeted lava. Luckily, the right is much better at low, peaking up and pitting, before shouldering off down beside the very busy boat channel into the harbour. Busy is the buzz word for this line-up and there's no parking anywhere near the waves. Works on N swells as well. **MALA WHARF** is a popular longboard and intermediate spot on wrapping S swells or a due N. Spokes around a reef opposite the disused concrete pier and shoulders off into deeper water. Gets very shallow at low and can be polluted by stormwater canal after a downpour. Roping rights skirt the reef at **RAINBOWS** on winter pulses from the north, serving up some barrel action and grunty hooks, plus a shorter, bonus left barrel. Shallow and powerful line-up with plenty of current, making it for experienced riders when bigger. Just south is Osterizers, another crisp A-frame that will always have some takers. **S-TURNS** sits between Honokowai and Kahana, this clutch of lava and coral reefs offer some nice peaks in less than perfect conditions and away from the heavy crowds of the surrounding well-known spots. At the north end of Napili Bay, **LITTLE MAKAHA** can do a fair impression of it's Oahu namesake. Sharp drop into bowly sections along a point-style reef that goes for some distance with tubes along the way. Fast and powerful on the right N swell day when E-SE trades groom the mid tide sessions. Big W can squeeze between the blocking outer islands. Classical outer island perfection that often puts **HONOLUA BAY** into the top five waves in the world list. The clue is in the name and **WINDMILLS** is very exposed to all wind and swell at this due north-facing set of reefs. Long lefts and a couple of rights pound the rocky shoreline and really need calm winds or light S quadrant. Good check on small windswells, but still for advanced riders only, especially at size. which it handles easily. Northeast of Honolua is the small town of **HONOKOHAU**, where a track runs down to a steep and deep bay. There's a righthand boulder-strewn reef to the east and some lefts on the other side, which both break on any N swell. By no means perfect and maxes out when above double overhead, but a fun and changeable line-up without the thick crowds of other waves. Watch out for rocks and strong rips at size. **WAIHEE** is a broad amalgam of reefy peaks just off the golf course north of Kahului. Aspect means the trades mash the waves so early or kona winds required. Intermediate spot. The built-up area of Kahului has some basic boulder beach peaks at **WAIEHU**, but just to the south, a brace of heavy localised reefs take plenty of N-NE swell, but need S-W winds. If the trades are blowing and the swell is maxing, there just might be a clean wave inside the Kahului Harbor, just a mile south. Water quality not great in this area. **KANAHA** is the start of the wind corridor,

HOOKIPA

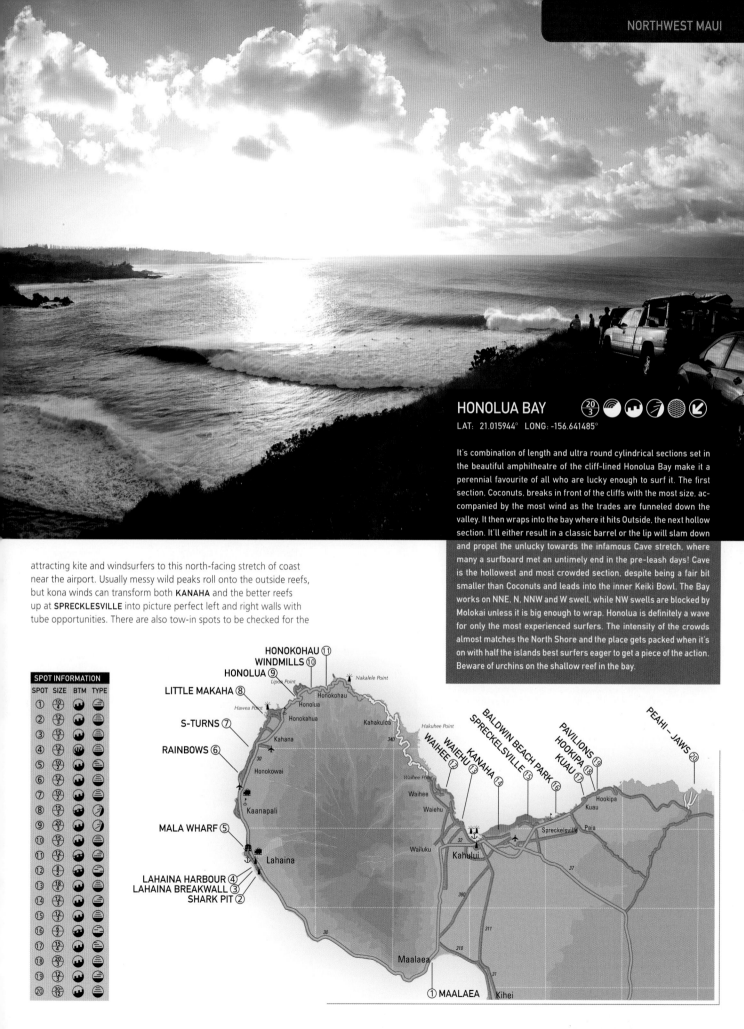

HONOLUA BAY

LAT: 21.015944° LONG: -156.641485°

It's combination of length and ultra round cylindrical sections set in the beautiful amphitheatre of the cliff-lined Honolua Bay make it a perennial favourite of all who are lucky enough to surf it. The first section, Coconuts, breaks in front of the cliffs with the most size, accompanied by the most wind as the trades are funneled down the valley. It then wraps into the bay where it hits Outside, the next hollow section. It'll either result in a classic barrel or the lip will slam down and propel the unlucky towards the infamous Cave stretch, where many a surfboard met an untimely end in the pre-leash days! Cave is the hollowest and most crowded section, despite being a fair bit smaller than Coconuts and leads into the inner Keiki Bowl. The Bay works on NNE, N, NNW and W swell, while NW swells are blocked by Molokai unless it is big enough to wrap. Honolua is definitely a wave for only the most experienced surfers. The intensity of the crowds almost matches the North Shore and the place gets packed when it's on with half the islands best surfers eager to get a piece of the action. Beware of urchins on the shallow reef in the bay.

attracting kite and windsurfers to this north-facing stretch of coast near the airport. Usually messy wild peaks roll onto the outside reefs, but kona winds can transform both **KANAHA** and the better reefs up at **SPRECKLESVILLE** into picture perfect left and right walls with tube opportunities. There are also tow-in spots to be checked for the

SPOT INFORMATION

SPOT	SIZE	BTM	TYPE
①	10/4		
②	8/3		
③	8/3		
④	6/2		
⑤	10/3		
⑥	12/2		
⑦	10/2		
⑧	15/3		
⑨	20/3		
⑩	15/3		
⑪	12/2		
⑫	6/2		
⑬	8/3		
⑭	8/3		
⑮	8/3		
⑯	8/3		
⑰	8/4		
⑱	20/4		
⑲	20/4		
⑳	30/12		

Map labels:

HONOKOHAU ⑪
WINDMILLS ⑩
HONOLUA ⑨
LITTLE MAKAHA ⑧
S-TURNS ⑦
RAINBOWS ⑥
MALA WHARF ⑤
LAHAINA HARBOUR ④
LAHAINA BREAKWALL ③
SHARK PIT ②
① MAALAEA

BALDWIN BEACH PARK
SPRECKELSVILLE
KANAHA ⑭
WAIEHU ⑬
WAIHEE ⑫
PAVILIONS ⑲
HOOKIPA ⑱
KUAU ⑰
⑮ ⑯
PEAHI – JAWS ⑳

Map place names: Nakalele Point, Lipoa Point, Honokohau, Honolua, Honokahua, Kahana, Honokowai, Kaanapali, Lahaina, Hawea Point, Kahakuloa, Hakuhee Point, Waihee Point, Waihee, Waiehu, Wailuku, Kahului, Spreckelsville, Paia, Hookipa, Kuau, Maalaea, Kihei

TRAVEL INFORMATION

LOCAL POPULATION	**COASTLINE** - 218km (136mi)
Maui - 156.674	**TIME ZONE** - GMT -10hr

GETTING THERE – Most flights arrive from Honolulu (HNL - see Oahu South Shore) at Kahului Airport (OGG) on Maui. although there are some direct flights from Vancouver. Canada and west coast mainland cities. Large planes can't land on Maui and airport expansion has met with strong local protests. Inter-island with Hawaiian Airlines. Island Air or Go!Mokulele (no boards over 6ft). All charge for boards + $35 e/w. While Lanai seems so close, it is actually cheaper and quicker to fly from HNL than OGG. There's also several ferry crossings per day at around $60 return. Molokai is a similar story, with flight connections from both Oahu and Maui. The Molokai-Maui Ferry departs 2x daily from Lahaina Harbor. Maui and Kaunakakai Harbor, Molokai.

GETTING AROUND – All the major rental companies available at the airport from around $30/day for an economy or compact model. Getting longer boards inside is a challenge - take straps/soft racks. Most car rental agencies require an age limit of 25. Gas is about 25% more expensive than the US mainland. Traffic gets thick through Lahaina and near the airport. Maui Bus links the main towns (fare $1), but bodyboards only. There are bike rentals available in Lahaina for both beach cruising and serious mountain riding.

LODGING AND FOOD – Accommodation prices are generally higher on Maui than Oahu. Good bases are Haiku or Paia near Hookipa in winter or Lahaina will have plenty of options in summer like Nani Kai Hale (fr $125 dbl). There are a couple of County Parks for camping near Hookipa. Avoid the low surf, tourist resorts on the SW coast around Kihei. Food is also pricey ($30+ per meal) so self catering is a good idea.

WEATHER – The stability of the temps is amazing. Between day and night, winter and summer, temps vary little from a near perfect 25°C (77°F). It's the same story in the water, which hovers around 24°C (75°F) year-round. The winter surf season has rainy periods, especially on S winds. When NE-E trades blow, skies are usually clear. The west shore is much drier than the easterly windward coast.

WEATHER	J/F	M/A	M/J	J/A	S/O	N/D
Total Rainfall (mm)	90	55	17	18	35	65
Consistency (d/m)	8	7	5	6	6	9
Temperature min. (°C)	19	19	21	23	22	20
Temperature max. (°C)	26	27	29	29	30	27

NATURE AND CULTURE – Haleakala Crater is the world's largest dormant volcano and. according to legend, is the soul of Maui. It has been a place of pilgrimage for centuries and check out the sunrise from the summit. Other flat-day activities include mountain biking, windsurfing. diving. and whale watching (March and April are best for the humpbacks). For nightlife, head to Lahaina or Kaanapali.

HAZARDS AND HASSLES – To avoid trouble with the locals, don't surf the big name spots at the busiest times of the day. Don't leave valuables visible in your car.

HANDY HINTS – There are plenty of surf shops in Paia, including Da Kine. Hana Highway Surf and Honolua Surf Co. or Ole's in Lahaina. run by legendary shaper Bob Olsen. You will need a big board for some of the points, but nothing like you would need on Oahu's North Shore. Honolua and others are real board snapping spots. Beginners should head to Nancy Emerson's surf school (fr $50/hr).

BEN THOUARD.COM

PEAHI – JAWS
LAT: 20.941597°   LONG: -156.259343°

The most notorious spot on Maui is a wave most surfers are extremely unlikely to ride. With the development of tow-in surfing in the early 90's, Jaws burst onto the scene. amazing the world with the sheer magnitude of the waves that were being ridden there by a select group of windsurfing and surfing hell-men. As big wave surfing has developed. Jaws has maintained the biggest and baddest tag. even providing 4 of the 5 nominations for the XXL awards and winning biggest wave in '03. '04. '05 and '10 plus monster paddle (x2). tube and ride categories in 2011 (and 2012/13). Takes any N swell, with more W favouring the long lefts, but it is the perfect, house-sized right tubes that most people associate with Jaws. Other waves have been discovered that challenge Jaws on height supremacy, but few can match its steroidal perfection. If you are thinking of tackling this wave, you will need far more knowledge of the spot than we can fit here and proper tow-in experience so as not to be a liability in the increasingly zooed line-up. A few of the hazards include trade wind cross chop and large speed-bump ribs that traverse the face, swatting surfers like bugs on a windshield. The impact zone is a washing machine all the way to the cliffs, regularly pulverizing boards, skis and bodies then punishing anyone fool enough to try and rescue their equipment off the slippery grinding boulders. Then there's launching at Maliko Gulch, where punching in and out of the closed out bay is a game of Russian Roulette. If a huge swell hits Maui, drive out to Peahi, find a park on the western headland then a comfortable spot on the cliff and watch the show below. Remember to bring binoculars and a long lens!

strapped crews. More offshore reefs at **SPRECKLESVILLE** are usually patrolled by the wind crew taking advantage of the cross-shore trades. Cleans up a treat in S-W kona winds and gives intermediates a real run for their money. All tides, but higher will see less tubes and close-outs. **BALDWIN BEACH** is a real assortment of waves for all types of crafts and abilities ranging from mushy longboard peaks to crunching shoredump. Absorbs plenty of crowd and wind, continuing to break during moderate trades. Consistently breaks through the tide up to headhigh, giving the beginners a chance over the sand and patchy reef foundation. There's more easy options nextdoor at Paia Bay. **KUAU** is a proper all out barreling left that will challenge most accomplished surfers and often win, thanks to it's shallow, unpredictable nature. Easily blown-out and lashed by currents, the long paddle keeps the local crowd down a bit. The sort of break where keeping your feet up seems a good idea. **HOOKIPA** is home to some of the best wavesailing in the world, so expect strong cross-shore trade winds on most days after 11am. Hookipa is the centre of kite/windsurfing activity in Hawai'i, but on windless mornings, this clutch of quality reefbreaks is always rammed. Furthest west is Lanes lefts, then there's shallow rights and lefts at the Point, just next to the main peak of Middles. The sailors are usually forced downwind on the rights, leaving plenty of long, roping lefts for packs of surfers to fight over. Hookipa is super-consistent, year-round, evidenced by the constantly jammed car parks of the Hookipa Beach Park off the Hana

Hwy. Rips, rocks and windy-rigs falling from a great height are all part of the deal. The **PAVILIONS** section runs down the eastern point, crouched out of the wind and walling up beautifully into the defined channel, making the paddle back out easy. Ultra-performance walls that can barrel off on low, over a well-covered reef. Won't handle above double overhead, when Middles starts motoring, and it's fun, ripable nature makes it super popular with the locals, to the exclusion of all others, including the windsurfers. **PEAHI - JAWS** (see above).

WIND AND SWELL

The Hawaiian Island chain is the most isolated archipelago in the world and swell exposure is second to none. Unfortunately, Maui is sheltered from many of the big SW, W, and NW swells by the smaller neighbouring islands of Molokai, Lanai and Kahoolawe, and the Big Island creates a very large shadow on the rare SE swells generated by cyclones pinwheeling into the Pacific from Central America. Generally, Maui receives less swell and more wind than the North Shore on Oahu, but figures for swell consistency are 99% from Nov to Feb, averaging

8-10ft at 12secs. ENE-E trades are dominant and strongest from May to Aug, but winds can be much lighter in the mornings. The best winds for the N coast come from the ESE-S quadrant, but they only blow for 19% of the time at best in mid winter. The south coast is usually offshore, however it only gets surf on the rarer SW swells. Tidal range is small, but can have a drastic effect on shallow spots. Tide tables are widely available in surf shops. ●

SURF STATS		J F	M A	M J	J A	S O	N D
SWELL	Dominant swell	◉	◉	◔	◕	◑	◉
	Size (m)	7	5	3-4	2-3	4-5	6
	Consistency (%)	80	60	50	60	50	70
WIND	Dominant wind	◷	◷	◷	◷	◷	◷
	Average force	F4	F4	F4	F4	F4	F4
	Consistency (%)	63	66	76	88	77	77
TEMP.	Wetsuit	🏄	🏄	🏄	🏄	🏄	🏄
	Water temp.	24	24	25	26	27	25

NORTHWEST PACIFIC

The Asian corner of the Pacific may not have the same depth of surf culture that is apparent among the Polynesian nations to the east, nor does it benefit from both the booming northern and southern hemisphere swells, yet it is an enigmatic, challenging and ultimately rewarding surf destination when the conditions conspire. The biggest storms on earth (super-typhoons) travelling over the deepest water (Mariana Trench) can magic up swell events that awaken a host of waves throughout the Philippine and South China Seas. Typhoon swells are different to groundswells, often boasting around 8-10 waves per set, or sometimes as many as 12-15, reflecting the raw energy and power that these massive storms exert on the ocean.

SOUTH CHINA SEA

The southern tip of **TAIWAN** extends into the tropics, overhanging the Tropic of Cancer and facing out towards the favourite path of many a tropical storm. Despite the confusing relationship between the Taiwanese Republic of China (ROC) and the government of the People's Republic of China (PRC), when martial law ended in 1987, surfing came out of the shadows and is now practised by 30,000 across the island. North and east of Taipei, there is a bunch of consistent, crowded and sometimes polluted spots that are easily accessible, many by public transport, including Jin Shan, a super-popular summer spot with huge crowds of beginners and a beach

party vibe. Down the east coast, more serious, powerful waves are found at Bashien Dong, a long, left pointbreak. Mainland **China** also has seasonal surf opportunities in Guangdong Province and Hong Kong, as the NE monsoon whips up waves throughout the South China Sea from November to March. Waves like Big Wave Bay may not be household names, but they are a favourite haunt for the growing crowd of locals and ex-pats that surf this corner of SE Asia. **HAINAN** is now the established international face of Chinese surfing since the ISA brought top-level mainstream competition to the peeling points of Riyue Bay. With so much of the surf industry reliant on Chinese manufacturing for equipment and apparel, many are keen to tap the biggest market in the world and the Chinese regions are even keener to create the right tourism infrastructure.

The east coast of Taiwan is riddled with rivermouths, flowing from the mountainous interior, sculpting many an Asian beauty.

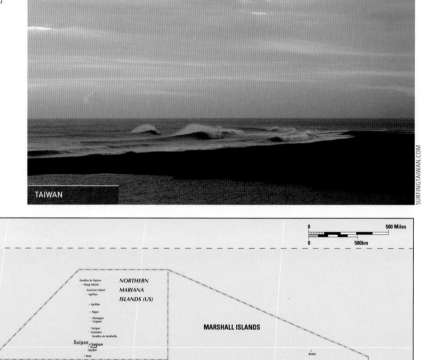

TAIWAN

SURFINGTAIWAN.COM

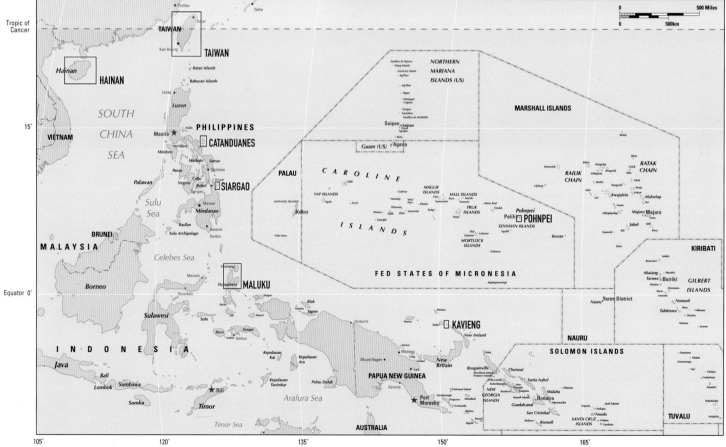

OTHER ISLANDS TO CONSIDER

+ GLASSY, TROPICAL PERFECTION
+ QUALITY REEFBREAKS
+ HUNDREDS OF SECRET SPOTS
+ WORLD-CLASS DIVING

– ERRATIC SEASONAL SWELLS
– SHALLOW REEFS & SHARKS
– HIGH RAINFALL.
– MALARIA
– EXTREMELY REMOTE ACCESS

STÉPHANE ROBIN

SANTA ISOBEL

SOLOMON ISLANDS

Composed of 992 rugged volcanic islands and tiny low-lying coral atolls, the Solomon's are the 3rd largest archipelago in the South Pacific. With soaring mountain peaks, dense tropical rainforest, cascading waterfalls, palm-fringed beaches and traditional villages, the Melanesian Islands are known for their unspoilt beauty and relaxed pace of life. The Solomon's may not be in the ideal location to get the best Pacific swells, but there are some quality coral reefbreaks throughout the archipelago. **Malaita and Makira** face NE, picking up a variety of swell directions, but the main problem is access in this undeveloped region. Good waves have been ridden by a lucky few who have overcome the challenge of travelling to this tropical wilderness, scoring long, peeling rights at waves like Tawarogha in both NE and SE swell. Surprisingly, the majority of discoveries have turned up on the SW-facing coasts, when the Coral Sea cyclones kick in. The group's capital, Honiara, on Guadalcanal is the gateway to the Solomon's and under the right conditions, there's surf at Beaufort Bay and Yandina on Russel Island. The Western Provinces is where surfing has expanded, on the back of the diving resorts infrastructure, set up to explore the world's largest lagoon – Marovo, which is blessed with 30m (100ft) visibility and countless WWII underwater relics. Gizo is the capital of the Western Province and the starting point for riding some of the established waves on **New Georgia** like Skull Island, which is probably the longest righthander in the Solomons when a decent SE-SW pulse arrives from the Solomon Sea.

PACIFIC INDONESIA AND PNG

NORTHERN MALUKU is the next stop on the Philippine swell train as it rolls south and represents the best exposure Indonesia has to Pacific NE swells. Between here and the hulking mass of PNG, there is a flotilla of islands moored in the deep blue, from tiny Pulau Fani to supertanker sized Pulau Waigeo and the Biak Islands. All you need is a long distance, open ocean vessel, a lot of time and money, plus a real spirit of adventure to see what secrets this quiet corner of Indonesia hides. **Papua New Guinea** is a fascinating kaleidoscope of different peoples, cultures and landscapes. The fact that there are over 750 different languages and that over time it has been wrestled over by Germans, English, Australians and Indonesians only gives a hint to the diversity of this country. The mainland is endowed with plenty of surf, but it is the far-flung Bismarck Archipelago where most surfers head and KAVIENG is the most established surf town on the map.

MICRONESIA

Festooned across the empty vastness of the Central Pacific and Mariana Basin, Micronesia incorporates the **Marshall Islands**, **Gilbert Islands**, **Caroline Islands**, **Mariana Islands** and a few outposts like the world's smallest republic **Nauru** and the US restricted zone of Wake Island. Within this region of Oceania, the Federated States of Micronesia contain the most documented spots, including the poster pin-up righthander of P-Pass on the volcanic island of POHNPEI, plus N and S swell options on populous **Guam** and **Kosrae**. Further east the 34 atolls and islands of the **Marshall Islands** rely on US aid and missile base rent to fund the republic, while the few local surfers rely on scraps from both hemispheres on the crowded atoll of Majuro, where a glance at the map suggests great potential, but the reality is a

The seasonal nature of Pacific Indonesia has kept down visitor numbers and left many islands unexplored, despite their obvious wave potential.

dearth of top quality waves on the main island. North swells coincide with NE winds and most spots are on the south coast, so it's really inconsistent, with no clear surf season. One other deterrent is the Marshalls are the world's biggest shark sanctuary, covering nearly 2M km² (772,000 mi²) of deep blue Pacific.

HENNER THIES/SAMASAMABOATTRIPS.COM

NORTHERN MALUKU

PHILIPPINES

A glance at a map of the 7,107 islands of the Philippines could leave you feeling dizzy over the apparent possibilities this country offers to surfers. Drawing parallels to Indonesia, the quality of the reefs is similar, the climate much the same and the beaches as beautiful. It differs only in swell consistency, which is seasonally reliant on the monsoons and typhoons. **Luzon** is the birthplace of surfing in the Philippines, with US servicemen on the west coast, and actors dressed as servicemen at Baler on the east coast, where the famous surf scene from *Apocalypse Now* was shot. The film crew left their boards and the locals took to the water, creating a little surf scene and the first national champion. Zambales is fairly close to Manila on Luzon's west coast with sandy beachbreaks stretching for miles between major rivermouths at Botolah, San Felipe and Pundaquit, plus Capone Island has quality reef and beachbreaks, attracting city surfers in typhoon or SW-NW swells. There is more surf to sniff out in Illocos Norte around Pagadpud and in the northern part of Cagayan province at Aparri.

Natural disasters, civil unrest and gruelling overland travel haven't stopped surfers probing the endless wilds of the Philippines, searching for the next Cloud 9.

OTHER ISLANDS TO CONSIDER

NORTHWEST LUZON

Northwest Luzon is outlined by a beautiful coastline, airbrushed by constant offshores and lucky enough to pick up the wrapping NE swells on the South China Sea side of the archipelago. US airmen have been surfing Mona Liza Point in La Union since the early '70s, paving the way for surf resorts to set up on a few of the offshore

+ FREQUENT NE MONSOON SWELLS
+ VARIETY OF REEFS & BEACHIES
+ SCENIC SIERRA MOUNTAINS
+ REALLY CHEAP & ENTERTAINING
+ PINOY SURF CULTURE

− NO WORLD-CLASS WAVES
− OCCASIONAL CROWDS
− ONSHORE BEACHBREAKS
− TOUGH OVERLAND ACCESS
− LANDSLIDES, RAINS, ROBBERY

islands. Badoc Island is stacked with four quality, uncrowded reefbreaks nearby and a reliable beachbreak, but for those who prefer public access, there's plenty more along this coast down south in La Union province. If long, cruisey pointbreaks are your thing, then Urbitzondo, Mona Lisa and Car-rille are sure to impress, cementing this coast's reputation as a longboarder's favourite.

CAR-RILLE POINT

The NE coast of Cagayan and Isabela is a virtual wilderness, with the rough coastal road often washed out, but surf possibilities are high thanks to direct NE swell exposure, while hopefully finding protection from the following wind. The large islands of surfless Quezon province are open to the north and east, as is Camarines Norte and Sur where there is a good rivermouth near Daet, but shallower offshore waters cut potential, compared to the regal rights of Majestics on nearby **CATANDUANES**. Eastern **Samar** represents a real discovery zone with some surfers around Borongan and Calicoan Island, but there are plenty of other waves to search for. Beyond the dreamy Cloud 9 peaks on **SIARGAO**, a myriad of potential exists on small offshore islands and major landmasses alike, throughout Surigao Del Sur and Davao on Mindanao's southeastern fringe. Northern **Mindanao** holds some serious peelers on rocky shelves and fringing reefs, plus the enigmatic Doot Poktoy, a rare rivermouth right that often attracts Mundaka comparisons. Finally, the long, thin flank of Palawan does get some small South China Sea N swell action with light offshore winds for 2-4 months (Dec-March) of the year.

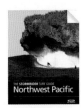

THE STORMRIDER SURF GUIDE
Northwest Pacific

For more information, check these other Stormrider Surf Guides and/or eBooks.

EASTERN LUZON

The Philippines are notorious for long, arduous journeys and the town of Baler, in Aurora province on the coast of East Luzon, is no exception, taking the adventurous on a nerve jangling road trip over the rolling Sierra Madre mountain range. The

+ CONSISTENT NE MONSOON SWELL
+ OCCASIONAL SW TYPHOON SWELL
+ MANY UNCROWDED BREAKS
+ CHEAP LIVING COSTS

− SMALL SIZE WAVES
− SOME MANILA CROWDS
− NATURAL AND SOCIAL DISASTERS
− SEX TOURISM

typhoon season coincides with the wet season from mid June to November and makes it a tough time to travel. Aurora province is hit by typhoons at least 3 or 4 times a year. The best surf season runs from October to March, when the NE monsoon produces larger waves in the 3-8ft (1-2.5m) range. This will awaken the mixture of all-abilities beachbreak at Sabang Beach plus the exciting coral reef grinders at Cemento. Winds will be onshore NE-E in the afternoon, but mostly calm in the mornings.

ALAN VAN GYSEN

+ TYPHOONS AND WINDSWELLS
+ UNDISCOVERED QUALITY BREAKS
+ WARM AND TROPICAL
+ CHEAP AND LIVELY

- ERRATIC TYPHOON SWELLS
- MESSY WINDSWELLS
- HEAVY RAINS
- NO TOURIST INFRASTRUCTURE
- TIME CONSUMING TRAVEL

EASTERN SAMAR

Out of the 7,107 islands of the Philippines, Samar is the 3rd largest volcanic island and both Northern and Eastern Samar boasts some undiscovered surf potential. Eastern Samar is 150km (94mi) long and only 40km (25mi) wide of rough and hilly terrain covered by lush tropical vegetation, yet local Borongan surfers think less than half the province's waves have been discovered. Photographer John Callahan has led boat expeditions from Siargao and made discoveries like Jurassic Point, but locals and visitors are scoring plenty of waves around Barongan and down on Calicoan Island where a surf camp caters to all abilities in a pristine environment. Choose between erratic typhoon swells and offshores (Aug-Oct) or consistent windswell and dominant onshores (Nov-Mar).

MINDANAO – NORTH

Mindanao is the second largest island of the Philippines and because wave-rich Siargao island is so close, there is little wonder that intrepid travellers have searched around and discovered some perfect, typhoon swell gems like Jelly's Point or Lanuza's Doot Pooktoy. A stop-off in Surigao Province during a decent NE swell makes a lot of sense, as it can be way

+ VARIOUS GOOD SPOTS NEAR LANUZA
+ WORLD-CLASS SANDY POINT
+ MOSTLY UNCROWDED
+ CLOSE TO SIARGAO
+ DIRT CHEAP. VIRGIN MINDANAO

- INCONSISTENT SWELLS
- SHORT SURF SEASON
- LACK OF TOURISM INFRASTRUCTURE
- DIFFICULT ACCESS
- UN TRAVEL WARNINGS

JS CALLAHAN/SURFEXPLORE

PUNTA LEFT

less crowded than Cloud 9, and some of the waves are almost as good. Getting it good at Lanuza is not easy, as the requirements are a powerful typhoon swell to push into the sheltered location, good sandbars and dead low tide. When it's on, it's a legendary wave of awesome dimensions, from deep throaty barrels at low tide, to endless off the top and cutback combinations at high tide. Other spots like Moshi-Moshi or Cauit require less swell and any NE swell will do. SW *habagat* monsoon wind is straight offshore.

TAIWAN

+ SE TYPHOON &
  NE MONSOON SWELLS
+ POWERFUL BEACHES & POINTS
+ CHEAP, EASY ACCESS FROM ASIA
+ BEAUTIFUL EAST COAST

– NO WORLD-CLASS BREAKS
– SUFFOCATING SUMMER HEAT
– DENSELY POPULATED TAIPEI
– RISK OF DESTRUCTIVE TYPHOONS

When Portuguese sailors stumbled upon Taiwan in 1547, they named it Ilha Formosa meaning "Beautiful Island". Taiwan is only 160km (100mi) from the mainland where the government of the People's Republic of China (PRC) have ruled since winning the civil war against the Republic of China (ROC) in 1949. The ROC government withdrew to Taiwan and continue to dispute the political rights of the PRC and maintain some sovereignty over Taiwan and the 90 small islands of Penghu (Pescadores). Despite the confusing situation, surfing in Taiwan has a long history and surf arrives from a generous 225° swell window hitting all sides of the island. US soldiers were the first to ride the north coast beach of Jin Shan in 1965 and local pioneers like Mao Guh and his brothers ignored the Taoist suspicions of the sea and government ban on access to the ocean, to take up surfing. Mao Guh opened the original and still popular Jeff's Surf Shop near Honeymoon Bay and with the lifting of Martial Law in 1987, surfing clubs popped up across the island and Jung Wen-Chen, founder of R.O.C Surfing Association, estimates that there could be 30,000 people riding waves across Taiwan. This is no surprise as the seasonal monsoons bring consistent waist to headhigh waves and a pair of boardshorts will do for all but the depths of winter, making Taiwan an increasingly alluring tropical destination.

ANDREW SHIELD

HOUBIHU HARBOUR

In Danshuei, **PAISHAWAN** is consistent in winter N swells, often offshore and easy to get to on the metro train system. Lacks power and shape so perfect for beginners. **JIN SHAN** aka Green Bay or Golden Mountain is super popular in summer with huge crowds of clueless beginners and a beach party vibe, but the rivermouth brings bad pollution. Also check Wan-Li. The eroding golden sands of **FULONG BEACH** are split by the large Shuangshi rivermouth, which often floods the end of the access bridge. Weak, shifting peaks so surf next to the harbour wall for cleaner conditions. **DASHI**, aka Honeymoon Bay, benefits from clean water and some good, but unreliable sandbanks. Favours rights toward the southern end and is often the best option in the area. Gets crowded and a few rogue locals have been known to be aggressive to foreigners. Just north of Toucheng is **WUSHI**, a decent black sand beach with south end jetties and some decent rights in winter NE'ers. Gets crowded because it has the best waves along the heavily armoured coast. Miles of sandy shoredump and rocky coast leads down to Hualien and 17km further south is **GONGS**, an inconsistent low to mid tide outside reef peak, that handles some size and N winds. **JICI** is the sandiest beach in rocky

Hualien, with average, often sloppy peaks in the southern corner. May pick up some power in a SE swell, but readily closes out. Serviced by Hualuan Surf shop and there's a school for beginners. The coast road overlooks a stretch of rocky reefs down to and beyond **FONGBIN**, a rivermouth beach with good form, but watch out for rocks and the vicious shorebreak. Catching classic **BASHIEN DONG** lefts, at Eight Fairy Cave, will convince visitors of the power of Taiwanese surf. It's a long, boulder pointbreak that lines up great walling lefts on big NE swells, combined with NW winds. Usually soft shoulders outside and the odd short peeler on the rocky inside, before the heavy shorepound. The rivermouth can create intense rips and some rights to the north. South of Three Fairy Platform is **CHENG GONG** an epic left reef/point, breaking close to shore, but only on typhoon Category 4 or 5 from the E-SE. **DONGHE RIVERMOUTH** is extremely consistent and a swell-magnet, picking up all available seasonal swell onto shifting, river sculpted sandbars. There are two main peaks, either side of the rivermouth offering long walls with plenty of open face to dissect, plus some short barrel sections. It can hold a lot of swell and maintains good shape even on the bigger days. Wave quality is often the best on the island, so it's not the best place for beginners, especially as crowds are increasing, fed by a few new local surf shops nearby and visiting rippers looking to film and showcase Taiwan's surf. Further south the number of sandy beaches and reefbreaks increases, but the swell is less consistent. The wide beach at **JIALESHUEI** may be Taiwan's most reliable spot, with a range of waves for the regular crowds of surfers of all abilities. There are shapely rights near the rivermouth, while the lefts are almost always breaking, even in the regular onshores. Facing SE, **NANWAN**, aka Binglang Beach, stands out as a shapely right reefbreak with nice curves and a sculpted face, but only on low-mid tide and S-SW swells. If the sand mix is just right, barrels are a given when it's bigger, which should help clear the water of weekend learner crowds. Summer typhoons should awaken a number of other reefs in the bay (Windmills, Houbihu Harbour, Banana Bay) where the

Map labels:
- ① PAISHAWAN
- ② JIN SHAN
- ③ FULONG BEACH
- ④ DASHI
- ⑤ WUSHI
- ⑥ GONGS
- ⑦ JICI BEACH
- ⑧ FONGBIN
- ⑨ BASHIEN DONG
- ⑩ CHENG GONG
- ⑪ DONGHE RIVERMOUTH
- ⑫ JIALESHUEI
- ⑬ NANWAN
- ⑭ SUNYATSEN BEACH
- ⑮ SANSHUEI
- ⑯ CHU NAN

KENTING BEACH

ANDREW SHIELD

barrels and the coral reef are sharper. The nuclear plant discharges cooling water into the bay! In Kaohsiung, go to **SUNYATSEN BEACH** facing the university for a short, bodyboard style shorebreak. Escape to the Penghu Islands (64 tiny dots) on a good S swell – it's easy to fly there with boards. **SANSHUEI** is one of those picture-perfect beaches, ready to catch the occasional SE-SW summer swells. Back on the heavily populated and usually flat NW coast of Taiwan is **CHU NAN**, a slow, mushy, beginners beachbreak that's protected from NE winds by the harbour wall, just avoid lower tides.

SWELL AND WIND

Taiwan sits smack dab in the middle of Typhoon Alley and the biggest swells of 8-12ft (2.5-4m) usually occur from July to October. Category 1-3 storms can appear in less than 24hrs, while super-typhoons Cat 4 and 5 usually take days to wind up, with potential for destruction, depending on the storm's track. Any violent storm activity in the western Pacific can create some waves, but consistency varies greatly, year to year. In the summer, knee to waist high is the average surf height pushed in by the SW monsoon winds without any typhoon activity. The most consistent surf is generated in winter from NE monsoon winds, which bring chest to headhigh waves almost everyday with potential 8-10ft (2.5-3m) peaks. North and east Taiwan

SPOT INFORMATION

SPOT	SIZE	BTM	TYPE
①			
②			
③			
④			
⑤			
⑥			
⑦			
⑧			
⑨			
⑩			
⑪			
⑫			
⑬			
⑭			
⑮			
⑯			

SURF STATS

		J F	M A	M J	J A	S O	N D
SWELL	Dominant swell						
	Size (m)	4-5	2-3	1-2	3	3-4	4-5
	Consistency (%)	80	50	30	60	70	80
WIND	Dominant wind						
	Average force	F5	F4-F5	F4	F4	F4-F5	F4-F5
	Consistency	64	51	40	38	74	91
TEMP.	Wetsuit						
	Water temp.	23	24	27	29	28	25

NANWAN BAY

ANDREW SHIELD

has many spots that pick up even a sniff of swell (Yilan, Hualian) while the southern region has a myriad of breaks that need a bit of a look around to find (Taitung). Tides are semi-diurnal with diurnal inequality but hardly reach more than 3ft (1m). ●

HAINAN, CHINA

+ CHINA'S BEST SURF	– LACK OF POWER
+ QUALITY LEFT POINTBREAKS	– AVERAGE BEACHBREAKS
+ CONSISTENT IN NE MONSOON	– RARE TYPHOON SWELLS
+ WARM WATER AND TROPICAL	– DIFFICULT TRAVEL WITHOUT GUIDE
+ CULTURAL ADVENTURE	– SOME AREAS OFF-LIMITS

Hainan, the second largest of the Chinese islands after Taiwan, extends 1,500km (930mi) of coastline into the South China Sea, with an eastern side exposed to consistent NE monsoon swells and seasonal typhoon swells. Hainan is advertised throughout China and Russia as a tropical holiday paradise, attracting around 10 million Chinese tourists every year, mainly to Sanya in the south of the island. The surf potential is still relatively unexplored, with hundreds of beaches and consistent left points. Long stretches of sand are divided by occasional headlands, with a backdrop of volcanic mountains. The pointbreaks have been ridden by a small group of visiting foreign surfers for decades and recently a small, but growing mix of Chinese and expat local surfers. The waves have been deemed good enough to hold top level ISA contests at Riyue Bay, including an ASP Mens 6 star event.

MAIN LEFT, RIYUE BAY

Between Haikou and Sanya, a 320km (200mi) long expressway occasionally skirts the coastline. However, once off this major route the road network is poor, so exploring is time-consuming. The NE coast of Hainan, around Wenchang, is hard to access. Tonggu Ridge is more of a sightseeing area than a surfspot, but the islet in the rivermouth at **MOON BAY** sometimes holds some punchy peaks. Getting to **BUDDHA BEACH** is a mission, but the 16m (50ft) statue lends a unique feel to the place. Like the next spot south, **DA'AO BAY**, Buddha Beach is generally surfed on typhoon swells with SW winds, as the NE monsoon is onshore. Further south, **DA HUA JAIO** breaks near a military camp under similar small NE conditions. More spots around Wanning may be worth investigating, such as **XING TAN WAN**, an exposed beach with difficult access. South of here, the coast faces more SE and the likelihood of consistent, offshore surf soars. **RIVERMOUTH BRIDGE** can produce nice peeling rights at lower tides with good access. No good in NE-E winds. The next three bays – Shimei Wan, Riyue Wan and Xiangshui Wan (wan means bay) hold major surf potential. **GOLF COURSE**, in Shimei Wan, is a long left breaking down a sharp, rocky point by the Ocean Bay Golf Club. Best in bigger NE swells with N quadrant winds, it's a big paddle against sweeping currents to score the fast inside section. Small days are mellow, perfect for longboarding. At **KANI ROCK**, powerful, low tide

rights and lefts throw out close to shore over boulders and sand. **KAME ROCK** is a hollow beachbreak with a good right next to the large rock. Some close-outs, but good barrels when the sandbars are right. **BACK BEACH** is just north of the headland in Riyue Wan and is a good option when the point is small. Powerful A-frames with great barrel potential are possible along this NE exposed stretch of sand on medium NE swells, low tide and offshore winds. The **MAIN LEFT** off the point of Riyue Bay can offer a low-mid tide 100m+ (330ft) left with a sucky, barrelling take-off and steep, ripable sections. NE winds are not a problem, making it the most consistent wave in the area and an international contest site. Handles size during typhoon swells, when currents can be strong, but user-friendly for improvers up. Further south from the point in Riyue Wan, a cluster of mussel encrusted rocks hold the sand and create **CAMEL LEFT**, a low tide-only potential barrel when big NE swells wrap and winds blow N. **NIULING** is a left shorebreak opposite restaurants plus a punchy left at the harbour entrance, where the ferry goes to Fenjiezhou Island. If the wind is up from the NE, **ABALONE FARM** offers sheltered lefts tucked into a cove. At **SANDALWOOD** in Lingshui, a four star hotel caters to luxury seekers, and a good beachbreak is easily accessible from the highway. 45km NE of the tourist hub of Sanya, the small village of **HOUHAI** hosts a very consistent and powerful beachbreak, best on small to medium E and NE swells. Houhai is the winter hub for Sanya's booming surf scene with good wind and swell protection in the deep scalloped bay. Surfer friendly guesthouses and board rentals can be found here. Further south near the water sports haven of Yalong Bay, **WEST BEACH** will work in SE swells. Access is via dirt tracks through the virgin forest. The main city break in Sanya is called **DADONG HAI** and is located in its busiest tourist district. This wide bay looks like a run down version of Waikiki but offers punchy peaks with possible inside barrels during the frequent E and SE summer swell. This spot favors low tide and can be crowded both with surfers and tourists. In the next bay west, **XIAODONG HAI**, offers one of the best righthanders on the island. This long reef pass breaks on a sharp coral bottom and activates during S and SW typhoon swells producing high quality barrels, especially at high tide.

SWELL AND WIND

There are two main surfing seasons in Hainan. The typhoon season runs from August to October while the NE monsoon extends from November to March. November produces both early N swells and

SHELL BEACH

RIYUE BEACHBREAK

JS CALLAHAN/SURFEXPLORE

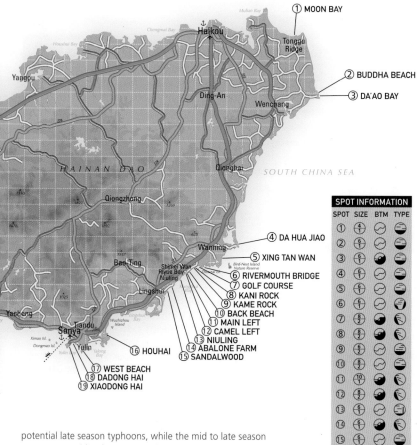

① MOON BAY

② BUDDHA BEACH

③ DA'AO BAY

④ DA HUA JIAO

⑤ XING TAN WAN

⑥ RIVERMOUTH BRIDGE

⑦ GOLF COURSE

⑧ KANI ROCK

⑨ KAME ROCK

⑩ BACK BEACH

⑪ MAIN LEFT

⑫ CAMEL LEFT

⑬ NIULING

⑭ ABALONE FARM

⑮ SANDALWOOD

⑯ HOUHAI

⑰ WEST BEACH

⑱ DADONG HAI

⑲ XIAODONG HAI

SOUTH CHINA SEA

HAINAN DAO

SPOT INFORMATION			
SPOT	SIZE	BTM	TYPE

potential late season typhoons, while the mid to late season monsoon provides the most consistent waves in January and February. The Taiwan Strait also produces regular NE swells while the Luzon Strait gets direct but occasional E swells. The NNE wind becomes side/offshore on the ESE facing shorelines, mainly in

SURF STATS		J	F	M	A	M	J	J	A	S	O	N	D
SWELL	Dominant swell												
	Size (m)	3-4		2		0-1		1-2		3		4	
	Consistency (%)	70		30		10		20		60		80	
WIND	Dominant wind												
	Average force	F4-F5		F4		F4		F4		F4		F4-F5	
	Consistency	77		91		74		61		62		95	
TEMP.	Wetsuit												
	Water temp.	24		26		29		29		29		25	

TRAVEL INFORMATION

LOCAL POPULATION: 8.6M
TIME ZONE: GMT +8h
COASTLINE:
Hainan – 1580km (981mi)

GETTING THERE – Get a visa at Hong Kong airport in less than a day. HK flights are more expensive and less regular than those from Shenzhen and Guangzhou. Hainan Airlines and China Airlines fly many times daily, although some aircraft might not take surfboards. Fly from Shanghai, or choose a direct flight from Osaka with Hainan Airlines. Gaungzhou airport connects with both Sanya (SYX) and Haikou (HAK) on China Southern Airlines, while from Singapore you can fly to Haikou with Tiger Airways. JetStar and Hainan Airlines. There's a ferry to Shekou from HK.

GETTING AROUND – The capital city is Haikou, but visitors can also fly to Sanya, closer to the main surf area. Individual tourism is still a strange concept, and tourists are not allowed to drive a car without a Chinese driving license.

LODGING AND FOOD – Stay in 4 star accommodation at Sandalwood in Xiangshui Bay or a run down, overpriced 21 Century chain Hotel in Riyue Wan. Riyue Wan Surf Club offers spartan dormitory style accommodation. Lots of hotels are being built. Chinese street food and restaurant cuisine is outstanding and very cheap. Try Wenchang Chicken, Jiaji Duck, Dongshan Mutton, Merry Crab. There is lots of fresh seafood available.

WEATHER – Hainan is a tropical monsoon zone, with average temperatures between 22°C and 26°C (72-79°F). Annual rain is 1.639mm (66in), but much less in the leeward coasts around Niuling. Forest cover exceeds 50%. Surf without a wetsuit is possible in the early season because the water remains warm (25°C/77°F), but N winds can get chilly so take a springsuit in Nov-Dec and maybe a light fullsuit in Jan-March. Because of the fairly shallow South China Sea, the water is colored by sediment.

WEATHER	J/F	M/A	M/J	J/A	S/O	N/D
Total Rainfall (mm)	7	21	150	180	240	25
Consistency (d/m)	11	12	13	13	12	12
Temperature min. (°C)	19	21	24	25	24	20
Temperature max. (°C)	24	27	32	32	31	25

NATURE AND CULTURE – There is plenty to see and do: Nanwan Macaque island and a Buddhist statue 108m tall, Xinlong Botanical Garden with 1200 plant species, Hainan Marine Tropical World in Haikou, the Hot Spring region, Yalong bay near Sanya, Tinanya Haijiao rocks, and the Sanya Zoological Garden. There is buzzing nightlife in Sanya, and karaoke and massage are commonplace.

HAZARDS AND HASSLES – There are few local surfers, so localism is currently not an issue, but pay respect to the expat surfing community, local Hainan surfers and regulars from mainland China. There are some sea-lice and low tide rocks to be aware of. Hiring a cab can be difficult. Some beaches are off-limits and guards or the military may prohibit surfing in some areas.

HANDY HINTS – Very few people speak English or Japanese, only Mandarin. Internet facilities are very limited. The surf conditions cater for both short and longboards. During typhoon season, it's really hot. Bring all surf supplies, including wax. Check chinasurfreport.com for more info.

Wanning, and can get strong at times. Winds shift a bit ENE in the afternoon but remain fairly offshore for the spots in the SE. During the SW season, from May to September, waves are rare and only found at south-facing spots. Typhoons can send awesome long period swells and sometimes the SW monsoon will produce 2-3ft (0.6-1m) of windswell on the south coast. Tide phases can get up to 5ft (1.5m), with very irregular changes between the two tides. A general rule of thumb is to favor the beachbreaks on high tide and the points on low tide. ●

CATANDUANES, PHILIPPINES

+ WORLD-CLASS RIGHTHANDER   – LONG FLAT SPELLS
+ EMPTY WAVES   – LACK OF QUALITY SPOTS
+ EXOTIC, TROPICAL PARADISE – UNSUITABLE FOR BEGINNERS
+ CHEAP AND MELLOW TRIP   – DIFFICULT ACCESS

MAJESTICS

JS CALLAHAN/SURFEXPLORE

Located just off the Bicol region of South Luzon, (the main island), Catanduanes island juts out into the Pacific and appears to be an ideal swell magnet for the NE typhoon swells. Intrepid travellers from Japan and Australia began searching the region in the early to mid '80s, before *Surfer* magazine published the story of a 1988 trip showing pictures of a palm fringed, white sand beach with a barreling righthander just offshore. Photographer Warren Bolster dubbed it Majestics, putting the Philippines under the surf world's spotlight. However, the pictures were deceiving, not showing how quickly the wave peeled or how shallow the reef was and most notably, how inconsistent the wave appeared to be. Many surfers have been drawn here by the pictures and ended up spending weeks waiting around for Majestics to do its thing, but those that do score it good, rate it as the Philippine's best barrel.

Puraran Bay is the local name for **MAJESTICS**, which hits an angled coral shelf, stands up beyond straight and vortexes off for a short, but intense ride with an impressive power to size ratio. Needs at least a 2-3ft (1m), swell to clear the coral and it is best surfed from mid to high tide on the push. Having a light SW wind to hold up the lips is also a crucial factor, limiting the season to *habagat* months, which luckily coincide with the typhoons that bring the ideal E-NE swell direction. Intermediates might have fun on small days,

but once it gets overhead, only tube-jockeys with an air-drop game will get into the heaving pits. Low tide can be ridden, but cuts are guaranteed to fallers and often result in infections and fevers, a long way from any hospital. Locals are usually cool and any hassles in the line-up may come from zealous regulars and transplants, irked by the wave's fickle nature. If conditions are too sketchy at Majestics, try **POINT B** further to the S, but beware of the exposed rocks. It can be a brilliant wave but it's not suitable for beginners. By renting a boat you can reach **LUCKY POINT**, an exposed fringe of reef that needs E swell to line up properly. When Majestics and Point B are onshore go to **MONING**, a tidy right peeler that only works at high tide. Hire a boat in Baras to get out there. On big stormy days there can be a fun left inside **VIRAC HARBOUR**, which has plenty of opportunities to bust out some big moves. An hour south on the tip of the island, **TWIN ROCKS** has some fun lefts and rights and easy accommodation in a chilled-out atmosphere. None of the spots here ever get very busy, as there are only a handful of local and visiting foreign surfers. The island is big and certainly hides more spots. Hire a boat in Virac and go and explore.

WIND AND SWELL

Swell exposure is not great, coming only from typhoons travelling in a W-NW direction towards Japan. They can form at any time, but the majority occur between July and Nov, the peak months seem to be Aug-Sept. There's an estimated 15-20 typhoons a year, each one providing 2-4 days of swell between 3-8ft (1-2.5m), with peak swells hitting 12ft (4m). The best time is from July to Oct when the swells are cleaned up by an offshore, SW wind. By Nov the wind is shifting round to an onshore, NE direction, although this transition period sees

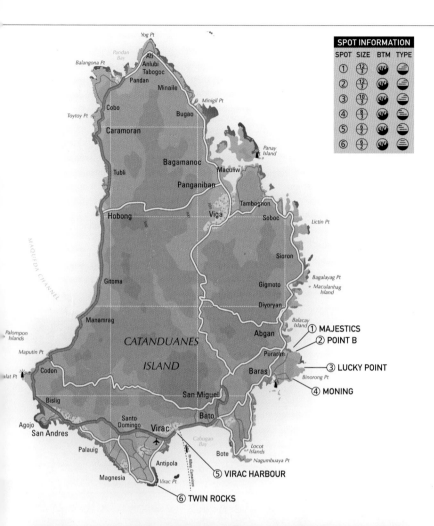

SPOT INFORMATION

SPOT	SIZE	BTM	TYPE
①	12/3	🖐	⬲
②	12/3	🖐	⬲
③	10/3	🖐	⬲
④	8/3	🖐	⬲
⑤	6/2	🖐	⬲
⑥	6/2	👐	⬲

Map labels: Yog Pt, Pandan Bay, Ati, Anlubi, Tabogoc, Pandan, Minaile, Minigil Pt, Balangona Pt, Cobo, Bugao, Panay Island, Toytoy Pt, Caramoran, Tubli, Bagamanoc, Maculiw, Panganiban, Tamboanon, Hobong, Viga, Soboc, Lictin Pt, Sioron, Bagalayag Pt, Gitoma, Gigmoto, Maculanhag Island, Manamrag, Diyoryan, Balacay Island, Palompon Islands, Abgan, Maputin Pt, CATANDUANES ISLAND, Puraran, Codon, Baras, Binorong Pt, Bislig, San Miguel, Agojo, Santo Domingo, Bato, San Andres, Virac, Cahugao Bay, Palauig, Bote, Locot Islands, Antipola, Nagumbuaya Pt, Magnesia, Virac Pt, MAQUDA CHANNEL, to Albay, Camarines, ☩lat Pt

① MAJESTICS
② POINT B
③ LUCKY POINT
④ MONING
⑤ VIRAC HARBOUR
⑥ TWIN ROCKS

MAJESTICS

Photo credit: JS CALLAHAN/SURFEXPLORE

quite a lot of swell activity. The NE monsoon only brings small, onshore windswells. The May-June transition period will bring E-S winds, which fluctuate in strength and direction all the time, but generally it's quite calm and a good time for beginners. The tidal range is large and most of the shallow reefs are only rideable from mid to high tide. ●

TRAVEL INFORMATION

LOCAL POPULATION: 232,757   **TIME ZONE:** GMT +8h
COASTLINE: 210km (131mi)

GETTING THERE – Most international flights go to Manila (MNL), from where a PAL, Cebu Pacific or AirPhil Express connection can take you to Legaspi (fr $20e/w), the nearest large airport. CEB will fly Manila-Virac ($40/ew; 5d/wk), but take no checked baggage or surfboards. Buses travel daily from Manila to Tabaco City (10hr), then ferry to Virac (3-4hr). RSL Bus does Manila to Virac daily, avoiding stopping over in Tabaco City. From Virac pier, jeepneys go straight to Puraran (1hr) or Baras.

GETTING AROUND – This is pretty much a one spot zone and you may find little reason to move around. Much of the coastline is accessible only by foot, down muddy trails. Hire a boat to scout out the hidden reefs; much of the E coast is unchartered. Local transport includes jeepneys (rebuilt jeeps), metered taxis, sidecar motorbikes, PU-cabs (small taxis, no meters) and trishaws.

LODGING AND FOOD – Puraran Surf Beach Resort has beachfront huts on stilts (fr $12/n) and various rooms for less. Puting-Baybay Resort has similar local nipa huts (fr $8-10/n) as does Majestic Resort. Food is also cheap at $4-5 for a basic meal. Lots of seafood and rice.

WEATHER – The Philippines are hot and extremely humid year-round. The Pacific side of the island is open to two different monsoons. The NE monsoon, *amihan*, lasts from Nov-April and not only brings onshores and small windswells, but also huge amounts of rainfall. After the May-June transition period, the SW monsoon, *habigat* starts blowing, bringing drier weather and offshore winds. Even though the swell comes from typhoons they rarely make landfall in the Philippines, although there is always the risk between July-Nov. If they do hit be prepared for devastation: super typhoon Loleng flattened every beach hut in Puraran in 1998.

WEATHER	J/F	M/A	M/J	J/A	S/O	N/D
Total Rainfall (mm)	460	380	141	154	220	524
Consistency (d/m)	21	20	11	12	15	22
Temperature min. (°C)	23	23	24	24	24	23
Temperature max. (°C)	29	31	31	31	31	29

NATURE AND CULTURE – Don't miss the 2500m Mayon Volcano near Legaspi. The beaches here are some of the best in the world and the crystal clear water makes for excellent snorkeling and diving conditions. Climb up to the Puraran pass for some amazing views.

HAZARDS AND HASSLES – Reef cuts and malaria are your biggest enemies. Be prepared for flat days. Crowded line-ups are rare. There is the risk of civil unrest, especially in the cities.

HANDY HINTS – Don't expect to find any surf gear available here. The local surfers, who are friendly and dedicated, always appreciate new gear. The annual Majestic Surfing Cup is usually held in October, contested by 48 surfers from around the country.

SURF STATS	J	F	M	A	M	J	J	A	S	O	N	D
SWELL Dominant swell	-		-		-		◔		◑		●	
Size (m)	1		1		1-2		3		3-4		3-4	
Consistency (%)	10		10		20		50		60		40	
WIND Dominant wind	◑		◑		◔		◔		◕		◑	
Average force	F4		F3		F3		F3-F4		F3		F3-F4	
Consistency	79		70		57		63		76		75	
TEMP Wetsuit	🩳		🩳		🩳		🩳		🩳		🩳	
Water temp.	24		24		24		26		25		24	

SIARGAO, PHILIPPINES

+ WORLD-CLASS REEFS
+ PLENTY OF UNCROWDED SPOTS
+ TROPICAL CONDITIONS
+ CHEAP LIVING COSTS

– GENERALLY SMALL SURF
– LONG FLAT SPELLS
– LONG TRANSFER JOURNEY
– POLITICAL INSTABILITY

Perfectly positioned as close to the plummeting depths of the Philippine Trench as possible, Siargao represents the highest concentration of good surf to be found in the 7,107 islands of the archipelago. There are a number of world-class reefs on the 27km (17mi) of coastline exposed to swell, where many of the spots are outside reefs and islets that can only be accessed by boat, while others break closer to the beach on a fringing reef. General Luna is a good place to be based during the SW monsoon and Pilar is better during the NE trades.

Near San Isidro is **PACIFICO**, a long, hollow and consistent left that likes N in the swell to stop closing-out. Long walk over the weedy reef lagoon best done in booties. Further north, Burgos and Alegria also have empty waves and pristine beaches. On SW winds with a good swell and full tide, **CARIDAD** reveals a perfect left with a low crowd factor. The place to be based during the NE trades is **PILAR**, only 7 miles from General Luna, but a long boat or car ride. The Pilar area is generally not as crowded as the General Luna region and the deep bay holds a selection of good left reefs that can be surfed during NE storms. **STIMPY'S** can be a ferocious, unpredictable left barrel that wraps around the coral heads and explodes with board-breaking power on overhead swells. Can also be mushy, fun walls and shoulders on smaller days when the regular NE blows, but there is usually something at this consistent, advanced spot. Take a longer board to make the drop. **TUESDAY ROCK**, Rock Island and Pancit Reef have all been used to describe this long, consistent, soft-peeling right that breaks in the shadow of a rocky islet, across the deep channel from Stimpy's. N-NE swells hit it perfectly and the SW monsoon is dead offshore, so it can hold double overhead waves and

is best at lower tides when cutbacks can transform to cover-ups. Boat access only so crowds are variable. Improvers at high, intermediates up at low. It takes about an hour to walk from General Luna to **CLOUD NINE** and on the way there are several other good spots. **TUASON POINT** is a seriously heavy left that breaks hard and hollow down the fringe of exposed reef. **HORSESHOE** is another spot on the way to Cloud Nine; it's a wedgy, high tide peak that is well regarded. General Luna itself is hardly ever rideable but it serves as a good swell size indicator. Daku Island is only 4km (2.5mi) south from General Luna, home to a long, fun right called **BARRIO** that breaks out in the channel. Rent a pump boat to get there and hope no more than 2 boat loads arrive. There are lots more sectiony rights on the islands northern fringe of reef that are offshore in the SW monsoon, plus loads more potential on the exposed eastern tip. **PANSUKIAN** faces the plush resort of the same name and was one of the original waves ridden on Siargao, but these days is usually empty despite having some clean peelers over the obligatory coral shelf in NE winds and E-SE swells. Daku blocks the NE swells. Short ride out via the bright white sands of Naked Island.

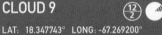

CLOUD 9

LAT: 18.347743°   LONG: -67.269200°

Cloud Nine is a perfect, top to bottom, barreling peak that's short but sweet when the conditions align. The more W in the swell the better as this will keep the door open to the safety of the channel, while N-NE tends to slam it. Higher tides also improve makeability as the coral lurks challengingly close to the open air. The rights are most coveted, while the lefts are shorter, yet just as hollow off the peak, before quickly shutting down. Sucks in the swell and can handle pretty large faces before maxing out. Confident, nimble, experienced surfers will love it, while intermediates may struggle. The walk along the snaking, monsoon and typhoon battered pier gets you within 200m of the peak and avoids a lot of coral reef. The annual pro contest is a big event for Siargao, when it is a good time to visit for the party and pageantry, but not for getting shacked at Crowd 9! The tight take-off zone can be a hassle with locals and expats fighting for the bombs, but patience will be rewarded by the generally friendly local crew. If it is too packed, try the nearby options of Jacking Horse or Quicksilver.

TUESDAY ROCK

JS CALLAHAN/SURFEXPLORE

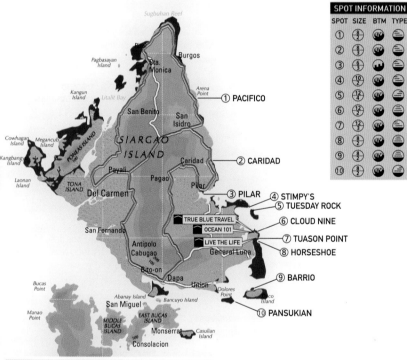

SPOT INFORMATION

SPOT	SIZE	BTM	TYPE
①			
②			
③			
④			
⑤			
⑥			
⑦			
⑧			
⑨			
⑩			

① PACIFICO
② CARIDAD
③ PILAR
④ STIMPY'S
⑤ TUESDAY ROCK
⑥ CLOUD NINE
⑦ TUASON POINT
⑧ HORSESHOE
⑨ BARRIO
⑩ PANSUKIAN

TRUE BLUE TRAVEL
OCEAN 101
LIVE THE LIFE

WIND AND SWELL

The Philippines doesn't have great swell exposure, because the only real swell generator is from typhoons travelling W-NW towards Japan. They may form at any time but July-Dec is the prime time, peaking through Sept-Oct. There is an estimated 15-20 swells in each season, that provide several days of E-NE swells between 3-8ft (1-2.5m) with occasional 12ft (4m) days. The best time for clean conditions is during the SW monsoon from July-Oct when the wind is

SURF STATS		J	F	M	A	M	J	J	A	S	O	N	D
SWELL	Dominant swell												
	Size (m)	7-8		4-6		2-3		2		2-4		6-7	
	Consistency (%)	94		86		23		6		39		97	
WIND	Dominant wind												
	Average force	F4		F4		F3		F3-F4		F3-F4		F4	
	Consistency	85		80		67		59		56		65	
TEMP.	Wetsuit												
	Water temp.	24		24		24		25		24		24	

TRAVEL INFORMATION

LOCAL POPULATION:	COASTLINE: Siargao - 122km (76mi)
General Luna - 13,385	TIME ZONE: GMT +8h

GETTING THERE – No visa required for less than 21 days. Extensions are really easy. Plenty of charter flights from Asian cities, Australia, Europe and USA. Cebu Pacific fly small planes from Cebu City to Del Carmen on Siargao, but boards may not fit in hold. Air Philippine Express and Cebu Pacific fly Cebu-Surigao City or Manila-Surigao City daily (fr $70 + $24/15kg boardbag e/w). Or Cebu-Surigao City (Cokaliong overnight ferry fr $20). Surigao City to Siargao Island is a 3hr ferry ride to Dapa (fr $6) and a 30min bus ride to General Luna. Departure tax is $18/750PHP)

GETTING AROUND – Pump-boats (or banca boats) are fast, noisy, uncomfortable outrigger dug-outs for hire, ($20/h) to access the Siargao reefs. Jeepneys, (local buses), are reliable and frequent for the hop between General Luna and Pilar as well as almost all barrios, (villages). It's easy to walk between the different spots or if you are staying at one of the surf camps then a guide will drive you around. Keep some spare money on you for banca rides, they're cheap, and there are loads of them.

LODGING AND FOOD – Plenty of accommodation options. There are a number of surf camps on Siargao Island at Cloud Nine; choose from Ocean 101 ($10-43 dbl), Sagana Resort (fr $80/n/dble full board), Turtle ($36/n/dbl), or the Tuason Cottages ($35/d). Closer to General Luna is Buddha's Surf Resort (fr $47/n) and the luxury Pansukian Tropical Resort (fr $140/p/n/dbl full board) plus dozens more surf/guest houses. In Pilar try Lucod Beach Resort, Jafe Surf in Pacifico and White Sands in Burgos. Food is very cheap and revolves around fish and rice; $5-10 a meal.

WEATHER – The Philippines is hot and extremely humid year-round. The Pacific side of the Philippines is subject to two monsoon patterns, the NE monsoon called amihan from Nov to April not only brings onshores and small windswell, but also huge amounts of rainfall. In July the SW monsoon habigat starts blowing, this brings less rain and better wind patterns. Typhoons rarely make landfall this far S, but if they are going to then July-Dec is the risk period. The water is warm all year, so take boardshorts, a rash vest and booties for the reef walks.

WEATHER	J/F	M/A	M/J	J/A	S/O	N/D
Total Rainfall (mm)	460	380	141	154	220	524
Consistency (d/m)	21	20	11	12	15	22
Temperature min. (°C)	23	23	24	24	24	23
Temperature max. (°C)	29	31	31	31	31	29

NATURE AND CULTURE – The SUP, kite-boarding, kayaking, diving, snorkeling, fishing and jet-skiing are all excellent and many camps/hotels arrange hire and tours. Jump in a banca boat and go explore. Siargao Island has some natural hot springs near Lake Mainit, giant caves on Hikdop Island or whirlpools in the Surigao straits. For night-time entertainment go to General Luna.

HAZARDS AND HASSLES – Siargao is hard to get to. There is a growing band of competitive local surfers and quite a lot of foreign surfers, but everyone is spread out over plenty of different spots. Rain, intense heat and malarial mosquitoes are present.

HANDY HINTS – Bring all your own surf gear, including a semi-gun, although rentals and essential kit is becoming more widely available. Filipinos are usually very friendly, but there is the occasional bit of localism at Cloud Nine.

predominantly offshore. After this the wind switches around to the NE, bringing onshores and bigger NE windswells that peak in Dec/ Jan. The calm May-June transition period sees low winds blowing from a E-SE direction, while swell is almost non-existent. The tidal range is minimal, but most shallow reefs are better surfed from mid-high tide. ●

MALUKU, INDONESIA

+ REGULAR N MONSOON SWELL
+ QUALITY, MID-SIZED WAVES
+ CALM WINDS, SMALL TIDES
+ TOTALLY VIRGIN SURF AREA
+ SUPER SCENIC AND WILD

– SHORT SURF SEASON
– LONG DISTANCES BETWEEN SPOTS
– EQUATORIAL WET
– FEW ORGANISED BOAT TRIPS
– VOLCANIC ACTIVITY AND QUAKES

DAN HAYLOCK

SERENADE

The original Spice Islands, the Maluku (Moluccas or Molluques are alternative names) are part of the easternmost archipelago of Indonesia and the only Indonesian island chain in the Pacific. Magellan's expedition, which took a ton of spices back to Spain in 1521, first put Maluku on the map. Despite waves as good as the Philippines, these islands remain largely ignored by travelling surfers. Occasional forays into the region by boat have revealed an outstanding variety of breaks, most of which go unsurfed. A small number of feral surfers make the long trek through the jungles around Christmas time, to stay in remote villages and surf the better-known spots.

The east coast of Morotai and Halmahera is only likely to come to life in a major N swell, or in an ENE typhoon. Reports on this area indicate that the **ATOLL REEFS** off islets near Tobelo could go off, with two lefts witnessed but not surfed. **PULAU KECIL**, an island off the east coast town of Berebere, does have a long, wrapping righthander and a left. Both these spots have great potential, but are very fickle. Sopi, the northernmost bay on Morotai, is an obvious swell magnet for consistent north monsoon swells. **INDO JIWA**, named after one of the first boat trips to the area, is an epic right with fast outside sections and hollow walls, but needs plenty of size or N in the swell and higher tides. Inside, the **VILLAGE REFORM** is a super-fast right, which is on the shallow side of rideable at low and fun, but sectiony at high. A few other reef and beach options exist close to the village where most surfers hang out. They are here to ride **SERENADE** (also named after a pioneering boat) a stunning left 40mins walk from Sopi. Breaking on all tides, almost every day, this spot has an incredibly ledgy take-off into an angular barrel section that regularly slams shut, before leading into smooth, variable speed walls mixed with clean tapered shoulders. This easier wide section peaks up and runs off down the reef, leaving plenty of room for lip-tapping and roundhouses. The two sections are distinctly separate on smaller swells and the fairly benign reef can get sketchy on the inside shut down section close to the tall, jungled shoreline. The nearby **SHORT LEDGE** right is a thick high tide barrel on the east side of a deep bay with good anchorage and more possibilities. Land access is impossible. The western shores of both Morotai and Halmahera are steep, but many bays have the right topography and reef set-ups to hold some fast peeling rights if the swell is big enough. **TANJUNG PADANG** is a great set-up, with long, fast rights over the reef, flanked by a deep-water channel. Pulau Rau has a couple of excellent lefts dubbed **NACHOS**, a fun high tide peak/left and **TACOS**, a super fast left fringing reef over super sharp coral. The first spot on Halmahera is **HEAVY'S**, a long and sucky left that needs perfect SE winds to be makeable and may still be unsurfed. Nearby **DOUBLE DOME** is ridden by local surfers on village shaped wooden planks and the odd visitor

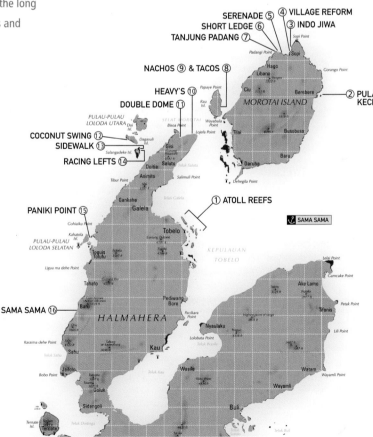

SERENADE ⑤ ④ VILLAGE REFORM
SHORT LEDGE ⑥ ③ INDO JIWA
TANJUNG PADANG ⑦

NACHOS ⑨ & TACOS ⑧

HEAVY'S ⑩
DOUBLE DOME ⑪

② PULAU KECIL

MOROTAI ISLAND

COCONUT SWING ⑫
SIDEWALK ⑬
RACING LEFTS ⑭

PANIKI POINT ⑮

① ATOLL REEFS

✓ SAMA SAMA

SAMA SAMA ⑯

HALMAHERA

OLLIE FITZJONES

SAMA SAMA

TANJUNG PADANG

DAN HAYLOCK

TRAVEL INFORMATION

LOCAL POPULATION: 2.1M	COASTLINE:
TIME ZONE: GMT +8h	Indonesia – 54,716km (34,000mi)

GETTING THERE – A 30-day visa costs $35. Flights run with Merpati to Ternate (daily), Galela (3/week) or Daruba (weekly). The *Sama Sama* does 10 day charters from Ternate Dec-March. Some fly to Manado (MDC) in Sulawesi, then arrange a charter.

GETTING AROUND – The *Sama Sama* takes up to 10 people and is the only scheduled charter in this area. The distance between spots can be long and the sea can be rough, so a good boat is essential. Land access is long and slow, but small numbers of ferals head to Sopi and get a homestay, making the 40 min walk and 10 min paddle to Serenade every morning. The promise of a reliable ferry service around Morotai is yet to be realised. There are inter-island ferries to Rau from Morotai.

FOOD AND LODGING – In Manado, stay in town for $30-110/d, at hotels catering for divers. Most hotels are 30-45min from Manado, but the best resorts are on the small Siladen Island in Bunaken Marine Park. There are cheap hotels ($5-10) in Ternate, Daruba or Tobelo. Food is fresh and cheap, boat menus have lots of fresh fish (yellow fin tuna). Expect to pay $3 for a meal in town.

WEATHER – With a thousand odd islands, the climate in Maluku is heavily influenced by the monsoon trends, elevation, proximity to volcanoes, and coastal exposure. The weather varies from one island to another. However, humidity is the rule with over 2.5m (100in) of rain a year. Usually, north of the Equator, Nov-March NE monsoon clears up the skies while April-Oct SW monsoon brings downpours. Wind squalls are frequent and thunderstorm activity is amongst the highest on earth. Transition months like October or April are characterised by heavy rainfall as well. The surf season is somewhat clearer. Daytime temperature variation is small; expect it to be hot and humid year-round. Water is amongst the warmest on earth, at 29°C (84°F).

WEATHER	J/F	M/A	M/J	J/A	S/O	N/D
Total Rainfall (mm)	123	207	577	501	198	123
Consistency (d/m)	13	17	23	21	14	12
Temperature min. (°C)	24	24	23	23	23	24
Temperature max. (°C)	31	30	28	27	28	31

NATURE AND CULTURE – Apart from old rusty jeeps and remnants of WW2, there is not much on Morotai except thick jungle. In 1988, most of the rusted remnants were removed. Underwater, there remain sunken ships and bombed planes for divers to visit. Halmahera has more WW2 evidence, and Ternate and Tidore are popular sightseeing spots. Smoking volcanoes dominate the skyline. The waterfall shower at Paniki Point is a gem.

HAZARDS AND HASSLES – This is a virgin area with a really low population. For the rare traveller opting for land access, be aware, malaria is present and humidity levels are high. Travelling even short distances on the back of motorbikes can take hours as the tracks follow the steep contours of the land. Earthquakes, tremors and volcanic eruptions, albeit small ones, are an almost daily occurrence.

HANDY HINTS – Take at least 2 everyday boards and a semi-gun in case of a bigger swell. A longboard opens up a variety of long, fast, peeling waves. The water is extremely warm, so pack plenty of wax.

making the long overland trip from Tobelo. Lefts break down the angled reef into the town and are offshore in westerlies. Offshore, islands known as Loloda Utara have many surf spots. At **COCONUT SWING**, a savage left breaks, but few waves are rideable. The main attractions in this area are at Salandageke Island. **SIDEWALK** can be a perfect, long and mellow righthander, or an angry fast tube full of shut-down sections. This spot breaks down a natural rock spit, is ideally exposed to the NNE, and is a lovely longboard wave when small. The **RACING LEFTS** across the channel are long and sectiony. Further south, Halmahera hides a bunch of great waves including the incredibly long, cruising walls of **PANIKI POINT** that bend through 130° and bring you almost back to the peak. Finally, the reliable rights of **SAMA SAMA** are a great option, close to the main town of Ternate. Beneath the steep headland cliffs, the sets rear-up, peel for about 2 or 3 turns, then close-out through the connecting section that would have led to the channel shoulder and a series of cutbacks. Sit wide or way inside as it changes constantly through the tide. Local groms rip on rudimentary wooden bellyboards.

SWELL AND WIND

Although the NW Pacific typhoon season must give rise to some epic days, it's much safer to hit these islands at the heart of the North Monsoon season (Nov-March) for maximum consistency. Sept-Oct is the ideal time of year for a low latitude typhoon developing off Mindanao, Philippines. During winter NE monsoons, the usual size is 3-6ft (1-2m) of wind-driven waves, with potential for bigger days at the more exposed spots. Wind patterns at this equatorial "doldrums" latitude are very light and variable and glassy days are the norm, apart from the frequent rainy squalls. Some offshore ENE winds do occur, shifting NNW if the sun is shining. Transition months of April-May and September-October are usually calm with light winds, but hardly any swell. The unlikely question of whether the Maluku straight produces SW windswell from July to Sept is yet to be answered. Tidal range varies up to 3ft (0.9m), and affects almost all the known spots. Tides are difficult to gauge and accurate information is hard to find – ask the local fishermen. ●

SPOT INFORMATION

SPOT	SIZE	BTM	TYPE
①			
②			
③	10		
④			
⑤			
⑥			
⑦			
⑧			
⑨			
⑩			
⑪			
⑫			
⑬			
⑭			
⑮			
⑯	10		

SURF STATS		J	F	M	A	M	J	J	A	S	O	N	D
SWELL	Dominant swell												
	Size (m)	4-5		2-3		0-1		1-2		2-3		4	
	Consistency (%)	90		60		10		20		40		80	
WIND	Dominant wind												
	Average force	F3		F3		F2-F3		F3		F3		F2-F3	
	Consistency	65		54		40		66		49		48	
TEMP.	Wetsuit												
	Water temp.	28		28		29		28		28		29	

KAVIENG, NEW IRELAND, PNG

+ CONSISTENT, SEASONAL SWELLS
+ CLEAN, TROPICAL WAVES
+ UNCROWDED, PERFECT SURF
+ SHORT IDYLLIC BOAT RIDES
+ MELANESIAN AND PAPUAN CULTURE

– OFTEN SMALL
– VERY RAINY SURF SEASON
– DIFFICULT AND EXPENSIVE ACCESS
– HIGH MALARIA RISKS
– CIVIL UNREST IN CERTAIN AREAS

Papua New Guinea may rank as the world's 2nd largest island, but some of the best waves in the country break on tiny coral specks scattered throughout the Bismarck Archipelago. Decidedly Melanesian in flavour, it is these islands, bearing unlikely European names such as New Britain, New Ireland and New Hanover that hold the best potential for maximizing the power of any available WNW to ENE swells. Kavieng is the main town and jump off point for the islands that nestle not too far offshore.

tolerance over the coral and getting caught behind will require booties to escape a pounding. Usually smaller and less fraught closer to Kavieng harbour, where the local kids paddle out on lumps of wood. All the waves in Kavieng are classified as rarely crowded, because there is a maximum of 20 foreign surfers quota system in place for the whole region, spread over nine different surfing spots. **NUSA LEFTS** hit the northern tip of reef attached to the island where most surfers stay. The exposed nature of the spot makes the waves jack up out of deeper water, then bowl out in places as the wall bends

Skirting around the town and heading up to the exposed Mongol Point is a shallow layer of reef known as **PIKININI**. Consistently rideable in shorter sections, it shows true class when a moderate WNW swell links up the speed runs into one, long racy barrel. All tides are doable, but high doesn't give any more

ANDREW SHIELD

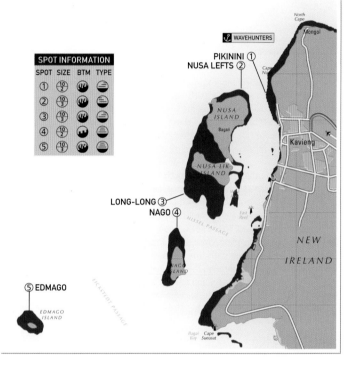

EAST OF KAVIENG

ANDREW SHIELD

ANDREW SHIELD

around the shelf. Fast and fluid with a nice coping, until the inside section turns inside-out over the barely drenched coral. Again prefers more W than N in the swell with S quadrant winds and a mid tide. A short boat ride from Nusa Island Retreat is **LONG-LONG**, properly named for it's length of ride. It's a bit rare since the swell has to be strong from the W-NW and winds from the N-E, but when it does work, fun is the operative word. Deep water roll-in to a generous wall that invites all-comers to tag and spray or throw on the anchors for some shade time. Perfect intermediate relief from the shallow barrels nearby. Across a short channel is **NAGO**, a more consistent reef and more likely to work in swells from a N direction. The left is usually the go, making the most of small swells with lip-bashing walls and an inside tuck section. The right is more fickle, needs more swell and can be a charging barrel. Both prefer low to mid tides and the left even handles some onshore ruffle. A short 4km cruise to the SW arrives at **EDMAGO**, a pretty oval of glinting white sand, palms and a top-drawer lefthander that needs W in the swell and SE winds to be any good. The adjacent right is more reliable, but far less impressive and neither spot likes the extremes of tide. When swell is in short supply, a longer trip to Ral is the call, since it sits in splendid isolation, open to all swells directions including NE and will have something to ride when all else is flat. Easy, fun and mushy when small, the rights on the western fringe of reef can be peaky or lined-up runners, depending on swell direction, which helps spread out the crowd on small days. The left is less reliable, but both will become punchy and heavy over headhigh, when other spots closer to home are going to be better.

SWELL AND WIND

The bulk of Papua New Guinea's waves come from NW-NE windswells, which provide regular 3-6ft (1-2m) waves from Nov-April. While NW swell is ideal for many of the breaks, NNE-NE is far more prevalent. The more exposed spots will only be surfed early in the morning, as the offshore mornings turn WNW-NE onshore most afternoons. Nov is the month with the lightest winds and the winds turn increasingly E towards the end of the season. While the supposed dry season (May-Oct) sees offshore ESE winds, there is far less swell and May-Aug are usually flat. The tides are semi diurnal odd (2 daily tides with a different range) and the big tide averages around 1m (3ft) between

TRAVEL INFORMATION

LOCAL POPULATION: Kavieng - 17,248
TIME ZONE: GMT +8h
COASTLINE: New Ireland – 1334km (829mi)

GETTING THERE – Air Niugini fly into Port Moresby (POM) from Australia (Sydney, Brisbane & Cairns), Hong Kong, Tokyo, Manila, Honiara, KL and Singapore. Qantas and Air Niugini do selective Australian cities. Air Niugini flies POM-Kavieng-Rabaul triangle from $425/rt. Domestic flights - 16kgs (35lbs) plus an additional 15kgs (33lbs) per person for sports equipment (scuba).

GETTING AROUND – Transport is very limited because of poor roads and 4WD rental for driving the one road on New Ireland is astronomical ($150/d min). Most travel is by public transport PMV (Passenger Motor Vehicle) which includes cheap crowded buses, trucks or even motorboats. There are regular boats from Rabaul to Kavieng, but schedules are short term and unreliable. Local trade and banana boats can be hired, but not as cheaply as the official PMV boats at $15/hr.

LODGING AND FOOD – There are a few hotels, B&B's and resorts in this area and they're all expensive. A basic hotel costs about $50/d, but most surfers stay at the Nusa Island Retreat on Nusa Lik, which will take no more than 12 people at a time and provide transport to the breaks. Beach and waterfront bungalows, good restaurant and surf transfers are all part of the package. The fresh seafood is excellent.

WEATHER – Dry season is a bit of a misnomer as it's very wet year round with a yearly average of 3.2m (10ft). Also, with a surf season that corresponds with the NW monsoon you can be sure of a good soaking. It also gets very hot and is constantly sticky. Port Moresby is much drier, whilst the W of New Britain island has up to 6m (20ft) of rain a year! Cyclones actually hitting this area are a rare occurrence.

WEATHER	J/F	M/A	M/J	J/A	S/O	N/D
Total Rainfall (mm)	434	368	169	154	178	283
Consistency (d/m)	22	21	8	6	7	14
Temperature min. (°C)	24	23	23	22	23	24
Temperature max. (°C)	30	31	31	30	30	31

NATURE AND CULTURE – The diving and fishing is world-class. On land you can play volleyball and snooker, visit the crocodile farm or the W.W.II relics. A totally unique experience is the "shark calling" - local people using coconut shell rattles and their voices to attract the sharks. Pidgin is a strange mix of local and English vocabulary, which can be hard to interpret. The Surfing Association of Papua New Guinea promotes sustainable development by implementing the Kavieng Area Surf Management Plan that limits the total number of visiting surfers to 20 per day. Fees apply, regardless of where you stay and are distributed among the surfside communities. Book your place with the Kavieng Surf Club.

HAZARDS AND HASSLES – PNG has a reputation as a violent and unstable country, but the Kavieng area is pretty safe and the locals are friendly and hospitable. Even petty theft is quite rare, however remain vigilant. Reefs are super shallow and home to sharks, stonefish and sea snakes. A much greater health risk is malaria and infection from reef cuts.

HANDY HINTS – Take lots of cash as credit cards either attract a surcharge or don't work at all. There is no surf gear available anywhere. Bring your standard shortboard, a fish for small mushy days and some reef boots. There is reasonable hospital care in Kavieng. Contact World Surfaris for package trips to Nusa Lik and also Rubio Plantation, a frontier camp halfway down New Ireland, or Wavehunters for PNG Explorer.

SURF STATS	J	F	M	A	M	J	J	A	S	O	N	D
SWELL Dominant swell	🌀		🌀		🌀		🌀		🌀		🌀	
Size (m)	4-5		3-4		1-2		0-1		1-2		3-4	
Consistency (%)	80		70		30		10		30		70	
WIND Dominant wind	🧭		🧭		🧭		🧭		🧭		🧭	
Average force	F3		F2-F3		F3		F3		F3		F3	
Consistency	60		58		62		75		63		57	
TEMP Wetsuit	🏄		🏄		🏄		🏄		🏄		🏄	
Water temp.	28		28		28		27		28		28	

high and low. Most spots favour mid to low tide although high will be rideable, but mushier. It's not too hard to get a tide chart from Kavieng Harbour or the numerous diving resorts. Don't visit during El Niño years, as the waves are very inconsistent. ●

POHNPEI, MICRONESIA

+ NORTH PACIFIC & TYPHOON SWELLS
+ WARM, CRYSTAL CLEAR WATER
+ P-PASS PERFECTION
+ ISLAND SIGHT-SEEING
+ SAFE, POLITICALLY STABLE & CLEAN

– INCONSISTENT N SWELLS
– NOT FOR BEGINNERS
– OCCASIONAL CROWDS & RIPS
– EXTREMELY RAINY
– VERY EXPENSIVE TRIP

Pohnpei is part of the Federated States of Micronesia (FSM), lying more than 5000km (3,200 mi) southwest of Hawaii. The FSM is one of 8 island nations inside the region of Micronesia including, Kiribati, Marshalls, Palau, Nauru, the Northern Marianas, Guam and Wake Island. The FSM is made up of more than 600 islands scattered across over 3.9 million square kilometres (1.5M sq/mi) of the Pacific, divided into the four states of Yap, Chuuk, Pohnpei, and Kosrae. Pohnpei is the tip of a 5 million-year-old extinct shield volcano. The entire island is made up of black basalt rock, surrounded by a deep lagoon up to 8km (5mi) wide, circled by many linear, patch and pinnacle reefs. Secretly surfed by a lucky few until a Surf Report Issue in Feb 1998, the media have frenzied over some of the photos depicting the smoking barrels of P-Pass, generally considered as the best wave in Micronesia.

Waves break out on the barrier reef or near a reef pass, so it's boat access only and it's always shallow on the inside. Up to 4ft (1.2m), the waves are user-friendly, but once the surf gets bigger, things get serious quickly. Late take-offs, fast down-the-line rides, and hollow barrels are what most surfed spots offer and the best of them is **P-PASS** (Palikir Passage). It is only a 5min boat ride from the Pohnpei Surf Club (PSC) to **SOKEHS PASS**, where small outside rights are rideable at high tide from 2-4ft, but there's nothing easy about the treacherous inside. **LIGHTHOUSE** breaks under the same conditions as P-Pass, but it is always bigger and has a super-shallow inside section. It's a challenging spot in big waves,

with a west and a north take-off spot, a long wall and an incredible inside barrel section, inevitably drawing comparisons to Sunset Beach in Hawaii. Holds chunky swells and bigger is always better, because the reef can go dry at any tide on smaller days, when nearby Middle Pass may be working. The east side of Pohnpei has three different passes that work in totally different conditions from one another. A 20min boat ride to **MWAHND LEFTS** will reward early season forays when the trade winds are low. It holds big swell and can offer fun walls, good hooks and quick barrels. Across the channel, **MWAHND RIGHTS** also work without tradewinds, plus any size swell from small to triple overhead. Reminiscent of Macaronis in Indo, **ARUH** sees spinning lefts that require a huge N swell or an E swell without the E winds. Sharp bottom. The next big reef pass is **NAHPALI**, a long sectiony right, which always has waves, but is usually blown out. It's rippy, sharky and a 40min boat ride. On the other side of the famous ruins of **NAN MADOL**, more wind exposed rights peel and section off into the bay. **NAHLAP** has a fun right reefbreak ideal for beginners. The waves pick up in SE swells from July until October, with 3-4ft faces and light or no winds.

P-PASS

LAT: 6.98197°   LONG: 158.128°

This wave has become the star of the Western Pacific by occasionally churning out impossibly perfect righthand pits, attracting pros and chargers to this remote island when the forecast looks right. It takes any swell from W-NE, with straight N being the best direction to avoid close-outs from the NW or missing the reef from the NE. P-Pass works with no winds or with light NE-E trades, which blow dead offshore as the swell lines wrap around the reef. These rights can be surfed at any tide, but it does get very shallow on a full low tide. Intermediates will enjoy the fun, consistent, headhigh, high tide sessions while pros will tackle the scary, rare, double-overhead, super-sucky days. It's a 20min boat ride from Kolonia.

LIGHTHOUSE

ANDREW SHIELD

TRAVEL INFORMATION

LOCAL POPULATION: 34,500   TIME ZONE: GMT +11h
COASTLINE: 67km (43mi)

GETTING THERE – 30 days visa issued on arrival. Passport needs min 120 days validity. Only United Airlines serves Pohnpei (PNI) from Honolulu (HNL) or Guam (GUM). Expect to pay at least $1645 (Mon/Tue) up to $1903 (Fri) for the 9hr HNL return flight or $1051 from GUM (4hrs). Don't forget the $200 e/w for your boardbag! Dep tax $10.

GETTING AROUND – No paddle spots so use Pohnpei Surf Club boats, leaving at regular times (7am/9am) to spread the crowd. All the boats are equipped with cell phones, radio, first aid kits, coolers for food and drinks, ice, shaded area, seat cushions, and fishing and diving equipment when needed. It's all included in the package.

LODGING AND FOOD – Pohnpei Surf Club costs between $205-225/night (peak season is Nov - Mar). 9 double rooms with private bathroom, hot water, A/C, TV, telephone and wireless internet. PSC is limiting surfer numbers to a maximum of 18. P-PassSurf Camp service the Aussie market from $155/d. Staying at the Village Hotel (fr $103) is possible, but finding a boat will be difficult and expensive. All-you-can-eat rotary Sushi for $8. Expect $15-20 for meals daily + stocking hotel rooms with supplies from the supermarket in Kolonia.

WEATHER – Pohnpei has a tropical, humid climate that keeps the fertile landscape lush and green year-round. Rain is a substantial part of the Pohnpei experience since it is one of the wettest places on earth with an average annual rainfall of 4860mm (191in). The largest part of the rainfall comes at night, when on-shore breezes are quickly cooled as they rise up the mountain slopes. Temps are constant, ranging from 23-30°C (74-86°F). Most of the year, there is a NE trade wind. A typical day in Pohnpei is cloudy with intermittent showers and the sun breaking through now and then. The mountains aren't quite high enough to act as a complete block, so the rainfall on the windward and leeward sides of the island does not differ greatly. Major windstorms and destructive typhoons are rare. Boardshorts only in the "Pool", the warmest ocean temperatures in the world.

WEATHER	J/F	M/A	M/J	J/A	S/O	N/D
Total Rainfall (mm)	283	411	463	427	427	417
Consistency (d/m)	17	22	25	22	20	19
Temperature min. (°C)	24	24	23	23	23	23
Temperature max. (°C)	30	30	30	31	31	31

NATURE AND CULTURE – Explore beautiful waterfalls, hike to the ancient ruins of Nan Madol, or try world-class diving. Visit Outer Atolls like Ant and Pakin, only 16-50km (10-30mi) offshore. Deep-sea fishing, snorkelling, bird watching, canoeing. Climb or visit Sokehs Ridge and the World War II historical sites. Check Rusty Anchor, the best bar on the Island.

HAZARDS AND HASSLES – Since boats are always in the channel, there is no reef walking when you paddle in and out. Most surfers do not use booties, but they can be very helpful at times. Above 5ft (1.5m), waves at P-Pass get dangerous for inexperienced surfers. Rips can get pretty intense at times.

HANDY HINTS – Small to mid-range boards (6'0"-7'0") work best in the barrels. PSC recommends bringing 4 boards and has a fleet of used hire boards for those who break all theirs. Bring everything with you including snacks. Island hopper flights go to Guam and Kosrae (Kosrae Surf Tours).

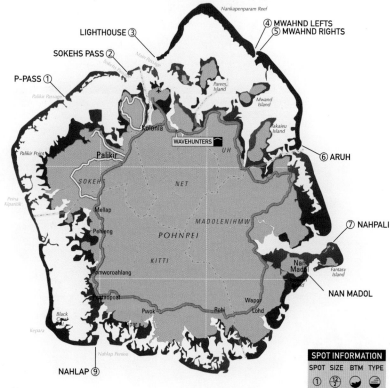

Nankapenparam Reef

④ MWAHND LEFTS
⑤ MWAHND RIGHTS

LIGHTHOUSE ③

SOKEHS PASS ②

P-PASS ①

Palikir Passage

Parem Island

Mwand Island

Kolonia

Takaieu Island

WAVEHUNTERS

Palikir

Palikir Point

UH

⑥ ARUH

Peina Kiparilik

SOKEH

NET

Mellap

MADOLENIHMW

⑦ NAHPALI

Pehleng

POHNPEI

Nan Madol

Fantasy Island

KITTI

Tomworoahlang

NAN MADOL

Wapar

Black Coral

Pwok

Rohi

Lohd

Dpar

Kepara

Nahlap Penieu

NAHLAP ⑨

SWELL AND WIND

Most of the swells that reach Pohnpei are generated by typhoons in the western Pacific or North Pacific winter storms, although it doesn't necessarily receive the same swells as Hawaii. Pohnpei surf season runs from early October thru to early May. June is usually flat, and by late July the winds die out, shifting from absolutely no winds to variable. During the months of August and September, some breaks on the exposed windward side come alive with glassy or offshore conditions

SPOT INFORMATION

SPOT	SIZE	BTM	TYPE
①	12/4		
②	4/2		
③	8/2		
④	12/4		
⑤	18/2		
⑥	6/2		
⑦	6/2		
⑧	8/2		
⑨	8/2		

SURF STATS		J	F	M	A	M	J	J	A	S	O	N	D
SWELL	Dominant swell												
	Size (m)	3-4		3		3-4		4-5		2-3		3-4	
	Consistency (%)	70		50		40		30		60		70	
WIND	Dominant wind												
	Average force	F4		F4		F3-F4		F3		F3		F3-F4	
	Consistency (%)	93		89		73		39		35		70	
TEMP.	Wetsuit												
	Water temp.	28		28		29		29		29		29	

and E swells generated by trade winds east of Pohnpei. SW swells can arrive with the strong monsoonal winds that blow in from western Micronesia and the Philippines. These waves hit the east to southwest sides of Pohnpei with less power and size. The trades pick up from late December all the way to late May and blow strong. Semi-diurnal tides with diurnal inequality, average 3-6ft (0.9m-1.8m) max tidal range. ●

Nemberala Beach Resort, **Rote**

Macaronis Resort, **Mentawais**

Kandui Villas, **Mentawais**

Indo Yacht Charters, **Indo**

Tavarua Island Resort, **Fiji**

Chaaya Island Dhonveli, **Maldives**

Namotu Island Resort, **Fiji**

Salani Surf Resort, **Samoa**

Maldives Yacht Charters, **Maldives**

Aganoa Beach Retreat, **Samoa**

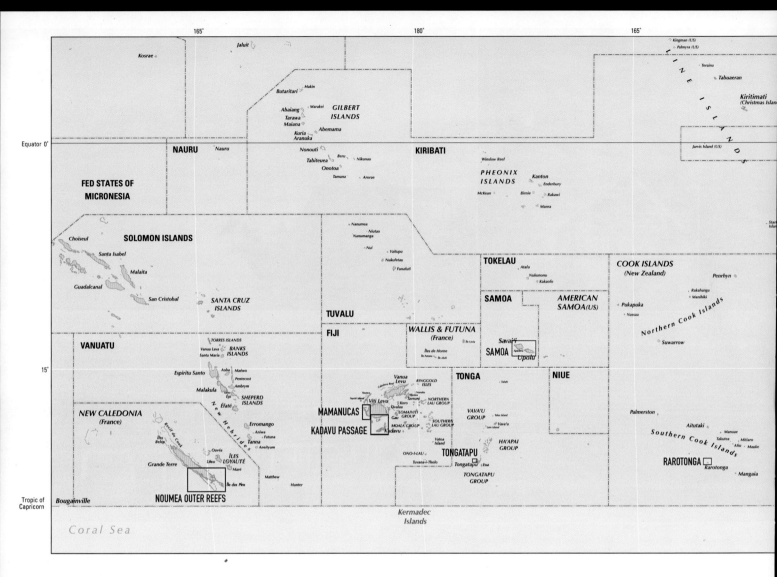

NEW CALEDONIA AND VANUATU

Triangulated with the Coral Sea and the Great Barrier Reef to the west and open to the Tasman Sea to the south, the elongated finger of **New Caledonia** is an unusual concoction of French chic and the Melanesian laid-back way of life. **SOUTH PROVINCE**'s outer reefs form part of an incredible 1500km barrier to the surf and encircle the world's largest lagoon, creating a spectacular playground for all types of water-sports lovers. Beyond the superb reef passes of Boulari, Dumbea, Tenia and Ouano lie dozens more to the south and all the way north beyond the land mass of Grande Terre. The coral defences continue on the east coast, but of course the trade winds and lack of any regular northern hemisphere swell kill off the chances of surf. Ile des Pins off the SE corner of Grande Terre has a few land accessible waves around the main bays of Kuto and Rouleaux, where a boat would allow access to some more reef passes, but much of the island is a nature reserve so surfers and kiters are interdite (prohibited).

There is little doubt that if New Caledonia didn't block all the SW groundswell, **Vanuatu** would have some top notch surf. As it is, Efate has some nice set-ups that offer early morning, high tide barrels before the trades set in. The trade winds blow E in southern and central Vanuatu, but turn more S in the far north where there is a clear equatorial climatic influence. These scattering of small

Trying to sum up or describe the definitive vision of "tropical paradise" that floats around most people's imagination is probably best done in two words – South Pacific. This gigantic expanse of the deep blue Pacific, warmly embraces the randomly scattered island groups that dare break the surface, providing perfect conditions for an abundance of coral life in the form of fringing, platform, patch, barrier, oceanic ribbon, atolls and drowned coral reefs. Where there's reef, there's surf and early Polynesian cultures quickly learned how to integrate that surf into their daily lives. It's not all plain sailing when it comes to catching some of these waves and many waves require a boat to reach them, high tide to cover them and above average skill to ride them.

OTHER ISLANDS TO CONSIDER

PANGO POINT. AKA POUNDERS

ÉFATÉ, VANUATU

Vanuatu, the "Timeless Islands" is a group of 83 islands, spanning 900km (563mi) on a north-south axis, just to the east of the Solomon's. Situated 2,250km (1400mi) northeast of Sydney, and 800km (480mi) west of Fiji, Vanuatu would be an idyllic surf island if New Caledonia was not blocking the main South Pacific swells. Capital city Port-Vila sits on Efate, pretty much in the middle of the Vanuatu archipelago and is more associated with honeymoons than surfaris. There are a few good reefs along the south coast near Vila, including Pango Point, where lefts pitch from take-off then offer tapering walls before shutting down over the aggressive polyps. In the next bay, Breakas peels off the peak before shouldering into the channel on the longer, dominant lefts, but both waves require two important ingredients - high tides and no wind. This means getting up in the dark and

+ QUALITY CORAL REEFBREAKS
+ YACHTING AND SAILING STOP-OVER
+ WARM AND EMPTY LINE-UPS
+ GOOD TOURISM FACILITIES

− S-SW SWELL SHADOW
− LACK OF CONSISTENT SPOTS
− SE SWELL/WIND EXPOSURE
− HIGH FLIGHT AND LOCAL EXPENSES

getting your waves before 9.30am when the SE trades blow in. SE swells are the main wave generator, along with E-SE windswell so mid winter should see the biggest waves, but also the strongest trades. March to June probably gives the best compromise of swell and wind, but there can be waves any time of year, especially on the more exposed east coast. Those with time and patience will undoubtedly score some nice waves, but the inconsistency, high tide and onshore wind factors make Efate a bit of a gamble for a week or two surf trip.

islands share more with the Solomons and are the frontier between Melanesia and Polynesia, suggesting N swell is a safer bet on the fringing reefs of the Torres Islands. The large mass of Espiritu Santo has some spots that a few locals ride, but it is extremely shadowed from E-SW and relies on W- NE swell for any action. There's some black sand beachbreak near Ipayato and Tasiriki in the southwest and rumours of a good reef on Sakau Island, but it takes huge effort to get there. Maewo and Pentecost Island have some windward coast potential, but will be blown out 90% of the time. Also inaccessible by land so only yachties willing to take the leap will surf these islands. The general consensus by those who have been is the surfing on Tanna is better than Efate as it picks up proper SW swell, sneaking round the tip of New Caledonia. In front of the wharf in Lenakel is one of a number waves in the area including friendly beachbreak and serious left reefbreaks that are offshore in the trades. Over the other side of the island, Port Resolution sees a massive expanse of reef, bend righthanders into the bay, plus small swell, wind exposed peaks nearby. Finally, Anelghowhat on Aneityum overlooks some very promising left reefbreaks including Mystery Island.

New Caledonia is a continental island that was part of Australia and its gargantuan barrier reef protects the world's largest lagoon.

SECRETS. NOUMEA. NEW CALEDONIA

OTHER ISLANDS TO CONSIDER

TUTUILA, AMERICAN SAMOA

The only US land below the Equator, the territory of American Samoa consists of seven volcanic islands, with Tutuila the largest and most populated. Despite being surfed by Americans since the early '60s, the surfing population is mainly ex-pat and no bona-fide surf camps have been set up. The waves are powerful reefbreaks with world-class potential, but the reality is that surf conditions are pretty fickle and surf spots dangerously shallow. Most breaks are located on the south coast, way too exposed to prevailing SE trades and the north coast of Tutuila is mostly sheer, black lava cliffs. Fortunately, the south coast has a relatively flat volcanic platform with fringing reefs and submerged coral banks, producing many surfable breaks. Sliding Rock is probably the epicenter of AmSam surfing since it handles the E trade winds, is close to shore and is a top to bottom throaty barrel with good length of ride that is also surfable on

+ RELIABLE SOUTH PACIFIC SWELLS
+ UNCROWDED, POWERFUL REEFBREAKS
+ SOUTH COAST SPOT DENSITY
+ NO SURF CAMPS

– SUPER SHALLOW REEFS
– LACK OF NORTH COAST SPOTS
– EXPOSED TO SE TRADES
– EXPENSIVE ACCESS
– INTENSE HEAT AND RAINFALL IN SUMMER

Sundays. The less developed eastern end of the island has a few gems out of the wind, including a top-class left behind the little island of Aunu'u, a short ferry ride away. The wetter summer season from Nov - April will have much less wind and less S swell, but may get some long distance, long period N swells that light up the breaks at each end of the island. One thing is for sure and that is AmSam is no place for a beginner and only those who like their waves fast, thick and hollow need apply.

BRYAN JACKSON

SLIDING ROCK

FIJI

Comprising 844 islands and islets, Fiji covers 18,274 km2 of solid land, but this doesn't include the staggeringly large 10,000 km2 of reef. The Fiji Barrier Reef marine ecoregion supports at least 300 species of coral, over 475 species of molluscs, and 2,000 fish species, below the waves that arrive from all directions. The SW flank of the main island Viti Levu has held the surf world's gaze for decades and the perfect lefts of Cloudbreak in the **MAMANUCAS** have become one of the most iconic stops on professional surfing's "Dream Tour". Further south, land-accessible spots were found on the fringing reef before Frigates fantastic lefthander emphasised the wave potential of the **KADAVU PASSAGE**. Exposure is the buzz word, but it also points out that the trade winds cause havoc for the swell drenched Eastern Division, so finding a pass or curve of reef that faces west is the challenge and only ocean-going yachties will get to explore the far flung islands of Lau and Lomaiviti provinces where traditional life continues without resorts. Islands on the outer edges filter the SE-SW swell, but plenty still punches up through the wide channels, hitting unlikely reefs like the ones on the southwest tip of Qamea, just beside the 4th largest

island Taveuni. A surf camp has set up at Maqai Beach in front of a handful of good waves including Maqai Wall, an all tide, intermediate plus, righthand carve-fest and across the channel is a gauntlet throwing left sprint, as well as a beginner-friendly inside reef. The myriad of small islands sprinkled to the east probably all have surf at certain times of the year and are open to both S and N swells, mixed in with the constant underlying ESE windswell. Nanuku is one such speck where fast closeouts comb the outer reef until a bigger swell wraps enough to create makeable lines on the western fringes at higher tides.

Snaking along the frontier of the Northern Division and Vanua Levu, Cakaulevu Reef is about 200 kms (120 miles) long and is the third longest continuous barrier reef in the world. While this Great Sea Reef is generally considered as diving territory, from November to March, NW-NE swells can arrive, helped along by the NE swing in the trade winds. Getting out to the reef takes plenty of time and money so few bother to explore during the N swell season. Labasa has direct access to the reef and there are enough curves and passes to expect to find some rideable waves, providing there is swell and the F4 winds haven't ripped it to pieces. Nukubati Resort boats out to Raviravi and Twin Passage, where lefts and better rights break with E wind protection in the shadow of Kia Island. Yasawa, Nacula and down to Naviti all face NW and are a little too far around the corner for any consistent S swell, making them another Nov-March N swell option, but far riskier than the Great Sea Reef. There are many fancy resorts, but none offer surfing, with flat water SUP, kite or wakeboarding more likely for the droves of honeymooners.

TONGA, SAMOA, TOKELAU AND TUVALU

The Kingdom of **Tonga** counts 174 islands spread over a 950km (590mi) axis, yet we only describe waves on the NW corner of **TONGATAPU**. This leaves literally hundreds of potential spots to be found on the other islands, starting with the main population centres in the Ha'apai, Vava'u and Niuas groups. High volcanic and low limestone islands characterize the Ha'apai, where the fringing, barrier and lagoon reefs catch the swell out of the Tonga Trench and there is enough variation in the reef architecture for good waves to appear. Same goes for Vava'u, where the west-facing reefs are always offshore, but reliant on more SW swell, making them fickle. Little exploring can be done without a boat, which explains why the short Ha'atafu stretch back on Tongatapu is so popular, with its easy 100m paddle to the reef. To surf the dredging peak at Ovaka takes a 1.5km paddle from private land and a sturdy, fast boat is essential to travel between the dozen known spots peeling off the circular reefs of uninhabited islands that dot the southern Vava'u seascape. The eastern reef gets way more swell and acts as a back-up for small NE or windswell days, but the SE trades usually frag it to hell. These winds and the exposed nature of the southern Vava'u islands make it hard for yachts to find safe anchorage.

The Tongan summer (Dec-Mar) offers better hope as winds slacken and N swells arrive. The Niuas Group is closer to Samoa and outposts like Niuatoputapu, Tafahi and Niuafo'ou are volcanic and lack reef passes, so surf potential is minimal. French led Wallis has a powerful, bowly, 200m left on the South Pass plus a handful of other fickle spots on the western outer reef. Futuna's rocky, ragged reef is much closer to shore, but set-ups are virtually non-existent.

Samoa is increasingly well-documented on **SAVAI'I AND UPOLU** although both island's northwestern coasts remain off the map, despite extensive fringing reef from Apia to the island of Manono. Apolima Island is far too steep with sheer cliffs dropping into the sea. Recent lava flows have engulfed large areas of land and reef around Mt Matavanu on the NE coast of Savai'i, wiping out some potentially prime surfing real estate by icing the reef in rugged igneous rock.

OTHER ISLANDS TO CONSIDER

KIRITIMATI AND TABUAERAN, LINE ISLANDS

+ CLEAN N & S SWELLS
+ VIRGIN, CRYSTAL CLEAR LINE-UPS
+ VARIOUS QUALITY SPOTS
+ GREAT DIVING & FISHING

– DIFFICULT ACCESS TO SPOTS
– INCONSISTENT IN SUMMER
– EXPENSIVE, INFREQUENT TRANSPORT LINKS
– REMOTENESS AND HIGH COSTS

Kiribati (pronounced kee-ree-bass), comprises of 32 low lying atolls plus 1 island, stretching for 3220km (2000mi) from east to west and covering a vast 3.5M km² (1.35M mi²) swathe of the Central Pacific. Hawaii is the closest neighbour and most visitors arrive by cruise ship, mainly for spectacular diving, awesome bone fishing and very occasionally for surfing some freight-train reef passes. Tabuaeran (Fanning Island) is blessed with year-round swell, while Kiritimati (Christmas Island) is way more consistent from November to March, when it receives the same winter swells as Hawaii, only at a smaller size, but with longer periods and constant offshores. There are breaks for all skill levels, from beginner to experts with gentle bathymetry on Kiritimati, which means close-outs when big, but fun when small. On Fanning, surf is consistent, overhead and much larger at times from November through March. English Harbour is a world-class left in S swells and there's a lesser right across the channel on W-NW swells. The bottom is user-friendly coral rubble strewn on flat reef, as opposed to jagged live coral common to so many other Pacific spots. Offshore E trades winds blow NE in Northern Hemi winter and more SE for the rest

BRIDGES POINT

MICHAEL KEW

of the year. Despite minimal tidal range, waves are often better at high tides and at Fanning's English Harbour, there is a strong side-shore rip to the wave on incoming tides. All water sports can be practiced on the lagoon, where as ever, there will be sharks cruising around the passes, currents and sharp coral to avoid. This is an ultra-remote archipelago that takes some serious effort to get to since no domestic and only one international flight services Kiritimati as a stopover between Fiji and Hawaii, unless you travel by the infrequent supply ships.

Sitting 500km north, **Tokelau** is three low-lying atolls that should have great waves, if only there was a break or pass in the reef. This leaves a few sharp bends reliant on swell and wind direction to not close-out and east Atafu has an exposed, boat access only reef that should work in both N and S swells, wind permitting. Further west and the tiny nation of **Tuvalu** suffers a similar fate with unbroken atoll rings like Vaitupu lacking any shape, or even a harbour for the ferry to dock. Funafuti is the capital where a total land area of 2.4km² thinly encircles a lagoon area of 275km² with many openings in the reef on the N and W sides. **Niue**'s rugged fringing reef sucks for surf.

Like so many Pacific Island nations, the sheer volume of Tongan islands almost guarantees there are waves to be found all over the archipelago.

its circumference, enjoyed by low numbers of locals and tourists on round-the-world tickets. On Aitutaki, the ring of coral protecting the island is virtually unbroken, continuing the Cook Islands theme of shallow, sharp and prone to closing out unless conditions are just right, plus the added hassle of needing a boat to access the waves. Many of the other islands are volcanic platforms with no appreciable surf. Classic atoll architecture returns on the northern outposts of the chain where the uninhabited Suwarrow atoll has a proper north-facing pass righthander and even further flung Penryhn has another couple of tidy set-ups at the Takuua and Tekasi passes, but only those lucky enough to have an ocean going yacht will ever see them.

KIRIBATI AND THE COOK ISLANDS

The Republic of **Kiribati** is sprawled over an area of ocean way bigger than India, with a mere 3300km (2050mi) between the two main island groups of the Gilberts and the Line Islands. The Phoenix Islands make up the second biggest marine reserve in the world (part of the Pacific Oceanscape initiative) and Kiribati is the only nation to straddle the 4 hemispheres (equator and date line), so it stands to reason there must be some waves somewhere amongst the 32 atolls. Most documented spots are on the planet's largest atoll, Kiritimati and Tabuaeran, which are closer to Hawaii than the Gilberts and where powerful, serious line-ups hold some epic waves for a small local crew. The Gilberts are less consistent, but the northern tip of the Tarawa atoll does hold a long, walled up, high tide right at Naa, that relies on NE swell to fire and is a long way from help if you hit the reef. Other small islands like Abaiang are rumoured to have a wave in S swells at Ouba, but the absence of deepwater passes limits the Gilberts and many of the Line Islands severely.

Another few thousand kilometers to the south, the **Cook Islands** would appear to be an ideal destination, but the island's geology is less than ideal. **RAROTONGA** has a few fun reefs around

MICHAEL KEW

VAVA'U GROUP, TONGA

OTHER ISLANDS TO CONSIDER

FRENCH POLYNESIA

French Polynesia is perfectly centered in the South Pacific, free from any swell shadowing and extremely welcoming to swells from either hemisphere. Once again, the numbers are staggering when simplified; 6 island chains made up of 130 islands spread over 2.5 million square kilometres of primo wave real estate, roughly equivalent to the size of Europe. Best known are the **Society Islands** and its Leeward Group of Huahinè, Raiatea /Tahaa, Maupiti and Bora Bora sit only 200km (125mi) west of Tahiti. Maupiti and Bora Bora have only one pass each and outriggers, canoes and SUP's rule the inshore waters, however the rest of the group is blessed with multiple openings in the fringing reef. While Huahine and Raiatea have a reputation for fierce localism, the islands of the Windward Group, namely **TAHITI AND MOOREA**, are world famous for awesome waves like Teahupoo and Taapuna. The north and west coasts are rich in reefbreaks, gyrating down the many deepwater passes, offering a range of lefts and rights with varying degrees of difficulty. There is also the occasional opportunity to ride fun reef, point and black sand beachbreak type waves on the windward coast at little bays like Tiarei and Faaone, while the offshore motus could be holding for those with a boat and the right angles of swell and wind. The 7 Austral Islands sink deep to the south, leaping the Tropic of Capricorn in a stormier, angry sea. Those seeking adventure will be relatively disappointed and only the twin passage on the south coast of Tubuai will tame the booming SE to SW swells into some manageable rides.

Heading to the north of the Society Islands, the **Tuamotu Archipelago** barely breaks the surface with a procession of ringlet atolls that Darwin correctly guessed were the tips of old volcanoes. The western extremities have been shown to hold seriously good surf, so it makes sense that the impossibly remote central and eastern atolls and the far-flung Gambier Islands are similarly blessed. Of course avoid Mururoa and Fangataufa atolls, the site for the now infamous nuclear testing program run by the French Government in the SE

Tahiti is not just Teahupoo. There are other slabs of coral to test one's commitment, even on the windward coasts.

HUAHINE AND RAIATEA, FRENCH POLYNESIA

Tahiti may be the crossroads of French Polynesia, but French Polynesia's second largest island, Raiatea, is considered the traditional center of religion and culture, where many voyages of Pacific discovery started. The surf spots are more remote and quality is highly dependent on swell direction and wind exposure.

+ YEAR-ROUND SWELL
+ POWERFUL REEF PASSES
+ POSTCARD SCENERY
+ ALL TYPES OF ACCOMMODATION

– FIERCE LOCALISM
– REEF PASS DANGERS
– DIFFICULT ACCESS
– VERY EXPENSIVE TRIP

Huahine is smaller, but packs just as much punch in the surf department, boasting a number of quality reef passes including the matching pair of Fare Left and Fare Right, the region's most surfed waves. They work on a wide swell window, all tides, E trades and it's possible to paddle from land, plus there are some fun reforms on the beach for the kids and beginners. Most local wave-riders have escaped the Tahitian crowds to enjoy a privileged environment of idyllic tubular waves with a handful of close friends, so a strong feeling of ownership of the spots, namely localism, has developed. The "Black Shorts" on Huahine and Raiatea will only let outsiders surf with them once they have proved themselves to be respectful. Surfing very early and preferably alone will help, coupled with a cool attitude, a very low profile and a willingness to leave the surf if harassed are all essential ingredients. Also beware the heavy currents at the passes. It's a year-round destination, favouring north winds (Nov-April) for the epic righthanders like Fitii. North Pacific swells arrive 3-5 days after hitting Hawaii and despite the large distances travelled, there's no shadowing en-route, delivering anything from 3-10ft (1-3m) reef perfection. The S swell season lasts the majority of the year, with the peak months being May-September, entering through a broad swell window spanning from SE to SW. Dominant winds are E-SE trades, strongest from July-Sept, before shifting NE and calming down in summer (Jan-March).

TAHITI

BERNARD TESTEMALE

BEN THOUARD.COM

TUAMOTU, FRENCH POLYNESIA

The vast majority of the world's 400 atolls are located in the Pacific and the Tuamotu, which cover a territory as large as western Europe, is home to 77 of them. This dusting of islands is also called The Labyrinth, or the Archipelago of the Rough Sea and has remained essentially uncharted due to the difficulty of navigating the local waters. To the east are the younger atolls, but it's the older atolls that are most likely to contain a reef pass, cut through the fringing reef to the inner lagoon. Out of 77 atolls, only 32 have at least one pass, only 10 have several, and most of these are found in the NW corner of the territory. The main atoll is Rangiroa, where the northern pass of Avatoru holds a long, hollow right that is regularly ridden by local surfers and bodyboarders, since it is accessible without a boat. It should be noted the rip in the pass averages at 5km/h

(3mph) and flows into the lagoon 35% of the time, while outgoing flow is 55%. This major current is a factor at all Tuamotu passes, including Tikehau, which is where most surf charters end up. The majority of N swells produce clean, mid-size rights while South swells generally result in punchier lefts. Some waves are hollower on the outside reef and then actually back off into a mushier bowl as they wrap into the deeper passes, giving less experienced waveriders a chance, while the hardcore tube charger takes off deeper, further up the reef. It's a year-round destination, but N swells provide the best quality surf from Nov - April, getting to the Tuamotu 3-5 days later than Hawaii. Despite the large distances travelled and because they come out of deep water with nearly no shadowing en-route, they arrive with surprising ferocity and consistency, lasting about 2-3 days. The S swell season

+ YEAR-ROUND SWELLS
+ JUICY REEF PASSES
+ WORLD-CLASS FISHING AND DIVING
+ LUXURY BOAT TRAVEL

– OCCASIONAL FLAT SPELLS
– NO SHELTER FROM TRADE WINDS
– LARGE DISTANCES BETWEEN BREAKS
– EXTREMELY EXPENSIVE SURF TRIP

lasts the majority of the year, with the peak months being May-September, but it is not uncommon to have classic SE to SW swells during the N season. E-SE trades can be damn strong, Jan-March being the weakest and July-Sept the windiest. The Tuamotu Archipelago takes a lot more effort and money to get to, but rewards those surfers lucky enough to make it there, with an intense tropical experience in the Pacific wilderness.

corner of the Tuamotu's, but don't discount an atoll just because it is surrounded by others, because the swell seems to find a way in, as proven by the reef passes on the west side of Apataki. Mere mortals will never get this far in some of the most dangerous waters in the Pacific, where big sharks hunt in the passes and the rips take Herculean shoulders just to stay in position, in order to catch waves that will often test even the best riders. Skipping to the northeastern frontier of French Polynesia, the **Marquesas** couldn't be more different as monolithic basalt mountains rise from the submarine volcanic plateau and an arid, rocky landscape meets the South Equatorial Current. Plunging cliffs line deeply indented bays, where rocky beaches like Hanaiapa and Puamau are good starting points for exploration on the north coast of Hiva Oa and Atuona beach on the south. Ua Pou has a fun peak in Hakahau Bay, while kids bodysurf beside the wharf at Hakahetau and wind exposed Nuku Hiva picks up E swell at the pristine, white-sand beachbreak of Haatuatua.

THE STORMRIDER SURF GUIDE
South Pacific

For more information, check these other Stormrider Surf Guides and/or eBooks.

There is a small local surf population on all the islands who may choose to show visitors what the Marquesas have to offer to dedicated travellers willing to go to the ends of the earth.

GALAPAGOS ISLANDS

The Galapagos Islands are an anomaly for the equatorial Pacific as cool Southern Ocean water is piped in from the depths of the Humboldt Current, feeding a cacophony of weird and wonderful wildlife and creating a surfing zone on the equator where you may occasionally need a light steamer. **SAN CRISTOBAL AND SANTA CRUZ** are the main attraction but there are some beachbreaks that have been regularly surfed around the hotels at Puerto Villamil on Isla Isabela, which is also popular with any yachties heading to the Marquesas. Many of the smaller Galapagos isles are either too steep, rocky or off-limits to all tourist activity. ●

SOUTH PROVINCE, NEW CALEDONIA

+ PERFECT REEF PASS WAVES
+ VARIETY OF BARRIER REEF SPOTS
+ EXOTIC YACHT TRIP
+ LOW CROWD FACTOR

– MOST SPOTS ONLY ACCESSIBLE BY BOAT
– EASILY BLOWN-OUT
– VERY EXPENSIVE
– INCONSISTENT

Nouméa sits on the edge of the largest lagoon in the world and has traditionally been a big windsurfing and more recently kiteboarding destination. It's only in the last couple of years that New Caledonia has begun to reveal its potential for outer reef barrels to a waiting surf world. Though the waves that have been found here are the equal of anywhere else in the South Pacific, it is unlikely that New Caledonia is ever likely to become as popular as some of its neighbouring island states. The reason being is that these waves break on reef passes between 5-20km (3-12mi) offshore and are stretched along a 700km (435mi) ribbon of barrier reef, which is way too far for even the most hardcore of paddlers! This means that unless you can afford to be on an expensive charter yacht, or spend a couple of hours each day commuting, then you aren't going to do a lot of surfing.

There is only one paddle accessible spot on the island near Bourail, at Nera rivermouth in the southern corner of **ROCHE PERCÉE** beach. Stronger SW swells will punch up the wide estuary and break left over shifting sandbars on the outside before reforming and hitting the inside shoredump. Usually soft and forgiving, perfect for beginners and SUP, until high tide makes it close-out on the beach. Gets quite busy at weekends, but it's a relaxed, family scene. Directly across the Baie des Tortues the fringe of coral holds a decent right at **GOUARO**, but don't think about paddling the 2km there, especially since the rivermouth attracts sharks. It's a fun, consistent right and less threatening than the outer reef waves, working in most swell directions. Also inside the Passe de Bourail is a left and another right offering big swell options. Sometimes a weekend crowd as locals join the Nekweta Surf Camp visitors just a short hop across the bay. On the southern tip of the gaping entrance to the Baie des Tortues, **GREEN ISLAND LEFT** enjoys a prime position for attracting S-SW swells and remaining clean in moderate trade winds. Three short sections that may wall or barrel and it can link up on the good days. Confident intermediates will manage, especially on higher tides. The left at **SECRETS** is definitely not for the faint-hearted as it smacks the reef hard and tries to turn inside out on the overhead days. Fast, fluid and technical barrels spin through the gin-clear water, blurring the corals and fish into a riot of colour. Since it is a

promontory of reef and not a pass, getting caught inside is more likely. Rarely crowded and a regular haunt of the Nekweta camp. Out on the Passe d'Ouarai, one of New Caledonia's best lefthanders uncoils down the coral at higher tides, hitting three sections of tubing, lip-smacking splendor. **OUANO** handles any E wind, as NE hits the outside square-on and SE smoothes the inside, but morning glass is the real treat. Across the other side is the mirror right, which is shorter, faster and heavier and usually blown out by the SE trades. Sometimes crowded with locals and visitors who stay in La Foa accommodation and hire a boat for the 20min ride. Experienced reef surfers only who don't mind the abundant sea-life and coral under fin. There are some much shorter lefts at Shipwrecks on smaller days and speedy rights across the Passe d'Isie. You can camp on **TENIA** Island and surf the left on the Passe de St Vincent, a half hour boat trip from the mainland at Bourake. It's not the hollowest left, but has long carvable faces and crumbling lips for the wind crew who descend for the afternoon trades. Handles plenty of size and packs a punch as it shifts around the long line-up. Ideal in SSW swell and

TENIA

ANDREW SHIELD

ENE wind with an incoming tide. There is another left (Little U) and smaller right on the reef protecting the island. Intermediates will handle the average days. Strong currents on dropping tides. **DUMBEA RIGHTS** are longish, predictable walls that march along the reef edge, especially when there is some W in the swell, allowing turns galore in the 3-6ft (1-2m) range. As the swell goes overhead, so do the lips and this becomes a faster, tube riding experience. Any N wind should be ok with an incoming tide. Almost 2km across the channel, **DUMBEA LEFTS** are regularly firing, attracting regular crowds to its multi-faceted line-up. Like most New Caledonian waves, up to headhigh is fun, slashable, walls and ramps with little pockets appearing along the 200m playground. Once the swell kicks on past 6-8ft, things start getting serious and throaty tubes scour the coral that gets drained on the inside. Short close-out sections allow multiple take-off zones and ENE is bang offshore. If it's too small or crowded, head up the reef to False Pass for some seriously horseshoe shaped tubes. On the north side of Passe de Boulari, **LIGHTHOUSE** is another edgy righthander that sucks hard from take-off and races for up to 100m if there is a good dose of SW swell and NW-N winds. Gets super-shallow on the inside so caution and experience required. One of the closest passes to Nouméa, yet it's still a 45min journey, leaving precious little surfing time before the trades blow out the rights by 10 or 11am. Sitting slightly inside the wide Passe de Boulari, **SKATEPARK** is a bit misleading since this highly consistent left reef is no easy ride. On smaller swells, the reef is barely dampened and from 6-8ft, this wave can be thick

ANDREW SHIELD

GOUARO

FALSE PASS

ANDREW SHIELD

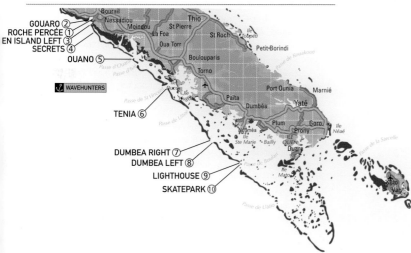

GOUARO ②
ROCHE PERCÉE ①
EN ISLAND LEFT ③
SECRETS ④
OUANO ⑤

WAVEHUNTERS

TENIA ⑥

DUMBEA RIGHT ⑦
DUMBEA LEFT ⑧
LIGHTHOUSE ⑨
SKATEPARK ⑩

Bourail
Nessadiou
Moindou
La Foa
Oua Torr
Thio
St Pierre
St Roch
Petit-Borindi
Ile Tolpeti
Passe de Kouakoué
Bouloupari
Torno
Port Ouina
Marnié
Païta
Dumbéa
Yaté
Plum
Goro
Ile Néaé
Prony
Passe de la Sarcelle

SPOT INFORMATION

SPOT	SIZE	BTM	TYPE
①	⅜	〰	◖
②	10/3	◍	◖
③	10/3	◍	◖
④	10/3	◍	◖
⑤	12/3	◍	◖
⑥	12/2	◍	◖
⑦	12/2	●	◖
⑧	12/3	◍	◖
⑨	10/3	◍	◖
⑩	⅜	◍	◖

and powerful. In between can be a mix of caves, cracks and cutbacks as it pitches, walls and shoulders down the line, with a reputation as a grower as it bends towards the end bowl section. Fast minds and boards required, plus it can attract a weekend crew. Beyond here to the south is an ocean playground where 14 more major passes beckon to those with the right vessel and navigation skills to sample some more of what the New Caledonia barrier *récif* has to offer.

SWELL AND WIND

Swell comes primarily from the Roaring Forties and is funneled through the Tasman Sea and onto the SW-facing coast of New Caledonia. May to Sept is the prime time with consistent SE-SW swells producing 2-10ft (0.5-3m) waves. The swell shadow cast by New Zealand makes for shorter swell duration. During summer (Nov-Mar), swell consistency drops, but smaller 3-6ft (1-2m) SE swells will break on exposed passes. Coral Sea cyclones can bring NW swell, along with rain and destructive wind and also occasional E swells, but they're fickle and the spots that break on these swells, like Ile des Pins, are hard to reach. Year-round the wind blows primarily from the SE, around 71% of the time in Jan-Feb and 44% of the time in Aug. Most of the reefs face SW, so SE winds are cross or offshore for the lefts (which can handle 15-25kmh) and destructive for the rights. From Sept to May the wind has more of an E-SE direction, which is more offshore, but not the prime swell season. During winter the wind varies a lot more and can blow anywhere from dead offshore NE round to blown out SW. Most of the reefs are affected by the tide with many preferring mid incoming. ●

TRAVEL INFORMATION

LOCAL POPULATION:	COASTLINE: 2,254km (1,408mi)
Noumea - 163,723	TIME ZONE: GMT +11h

GETTING THERE – New Caledonia is expensive to get to with major airlines including Qantas, Air New Zealand plus some charter flights from France or local carriers like Air Calin and Air Vanuatu, who code share with Qantas, Air France, KLM, Cathay Pacific, Singapore Airlines. So direct links to France, Australia, NZ, Korea, Japan, Vanuatu, Fiji, Wallis and Tahiti. Tontouta Airport (NOU) is 45k's (30mi) from Nouméa. A passenger and cargo boat links Vanuatu monthly, along with regular cruise ships from Sydney.

GETTING AROUND – Rental cars are much more expensive at the airport - prices from $15-22/day + per km charge or all in from $220/wk. Boats to get out to the waves are expensive. You can rent a 7m, 7p zodiac from Nouméa for $2266/wk. Taxi-boat prices fr $62.50 (Jayak; Ouano), but much more in Noumea. For more surf time, but a bigger dent to your wallet, stay on a charter boat out by the waves (Black Lion $1700/7n; Kuare fr $2000/d private charter, sleeps 8); book through Wavehunters.

LODGING AND FOOD – Nekweta in Bourail has package deals - full board accommodation + surf charter (up to 6 hours surfing) is $150/p/d. Ouano Safari Camp has camping ($18/p/n), safari tents ($75/dbl/n) or bungalows ($115/dbl/n). The luxury class charter boats are usually catamarans so somewhat cramped. Nights at sea can be noisy and rough. Food on board will have huge helpings of the freshest seafood available. Imported food is 65% higher and the cost of living is 34% higher than Europe.

WEATHER – The warm, sticky wet season lasts from December to April and the chances of torrential rain and cyclones are always present. The best surf months (May-Sept) coincide with winter (Jun-Aug) when temperatures drop to 15-21°C (59-70°F) and can feel a little cold for a tropical destination. In deep winter, a light shorty for early or windy sessions is recommended, since water temps vary a lot from 22-26°C (72-79°F).

WEATHER	J/F	M/A	M/J	J/A	S/O	N/D
Total Rainfall (mm)	110	135	95	83	47	60
Consistency (d/m)	10	11	11	9	6	6
Temperature min. (°C)	23	22	19	17	18	21
Temperature max. (°C)	29	27	24	23	25	28

NATURE AND CULTURE – If you're not surfing then onboard activities are limited to snorkeling, fishing or scuba diving. On land there is trekking, horse riding and exploring the many caves.

HAZARDS AND HASSLES – The only worries are the standard tropical surfing hazards of reef cuts, sun stroke and marine life. There are a lot of sea snakes and sharks, with a 15yr old kitesurfer killed by a tiger shark in 2011 and a 19yr old surfer by a great white in 2009 at Bourail. The strong trades regularly hit 25 knots, which is why kitesurfing is so big.

HANDY HINTS – The French influence in New Caledonia is very strong and the standard of living is high. There are a few pricey surf boutiques in Noumea, so bring all your own equipment and booties for the reef.

SURF STATS		J	F	M	A	M	J	J	A	S	O	N	D
SWELL	Dominant swell	🌊		🌊		🌊		🌊		🌊		🌊	
	Size (m)	2		3-4		4-5		5-6		4		1-2	
	Consistency (%)	20		50		70		70		60		20	
WIND	Dominant wind	🌀		🌀		🌀		🌀		🌀		🌀	
	Average force	F4		F4		F3		F3		F3		F4	
	Consistency	71		65		78		79		60		63	
TEMP.	Wetsuit	🏄		🏄		🏄		🏄		🏄		🏄	
	Water temp.	26		25		23		21		22		24	

MAMANUCAS, FIJI

+ SUPER CONSISTENT
+ VARIETY OF WORLD-CLASS WAVES   – DANGEROUS REEFS
+ CHOICE OF RESORTS   – STRONG CURRENTS
+ OPEN ACCESS TO CLOUDBREAK   – BOAT ACCESS ONLY TO MANY REEFS
+ FANTASTICALLY FRIENDLY FIJI   – EXPENSIVE RESORTS

The 322 islands of Fiji form the epitome of the surf travel dream. A magical archipelago of white sand beaches and tropical vegetation ringed by shallow coral reefs, which get bombed by heavy, hollow lefthanders that set the standard for wave quality around the world. Most of the waves break on barrier reefs in the Mamanuca group of islands to the west of Fiji's main island, Viti Levu. Surf camps and boat access only to the waves around the Mamanucas make Fiji, or more to the point, Tavarua, an expensive, but essential surf experience. Yachties discovered Cloudbreak, probably in the '70s and kept it hush hush, until 1984, when Dave Clark began setting up the exclusive Tavarua resort and exclusive surfing rights to the offshore reef that has since been regarded as one of the planet's top lefthanders.

To the N of Tavarua is **WILKES PASS** named after a group of village warriors who escaped from the authorities through the reef pass here. It's a high tide right with long, fast, barreling waves finishing with a bowly inside section. Like most of Fiji's rights, it is sensitive to SE trade winds, so consistency suffers. Further north is the peak at Desperations, an exposed tip of the Malolo barrier reef where everyone ends up on those small swell days. N winds or glassy for both breaks. **NAMOTU LEFTS** offer intermediates and longboarders a playful tapering wall on smaller swells from the S-SW. When it jumps well above headhigh, all bets are off as hefty barrels bend onto the reef, but it is still a notch down on Cloudbreak. Best with a bit of water covering the reef on the push and more NE wind than SE. Susceptible to very strong currents at low tide. On the other side of Namotu, **SWIMMING POOLS** can be a tad faster, hollower and shallower than the lefts, but keeps the emphasis firmly on fun as it is always smaller than the surrounding breaks. **RESTAURANTS** is the iconic wave that breaks off the resort island of Tavarua in full view of the diners and is the perfect back-up wave to big brother Cloudbreak. Always a bit smaller, but the utter predictability of the lip as it peels off means barrels and lip-smashing fun in equal measure. S to SW swell will wrap around the reef and S-SE winds will iron out the surface. It's still an experts only wave and gets way too risky at low as the corrugated coral contradicts the uniformity of the wave. Other waves on the island include Kiddieland, ideal rollers for beginners on soft-tops, SUPs and anything else, breaking regularly in close proximity to the Tavarua bar. On small swells, Tavarua Rights are ripable, fun-park walls, before rising to beautiful blue cylinders when the wind dies and glassy water envelops the southern tip of the island. All accessed by walking/paddling over reef or getting dropped outside by the resort boat. **CLOUDBREAK** (see next page). When the swell is bigger, a couple of waves break at the entrance to Momi Bay, in front of the Seashell Cove resort. The rare and fickle right by the Lighthouse is usually blown out by the SE winds, but across the Navula Passage at **MINI CLOUDBREAK**, it's offshore and firing fast barrels, providing there is enough SW swell and high tide to cover the hungry reef. Always much smaller than Cloudbreak, but just as powerful, hollow and mean.

JUAN FERNANDEZ

WILKES

RESTAURANTS

SCOTT WINER/A-FRAME

SWIMMING POOLS

JEREMY WILMOTTE

MAMANUCA ISLANDS

Lomolomo

Malolo
Nadi Waters
Malolo Lailai Island

Malolo Barrier Reef

Nadi

WILKES PASS ①
NAMOTU LEFTS ②
SWIMMING POOLS ③
RESTAURANTS ④
CLOUDBREAK ⑤

WATERWAYS
ATOLL TRAVEL
WAVEHUNTERS
Namotu Island
Tavarua Island
Nabila

VITI LEVU

MINI CLOUDBREAK ⑥

Momi Bay
Momi

WAVEHUNTERS
UNITY SURF

Uverite Point

Lomowai

Mbatiri

NATADOLA ⑦

Voua
Sigatoka
Korot

LULU'S BEND ⑧

SIGATOKA ⑨

QUEENS ROAD

NATADOLA is a beautiful resort beach with a shorebreak that's good for bodysurfing and an inside reef peak for longboarding in big swells. 2kms outside of this at high tide, lefts leap out of deep water and hit the reef pass, bending and peaking along a disorganised line-up. Can be long walls and tubes when smallish, scary and sketchy when big, but the main problem is the howling SE wind. It's a 1km paddle over to the lesser right, which also needs NE winds. **LULU'S BEND** is another deep bay with high tide barrels breaking on both sides at the entrance. The north side peaks and hisses across the reef, before shutting down on virtually dry reef, while the south side left is prone to the same fate. Any N wind for the rights, glassy or NE-E for the lefts. The **SIGATOKA** Sand Dunes National Park offers 5kms (3mi) of beachbreaks in wonderful scenery without crowds. If there are N quadrant winds, A-frames will huff and puff along its length, but the real action is at the Sigatoka Rivermouth, where long, zippy lefts and shorter rights spin back into the river flow. Downsides are strong SE winds, strong rips and currents, murky water and sharks. Upsides are all abilities waves, friendly locals, low crowds and no coral heads lurking below!

SPOT INFORMATION

SPOT	SIZE	BTM	TYPE
①	4⁄3	🌀	⬗
②	4⁄3	🌀	⬗
③	10⁄3	🌀	⬗
④	4⁄2	🌀	⬗
⑤	25⁄3	🌀	⬗
⑥	6⁄3	🌀	⬗
⑦	12⁄2	🌀	⬗
⑧	10⁄3	🌀	⬗
⑨	10⁄3	〜	⬗

TRAVEL INFORMATION

LOCAL POPULATION:	COASTLINE: 1,129km (705mi)
Viti levu - 600,000	TIME ZONE: GMT +12h

GETTING THERE – Centrally located in the S Pacific, Fiji is a main stop off point for trans-Pacific flights. Most int'l flights (Air New Zealand, Qantas, Air Pacific, Korean Air) arrive at Nadi (NAN), with a few Auckland and Vanuatu flights arriving at Nausori (SUV), near Suva, the domestic hub. Flying times are NZ 3hrs, Aus 4hrs, Hawaii 6hrs and west coast USA 9hrs. Departure tax is a huge $85 (F$150) and is usually included in the price of your ticket.

GETTING AROUND – Most people stay in one of the resorts, which provide airport transfers. Two local airlines (Air Fiji and Pacific Sun) serve 13 island airports daily from either Nadi or Suva. Car rental is around $380/wk, but unnecessary, since taxis can be rented for a similar day rate or less. Cheap, open-windowed buses stop in just about every village. Ferries or fast catamarans service the Mamanucas, but you will need to hire local boats to take you to the surfing spots with prices varying depending on distance and destination (fr $50/p per surf). Check Unity for boat hire. Most surf camp accommodations include 1 surf transfer per day.

LODGING AND FOOD – Resorts are expensive! To stay at the Tavarua (fr $1991/w) or Namotu (fr $1929/w) surf camps during the peak season, book well in advance. Natadola and Shangri-La Fijian Resort are way upmarket. Plantation Island resort is behind Wilkes and starts at $212/n/dbl for the cheapest hotel room. Budget options, which don't include food and boat rides out to the reefs, may not always work out lots cheaper than surfer packages. There are backpacker and locally run establishments that offer everything from campsite (fr $10), to dorm (fr $12) to family rooms (fr $42). The Seashell@Momi from $65/n dorm room inc. all meals, or Surf Package (7n/dorm, 5x4hr surf boat + a'port trans = $395). Club Masa is just behind Sigatoka rivermouth and prices start at $50/d. The food is good, revolving around fish, taro, rice and fruit. Try some kava, the local brew.

WEATHER – Fiji has a tropical climate that sees stable temps and ample rainfall, although compared to neighbouring island groups it is somewhat drier. The rainy season extends from Nov to April, peaking through Dec-March, when temperatures are at their warmest (32°C/90°F max). Humidity levels can reach an uncomfortable 100%. Cyclones are an occasional occurrence. When the SE trades increase in strength in May the weather becomes much drier and cooler, but it rarely falls below 15°C (59°F), so being cold is never an issue. Year-round boardshorts and a rash vest, maybe a shorty for the coldest days in July-Aug.

WEATHER	J/F	M/A	M/J	J/A	S/O	N/D
Total Rainfall (mm)	300	320	105	60	72	170
Consistency (d/m)	16	17	10	7	8	11
Temperature min. (°C)	23	23	21	20	21	22
Temperature max. (°C)	30	30	28	26	28	30

NATURE AND CULTURE – Fiji is a tropical beach paradise. Diving, snorkeling, fishing and sailing are all excellent. Kiting has become very popular in the strong SE'ers, with or without waves on the lagoons. Hike the Tavoro Falls, Taveuni, or through the rainforest at Abaca. Check the sand dunes at Sigatoka, where they keep uncovering historical artifacts.

HAZARDS AND HASSLES – Most surf spots are shallow so be careful of hitting the reef. Cover up from the sun, especially in the boats; take a surf hat and plenty of bottled water. Fijian people are very friendly, including those that surf.

HANDY HINTS – The Fiji Surf Shop is in Nadi stocking boards, rentals and accessories and is part of Fiji Surf Co that run a surf school, tours and local comps for the growing number of Fijian surfers. Fiji's 2010 governmental "Surfing Decree" allows anyone to surf anywhere in Fiji waters.

SURF STATS		J F	M A	M J	J A	S O	N D
SWELL	Dominant swell	🌑	🌑	🌑	🌑	🌑	🌑
	Size (m)	4-5	5	6-7	7	6	5-6
	Consistency (%)	70	85	90	90	80	70
WIND	Dominant wind	🧭	🧭	🧭	🧭	🧭	🧭
	Average force	F4	F3-F4	F4	F4	F4	F4
	Consistency	63	72	64	62	73	67
TEMP.	Wetsuit	🏄	🏄	🏄	🏄	🏄	🏄
	Water temp.	28	27	26	25	25	26

SWELL AND WIND

Fiji is blessed by one of the best swell exposures in the world. For the Mamanuca group, the major source of swell is from the SW, generated by low pressures in the Tasman Sea, off Australia's east coast. Although New Zealand can block some size and warp the direction of these swells between due S 180° and SSW 205°, most low pressure systems will continue spinning east, providing Fiji with lesser SE-S swells. Swells range in size from 3-15ft (1-5m), with occasional freak swells hitting 20ft+ (7m+) at 18 seconds, during the favoured March-Nov South Pacific swell season. This is when wave height averages out at 5-6ft (1.5-2m), with 10-12 second periods and

BERNARD TESTEMALE

JOLI

CLOUDBREAK

LAT: -17.8875° LONG: 177.185°

Once the exclusive domain of well-heeled surfers able to pay the hefty daily rate to stay at the Tavarua Island surf resort, the Fijian government recently changed the law which allowed the resort to control access to this now legendary reef pass. While the perfect pictures of Cloudbreak suggest flawless left barrels for one and all, this is a tricky wave with multiple sections and a malevolent side that keeps even the best surfers on their toes. The outside section at the top "Point" of the reef holds plenty of size and the vertiginous roll-ins lead into a flying wall section where speed carves are possible. Middles is where turns are less useful and the barrel starts to wind up, covering a lot of distance in a short time. Insides, or Shish-kabobs, is where the reef gets extremely shallow and the tubes get extremely... extreme! Less confident surfers thinking they can pick off a few on the inside are not going to find any easy rides here and the fingers of razor sharp reef are far less uniform than further out. The 3 sections rarely link up, but when they do, usually on a long period, SSW swell of epic proportions, it is one of the seven wonders of the surf world. So advanced to expert surfers should be able to deal with the heavy waves, currents and bump-inducing frisky trades, but there are other hazards. The live coral is slasher sharp and cuts have the tendency to flare up. The reef attracts some fauna that is also best avoided like sea snakes, stonefish and the odd well-fed shark, but the unavoidable bogieman is undoubtedly the sun. Once you have negotiated a seat in a boat (for a handsome sum), remember to take lots of water, sunscreen and a surf hat!

consistently does so for 90% of the time. Despite year-round swell activity, the summer rainy season (Dec-Feb) has smaller, less consistent N-NE swells in the 2-6ft range. These are generated from remote NW Pacific lows which will hit the archipelagos N shores (Yasawa, Vanua Levu). Through summer (Nov-March) the winds are generally lighter and from a SE-NE direction – NE is bang offshore in the Mamanuca's. Trade winds increase slightly in strength from May to Nov, averaging 10-20 mph (16-32km/h) and blowing mainly from the ESE to SE. Despite minor tidal ranges, most spots are very shallow and will be affected by low tide. ●

KADAVU PASSAGE, FIJI

+ POWERFUL AND CONSISTENT
+ QUALITY TUBULAR LEFTS
+ WARM BULA SPIRIT
+ RESORT CROWD – FEW LOCALS
+ DIVING HEAVEN

– BIG AND WINDY IN WINTER
– RARE SUMMER RIGHTHANDERS
– COSTLY DEALS
– HEAVY RAIN
– OUTBOARD ACCESS ONLY

PIPES

WWW.WAIDROKA.COM

Until Cloudbreak made magazine cover shots, Fiji had been missing from the surfing map. Unlike French Polynesia, the surfing tradition was frowned upon by early Christian missionaries and had been all but wiped out. Surfing re-started in Suva in the early '80s, then ex-pats searched the archipelago of 344 islands, starting in the Mamanucas with Tavarua/Namotu. The great distance to the breaks out on the barrier reef means spending more time in an outboard powered dingy than in a car, whereas the southern coast has a fringing reef, closer to the white sand beaches of the resort studded Coral Coast. Powerful waves come surging in from deep water, hitting shallow reef ledges that unfortunately, are very exposed to the strong trade winds that buffet this coast. In order to find offshore conditions requires more long journeys in boats out to Frigates Pass or else an island-hopper flight to Kadavu Island where the contorted reef offers a selection of waves for all wind directions.

A 500m paddle from the resort's sun-loungers are **HIDEAWAY'S** rights, where guests hope the winds are N, the tide is high and the swell is not too big. A fast, tight barrel, prone to pinching that gets throaty when it's headhigh plus. Rips scour the narrow channel, the coral is sharp and intermediates will need a quick take-off. The SE trades cause havoc along this stretch where kiters will get more joy at the reef channels and lagoons near the Warwick, but there is a good reef in front of the **BEACHOUSE** budget resort. Rights that gather speed and suckiness as the water drains off the high tide only reef and it's usually smaller than surrounding spots until it implodes at 6-8ft. Inconsistent thanks to small ideal tide, wind and swell window. Surf school on the inside reforms. **VUNANIU** pass has 2 rights, 800m apart, where the outside peak at Shifties does just

that, as it picks up any hint of swell at any tide. Powerful, pushy and often real large at the initial peak, the refracting walls encourage big wrapping cutties back into the power source. It's a long wave over a wide area and handles some size, in any winds from W-NE. Way inside is Jays, that will always be much smaller, but an out and out barrel when there's more W in the swell and wind. Needs much higher tides to avoid getting caught inside and positioning is crucial. Intermediates will have fun on small to medium days at Shifties, while Jays is a full-on fast barrel for experts only. Across the channel Black Rock offers more high-octane ledgy rights. **PIPES** lives up to its name when a moderate SSE swell hits the bend of reef, sucks hard and throws lip for some pedal-to-the-metal tube rides. Thick, vertical take-off is challenging and the barrel is quite technical, especially if there's too much W in the swell and the tide is dropping. Handles E trades quite well so it's vey consistent. **WAIDROKA LEFTS** graces the channel that leads to its namesake resort and peaks up in deeper water, making it longboard and improver-friendly. Can get sizeable, when the steep-sloped take-offs lead to a hollow bowl before shouldering off into the deep channel. All tides and handles a bit of E wind. Consistent, fun spot. **SERUA RIGHTS** can be a long ride from the angled roll-in through the middle cutback shoulders to the sucky backdoor section as it hits the shallow inside reef. Tide is no problem, but the wind usually is. Across the pass, 420's is a left that can mirror the rights with equally fun, long rides. There's a surprisingly decent right called **LIGHTHOUSE** (not to be confused with the one near Mini Cloudbreak) at the entrance to Suva Harbour. It's a few minutes boat ride from the Suva yacht club, but it's inconsistent and with all the maritime traffic plus city population, theres a chance of some pollution.

To get to Kadavu Island requires the added expense of an extra flight, but provides crowd-free line-ups and an amazing, light aircraft flight over **FRIGATES**, landing on a short narrow airstrip at Vunisea. Many take a 45min boat ride to Nagigia Island (Naninya) on the SW tip, where there are several spots within a 5min boat ride or paddle from the private resort. **KING KONG LEFT** hits a notch in the otherwise straight fringing reef and wedges up a horseshoe peak that quickly

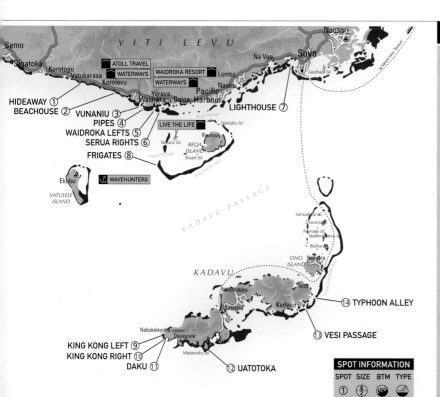

LOCAL POPULATION: Kadavu - 8700	COASTLINE: 237km (148mi) TIME ZONE: GMT +12h

GETTING THERE – Mamanucas for international flights to Nadi. Get a taxi or an express bus down to Hideaway (1h), Waidroka (2h) or Pacific Harbour (3h). Daily flights with Pacific Sun from Nadi to Kadavu ($282r/t). Max 2 boards up to 7ft cost $60e/w. Suva/Kadavu freighter is cheap ($25 e/w) but be flexible and the crossing can be long (4-48hrs!) and rough.

GETTING AROUND – Don't rent a car ($55/d). Devote your budget to boat transfers. Durations depend on sea conditions. Frigates is 45min from Waidroka ($25), 30min from Yanutha (1h from P/H). Outboards in Fiji matter a lot – without one you won't be surfing much. Departure times, rotation, schedules, carrying capacity, engine power, safety equipment, comfort factor and number of boats in operation are all important factors. Since most anticipate a rising wind, many surf in the morning, leaving the afternoon boats gambling on empty, but rideable waves.

LODGING AND FOOD – Matanivusi Eco Surf Resort at Vunanui fr. $2100/wk full board. Waidroka Bay starts from $130/dbl/n and surfing will cost $40-50/day on top. There are budget options here and there - dorms from $12/n while doubles in 'bures' average $50. A meal plan, accommodation and transport to the surf will be at least $80-100/day. On Yanutha Island, Batiluva does all inclusive with great food and 1 daily trip to Frigates from $100/n. Naninya Island Resort (Nagigia) $165/n + $10 for each boat trip.

WEATHER – Fiji has a tropical climate, tempered by the ocean and trade winds. The leeward or western side of Viti Levu where most resorts are located averages an annual rainfall of 1700mm, while windward Suva gets 300mm in Jan alone. Down by the coast and by islands like Beqa or Kadavu, rains are slightly lighter, but expect lots of humidity. The cool and relatively dry months from May to October provide the best weather, but swells and winds are the wildest. In July and August, temps may drop to 18°C (64°F). Spells of cloudy, cool weather with occasional rains alternate with warm, sunny, humid days. The hot, wet season starts in November, but the stifling days are Jan-March. In winter, you could take a bit of thin neoprene for the windchill.

WEATHER	J/F	M/A	M/J	J/A	S/O	N/D
Total Rainfall (mm)	300	350	210	160	210	280
Consistency (d/m)	18	20	15	15	16	17
Temperature min. (°C)	23	23	22	20	21	22
Temperature max. (°C)	30	29	28	26	27	29

NATURE AND CULTURE – Diving, snorkelling, fishing and island hopping are the main extras. Beqa is Fiji diving spot #1 for pelagics and Kadavu Astrolabe Reef and Nagigia Island is world-class. Research has recorded close to 300 species of coral, 475 species of molluscs, and almost 2,000 fish species. Kava ceremonies with music and Meke dance are a must. Fijian people are amazingly friendly. Don't miss the fire walkers.

HAZARDS AND HASSLES – Surf conditions can be sketchy, as gutsy swells, gusty winds, rapid rips and scary suck-outs on razor-sharp reefs conspire to injure the unprepared. Crowds only occur at Frigates when several boats overpopulate the break. Waterproof bags and adequate clothing are a must as getting wet is a major factor. Surfing on Sunday was only allowed by the village leadership in December 2002.

HANDY HINTS – There are only the surf shops in Nadi, but Fiji Surf Co plan to open in Suva soon. Many resorts have boards for rent and some like Nagigia give discounts to leave one behind. Surf lessons for learners are increasingly available. Before missionaries arrived to crush the surf scene, everyone, including women and children, practised "vakavodo ua"- 'vaka' means to do something, 'vodo' meaning to jump on and 'ua' means wave.

opens up and barrels, before backing off then pitching again on the shallow inside. It's short (40-50m), but consistent, holding great shape when small and wild tubes over 6-8ft. (2-2.5m). Intermediate to expert, depending on tide, size and the cross-shore trades. The fast, gnarly **KING KONG RIGHT** picks up a lot of swell, but it's usually blown out in the SE trades, so early or late is the go. SE swell and N/NE winds should see some big caverns for experienced riders. **DAKU** sees a split peak over a reef closer to the beach with fun rights and a few lefts in the morning before the wind gets up. Needs higher tide, as does the Daku beginner reform. If there is a N wind and a SE-S swell, pay for a long boat ride to **UATOTOKA**, a superb right with long, makeable barrels. Exposed to lots of swell and wind, so low score for consistency, but worth the effort when conditions align. On the Great Astrolabe Reef, three main passes are worth considering, including

SHIFTIES, VUNANIU

WWW.WAIDROKA.COM

KING KONG LEFT

the left at **VESI** that needs rare NW winds and some wrapping SW swell. **TYPHOON ALLEY** is on the narrow Naiqoro Passage which faces SE, so it only breaks occasionally, when the wind comes from the N to W quadrant. It'll be empty except for the sea-life using this major lagoon entrance.

SWELL AND WIND

This southern region receives all the same swells as outlined in the Mamanucas zone and in fact it has far better exposure to the residual SE swells that arrive off the back of a Southern Ocean low pressure system heading east. Being more exposed to the SE trade wind belt,

WWW.WAIDROKA.COM

FRIGATES

LAT: -18.475734°   LONG: 177.925401°

Like Cloudbreak, Frigates boasts an impressive size range from small to huge. Up to 6ft, it's not too radical with wrapping hollow walls, very sensitive to swell direction. At size, truly frightening barrels can be had at the inside "Bowl" section, as unpredictable swell lines bend and leap over the knuckle of coral, protruding from the seemingly mid-ocean barrier reef, 22kms (14mi) from land. Words like thick, bowly, fast and hollow reserve Frigates for the experienced surfers, who will mostly stay at the couple of surf camps nestled on Yanutha Island, halfway back to Viti Levu. Wind can be strong, chopping up the face making the easy roll in much harder and E wind is probably best although NE will be fine outside while SE is dead offshore on the inside benders. High tide will improve makeability, especially on the inside section which can dredge out at low and help extend what is already a long, long ride. World-class? Hell yes! If all the surfcamp boats are there at the same time, then it can get a bit crowded, but the length of the line-up helps spread the crew. Beware pushing it too far on the inside - it's a long way from nowhere. Rips, sharks, coral and the relentless sun are all to be avoided.

most reliable Kadavu Passage spots are lefts as the occasional rights get fully blown out by the trades, which average 15-25kph (9-16mph). Summer (Dec-March) is the main season for glassy days and N-NE winds that favour the rights, but the E-SE breezes still blow for over 70% of the time. Swell size drops a bit and windswells increase, yet most beginner to intermediate surfers should consider summer as a reliable season, especially on the south coast. Southern seas are very active and summer gets a lot of headhigh to overhead days. In winter, the surf can get pretty intimidating at exposed surf spots. One of the surprising factors at this latitude happens to be the tides, reaching 8ft (2.5m) at spring tides, not only affecting reef shallows but also boat movements. ●

SURF STATS		J F	M A M	J J A S	O N D		
SWELL	Dominant swell	●	●	●	●	●	●
	Size (m)	3	5-6	6	7-8	7	2-3
	Consistency (%)	60	80	70	50	70	60
WIND	Dominant wind						
	Average force	F4	F3-F4	F4	F4	F4	F4
	Consistency	63	72	64	62	73	67
TEMP.	Wetsuit						
	Water temp.	28	27	26	25	25	26

TONGATAPU, TONGA

+ UNCROWDED SPOTS   – LIVE CORAL REEF DANGERS
+ PERFECT REEFS   – COOLER WINTER WATERS
+ GREAT CLIMATE   – LACK OF VARIETY IN ORIENTATION
+ LAID-BACK VIBE   – EXPENSIVE LOCATION

The Tonga archipelago includes 170 islands divided into 4 separate groups. Starting with Niuas in the N, working S through Vava'u, Ha'apai and finally Tongatapu, at the southern end of the archipelago. Lying about 3,000km (1,875mi) to the E of Australia, Tongatapu is Tonga's main island, including the capital Nuku'alofa. Tongatapu is made up of a raised coral platform, where constant wave action has cut a shelf into the cliff bound south coast, but to the north there are some low lying coral reefs with many offshore islets. Most surf spots are all squeezed onto a remarkable reef bend on the W side of the island, where trade winds blow straight offshore. SW swells produce grinding lefts through the S hemisphere winter, (April-Oct), whilst less consistent N swells favour the shorter, shallow rights and offshore reefs from Nov-March.

bang on. Like many waves along this stretch of reef, 3hrs either side of high tide is the limit. Deep barrels on offer for those with the skill and possibly the skin to spare. Use rubber! **CORNERS** lefts work in both seasons, flipping between winter's short, sucky, intense barrels in due S swells and fun, ripable hotdog walls during summer NW-N pulses. Any W in the winter swell will make this the most dangerous left, while the summer version promotes big slashes and airs on the soft inside close-out. **LIGHTHOUSE** is a dangerous, barreling righthander, split into two sections by a straight bit of nasty reef. The outside section starts fast and doesn't let up for a good 50m dash and works at low tide even when it's small. The Surgeons Table interrupts things before the short inside section demands higher tides to make the air drops into a short winding barrel ending in the safety of the channel. Proper experts only wave in summer NW-N swells. **THE BOWL** doesn't break very often but when it does it's an exceptional ride, holding almost any swell size and bending around the reef with a heavy bowl section, similar to Hawaii's Ala Moana. Needs straight S for length of ride and is rideable at low tide if you are overly keen. Take-off is next to the outside peak of Lighthouse. **FISHTRAPS**, another rifling left, is a case of the bigger the swell, the better and longer the wave. Variety of moods from tapered corners, through flying walls to nice hollow barrel sections. A rare all tides spot, but again low is really sketchy closer to the reef. Intermediates to advanced riders looking for some speed runs. A string of circular and barrier reefs extend to the NE where some fickle, but classic spots can be ridden in summer N swells. **E.T'S** is a class act in summer NW-N swells and light NE-E winds, but is easily blown out and really inconsistent. Other spots with names like Loonies, Sharkie's and Razors are just as wind sensitive and require a long boat trip out to them. On nearby Eua Island there is a rare wave that breaks down the cliff side at Ufilei, plus a couple of high tide lefts and a right south of the harbour on moderate SW swells. The ragged, rocky, pushed up coral shelf is not ideal for surfing and is pocked with tidal pools, blowholes and caves.

JODY MACDONALD

OUTER ISLAND PASS

Just out from the Likualofa Beach Resort, **THE PASS** serves up a hollow left which is the most consistent small swell wave on the island, but it closes out over 6ft. One of the few reefs that improvers will handle as the steeper take-off quickly fattens up in to a nice rolling shoulder at mid to high tide. Across the channel, **PASS RIGHTS** (sometimes called the Alley), break in a similar, stress free fashion during the summer season. It's gets quite treacherous and sectiony in W-NW swells, but due N is fun for most abilities. Starts off a bit faster and hollower before hitting the deep channel where cutbacks are the order of the day. Both waves have generous depth and little current until it gets overhead. The other side of the peak can have an average left in winter S swells called Leftovers. The consistent lefts at **MOTELS** are fairly long with variable speed walls allowing big turns between the tuck sections before it ends on the reef fringe. Works on the smallest of swells and is user-friendly at small to medium sizes. Handles up to double overhead when it gets much heavier for advanced surfers. Straight in front of the main surf hang out Ha'atafu Beach Resort. Next wave north is **THE PEAK**, a small swell right that lines up a N swell into a high energy performance wall for lip-smacking and punting. Ends at a narrow crack in the reef so beware the end close-out section. **KAMIKAZES** is a tricky lefthander that often ends up being a straight-hander if the swell direction isn't

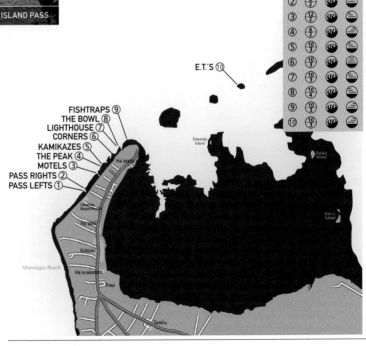

SPOT INFORMATION			
SPOT	SIZE	BTM	TYPE
①	6/2	〰	⊜
②	8/3	〰	⊜
③	8/2	〰	⊜
④	6/3	〰	⊜
⑤	10/3	〰	⊜
⑥	10/3	〰	⊜
⑦	10/2	〰	⊜
⑧	10/3	〰	⊜
⑨	10/3	〰	⊜
⑩	10/3	〰	⊜

E.T.'S ⑩

FISHTRAPS ⑨
THE BOWL ⑧
LIGHTHOUSE ⑦
CORNERS ⑥
KAMIKAZES ⑤
THE PEAK ④
MOTELS ③
PASS RIGHTS ②
PASS LEFTS ①

MOTELS

SEAN DAVEY

SWELL AND WIND

With good exposure to Roaring Forties swells and the deep water Tonga Trench just to the east, Tonga should be much more consistent than it actually is. However, for the swell to hit the NW facing breaks, it has to wrap in from the S-SW and loses size, whilst E swells don't register at all. New Zealand has a blocking effect so the best swells are those produced by rare lows forming to the N of New Zealand's North Island. SSW to SW is the dominant swell direction, year-round, with winter tending more S and summer seeing some W. Only the strongest NW Pacific lows will register on the northern coast and can get crossed up by opposing SW swell. Trade winds blow from the E-SE, year round, but from Jan to April, there's a lot more NW to NE quadrant winds, including the occasional gale force blast from the W-NW, which never lasts long. The tidal range is minimal, but low tide is still too shallow for many spots. ●

SURF STATS		J	F	M	A	M	J	J	A	S	O	N	D
SWELL	Dominant swell	◑		◐		◐		◐		◐			◐
	Size (m)	4-5		5		6-7		7		6			5
	Consistency (%)	60		80		90		90		80			60
WIND	Dominant wind	◕		◕		◕		◕		◕			◕
	Average force	F4		F4		F4		F4		F4			F4
	Consistency	65		65		55		64		73			68
TEMP.	Wetsuit	🏄		🏄		🏄		🏄		🏄			🏄
	Water temp.	26		26		24		22		23			24

E.T.'S

DAVID SPARKES

TRAVEL INFORMATION

LOCAL POPULATION:
Tongatapu - 69,000
TIME ZONE: GMT +12h

COASTLINE:
Tongatapu - 136km (85mi);

GETTING THERE – You can fly direct to Tongatapu from Australia, New Zealand and Fiji with Virgin Australia (boards free within baggage allowance), Air NZ ($150 e/w/bag; free if only bag) and Air Pacific ($50 e/w/bag max 9'6"). USA connections via Fiji, while Europe or Asia via Sydney or Auckland. Departure tax from Fua'amotu International Airport (TBU), is (TOP)$25 payable in Tongan Pa'anga cash only.

GETTING AROUND – Most of the breaks lie within 10 minutes walk of each other and are rarely more than a 100m paddle from the shore. A boat trip to the offshore reefs costs from $20 per person. Rental cars are unnecessary ($25/d), and require getting a local license at the police station. Inter-island flights were with Chathams Pacific, the 11th airline to cease flying in Tonga. A Chinese backed fleet is due to start routes late 2013. Two ferries ply the 3hr waters to Eua Island ($15/ew). Shipping Corporation of Polynesia operates a weekly ferry service from Nuku'alofa to Ha'apai and Vava'u (16hr/262km $35 e/w).

LODGING AND FOOD – Aussie expat Steve Burling and his Tongan wife Sesika have excellent rooms available at the Ha'atafu Beach Resort (fr $75/n/p) including great breakfast and dinner. Outhaka do rustic huts, backpacker style from $30/n. Royal Sunset resort on Atata Island from $130/n/dbl.

WEATHER – Tonga's low latitude means subtropical conditions of less rain, but cooler temperatures. The difference between the wet and dry seasons is not as significant as on neighbouring islands. The rainy season begins in Dec and runs through to April. Temps are high at this time and there's lots of rain, especially in March and April. Tonga lies within the cyclone belt. There is on average a major cyclone strike every 20 years, moderate ones every three years and small ones twice a year. The dry season is cooler, around the low 20°C's (68°F's) and occasionally a strong S wind bringing cold, wet spells. A springsuit is needed through the colder periods from June-Oct.

WEATHER	J/F	M/A	M/J	J/A	S/O	N/D
Total Rainfall (mm)	210	287	102	107	112	120
Consistency (d/m)	11	13	11	8	9	9
Temperature min. (°C)	22	22	19	18	18	21
Temperature max. (°C)	29	29	26	26	26	28

NATURE AND CULTURE – Life in Tonga revolves around the beach and the sea. Easy snorkeling inside the reef and outside on flat days, but beware currents in the small channels on ebbing tides. Diving, excellent pelagic fishing and swimming with whales or watching from the boat. On land there are some old stone tombs and possibilities for caving. Eua Island has some good hiking. Ha'atafu is a 15km (10mi) Protected Beach Reserve. The clubs and bars in Ha'atafu and Nuku'alofa can be pretty lively.

HAZARDS AND HASSLES – All of the reefs are live coral, so boots and a springy are a good idea. Reef cuts can be easily infected and medical help is rudimentary. There are a few locals and the atmosphere is usually cool as crowds spread out a bit along the Ha'atafu stretch, but more than a couple of boats at E.T.'s will put stress on the line-up.

HANDY HINTS – Bring everything that you need with you, including spare boards. The Tonga Surfriders Association are based at Ha'atafu Beach Resort, but equipment is hard to find, so think about donating hardware. There are some inner reef reforms for kids or beginners. The "friendly islands" are the last Kingdom left in Polynesia. Respect local religious beliefs and try to adapt to the slow pace of life, especially on Sundays.

SAVAI'I & UPOLU, SAMOA

+ YEAR-ROUND CONSISTENT SWELL
+ POWERFUL BARRELS
+ WARM AND UNCROWDED
+ SAMOAN CULTURE

– MANY BLOWN OUT-DAYS
– REMOTE, DIFFICULT ACCESS
– WET CLIMATE
– SHARKY
– NO SURFING ON SUNDAYS

The main islands of the Independent State of Samoa are actually a couple of ancient volcanic cones rising up from the ocean bed. They are amongst the largest of the South Pacific islands with a dramatic and mountainous terrain that ample rainfall keeps lush and green. The two islands of Upolu and Savai'i, are well situated to receive numerous swells from both the N and the S. Upolu is the more developed of the two islands with the majority of the resorts and decent surf spots. The western island, Savai'i is much wilder with fewer known breaks and one-quarter of the coral reefs, but potential for discovery. Generally, the waves are very hollow and powerful, breaking over shallow barrier or lava reefs usually within 500m of the shore. In a few spots big gaps in the barrier reefs allow the surf to break on lava reefs fringing the shore. The southern facing coasts hold the best quality waves, which are uniformly shallow, break at mid to high tide and more suited to experienced surfers. The N coast has fewer spots and receives less swell, making it more suitable for intermediate level surfers.

hour's drive like Middles peak, K-Land lefts, The Cross and Coconut Grove, which is offshore in the SE trades. Between the islands, **THE WHARF** reef at Salelologa has clean rights on a moderate SE-S swell. Unfortunately it is dead onshore in any E wind. An extensive fringing reef sits 1km offshore, curving towards the north and picks up Northern Hemisphere NW-NE winter swells from Nov - April. Aganoa surf camp access the bends, corners and passes of the reef by boat, usually surfing Blue Pools, a shapely large swell left. The north coast is also ringed with reef from **FAGAMALO** to Sasina, then it's rocky lava until the coral returns at Asau. There are at least a dozen spots named from easy left walls to Sunset style, big swell rights, where the vagaries of swell direction will decide the venue and most are paddle accessible from land.

Upolu is way more populated with people and waves and the main spots all have a surf camp nearby. **SALAMUMU** is no exception, with swell direction dictating whether it's rights or lefts peaking up over the reef in front of Sa'Moana resort and a quality, quicksilver left peeling down a slight bend in the reef in front of the village. The fringing reef heads offshore and a number of breaks hug the curves of the coral including **SPECIAL K**, a walled up right that bends and bowls out at the end section. It's another mid to high tide spot and SE trades are dead onshore. Across the channel, Pebbles offers the goofies a

On Savai'i, **SALAILUA** has a deep channel and manageable walls breaking both ways. The lefts prefer more S in the swell and will handle the SE winds better. Fun and intermediate-friendly in the headhigh range, plus there's more waves around Satuiatua. **AGANOA** is both a bowly righthander and screaming fast left situated right in front of the family run surf camp. The shorter rights can A-frame heavily, with barrels from take-off, before skirting the reef and bending through to an inside shut-down section where a coral head lurks. The lefts fly down the line with backdoor barrels aplenty, but no defined channel and sharp fingers of coral populate the straight reef. Swell direction dictates whether it is a nice barrel or a nasty close-out. Strong SE trades mess up both waves, but E should be cross-shore and fine. Adept intermediates will handle the rights at mid to high tides until size makes it an experts only challenge and the left works at low on small swells. Surf camp crowds are few and mellow, as they have plenty more south coast options within an

AGANOA

JEREMY WILMOTTE

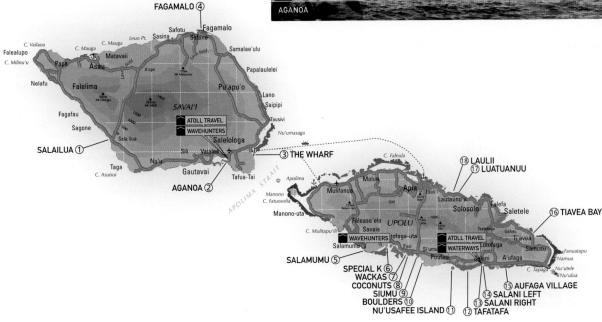

WACKAS

JEREMY WILMOTTE

TRAVEL INFORMATION

LOCAL POPULATION:	COASTLINE:
Savai'i - 46,000; Upolu - 129,000	Savai'i - 211km (131mi);
TIME ZONE: GMT +13h	Upolu - 188km (117mi)

GETTING THERE – There are direct flights to Faleolo Int Airport (APW) from New Zealand, Australia, Hawaii and Fiji with Polynesian, Air NZ, Virgin, Air Pacific and Samoa Air. Most resorts do pick-ups from the airport which is 40kms west of Apia. Dep tax is $29 ($65 Samoan Tala).

GETTING AROUND – Samoa Air operates frequent domestic services between Fagalii and Faleolo on Upolu and Maota and Asau on Savai'i as well as inter-island to Pago Pago with fares on a per kilo basis, including passenger body weight! The ferry service to Savai'i from Upolu leaves from Mulifanua and takes 1h (fr $5 passenger; $35vehicle). The reliable, unscheduled bus service reaches most of the mainland spots, but boards will be a hassle if crowded. Renting a car is expensive from $45/d and Samoa recently switched from driving on the right to driving on the left, yet most older cars remain lefthand-drive. Hitch-hiking is possible. Most resorts have a tour vehicle and often tow a boat to more remote spots. For offshore spots a boat is needed, costing around $20/rtn from local tour operators (Manoa) or fishermen.

LODGING AND FOOD – W Samoa is one of the cheapest countries in the South Pacific. If you're willing to rough it then there is accommodation fr $20 a night for a falé (thatched hut). To maximize water time, stay at one of the major surf camps on the south coast; Salani Surf Resort, Vaiula Beach, Maninoa, Coconuts, Samoana and Aganoa Beach on Savai'i. During the N swell season a good place to stay in Apia is the Samoan Outrigger Hotel. Green bananas, breadfruit, taro, fish, and lu'au (taro leaves and coconut) are cooked on the stone fire (umu). Samoan sushi is called oka.

WEATHER – W Samoa has a wet tropical climate with the rainy season occurring during the summer (Nov-April). The remainder of the year is dry with occasional showers. These showers will affect whichever coast they hit first, since the central mountains create perfect orographic conditions. Savai'i usually has higher rainfall figures. Samoa sits on the edge of the cyclone path, so they are a rare possibility, along with earthquake generated tsunamis (2009). Coastal temps are idyllic at around 27°C (80°F) year-round, water temps also never drop below 27°C (80°F), which is slightly above the South Pacific average. Even the trade winds are lighter than in many other South Pacific islands.

WEATHER	J/F	M/A	M/J	J/A	S/O	N/D
Total Rainfall (mm)	397	300	152	100	162	315
Consistency (d/m)	20	16	10	9	12	9
Temperature min. (°C)	24	23	23	23	23	23
Temperature max. (°C)	30	30	29	29	29	30

NATURE AND CULTURE – Most Samoans attend church and Sunday surfing is frowned upon, especially if it is in sight of the village. Diving, snorkeling, deep-sea fishing, hiking, waterfalls (Papapapa Tai, Sauniatu, Sopoaga, Falefa) exploring caves, blowholes and lava tubes, freshwater swimming holes, To Sua Ocean Trench, Papase'ea sliding rock and just about every other watersport can be experienced. There's very little to do at night.

HAZARDS AND HASSLES – Many of the reefs are super-shallow and dangerous and hospital care is fairly rudimentary. Infections from reef cuts are a problem. There are lots of reef and some tiger sharks, but no recorded attacks on surfers (Poutasi fisherman mauled in 2010). Mosquitoes are plentiful, but there's no malaria. Drink only bottled water.

HANDY HINTS – Bring all your surf gear with you including at least one or two spare boards, reef boots, rash vests and antiseptic for reef cuts. The wilds of Savai'i are best seen on an organised tour with Savai'i Surfaris.

much harder and hollower option. The rivermouth at Tafitoala village feeds into a bay where the fun, walled up lefts are called **WACKAS** (aka Sales) and although they bend a bit, are not quite protected enough from the SE trades. Can get an early morning crowd from the nearby resorts and watch the shallow inside section. On its day, **COCONUTS** rivals and usually trumps the best waves on the island. Fully exposed on the tip of the fringing reef, Cocos cracks the coral with full-blooded lips that hiss and spit down the line, offering ample tube time and powerful pockets on the right side of the peak. The lefts can be doable when smaller and more SE in the swell. Unfortunately, it's very sensitive to wind, tide and swell direction to fire, so catching it at its best requires luck and timing. Glassy, high tide and SW swell are the ingredients to cook up a memorable session. Experienced intermediates will handle smaller days when it can be hard to read with plenty of close-outs that put you on the inside just when the rogue sets arrive on a sharp, unforgiving reef. It's a hell of a long paddle from the resorts of Coconuts or Maninoa and returning on the dropping tide exhausted is not recommended so hire a boat. There are more waves on this stretch of reef depending on swell size and direction. Fresh water has gouged a deep inlet in the reef, providing easy boat and not so easy 10min paddle access to the lefts of **SIUMU**. Another high tide reef with bowly lefts popping up, translating into good barrels and perfect lip lines on the best days, or shorter irregular ripable walls when the swell direction isn't ideal. Outside Siumu is another 300m up the reef offering more lefts, but a bit more wind exposure. **BOULDERS** (see next page). Salani Village has a long established surf resort thanks to the top drawer rides on either side of the channel. **NU'USAFEE ISLAND** is a real swell-magnet and makes the most of small swells, yet some think it is better when size starts to allow the 3 sections to pull off the reef a bit. Also named Devils Island and burning in coral hell is a real possibility on the exposed first section where speed and barrel riding skills are required in bulk and the higher the tide the better. The middle and end section rarely link, but the curve of reef makes it offshore in E winds and the barrels a bit more manageable. Boat access only with rentals available from Poutasi. Natural footers can motor east to Vaiula Beach where the fast righthand peelers of **TAFATAFA** can be a long ride on SW swells or sectiony on a SE. Needs N winds so early or late for this rarely crowded spot. **SALANI RIGHT** will consistently barrel and fizz along the reef edge in any S swell and hopefully any N wind. More E in the swell will split the line-up with shorter, bowly hooks arriving from deep and shifting the take-off spot around, while SW will lengthen the ride and open up the face for turns. A little more flexible with lower tides and even onshore winds on certain days. Like most Samoan waves, plucky intermediates will handle the average days, but beyond overhead is for more experienced riders. There's another longer, larger and less-reliable right on the outer reef nearby. **SALANI LEFT** is a typical south coast left, requiring SE swell to wrap around and give a better chance of making this tube express that doesn't slow down until it hits the

SPOT INFORMATION

SPOT	SIZE	BTM	TYPE
①	6/3		
②	4/2		
③	6/3		
④	5/2		
⑤	9/3		
⑥	6/3		
⑦	6/3		
⑧	6/3		
⑨	9/2		
⑩	18/3		
⑪	6/3		
⑫	9/3		
⑬	6/3		
⑭	10/3		
⑮	9/2		
⑯	9/2		
⑰	9/2		
⑱	8/3		

COCONUTS

PHOTOS: TOM CAREY/A-FRAME

buffers 150m down the line. Onboard speed and taking the right track essential to reaping the long shade-time on offer. Compared to the right, it's less tide tolerant, handles less size, over a less user-friendly reef and is way less consistent. This means less people, albeit at a higher standard, striving to avoid the shallow inside shutdowns and dodging swinger sets on the paddle back out. On the S coast, the broken up reefs off **AUFAGA VILLAGE** attract some smaller swell lefts and rights before the trades blow it out. West of town, more rights break on reef passes carved out by the concentration of rivers here. The waves are close enough to paddle, but few ever bother. Various good quality breaks can be found in **TIAVEA BAY** a long, slow drive through the Uafato Conservation Area. The rivermouth is popular as a rest from the hazards of coral, peaking both ways with ramped-up walls and cover-up sections at mid tides. Further east is a powerful, fickle right peak and a distant right reef holds fun walls. At the western end there is also a fast sketchy left. The north-facing coast up to Apia is a mix of more extended fringes of coral and some steep, rocky volcanic coastline bringing the surf closer to the road. Fagaloa Bay is full of possibilities if you can get down to them and a boat becomes really handy. There are also a string of righthanders at Solosolo that are OK in E winds. Further east, **LUATUANUU** holds two short, rocky rights close to shore on either side of Pudding Rock and the suckier Waterfalls is actually better on low tides, which is a rare bonus in Samoa. **LAULII** rights need a bigger swell to break so it can wrap around the reef and it handles plenty of E in the wind. Fun and ripable walls that pitch on the big groundswells. A bit closer to Apia is Dragons Breath, a full-on, top-to-bottom, righthand barrel machine that breaks a long way offshore (20 mins paddle) and will test the best on their tube-riding skills. There's also a left for the insanely brave. Headhigh and a bit of NE swell, SW winds and full tide should see the dragon breathe some fire. Laulii is fine for average surfers, while DB is not.

WIND AND SWELL

Centrally located in the South Pacific, Samoa is an excellent swell magnet picking up swells from any direction with little loss in size or power. SW-NW swells can be slightly filtered by neighbouring Tonga, Fiji, Tuvalu and the remote Gilbert Islands, but generally, Samoa doesn't suffer from flat spells. The primary source of Southern Ocean swell arrives from April to October when SE-SW swells coming off

Antarctica lows generate regular 3-12ft waves. In fact, these swells can arrive year-round and the most prevalent direction is SSE with moderate 10-12sec periods. From Nov-March Samoa receives NW-NE swells generated by major northern hemisphere storms, and are the same winter swells that rock the North Shore of Oahu. While NE is more common, NW-N swells also occur and the period can be much longer than the S coast, helping with wave-height. The islands are also open to occasional cyclone swells coming from any direction as the storm tracks are wildly unpredictable. The good news is that the

BOULDERS

LAT: -18.475734°   LONG: 177.925401°

As the name Boulders suggests, this left breaks over a rocky mix of lava and the odd coral head, in pointbreak style, close to the headland. It is one of Samoa's classiest waves and handles as much size as the Pacific can throw at it, with triple overhead plus days a real possibility. A steep roll in leads to a flying wall that's thick and grunty, before turning totally tubular on the shallow end section. Major positive factors include rideable on lower tides and it's nicely tucked in out of the SE trade winds, which is also the ideal swell direction so only bigger pulses on the wrap will line-up properly. Negatives include: crowds of advanced surfers on big swells as all the surf camps descend by boat and road; getting too close to the cliff at high tide or the inside coral heads at low tide; being under-gunned; the regular shark sightings in the vicinity. Can be friendly enough on smaller, messed up S-SW swells and surfing in the remote bay on Sundays is usually OK.

E-SE trade winds are rarely too strong to surf, especially during the wet season when they are 15-25kph rather than 25-35kph in the middle of the year. ESE is the predominant direction, with the E to SE quadrant accounting for 31% of the time in Feb before ramping up to 84% in Sept. The slim shoulder seasons may provide the right blend of swell with lighter winds and both coasts can receive different swells at the same time. The tidal range never exceeds 1.5m, but even small changes effect the shallow reefs and many of the south coast breaks are mid to high tide only. ●

SURF STATS		J F	M A	M J	J A	S O	N D
SWELL	Dominant swell	🌀	🌑	🌑	🌑	🌑	🌀
	Size (m)	4-5	5	6-7	7	6	5
	Consistency (%)	70	85	90	90	80	70
WIND	Dominant wind	🌤	🌤	🌤	🌤	🌤	🌤
	Average force	F3	F3	F3-F4	F4	F3-F4	F3-F4
	Consistency	56	68	72	82	76	60
TEMP.	Wetsuit	🏄	🏄	🏄	🏄	🏄	🏄
	Water temp.	28	28	29	27	27	28

RAROTONGA, COOK ISLANDS

+ UNCROWDED REEF PASSES
+ N AND S SWELLS
+ EASY PADDLES FROM SHORE
+ OUTER ISLAND POTENTIAL

– LIMITED REEF PASS SET-UPS
– SHALLOW HIGH TIDE REEFS
– TROPICAL DOWNPOURS
– EXPENSIVE LOCAL COSTS

Many a round-the-world ticket includes the option of stopping in the Cook Islands, evoking thoughts of Pacific perfection. Considering these 15 islands sit in between world-class locations like Fiji, Tonga, Samoa and Tahiti, you would be forgiven for thinking that they must have awesome waves somewhere. The fact that they bear the name of the ultimate surf discoverer, James Cook, is not a guarantee of good surf and like Tubuai or Niue, the underwater topography doesn't suit epic surf requirements. However, devoting a few weeks should ensure sampling some decent and definitely uncrowded high tide waves.

The majority of the population lives in the southern group. The capital Rarotonga is volcanic with a rugged, eroded centre of peaks and ridges, surrounded by flat lowlands about 1 km wide. Since Rarotonga is the youngest island, it is physically unlike its other volcanic neighbours where erosion and periodic submersions have reduced mountains to gentle hills. Compared with other atolls, the lagoon surrounding Rarotonga is quite small, covering only 8km² (5mi2) and is relatively shallow. The fringing reef defines the lagoon, which is broad and sandy to the south, and narrow and rocky on the north and east. Most of the reef passes are too narrow, preventing waves from wrapping properly, and explains why there is only a handful of surf spots in the Cook Islands. The waves break over shallow reef, so it's usually safest to surf at high tide and a decent-size swell will also help the waves to break in deeper water. All the reefbreaks are easily accessible by paddling out of one of the passages or directly over the reef.

Despite being on the windward side, one of the most surfed spots is AVANA, breaking off the tip of Motutapu, helpfully located close to the popular accommodation at Muri Beach. The break is quite short and requires patience in selecting waves. The surf is neither that reliable nor challenging, even though it breaks over shallow reef, making it a bit too dangerous for beginners. Opposite the passage is a smaller right which is popular with bodyboarders. On moderate SW swells and summer NE winds, the thick, ferocious rights off the AVAAVAROA PASSAGE provide pits for determined tube riders. Direction, size and period will be crucial to prevent the skinny channel closing-out and a dropping tide will see the currents race, so paddle

in over the reef, well before mid tide approaches. RUTAKI PASSAGE, facing Rarotongan Resort favours the left side of another, thin 50m wide channel through the coral shelf. SE-S swell will help with the angle to the channel, but any wind lacking north will kill it. Bring a fast, sleek barrel board to out run this one. There's also a right on the other side when there's more W in the swell. Inconsistent, rarely crowded and not for intermediates. Just to the east, check anorexic Papua Passage on small, clean, organised swells. On the leeward side,

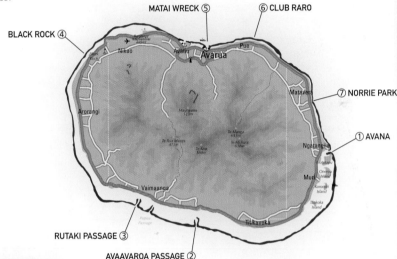

SPOT INFORMATION			
SPOT	SIZE	BTM	TYPE
①			
②			
③			
④			
⑤			
⑥			
⑦			

the best spot is undoubtedly BLACK ROCK by the Golf Course, next to the airport. It's not a pass, more a curve in the reef that will bend prevailing swell into some slabby shacks on the rights. The lefts get really good too, barreling fast from a wedging take-off, but beware the coral heads and pitching lips. Plus points are it is really consistent because of its wide swell window, constant offshores, mid to high tide range and easy access. Minuses include short rides, close-outs, getting pitched, sharks and scrabbling over the reef on a dropping tide. This wave exudes true Polynesian power and although it is uncrowded, negotiating its imperfections requires skill and guts. Respect the local bodyboard crew. "The Boiler" of the MATAI WRECK (1916) sticks up off the Avarua Harbour reef and has long been surfed, creating hollow lefts on major NW swells. Easier lefts peel down the harbour entrance on the inside, but NE winds are dead onshore. For righthanders, head to the reef off CLUB RARO, which regularly produces some good waves in smaller N swells. It's an ill-defined line-up and there's a good chance of taking a few on the head crossing the straight reef line. There's not much to recommend the east coast when the trades are shredding the waves to pieces, but on those rare, slack wind days, little scallops in the reef like NORRIE PARK can hold a decent right at high tide. The reef is closer to land here so it's a shorter paddle out.

WIND AND SWELL

The Cook Islands are blessed by one of the greatest swell exposures on earth, but the coastline sucks! The South Pacific provides most of the swell in the shape of 3-15ft (1-5m) SE-SW swells, from March-November, which peak in winter with 6ft+ (2m+) swells for over 60%

NEAR MURI

RONAN GLADU

SOCIALS, WEST COAST

JEREMY WILMOTTE

RUTAKI PASSAGE

JEREMY WILMOTTE

TRAVEL INFORMATION

LOCAL POPULATION: 13,095
TIME ZONE: GMT -10h
COASTLINE: 33km (20mi)

GETTING THERE – Three airlines fly to the Cook Islands; Air New Zealand, Virgin Australia and Air Tahiti. Air New Zealand is the main airline offering flights to Rarotonga (RAR) with direct flights from Auckland (and sometimes Christchurch), Sydney and LAX. Most flights arrive and depart in the early hours of the morning. Dept tax is NZ$55 cash.

GETTING AROUND – Air Rarotonga operates flights to 8 islands. Aitutaki fr NZ$188 o/w. Rarotonga's coastal road is 32km (20mi) long; cycling takes 2h. All drivers need their own license, plus a local driver's license (NZ$20), from Avarua Police Station. Motorbike License test is $5. Car hire fr $34/d, while moped hire from only $15/d. Drive on the left. Buses run anti-clockwise or clockwise (NZ$7/rt). Low quality bicycles are available for hire in "town" (Avarua).

LODGING AND FOOD – Prices are on the high side for the South Pacific. Muri Beach Resort (from $165/n/dbl). Avana Waterfront apartments (fr $245/n sleeps 4). Avarua has the Paradise Inn from $63/n/single. Tiare Village is a cheap $17/n dorm; $21/n single; $37/n/dbl near the airport. Palm Grove for the south coast waves (fr $197/n/dble). Expect $15-20 for a meal.

WEATHER – With 2116h of sunshine and 2087mm (82in) of rainfall annually, the climate is tropical. Rarotonga is almost opposite Honolulu in latitude and unlike the wet and dry extremes experienced by most equatorial nations, Rarotonga enjoys a pleasant climate year-round with relatively minor fluctuations. The surfing season, May-Sept, has the 'cooler' months, with average daily temps around 25°C (77°F), down to 19°C (66°F) at night. The summer rainy season, Dec-April, can be hot and humid 29°C (84°F) by day with bright sunny mornings and late afternoon downpours. As the heat accumulates over the Pacific Ocean, lows bring torrential rains, strong winds and the occasional tropical cyclone, which means high humidity, sticky nights and more mosquitoes. Bring a shorty for windy winter days when water gets down around 22-23°C (72-74°F).

WEATHER	J/F	M/A	M/J	J/A	S/O	N/D
Total Rainfall (mm)	238	226	170	109	114	187
Consistency (d/m)	15	14	12	10	9	11
Temperature min. (°C)	23	22	20	18	19	21
Temperature max. (°C)	29	28	26	25	26	27

NATURE AND CULTURE – Rarotonga is a lush, beautiful place, enjoy its peace. Go to Saturday morning's Punanga-nui Market. Fishing is world-class! Common catches include bonefish, trevally, mahimahi, paara, marlin (local record 277kg), snapper and tuna. Do Captain Tama's glass-bottom boat tour of the lagoon. Visit the other Cook islands who have joined the massive Pacific Oceanscape project along with 15 island nations to create the largest protected area network on the planet!

HAZARDS AND HASSLES – Watch the tides and currents in the narrow passes and surfing over shallow reef usually means reef cuts and urchins - booties essential. Most local riders are cool bodyboarders! There is no malaria but occasional outbreaks of dengue.

HANDY HINTS – Bring 2 boards for mid-size surf, contact Big Dave at Niki's Surf Shop in Tupapa (East Avarua) near Paradise Inn. It is a small shop with second hand boards. High season is December to February. The Cook Islands are located across the dateline from New Zealand and Australia, so it's a day behind!

of the time. This swell source continues year-round and can pop up in mid summer, when the focus has shifted to huge North Pacific NW swells making it this far south with enough size. January will see nice 4-10ft (1.2-3m) for 1 day in 3 so there's a lot of flat days on the north and west coasts, unless a big S-SW is wrapping around to Black Rock. The prevailing trades oscillate between ENE in Jan to ESE in July, which is also the windiest month with speeds exceeding 12-25mph (20-40kmh) for 50% of the time. The E wind favours lefts on the southern passes, while the rights get blown out until summer (Dec-March) N winds blow, which is also the season for glassy days on the windward east coast spots like Avana. Mid-sized, winter swells create the best chance of quality waves, breaking a bit further off the reef. Tidal range never goes over 1m, even on spring tides, but it's crucial to combine morning high tides with as much range as possible to maximise water-time. Check with Flinders National Tidal Utility for monthly tide tables or ask at Niki's shop in Avarua. ●

SURF STATS		J	F	M	A	M	J	J	A	S	O	N	D
SWELL	Dominant swell												
	Size (m)	4-5		5		6-7		7		5-6		4-5	
	Consistency (%)	40		50		60		60		50		40	
WIND	Dominant wind												
	Average force	F4		F4		F4		F4		F4		F4	
	Consistency	71		54		58		49		60		66	
TEMP.	Wetsuit												
	Water temp.	26		26		25		23		23		25	

TAHITI & MOOREA, FRENCH POLY.

+ POWERFUL WAVES
+ YEAR-ROUND AND CONSISTENT   – VERY EXPENSIVE
+ BARRELS!   – DIFFICULT ACCESS
+ BEAUTIFUL LANDSCAPES   – LOCALISM AT SOME SPOTS
+ CHILLED-OUT ISLAND LIFESTYLE   – SHARP CORAL REEFS

Tahiti sits at the centre of French Polynesia and now, thanks to the relatively recent discovery of Teahupoo, has become an undeniable focus for the surf world as the most challenging of playgrounds. There are dozens of islands in the Society Island chain that receive classic waves, but it's not all scary square barrels with some fun walls at various passes and even the odd beachbreak style wave to be found. On the whole, the quality of the spots is exceptional and the waves are varied, as swells arrive from both hemispheres, lighting up the coastlines of Moorea and Tahiti.

When the N swells roll in, Moorea Island is worth the effort for its quality north coast reef passes. COOKS BAY PASS has what some call a fun left, despite the coral reef being close under fin. Too much E in the wind will mess it up although the shallower, nastier right across the channel will be cleaner. Take a dugout as currents and distance rule out paddling. HAURU is a narrow cut in the fringing reef near the Intercontinental on the north coast, which seems to favour lefthanders with a bit of W in the swell. Fast and shallow is the theme while the right is even worse and only for chargers with little regard for the boiling shut down sections. There is an easier left back at the entrance to Opunohu Bay. Currents get really strong and the nearby motu's are shark diving hotspots. At headhigh, HAAPITI is an easy roll-in to a very long, slopey wall as it tours the curve of coral that is always deeper than the gin-clear water makes it seem. Even improvers can manage, but things hot up as the size increases to double overhead, when the drop steepens, the odd barrel section beckons and the river-like current heading out to sea cranks up. Extra inches of foam and shoulder muscle helps with the 20-40min paddle from town - better to hire canoes to get out there safely and quickly. Attracts plenty of surfers, but the vibe is often friendly and inclusive for all abilities. Wind can mess it up and kiters will descend in the afternoons. Moorea also gets plenty of decent waves through the S swell season, and if it's big enough, SE-SW lines will slip through the Chenal de Moorea then wrap around the eastern point near the airport. TEMAE hugs the coralline shelf, very close to shore, providing a righthand barrel spectacle on a par with Backdoor, but much longer. When it's on, which isn't often since it needs non-trade-winds, expect air drops into multiple caverns as it parallels the shoreline, getting shallower and uglier as it turns inside out. There can be problems when surfing Temae because the locals covet this inconsistent right, so tread lightly and be sure of your abilities.

On Tahiti PAPENOO can provide a fun, hollow range of peaks around the rivermouth, which helps shape some sand and rock bars, along with bringing pollution and a shark problem after rains. Holds the crowd that come in N swells and is usually cool, but there might be some vibe when the left is really firing. Cops the trades pretty bad so check it early. Out on an exposed, hammerhead reef, POINTE VENUS follows the trend of Tahitian rights by being shallow and sketchy, requiring more than a little skill to negotiate the rapid tubes. Needs a small to moderate NE swell and S quadrant winds as it will get out of control in bigger swells. Further east, there's more waves at PK 15, Rocky Point and the less challenging beachbreaks of Papenoo. While the Bay de Matavai is famous for being Cook's landing spot, its

TEMAE

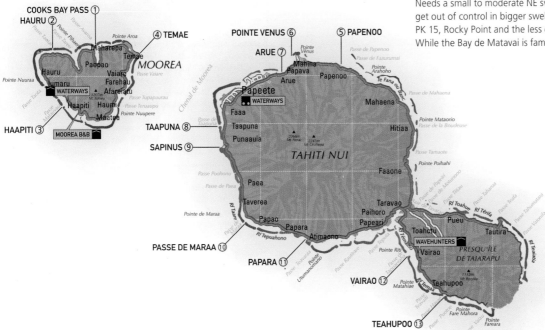

SPOT INFORMATION

SPOT	SIZE	BTM	TYPE
①	10/3		
②	8/3		
③	15/2		
④	10/3		
⑤	10/2		
⑥	6/3		
⑦	6/2		
⑧	10/3		
⑨	13/3		
⑩	10/2		
⑪	8/3		
⑫	12/3		
⑬	18/3		

LUIS BLANCO

SAPINUS

BERNARD TESTEMALE

TEAVAITI

LAURENT MASUREL

TRAVEL INFORMATION

LOCAL POPULATION:
Tahiti - 178,133; Moorea - 16,191
TIME ZONE: GMT -10h

COASTLINE: French Polynesia –
2,525km (1,578mi)

GETTING THERE – Fly to Papeete (PPT) with Air New Zealand, Air France, Hawaiian from Honolulu, LAN Chile or Qantas from Oz. Air Tahiti Nui fly direct from Tokyo, Auckland, LA and Paris, with links to Australia. They are board friendly and co-sponsor the WT contest.

GETTING AROUND – Tahiti and Moorea local trucks (Le Truck) provide good cheap transport around the island. Getting from the shore to the waves usually involves paddling for 30-45 min across the lagoon or more sensibly renting a dugout for $10rtn. A rental car costs about $65-75/d. The ferry to Moorea Island costs $33/rtn/p and $94/rtn/car on the Aremiti 5 and takes 30mins. The up-and-down domestic flight takes only 10mins!

LODGING AND FOOD – Like much of the S Pacific, Tahiti is not a cheap place to visit. At the bottom of the accommodation range are the dorm beds at Teamo (Papeete Youth Hostel), which charges at least $24/n. A mid-range favourite is Hiti Moana Villa near Papara (fr $110/n). In Teahupoo try Tauhanihani Village Lodge ($100/n), Vanira Lodge (fr$140/n), Te Pari Village or one of the other local "Faré" from $90/n. Moorea Surf Bed & Breakfast have dorm style beds starting from $50 inc. free use of boards, canoes, snorkeling kit and bicycles right at Haapiti. There's plenty of motu style high end hotels and also Camping Nelson from $12/n. Eat from the roulottes (rolling food trucks) where locals eat simple island meals from $10, but more frequently you'll spend around $20-30 on a meal.

WEATHER – During the wet season from Nov to April, there will be a heavy downpour every other day. El Niño years are very wet. Cyclones hit the country on occasions. In the dry season the high mountains effect the weather patterns and cause the S coast to see some rain. The temps are near perfect at 23°-30°C/74°-86°F year-round. The water hovers around 25-27°c (77°F-80°F).

WEATHER	J/F	M/A	M/J	J/A	S/O	N/D
Total Rainfall (mm)	300	170	95	67	75	195
Consistency (d/m)	14	11	7	6	7	13
Temperature min. (°C)	23	23	21	20	21	23
Temperature max. (°C)	30	30	29	28	29	30

NATURE AND CULTURE – If you need a break from getting barreled then head up into the beautiful mountains, visit some of the caves, go fishing, diving and snorkeling or just chill out amongst the lush landscape. Occasional dugout races are worth watching.

HAZARDS AND HASSLES – Respect the local's deep feeling of pride. The waves are super heavy and the reefs are shallow and full of fire coral. Currents at the mouth of reef passes can be very strong. Teahupoo is one of the most dangerous waves in the world and should only be tackled by the most advanced of surfers. It has already seen one surf-related death. Sharks although common, pose no real threat. Don't eat poorly cooked fish, as there is a chance of catching ciguatera, a type of food poisoning. There are lots of mosquitoes, but no malaria.

HANDY HINTS – Bring all your own surf gear, as equipment here is very expensive in the Papeete and Maharepa surf shops. Bring at least two boards, including a longer pintail made especially for local conditions (heavy barrels!). Other essentials include reef boots, sun cream and a helmet. Tahiti is a French speaking destination, but French people may find themselves the object of some bitterness. New live HD webcams for numerous spots on tahiti-webcam.com.

long curve of volcanic sand is fairly poor for waves with lots of close-outs, but the bays towards **ARUE** hold a few reefbreaks like Taharaa, surrounded by plush hotels and further on a very shallow left and right at La Fayette, where there is also some dumpy shorebreak, suited to bodyboards. Close to Papeete is **TAAPUNA**, the original Tahitian tube garden and popular destination wave for those who want a hollow, dredging and technically testing lefthander, a couple of notches below Teahupoo. Any W swell and any E wind will work, so it is consistent, crowded with good surfers and suited to experienced reefbreak surfers. Usual problems of being way out there, in waters strafed by current and a local crew who demand as much respect as the wave. Generally considered an easier alternative than Taapuna, **SAPINUS** can still throw a decent tube especially on its inside section and offers some nice walled rides on the pass opposite the Tahiti Museum. Deep in the bay is a fun beach/shorebreak type set-up near the rivermouth when big W swells are running and there's something

for everyone in a chilled out atmosphere. Just down the coast there's more waves in the bay and on the pass at Paea. Hollow, fast and shallow are often used to describe Tahitian waves and definitely apply to this distant fringe of reef at **PASSE DE MARAA**. Needs as much water

VAIRAO

as possible and some S in the swell to stop it shutting down horribly.
The bonus is a lack of crowds and occasionally the right across the
fast flowing channel will fire. Experts only. Beginners can head for the
good beachbreak in **PAPARA**, which is a nice rest from the intensity of
the surrounding reefs. Holds some curvy corners in larger swells and
attracts some high performance riders looking to cut loose without
getting cut. There's also some outside reef action for the chargers.
On the Iti Peninsula, the Tapuehara Pass holds the flawless lefts of
VAIRAO, yet another epic barrel spinning across the coral shallows.
It is less intense than Teahupoo, but still packs some serious punch
with the S swell window and NE-E wind combo that make it a reliable
performer without huge crowds. Maybe it's because of the near 2km
paddle, strong rips and sharky vibe....

BEN THOUARD.COM

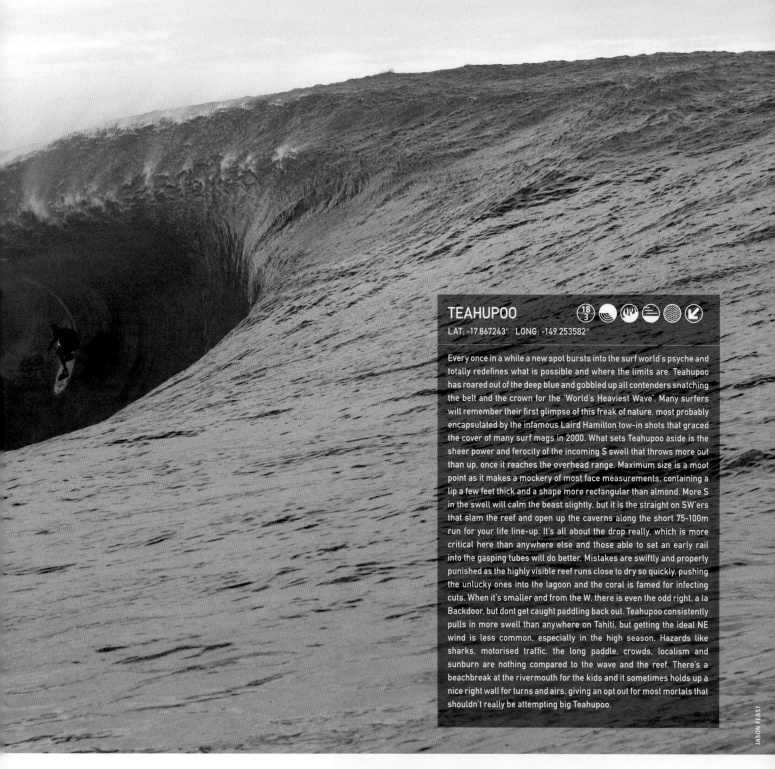

TEAHUPOO

LAT: -17.867243°   LONG: -149.253582°

Every once in a while a new spot bursts into the surf world's psyche and totally redefines what is possible and where the limits are. Teahupoo has roared out of the deep blue and gobbled up all contenders snatching the belt and the crown for the 'World's Heaviest Wave'. Many surfers will remember their first glimpse of this freak of nature, most probably encapsulated by the infamous Laird Hamilton tow-in shots that graced the cover of many surf mags in 2000. What sets Teahupoo aside is the sheer power and ferocity of the incoming S swell that throws more out than up, once it reaches the overhead range. Maximum size is a moot point as it makes a mockery of most face measurements, containing a lip a few feet thick and a shape more rectangular than almond. More S in the swell will calm the beast slightly, but it is the straight on SW'ers that slam the reef and open up the caverns along the short 75-100m run for your life line-up. It's all about the drop really, which is more critical here than anywhere else and those able to set an early rail into the gasping tubes will do better. Mistakes are swiftly and properly punished as the highly visible reef runs close to dry so quickly, pushing the unlucky ones into the lagoon and the coral is famed for infecting cuts. When it's smaller and from the W, there is even the odd right, a la Backdoor, but dont get caught paddling back out. Teahupoo consistently pulls in more swell than anywhere on Tahiti, but getting the ideal NE wind is less common, especially in the high season. Hazards like sharks, motorised traffic, the long paddle, crowds, localism and sunburn are nothing compared to the wave and the reef. There's a beachbreak at the rivermouth for the kids and it sometimes holds up a nice right wall for turns and airs, giving an opt out for most mortals that shouldn't really be attempting big Teahupoo.

JASON FEAST

SWELL AND WIND

At a southern latitude of 17°, Tahiti is perfectly exposed to the super-consistent S/SW swells, which hammer the S coast year-round, but peak between April and Oct. Expect the surf to range from 4 to 15ft in season and 2-5ft in the off-season. Exposure to the summer N/NW swells between Nov and March is less generous. Tahiti receives about half the swell of Hawaii. Even so, this time of year will still see plenty of 3ft-8ft swells. Dominant trade winds come from the E and blow from 40-60kph (25-40mph). During the May to Oct dry season (Maraamu), the wind has more of a SE to E angle, whilst the wet season (Toerau), sees the wind coming more from the N/NE. Even with these strong winds mornings will usually be glassy. Tidal range is very small. ●

SURF STATS		J F	M A	M J	J A	S O	N D
SWELL	Dominant swell	🌑	🌑	🌑	🌑	🌑	🌑
	Size (m)	5	5-6	7	7-8	6-7	5-6
	Consistency (%)	70	85	90	90	80	70
WIND	Dominant wind						
	Average force	F4	F4	F4	F4	F4	F4
	Consistency	75	78	60	62	70	72
TEMP.	Wetsuit						
	Water temp.	27	27	26	25	26	27

GALAPAGOS

+ POWERFUL REEFBREAKS   – INCONSISTENT
+ WAVES YEAR-ROUND   – COOL WATER
+ UNCROWDED   – FEW SPOTS
+ WILDLIFE MECCA   – TOUGH ACCESS

It was through observing the unique and diverse wildlife of the Galapagos Islands that led Charles Darwin to expand upon the theory of evolution. These 17 isolated, oceanic oases have been declared a national park and even today, only five of the islands are inhabited. The archipelago is the result of fairly recent volcanic surges from the sea floor that remain very active, particularly Isabela Island. The coastal fringe is made up of lava reefs and boulders, because the water is too cold for coral formation. Some islands don't have that many good spots thanks to steep and broken up lava outcrops, while other islands like San Cristobal have a concentration of top quality waves in a small area. Waves jack up suddenly out of deep water and have plenty of power, drawing the odd comparison with Hawaii. Further exploration may reveal more breaks, but many islands are off limits and permits are required to leave the main tourist areas. The predominant S-SE trade winds mean that the most consistent spots are to be found on the north-facing shores during the Northern Hemisphere winter, but there are also options to ride swells that have made the long journey from the Southern Ocean throughout the year. Most of the reefs are sharp and the very clear water makes it hard to figure out exactly how deep it is. The water is actually the coldest equatorial water on earth, due to the Humboldt Current working its way up the coastline of South America and past the islands, bringing with it water from Antarctica. This water is nutrient rich explaining the attraction for the prolific marine wildlife.

PAUL KENNEDY

TONGO REEF

Puerto Ayora is the centre of activity on busy Santa Cruz Island and there are some mushy beachbreaks to be had at Tortuga Bay, a 3km walk from town. The real action is 1.5hrs sail west, where there's a solid lefthander at **PALMAS GRANDES** with big drops into a longish, squared-off wall. This coast relies on S-SW swells and Palmas seems to receive and handle more size than other islands. **CERRO GALLINA** or "Chicken Hill" overlooks a rolling left that rumbles and crumbles down a long boulder point into a bay that offers afternoon wind protection. It's a fun, hassle free ride, with deeper

water, but enough power to keep all abilities happy. Very consistent in any S swell and only accessible from a surf tour boat. Baltra Island is the main airport and tourist arrival point, where most cruises start from. Baltra has a chunky left wall inside Aeolian Bay, plus a classic cruiser's righthander over sand, down the coast at Las Salinas. The main break is 20mins sail north on tiny **SEYMOUR NORTE**, where a top quality, 100m long, right pointbreak will peel over rocky reef and boulders in NW-N swells. There can be shorter, hollow peaks dotting the west coast and it is a fairly consistent bet for your first surf off the plane. On San Cristobal, Puerto Baquerizo Moreno, has the greatest concentration of decent surf spots in the Galapagos. It's also the administrative capital of the islands and holds the bulk of the islands accommodation. **CAROLA** is by far the most awesome, consistent wave, a righthander in front of the lighthouse, working on NW-N swells, plus a SW can also sneak in. It's a long, tubular wave, rideable from 4-12ft+, with a fast, heavy drop, made more difficult by the SE trades blowing into the barrel. The boulder strewn lava rock reef and semi-crowded conditions make this an experienced surfers spot. To surf **EL CAÑON**, you have to enter the military zone and leave your passport (or surf permit/i.d. from the San Cristobal Surf Club) at security! This left breaks close to the bouldered shore when small N pulses come in, but holds waves up to 8-10ft on wrapping SW swells. High and tight tuck-in moments between the open walls that shoulder into the busy bay. A kilometre offshore, the Outer Reefs have some great lefts and rights depending on the swell angle, for those with access to a boat. **TONGO REEF** is a 30min walk round the coast from Cañon, or a short boat ride if the military refuse entry. It's a multi-sectioned left that starts steep and keeps going with fast down-the-line walls that may get hollower at the last section or shoulder off into the bay. When it connects up in S swells it is pure stoke for fast driving goofies and breaks through the tides. On the southwest-facing coast, **LOBERIA** is another Galapagos gem that can hold epic barrels on its day. From the A-frame peak, it's thick and fast, pitching over a shallow, spiky lava reef and will rifle off both ways, depending on what flavour of S groundswell is hitting. It's not always barreling with plenty of smaller, high performance days and the left point opposite the right can be a fun, ripable wall. NW swell does wrap in, but won't line it up like a good SW. Scores a 6 for consistency and 5 for crowds. Aggressive male sea lions will bite surfers that get too close to the females and pups, especially during mating season. Loberia also has a few nasty rocks sticking up out of the line-up. It's a 10min cab ride from town. There are many more possibilities around San Cristobal like La Perdida, Puerto Grande, Crateres and Punta Pitt in the north, but access is always the issue and getting permits from the National Parks plus a surf guide (San Cristobal Surf Club or tour operator) is essential to travel to out of the way breaks. **MANGLECITO** is 15kms NE of Puerto Baquerizo by boat, where the point fires off fast lefts that are shallow and heavy at the peak before walling out into the bay. Long, fast and a real blast on an overhead NW pulse. Experienced surfers when bigger, plus there' a consistent A-frame reef nearby.

SWELL AND WIND

The good news about being located right on the equator is that the islands receive the cleanest swells from both N and S, but the bad news is that these swells are generated more than 5,000k's (3,000mi) away and can suffer from heavy decay. Nevertheless, during the peak season from Dec-Mar, NW swells throw up steady waves in the 2-8ft range, with occasional forays into the 12-15ft range and winds have more E angle at much lower speeds. During April to Dec, SW swells dominate, showing super-high groundswell consistency, long periods and greater wave height. At the same time, the trade winds pick up pace (15mph/25km/h) and clock around to the SE or due S, bringing cross-onshore winds to mess up exposed spots, so the early season

CAROLA

JUAN FERNANDEZ

SEYMOUR NORTE ③

Canal de Salvador

Isla Baltra

Isla Pinzón

Isla Santa Cruz

Puerto Ayora

Canal de Santa Cruz

Canal de Santa Fe

MANGLECITO ⑧

Isla San Cristóbal

ALMAS GRANDES ①

CERRO GALLINA ②

Isla Santa Fe

CAROLA ④
EL CAÑON ⑤

TONGO REEF ⑥

Puerto Baquerizo

WATERWAYS

LOBERIA ⑦

WAVEHUNTERS

SURF STATS		J	F	M	A	M	J	J	A	S	O	N	D
SWELL	Dominant swell	●		●		◐		◑		●		◑	
	Size (m)	4		3-4		4		4-5		4		3-4	
	Consistency (%)	60		50		60		70		60		50	
WIND	Dominant wind	◔		◔		◔		◔		◔		◔	
	Average force	F3		F3		F3		F3		F3		F3	
	Consistency	78		77		88		92		90		93	
TEMP.	Wetsuit	🏄		🏄		🏄		🏄		🏄		🏄	
	Water temp.	23		24		22		21		20		21	

SPOT INFORMATION

SPOT SIZE BTM TYPE

① ...
② ...
③ ...
④ ...
⑤ ...
⑥ ...
⑦ ...
⑧ ...

LOBERIA

JUAN FERNANDEZ

TRAVEL INFORMATION

LOCAL POPULATION: Galapagos - 25.000	**COASTLINE:** San Cristobal 127km (80mi)
TIME ZONE: GMT -6h	

GETTING THERE – No visa is required for most nationalities. Fly to mainland Ecuador first, either Quito or Quayaquil. Tame fly Quito - San Cristóbal and Quayaquil - Baltra (fr $290rtn), while AeroGal only fly from Quayaquil (boardbag $56 e/w). LAN offer Quito-Baltra from $550. Flights are frequently full especially during peak season (Dec-Feb, July-Sept). Book early!

GETTING AROUND – Emetebe flies inter-island from $160 e/w (no boards). Unless you stay on a surf charter boat, hopping between islands involves the use of ferries. If you land in Baltra, you'll need to take a combination of buses and ferries to Puerto Ayora, then a 2hr ferry to Baquerizo ($30e/w). To get to most spots, you'll have to walk or take a taxi ($2-3). Be careful of the sun, it's strong and shade is rare; people have died getting lost! Take strong footwear, hat and lots of water.

LODGING AND FOOD – Unless you stay on a boat, you have plenty of choice for Baquerizo Moreno basic hotels (Orca, Miconia, Casa Blanca, etc from $40/n), or the higher end Blue Marlin Hotel (Wavehunters package including boat transfers fr $1493/p/wk/dbl), or the Hotel Pimampiro, used by Waterways for all inclusive guided tours ($1407/p/5d/dbl). Cheaper hostels and home stays in Puerto Ayora from $20/n/dorm. Galapagos Vision catamaran from $850/p/3n. Food is generally fish & rice. Veggies and beers are expensive.

WEATHER – Despite its equatorial position, the Galapagos enjoys a relatively dry climate. The dry season, also called "Garua", causes low clouds, fog and drizzle on the hillsides from May to Dec but virtually no substantial rain. This is supposedly the cold season with constant SE to S winds. March and April are both the hottest and wettest months of the short wet season from Jan to May, when a springsuit should suffice, while around Aug/Sept, a light steamer is needed. El Niño years are much warmer in the sea and wetter on land.

WEATHER	J/F	M/A	M/J	J/A	S/O	N/D
Total Rainfall (mm)	57	60	9	4	7	6
Consistency (d/m)	7	4	2	3	6	8
Temperature min. (°C)	23	23	21	19	18	20
Temperature max. (°C)	30	30	28	25	25	27

NATURE AND CULTURE – The Galapagos is a World Heritage Site due to the amazing wildlife, which shows little fear of people. From midnight to 6am all electricity is switched off - don't expect any nightlife.

HAZARDS AND HASSLES – In the case of an emergency, adequate hospitals are far away. Most lava reefs are shallow and the rocks have sharp edges. A shark attacked a surfer at an Isabella break in 2007 and another hit occurred at Villamil beach on Isabela Island (both non-fatal). Male sea lions are swimming around and have been know to nip at surfers. The true local surfers are few and friendly.

HANDY HINTS – Bring everything you may need with you. A couple of boards (a semi-gun may be needed), leashes, fullsuit and springsuit, booties, hats, sunscreen, insect repellent, flashlight and a conservationist attitude, because the Galapagos is a very special place. The National Park entry fee is $100, payable in cash at the airport.

months (Apr-May) are the best bet for good conditions at southern spots. Deep in the Austral winter, water temps can drop as low as 18-20°C (64-68°F) due to upwelling, la niña and the Humboldt current. Be aware of the tides varying from 1-2.5m, which can make for a difficult time at certain spots, especially on small to medium-sized days when rocks can suddenly pop out of the water. ●

A RIDE
A DAY KEEPS THE
DOCTOR
AWAY!

ATLANTIC

CACIMBA DO PADRE, FERNANDO DE NORONHA

The Dos Imadoes (Two Brothers) loom over
the ballistic barrels that slam the sand on this
UNESCO World Heritage Site island.

OCEAN

INTRODUCTION

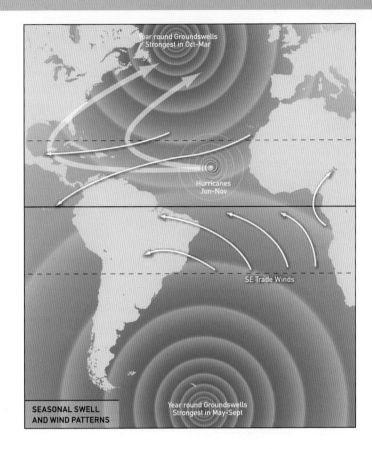

SEASONAL SWELL AND WIND PATTERNS

The Atlantic Ocean may play second fiddle to the Pacific Ocean in terms of size, depth and volume, yet it more than holds it own when it comes to other statistics. The Atlantic is the stormiest ocean, boasting the largest tides and the underwater Mid-Atlantic ridge forms the longest mountain range on the planet, equivalent to the Himalayas, Andes and Rocky Mountains combined. It covers 25% of the Earth's surface and holds almost a quarter of the world's water, accepting more freshwater river flow than any other ocean. It is the busiest stretch of water, supporting more human populations around its perimeter, as it incorporates bastions of civilization like the Mediterranean Sea, the Baltic Sea and the Caribbean Sea. The Atlantic also provided the proof for the theory of continental drift and plate tectonics, explaining the jigsaw symmetry that exists between the west coast of Africa and the east coast of the Americas. While modern resource exploitation begins to put pressure on this most important of environments and pollution issues have been rising to the surface, there is little doubt that mankind sees the Atlantic Ocean as the most important body of water on the planet and plenty of surfers agree.

SWELL

There are three distinct swell generators in the vast Atlantic with one for each hemisphere, plus the east to west travelling storms that bowl down "Hurricane Alley". The North Atlantic storms are steered across the ocean by an upper atmosphere wind known as the Jet Stream, hurtling from west to east at a height of 5-10kms. If the path of the Jet Stream is fairly straight, then deep low pressures will form and provide plenty of surf for Europe, North Africa and the east coast of North America down to the Caribbean islands. Known as a 'fluid' phase this is generally thought to be dominant in the winter, however, the 'blocking' phase can appear at any time, whereby the Jet Stream is forced to meander around a large, centrally positioned high pressure cell, which drastically reduces the size and frequency of North Atlantic groundswells.

Tropical disturbances form along a corridor of warm Central Atlantic water between about 5° and 20° latitude, spinning up storms that travel in the opposite direction to the North Atlantic depressions. They are a major swell source for the Caribbean and the eastern

seaboard of the USA, with the bulk of the swell issuing from the front right quadrant of the system, which usually means a strong SE pulse. Of course hurricanes are notoriously erratic and difficult to predict their exact path, but the slower and straighter they move, the more waves for everyone as swell propagates out in all directions. Hurricanes forming below the equator are virtually non-existent and the South Atlantic relies on Roaring Forties swells pushing up from the cold, forbidding waters of the Southern Ocean. These energetic ocean pulses can travel as far as the Azores, well beyond the tropics in the Northern Hemisphere, so African isles like Cape Verde receive great waves in what is essentially summertime and Sao Tome, along with the entire 'armpit of Africa' would be flat without them. Both Cape Verde and Fernando de Noronha look to the winter North Atlantic low pressures for the bulk of their waves, since S swells arrive on the steep, rocky Brazilian islands with little shape and onshore winds.

WIND

The Atlantic tropical belt is governed by the same wind bending, Coriolis effect that is in evidence across the Pacific. The easterly trades arrive in the Caribbean with a healthy dose of N in them, before briefly deviating to the SE for the warmer summer months. Unfortunately, unlike the Pacific, groundswell can only arrive from the N-SE, so the offshore western coasts are usually flat. Angled coasts that pick up NE swell and afford cross-offshore conditions are the focus in a region named after the constant trades (windward/leeward). These same NE breezes are even stronger across the ocean in the Cape Verde islands, maintaining a year-round force of F4, explaining why they have been so popular with wind/kiteboarders. Below the equator, SE reigns supreme in Fernando do Noronha, while Sao Tome is bang on 0° latitude and lighter S-W winds in the equatorial doldrums.

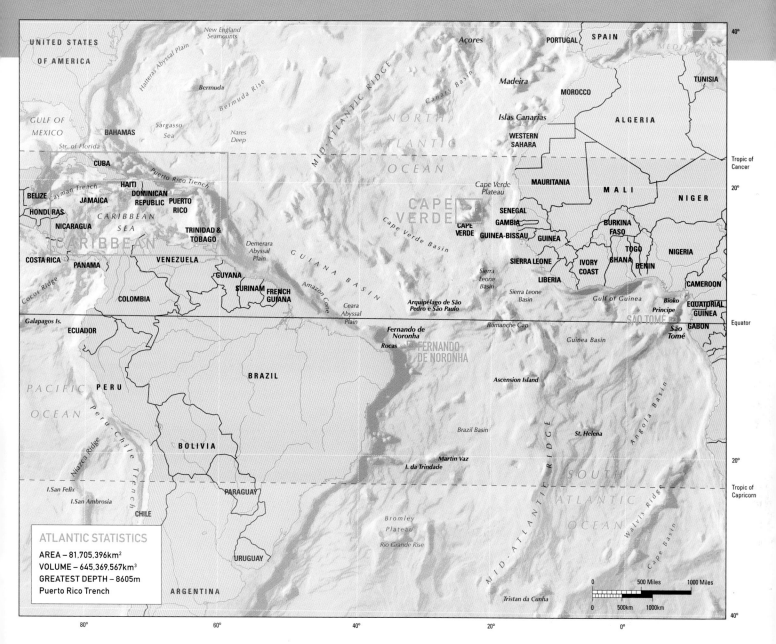

ATLANTIC STATISTICS

AREA – 81,705,396km²
VOLUME – 645,369,567km³
GREATEST DEPTH – 8605m
Puerto Rico Trench

TIDES, CURRENTS AND TEMPERATURES

Tides get extreme in certain corners of the North Atlantic, but between Capricorn and Cancer, most of the islands see a daily rise and fall of less than 4-5ft (1.2-1.5m). Many Caribbean countries barely see a 1ft/30cm change with a combination of semi diurnal even and odd tides, or the once a day diurnal pattern in parts of the Gulf of Mexico. Surf is generally unaffected throughout the Lesser Antilles and much of the Greater Antilles, where tide height grows and so does the affect over shallow reefs in Puerto Rico. Both Noronha and Cape Verde have a micro-tidal range around 3ft/1m, but it is enough to makes the reefs too shallow at low or break too close to shore at high respectively.

The famous Gulf Stream current powers-up in the Caribbean then snakes north and east, dumping its heat in Europe before returning as the cooler Canaries Current. This keeps the Cape Verde surfers in rubber during winter, but the rest of the Atlantic tropical swathe is boardshorts all the way and the minimum 26°C (79°F) sea surface temperature required for hurricanes to form is usually maintained or exceeded for most of the year, particularly further west.

Strong easterly trade winds dictate that the best waves are usually tucked away on the leeward Caribbean coasts.

CANE GARDEN BAY

THE CARIBBEAN

Strung out along a 1100km (685mi) oceanic front, the multitude of volcanic islands in the chain form an arcing Caribbean Sea barrier from the Atlantic swell train. Exotic, tropical, yet firmly Caribbean, each island group has its individual flavour in landscape, culture and also surf. Perfect pointbreaks over fire-coral, barrier reef passes, tabletop reefs and flawless sand point barrels are all fed with swell kicked up by the constant easterly trade winds or N swells from the cooler regions of the Atlantic. Throw in the possibility of hurricane swell from unusual directions and these Windward and Leeward Islands offer a rich diversity of wave-riding possibility.

THE GREATER ANTILLES

The biggest island in the Caribbean should be a carnival of waves, but the Bahamas puts a damper on the party, filtering out all but the biggest winter swells from the NE coast of **Cuba**. The Atlantic swells have to squeeze through the gaps between the islands, then traverse the continental shelf, so the most reliable coast is around the eastern tip where the window is widest. Gulf of Mexico storm fronts can bring some half-decent waves to Havana and when a hurricane winds up in the Caribbean Sea, proper S groundswell pours through between

Jamaica and Haiti, hitting the provinces of Granma, Santiago de Cuba and Guantanamo. The latter is particularly rocky and bristling with reefs, but good shape can be found at rivermouth pointbreaks like Rio Duaba in Baracoa and occasionally near Cajobabo on the south coast. Santiago de Cuba has plenty of beaches from the rivermouth peaks in the Bacomao reserve to Playa Mar Verde in town and will work on SE-S swells from August to November. It's often, weak, onshore junk, driven by the E-SE winds until a proper swell hits, when the south coast can host the most powerful and sizeable surf in Cuba. Urchins are common, the reefs are usually dead coral, but still sharp and sharks are definitely present, although the last of 9 fatalities was 1945. The rest of southern Cuba is very unlikely to receive any reliable surf and is a much better diving destination among the cays and islands.

Considering it's position next to wave-drenched Puerto Rico, the **Dominican Republic** should have a much longer history and established surf culture. It has managed to duck the spotlight and remain relatively low-key until recently, as north coast hotspots are now getting swamped by surfers from the US, Puerto Rico, Europe and a growing local contingent. THE AMBER COAST extends along the central, north-facing part of the island, picking up the constant N-E swells, either wind generated or from North Atlantic frontal and pressure systems. Either way, it's hard to avoid the wind, which blows hard from the NE or E most days from 10am or sometimes even earlier, resulting in towns like Cabarete becoming world-class kite and windsurfing centres.

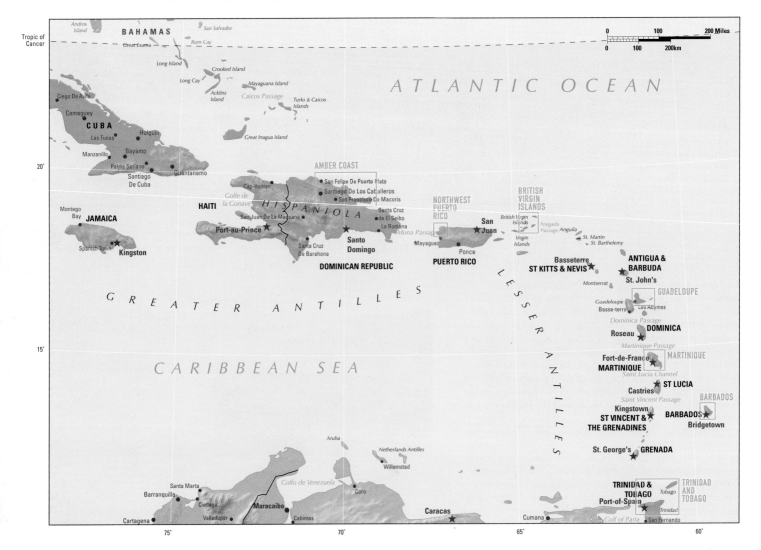

OTHER ISLANDS TO CONSIDER

ZANGLAIS

JS CALLAHAN/SURFEXPLORE

HAITI, HISPANIOLA

Little known as a surf destination and with a long history of social unrest, Haiti is generally off most surfer's lists, but nevertheless, it gets some fun and even challenging waves on its coral fringed north coast. While cruise ships stop at the deep-water anchorage off the sugar sands of Labadee Beach, passengers who have been riding the Flow-Rider onboard could be getting the real thing just around the corner at Haiti's best wave, Ginsu. There is still an element of the unknown about the north and south coasts, plus the cays and islands dotted around, but with no crowd pressure, there's little incentive to stray from the half dozen known spots in the country. Haiti hasn't had a shark fatality for as long as Jamaica.

+ EMPTY LINE-UPS
+ UNDISCOVERED WAVES
+ BEAUTIFUL LANDSCAPES
+ VARIETY OF SPOTS

– ONSHORE WINDS
– POLITICAL INSTABILITY
– DISEASES AND POVERTY
– INTER-ISLAND TRANSPORT

Eastward is the Samana Peninsula with friendly beachbreak at El Coson, Bonita and Nagua, towards the tourist town, La Samana. There's also a high concentration of hotels and resorts in Bavaro near Punta Cana and a few kilometers north is the reliably onshore, sandy peaks of El Macao, where straight N swells can produce short hollow waves plus there's some reef action at Caligula and more beachbreak at Uvero Alto. The south coast is far less consistent, particularly in winter, but more people are scoping the set-ups and new surf shops and schools have set up in the capital Santo Domingo. Close to the city and Las Americas airport is La Boya, the best right on the south coast, peeling over a rocky reef beside the polluted Boca Chica harbour. Lengthy, sucky, tapered walls are clean early in the morning, but it can still be ridden when cross-shore in the NE afternoon breeze, which is better for the left reef, Banzai. Complaints of foul water from harbor and sewage works. It can get busy plus Boca Chica beach attracts hundreds of holiday-makers to drink brown rum and listen to loud Bachata dance music. There's more pollution at the reefbreak peaks of Guibia in downtown Santo Domingo and the reef at 3 Tabacos works in SE swells also. Half an hour southwest of the city is the huge port at Haina and some barreling beachies at Chinchorro and Nigua. Najayo el Ojo and Palenquito are outer reefs in San Cristobal, La Punta is misleadingly a rivermouth left, while rocky Patho is more like a pointbreak as is El Derrumbao, way off near Las Calderas.

To escape the beach crowds, go west to the SW province of Barahona, close to the Haitian border. The mountain range meets the Caribbean in one of the least developed regions of the country, where a scenic coast road slowly winds through thick jungle, and colourful, neat villages beside the turquoise waters of steep pebble beaches. There is not much choice between budget guest-houses

and high-end hotels like Casa Bonita, overlooking Bahoruco, the best wave around. The cobblestone rivermouth peak gets pretty hollow, throwing up occasional tubes on the main left, which is in 26°C/79°F tropical water, but the right heads into the river flow, straight from the mountain at 19°-20°C (66-68°F), which makes for some thermal shock! There are a handful of locals there, mostly riding evenings and there are usually some kids bodysurfing waves at La Cienéga a sandy lefthander or over the pebbles of Los Patos down at Paraiso. No shark fatalities from 3 attacks.

Puerto Rico has so many surf spots it would be impossible to mention them all. For 40 years the surfing world has been well aware of the quality that resides on NORTHWEST PUERTO RICO and names like Gas Chambers and Tres Palmas have become synonymous with challenging, Hawaiian-style waves in the heart of the generally small-surf Caribbean. Judiciously aided by the second deepest ocean trench, just offshore, PR sucks in the lions share of winter ground and summer windswells to all its littoral extent. The north coast deserves its own map and is widely surfed by locals living in the capital, San Juan. There is no shortage of power and plenty of swell - it's just a matter of the wind, which blows some variation of E all year-long. This brought the ASP to the wave-stacked town of Isabella and the fast, chunky rights of Middles where Kelly Slater was crowned champ in 2010 and sadly, marked the passing of Andy Irons. Just down the road, Jobo's played host to another ASP 4 Star pro contest in 2013, reinforcing the fact that this coast has the goods in abundance. With break names like Los Tubos and Hollows, two spots near Arecibo, you know what you are going to get, along with a foot full of urchin spines. There are a bunch more reefs in this area, mostly all shallow, with treacherous rips and usually blown out by 11am. It's not all expert-only reefbreak and one of the main spots in San Juan is La Ocho, a reliable mix of waves for all abilities including a good righthander off a rock that is longboard-able and a left wall called Fiji off the other side. The NE coast is ecologically protected and despite being in the teeth of the trade-winds, has many breaks like Chatarra in Loiza, a dead ringer for Pipeline on those rare W swell, S wind days with the same gladiatorial vibe in the thick crowd. Just down the reef is the more consistent and achievable A-frame, Aviones, but it's also super-crowded. In Loquillo, La Pared is no stress, bumpy beachbreak, while the long walk into La Selva is worth it for punchy, turn-fest walls beside an exposed slab reef. Even the east coast gets great headhigh days when the trades reverse to W-NW. The SE coast has Inches, a coral reef left beside a deep channel and long, loping walls with the odd hollow part on the inside.

The Bahamas blocks off the bulk of the N swell from reaching Cuba, but there are some gaps to the east.

JUAN FERNANDEZ

CUBA

OTHER ISLANDS TO CONSIDER

JAMAICA

The Rasta island is bigger than Puerto Rico, but has far less breaks, receiving far less swell. All the known spots are clustered around the eastern tip of Jamaica on both the north and south coasts to pick up the corresponding NE and SE windswells that arrive in winter and summer respectively. The north coast has waves all the way to Montego Bay, but the trade-winds usually destroy the quality and without them, there's no waves anyway. A hurricane can bring SE and S groundswell to ignite bays and reefs that are usually flat year-round, especially along the southwest coast and the potential to ride junky wind-slop is always there, but generally speaking, stay east. Bad news is 2 shark attacks, 2 fatalities. Good news is no recorded attack since 1922!

+ USER-FRIENDLY WAVES
+ FEW CROWDS
+ WARM WATER
+ BEAUTIFUL SCENERY

– RARELY SURFABLE
– HIGH CRIME RATE
– WINDY
– LACK OF GOOD SURF SPOTS

RONAN GLADU

COPA

Can be long, fun and easy so it gets insanely crowded in summer, when a SE or S swell rumbles in. Also check out Patillas waves La Escuelita and Las Lajas. Dangers in PR are many and varied; the coral or lava reef is always ready for new flesh and the urchins are legion. Jellyfish and sea-lice add to the discomfort, but sharks are too well-fed to be a threat (last fatality 1924). Physical injury is far more likely if you get on the wrong side of the locals – choose your waves, sessions, parking and fights with the utmost care. Traffic can be hell.

THE LESSER ANTILLES

The Virgin Islands guard the northern border of the Leeward Islands and as such, is first to receive the winter NW -NE swells, which are crucial to the recipe for Tortola's west coast diamond, Cane Garden Bay in the BRITISH VIRGIN ISLANDS. Like Puerto Rico, a big N swell wrap and offshore NE-E is required and this can be replicated on the northwestern tips of islands like Jost Van Dyke and the far more accessible Saint Thomas in the **US Virgin Islands**. Hull Bay is the centre of the scene, holding a variety of fun, rolling waves over deeper water reefs, a long way from the beach and the tranquil waters of the yacht moorings, but expect austere wave heights as the 90° NE swell refraction saps plenty of size. There's fast, hollow, shallow waves at Caret Bay, where the locals are notoriously territorial. Over on St John, Trunk Bay holds guillotine lips over far out Johnson's Reef, plus there are a few SE swell options around Reef Bay and a couple of other rare south coast reefs.

Together with Anguilla, the Netherland Antilles islands of **St Martin** and **St Barthelemy** are the nicely placed on the northeastern corner of the Caribbean. The hilly interior is hemmed by 36 white sandy beaches, which fill a 60km (40mi) long strip of bays and coves. Good exposure to N swells and a mixture of sand, rock and coral breaks make these islands a quality Caribbean surf trip, if you can afford it. Both islands receive the usual mix of winter N swells, year-round trade wind E swells and of course some occasional hurricane action, mobilizing some south coast sleepers like Toiny on St Barts. Low consistency is the theme, especially on islands that are shielded by the outer chains and offshore islets and cays, like St Croix, **St Kitts and Nevis**, plus the steep, volcanic coasts of St Eustace, Saba and Monserrat. **Anguilla** is more exposed to swell and would seem to have the perfectly oriented NW coast, but the fringing reef way offshore is probably where the action is for those with a boat. Meads Bay has a left reef down near the dolphinarium and the southeast coast has some left reef set-ups like Junk Hole that may even be cross-shore in the NE trades.

Guadeloupe is the biggest land mass in this central zone and GRANDE TERRE benefits from a deeper offshore valley pointing towards the Atlantic NE swell source. Basse Terre is not as fortunate and NE swells will generally struggle to reach the north and west coasts, but a big due N or those rare W hurricane swells will hit some prime spots. Offshore islets hide some action so check Ilet a Fajou, Caret and Kahouanne, which has a long right and left off the SE tip. The west coast beaches around Deshaies usually look like a lake, otherwise they can be thumping shorepound plus the odd reef corner in a swell. Down on the south coast there's some black sand beachbreak at Trois Rivieres and at Bananier, the most reliable beach. There's more waves up towards Roseaux, but east-facing beaches are rarely clean. The Iles des Saintes and Marie Galante offer some real possibilities for the marine mobile.

A mere 25km south lies the relatively unspoiled island nation of **Dominica**, still cloaked in rainforest and the northernmost boundary of the Windward Islands. Cliffs make access tricky in places, but the 365 rivers cut valleys and build up black sand beaches, adding to the rocky reef inventory that dots the Atlantic coast. Check the mainly right reef of Calibishie up north, or the messy peaks of Pagua Bay beachie that has a few rivermouth paddling channels. Where the Rosalie river hits the coast can hold some shape providing the wind isn't too strong and there are many more potential waves down the east coast, but quality set-ups are few and far between. Scotts Head on the south coast can have waves in summer S swells and E wind is cross-off. The west coast is a very rare bird that gets a bit of swell in winter wrapping round to Portsmouth and a spot behind Ross University, or else it's destructive hurricane swells from the W. Next island south is the French department of MARTINIQUE, where the waves are concentrated on the unusually protruding Caravelle Peninsula, allowing for offshores on a windblown east coast that is freckled with nearshore islets, cays and reefs.

The French and the British battled over mountainous **St Lucia** 14 times, yet the island nation has remained low key as a surf destination. There are plenty of east-facing long sandy beaches that are joined by steep, plunging coastline that rarely provides the right bathymetry, but if the E wind stops blowing there are pocket beaches and rivermouths that may have good banks, like Comerette in the north and Fond d'Or near Dennery. Down south, the kite-friendly sands around Vieux Fort are protected by offshore reefs and the Maria Islands, but it may be worth a look at the reefs to the west of the airport runway. The west coast is usually flat until hurricane swell provides some rights in unlikely bays like Marigot, or a straight N wakes up Windjammer and the far more consistent lefts of Rodney Bay, that handle E winds. The Soufriere volcano erupted twice in the 20th Century, bringing widespread destruction to another French/British melange, **St Vincent**

and the Grenadines. The main island of St Vincent poses the best chance of surf and the buffeted black sand beaches of the east coast are usually rideable but messy and uninviting. Possibly the best spot on St Vincent is a consistent left wall out on the shallow, rocky, coral encrusted reef pass entrance to the Blue Lagoon on the south coast. It's a long paddle from the marina and there are currents to deal with, so once again, those with access to a boat are ahead of the game. The Grenadines is all about sailing between protected anchorages and avoiding the windward side surf which undoubtedly exists; it's just hard to get to. Park Point on Bequia has a left and there are plenty more offshore reefs preventing the surf reaching some of the pristine, ivory sand beaches, a theme that continues on Mustique, Canouan, Mayreau, Palm and the larger, but terminally shadowed Union Island. A W or NW swell would have no such barrier and there must be some good set-ups for those rare days. Over the border into the Grenada governed islands of the Grenadines sees little difference in the geology and outer reefs are the only reliable swell catchers, as seen on the biggest island Carriacou and its satellites, Petit St Vincent and Petit Martinique. The north coast of Caille Island has a proper, long, righthand reef setup that should be cross-offshore in a SE wind, but it is next to the world's most expensive private island. The water deepens off **Grenada** and the barrier reefs become less prevalent, but the long and short east coast beaches still fail to produce any class waves in the face of the trades and getting around the island when a swell is running is hard work on the slow road system. Check the south coast at Prickly Bay for some fast lefts and rights or be lucky enough to score the island's best wave, Cherry Hill, tucked away on the protected west coast. Out on the next oceanic ridge to the east lie the utterly reliable breaks of BARBADOS and the slightly less exposed shores of TRINIDAD AND TOBAGO where classy breaks like Soup Bowl and Mount Irvine keep a large local surfing population well-fed.

BVI is better known as an offshore tax haven than an offshore wave heaven.

GALLEY BAY

BARBUDA AND ANTIGUA

Antigua and Barbuda are renowned as a luxury tourist destination, ideally located on the NE curve of the Leeward Islands. Mostly low-lying, these islands lack the central range of mountains common to much of the Caribbean and the rocky coastline of the two islands has numerous bays, inlets and harbours for the fleets of visiting yachties. The water offshore is shallow, reducing the impact of the swell and cutting the number of surfable spots down to around ten. From Nov-April, winter storms and cold fronts should bring headhigh plus waves to the northwest coast of Antigua, which holds some decent shaped lefts at the more consistent spots like Galley Bay. The windward coasts are almost always blown-out, but receive constant NE-E-SE windswell throughout the year and hurricanes bring epic days to spots that are usually flat. Tides are tiny, so super-shallow is the theme for all the reefs and even the ultra-rare spinning rights of Palmetto Point on Barbuda break over barely covered sandbars, close to shore.

+ PERFECT PALMETTO POINT
+ UNCROWDED CONDITIONS
+ SAILORS PARADISE
+ DELUXE TOURISM SERVICES

– VERY INCONSISTENT
– SHALLOW, UNEVEN CORAL REEFS
– LACK OF LAND ACCESS SPOTS
– EXPENSIVE, NO BUDGET OPTIONS

BRITISH VIRGIN ISLANDS

For more information, check these other Stormrider Surf Guides and/or eBooks.

AMBER COAST, DOMINICAN REP.

+ INDENTED COASTLINE, GOOD REEFS
+ GREAT SURF/WIND/KITE COMBO
+ COMFORTABLE RESORTS
+ CHEAP FOR THE CARIBBEAN

– SHORT SWELL SEASON
– UNFAVOURABLE TRADE WINDS
– ONLY EARLY MORNING OFFSHORES
– SHALLOW, URCHIN INFESTED REEFS

The Dominican Republic is the second largest and most populous country in the Caribbean, occupying the eastern two thirds of the island of Hispaniola, adjacent to Haiti. To the east of the Dominican Republic is the Mona Passage, which separates it from Puerto Rico. Both the Atlantic Ocean to the north and the Caribbean Sea to the south produce rideable surf on an ideally indented coastline. While the Dominican Republic is a mountainous country, golden sandy beaches remain the main tourist attraction, which explains the high concentration of hotels and resorts on the Amber Coast, especially the 65km (41mi) zone between Puerto Plata and Cabarete.

Next to the colonial fort in the tourist hub of Puerto Plata, a channel splits the reefs of **LA PUNTILLA**, offering intense rights and lefts on a head high northerly swell. The city's other option, **COFFEE BREAK** is a reef peak worth checking when it's too small for La Puntilla. Compared to the developed Puerto Plata, Sosua is a real jewel of a beach town with coconut trees lining idyllic beaches. On the biggest northern swells when Encuentro spots start closing-out, peaks will appear in **SOSUA BAY**, groomed by the offshore trades, creating a short, clean, sucky ride that's best going left. Also check La Boca to the southwest. **EL CANAL** is an experts only reef that needs headhigh swell to start breaking and holds double overhead plus cylindrical left walls, as well as a short right over a rocky bottom. Encuentro is the Dominican Republic's surf hotspot with a concentrated variety of waves. **DESTROYERS** is a very shallow, urchin covered reef, holding fast, round lefts in N-NE swells up to 8ft (2.5m). **LA IZQIERDA** is a similar left with plenty of push and barrel sections in the same conditions, but both are very exposed to the wind. **LA DERECHA** is the most consistent and user friendly wave in Encuentro with long, walling rights in deep water good for both beginners and shredders. Same applies to **BOBO'S** rights and lefts which are a bit faster, but well covered and easy to get into. The treacherous peak at **COCO PIPE** is always less crowded since only experts can handle the heavy drop, barrel, get out quick sequence that the better rights demand. The whole Encuentro stretch usually gets blown-out by 10am in summer trades, yet winter can have plenty of glassy days. The large **KITE BEACH** hosts an outer reef A-frame that is a long paddle and handles the biggest 15ft (5m) N-NE swells. The rights are best and it's never crowded until the kiteboarders appear around midday, flying all the way down through Cabarete Bay, an official stop on the Kitesurfing World Tour. The strong winds will blow out any surf, but clean early morning sessions are common. Beyond Punta Goleta is **BOZO BEACH** a thumping, fast, experts only shorebreak that pits and spits, keeping bodyboarders and shut-down tube hunters happy. Just opposite the **POLICE STATION**, there's more sandy reefbreak that seems to line-up better in an E swell. Both **LA BOMBA** (opposite an old gas station) and **MANANERO** are curvaceous beachbreaks along an extensive playa leading down to the La Boca rivermouth kite spot and providing there is little wind, short barrels are plentiful amongst the shifting peaks. East of Rio San Juan, rights peel down a reef in front of the main entrance to the **PLAYA GRANDE** on N swell. Around the corner and a long paddle against the sweeping current, **LA PRECIOSA** peak is known to get picture perfect, especially going left. Needs more size than Encuentro, but gets real good in a due N without the same crowd factor. Tucked into the next bay east, the wreck of **EL BARCO** helps another A-frame reef sculpt some speedy rights in N-NE swells and it will handle a bit of E-SE wind. Even better protected is the experts only pointbreak **LA MUELA** that doesn't start breaking until it is overhead, but will hold shape as big as it gets, rumbling down the point with power and purpose.

OBDULIO LUNA

ENCUENTRO

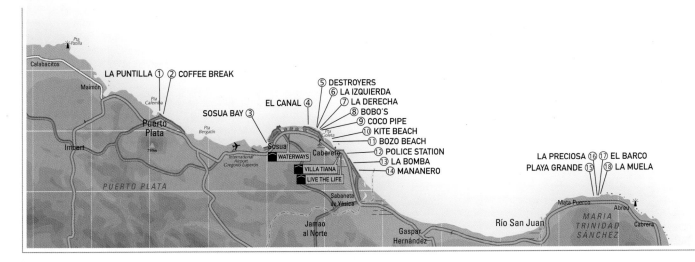

LA PUNTILLA ① ② COFFEE BREAK

⑤ DESTROYERS
⑥ LA IZQIERDA
EL CANAL ④ ⑦ LA DERECHA
SOSUA BAY ③ ⑧ BOBO'S
⑨ COCO PIPE
⑩ KITE BEACH
⑪ BOZO BEACH
⑫ POLICE STATION
⑬ LA BOMBA
⑭ MANANERO

LA PRECIOSA ⑯ ⑰ EL BARCO
PLAYA GRANDE ⑮ ⑱ LA MUELA

COCO PIPE

OBDULIO LUNA

SWELL AND WIND

The north shore, referred to as "La Costa" by the locals, receives consistent North Atlantic swells between November and March. N swells are perfect for the Amber Coast, arriving from lows located off Florida, usually tracking NE towards Europe. These 2-15ft (0.6-5m) waves hit the exposed northern coastline and the major breaks receive up to 15ft (5m) a couple of times a year. Early winter (November and December) is usually good despite rain making surfing less pleasant. Then the rains diminish, but the trade winds will pick-up from mid-January. Prevailing winds are E/NE all year-round, getting super strong in winter and only a few spots around Sosua will remain offshore all day, so surf early in the morning before the trades kick in. The Caribbean cyclonic swells only produce waves for the south coast of the Dominican Republic, where many spots will fire through the summer months. Tidal range remains micro, ie; under 0.6m (2ft). ●

SPOT INFORMATION

SPOT	SIZE	BTM	TYPE
1	8/4		
2	6/3		
3	10/4		
4	15/3		
5	8/3		
6	6/3		
7	10/2		
8	8/2		
9	10/3		
10	6/3		
11	8/3		
12	8/3		
13	8/3		
14	6/2		
15	10/3		
16	10/2		
17	10/4		
18	6/6		

SURF STATS

		J	F	M	A	M	J	J	A	S	O	N	D
SWELL	Dominant swell												
	Size (m)	3-4		3		1-2		1		3		3-4	
	Consistency (%)	80		65		30		30		60		75	
WIND	Dominant wind												
	Average force	F4		F4		F4		F4		F4		F4	
	Consistency (%)	79		76		89		81		84		79	
TEMP.	Wetsuit												
	Water temp.	25		26		27		28		28		27	

PLAYA GRANDE

OBDULIO LUNA

TRAVEL INFORMATION

LOCAL POPULATION:	COASTLINE: 1.288km (805mi)
320,000 – Puerto Plata	TIME ZONE: GMT -4h

GETTING THERE – Most visitors are required to purchase a tourist card ($10). It's best to fly directly into Puerto Plata's International Airport (POP), only 10km (6mi) away from Cabarete by minibus. Santo Domingo airport (SDQ) is 4.5h away by bus (Caribe Tours and Metro $8). Cheap flights from Europe and the USA (Condor, Jetairfly and Jet Blue, etc).

GETTING AROUND – The main roads are in good condition and a well-maintained, two-lane highway follows the north coast. Rent a car for $50/d or a motorbike for $15/day. Be aware that reckless driving is the norm and that traffic police may be open to corruption. Public transportation system is extensive with long distance bus operators and cheap "publicós" buses as well as "moto conchos" bikes within cities.

LODGING AND FOOD – There are various resorts scattered along the north coast between Sosua and Cabarete. Hooked Cabarete have apartments from $25/n behind the beach at Encuentro and offers rentals, guided tours and lessons. Cabarete Surfcamp offers budget cottage rooms (fr $15/n) to luxury two bed apartments ($100/n). More upmarket Villa Tiana boutique hotel in Cabarete has rooms starting at $97/n. Waterways offers packages with DR Surf Tours fr $125/n. Dominican dishes come with brown beans (habichuelas) and rice. Presidente is the local beer and the local Brugal rum is cheap and cheerful.

WEATHER – The Dominican Republic has a semi-tropical climate, tempered by prevailing easterly winds. The so-called "cool" season (November to March) is pleasantly warm with low humidity and a few days rain each month. On the coast, the temperature hovers fairly constantly around 29°C (84°F) during the day and drops to around a comfortable 20°C (68°F) at night. During the summer months, temperatures range between 28°C-35°C (60-95°F). The highlands are considerably cooler. June to September is the hurricane season, but chances of seeing one blowing through are minimal.

WEATHER

WEATHER	J/F	M/A	M/J	J/A	S/O	N/D
Total Rainfall (mm)	170	140	90	75	110	280
Consistency (d/m)	11	10	8	7	9	14
Temperature min. (°C)	21	22	24	25	24	22
Temperature max. (°C)	27	27	29	30	30	28

NATURE AND CULTURE – Cabarete is a busy town with bars, restaurants and nightclubs spinning Caribbean and American music. Take a trip to Playa Grande for fish meals on the beach and check Lake Dudu's tarzan swing and 10m cliff jump. Visit the beautiful island of Cayo Lavandado, in the Bay of Samana or travel through the highest mountain chain in the Caribbean. West of Puerto Plata, Damajagua has 27 waterfalls. Kitesurfing conditions are world-class in Cabarete.

HAZARDS AND HASSLES – Most locals are friendly and open when shown respect. Urchins cover many reefs, so bring booties (surf schools supply them). Most areas are quite safe, although Sosua's nightlife can lean towards the seedy.

HANDY HINTS – In Cabarete, there's a big surf shop (Carib Bic Centre) with leashes, wax, boardshorts, lycras and so on, but only a small selection of surfboards. At Encuentro you can find several surf schools with good board rentals and lessons. Buena Honda Surf School organises daily transfers from Cabarete to Encuentro and has a selection of good boards from $20 and lessons from $35. The peso is the national currency, but many businesses prefer US$.

NORTHWEST PUERTO RICO

+ CONSISTENTLY OFFSHORE
+ QUALITY POINTBREAKS
+ WARM, POWERFUL WAVES
+ EASY ACCESS
+ GREAT WEATHER

– WINDY
– HEAVY CROWDS AND LOCALS
– LOTS OF TOURISTS
– CAR CRIME
– POLLUTION PROBLEMS

Puerto Rico is to Florida what Hawaii is to California. It gets big, it's exotic, and it has fierce locals. Located in what is regarded as the best corner of the Caribbean for surf, Puerto Rico's premier surf spots are found on the northwest coast of the island. The eastern or windward side is blocked by the Virgin Islands, the south coast only breaks on rare hurricane swells while the north coast is consistent, but often onshore and right next to the capital, San Juan. A deep-water trench offshore (the second deepest in the world) means N-NE swells hit the north shore with little loss in size and power. Although the waves can get very big the average winter conditions are around 4- 6ft (1.2-2m). Most spots break on slab reefs of coral and lava.

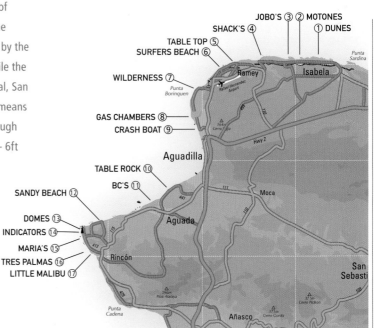

Since the '60s, surfing in Puerto Rico has traditionally centred around Rincon and today the area gets extremely busy. The standard of local surfing is high and the crowds have led most surf travellers to seek quieter spots further to the north, around Isabela. **DUNES** has many quality, wind-exposed reefs that are usually crowd-free. Playa **MOTONES** is a consistent, hollow wave - always worth a look and gets a bit of wind protection from the point. **JOBO'S** is a long right breaking onto a sand-covered reef plus a left and more peaks down the beach. Works best on small swells and gets

SURVIVAL

BERNARD TESTEMALE

GAS CHAMBERS

LAT: 18.461600°   LONG: -67.168027°

Uber-barreling right when the NW swell hits this outstanding line of sand-covered reef. The name alludes to the power and ferocity of the tube, but few have the skills to negotiate the frothing crowd, flying drop and full speed sprint to daylight. Only levitates when a decent W-NW materializes so it's super-low consistency and safer when it gets bigger. At high tide, waves bounce back off the cliff, adding an evil backwash to the already square shaped pits. It's always offshore and an easy park and paddle-out, but be very sure of your abilities.

a hassley crowd. **SHACK'S** is considered a windsurfing spot because of the consistent cross-shore conditions, but on windless days it is a well-shaped reefbreak. Watch out for the jagged coral heads. **TABLE TOP** is a heavy wave, also exposed to the wind with dangerous coral/rocks on the inside. Same goes for the adjacent Backdoor/Survival peak. **SURFERS BEACH** is a consistent, accessible reef peak on the Ramey Air Force Base, and ranges from fun shoulders to punchy barrels, but the rips, urchins, crowds and pollution are an issue. Most NW coast reefs are set up for rights in big wrapping NE swells, but often the lefts at **WILDERNESS** are more bowly. Spreads the crowd from Ruins down the reef. Holds huge faces over nasty reef, rips are strong, as is the local vibe. Aguadilla spots are only worth checking on big NW-NE swells when GAS CHAMBERS dishes out square, warp-speed barrels a dozen times a year. Crazed experts only have to deal with the drop, backwash, crowds and salivating locals, but the rewards are crack-high. **CRASH BOAT** is just on the south side of the jetty where wedgy rights line-up over the sandy reef bottom. Higher tides and decent swell needed. Lots of aggressive local bodyboarders. NW-facing Aguada area offers consistent waves at spots like **TABLE ROCK**, a righthand barrel that fizzes over an urchin covered reef and is another experts only spot. More consistent reef and sand peaks break

at **BC'S** in Aguada town. Sandy Beach lines-up a good left off the rocks plus there's some beachbreak in the area (Pools) that may suit beginner/improvers. Rincon is the surfing epicentre and **DOMES** is the first point to bend long rights onto its lava rock bottom. It's offshore in the trades, picks up the most swell (although it doesn't handle huge) and is often the only show in town, so crowds fight over the sectiony walls and odd left that bounces around in the small bay. Next point down is **INDICATORS**, a nasty stretch of shallow reef that tests the skills of those good enough to take it on. Exposed rocks, urchins and punishing paddle-outs, but no crowds compared to The Point at Domes or **MARIAS**, further down the reef. Marias draws the hordes

SPOT INFORMATION

SPOT	SIZE	BTM	TYPE
1			
2			
3			
4			
5			
6			
7			
8			
9			
10			
11			
12			
13			
14			
15			
16			
17			

STEVE FITZPATRICK

TABLE ROCK

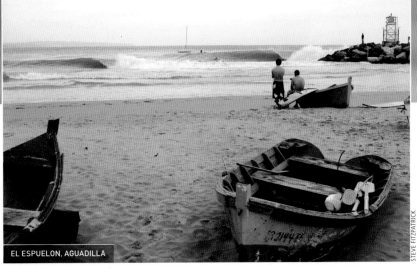

EL ESPUELON, AGUADILLA

STEVE FITZPATRICK

on all types of watercraft to a stretch of kinder reef that grooms the N swells into down the line walls perfect for high performance surfing. NW swell and lower tides will produce hollower waves. TRES PALMAS is Puerto Rico's big wave testing ground and can hold waves up to 20ft (6m) when a really big winter NW swell hits. Tough drops into the trade-wind offshores lead to wailing walls, coveted by the local chargers, but beware of wide sneaker sets. Tucked into a bay is **LITTLE MALIBU**, which has small, fast, tubey rights over a shallow, fire coral reef. Half the size of Rincon breaks and packed with local bodyboarders who don't have to worry about losing fins.

STEVE FITZPATRICK

TRES PALMAS

LAT: 18.347743° LONG: -67.269200°

Puerto Rico's big wave testing ground, which needs a really big winter swell, preferably from the NW to get going. The last stop on the unbroken reef that starts up at Domes is boosted by a submarine canyon that focuses and magnifies the swell. A gun will help overcome the chop hops down the face then wide open, rumbling walls provide a large canvas for large turns. Rips and sneaker sets keep the crowd to manageable levels and only a few will make it out when it is properly firing, which is hardly ever!

TRAVEL INFORMATION

LOCAL POPULATION:
San Juan – 1.6M

COASTLINE: 501km (313mi)
TIME ZONE: GMT -4h

GETTING THERE – Puerto Rico is the most accessible island in the Caribbean. Visas are not necessary for most visitors because it is an US territory. There are regular flights to San Juan from the East Coast US, London, Madrid and other Caribbean islands. It's also possible to fly from New York direct to Ramey Base. This will cut two hours of driving from San Juan.

GETTING AROUND – Local airlines don't take surfboards. Rental cars cost around $30/d for the cheapest model and are often targeted by thieves. The traffic gets hectic and the roads are dangerous. Fuel is cheap at 30¢/l. Use cheap 'publicos' (buses) for town to town travel.

LODGING AND FOOD – The best surf season is also the main tourist season and this means higher prices. However, compared to other Caribbean islands, it is quite cheap. Quality accommodation options include La Cima in Isabella, ($60/d), Cielo Mar in Aguadilla, ($55/d), or Surf & Board Surfari in Rincón, ($45/sgle/d). A good meal can be had for $15.

WEATHER – Puerto Rico has an idyllic tropical climate, with winter highs of around 24°C (75°F) and night-time lows that never drop under 15°C (58°F) at the coast. It rains a lot, especially in the mountains and in Sept-Oct. On the coast there is no distinct wet and dry season. From June-Oct strong hurricanes occasionally hit the island and can cause considerable damage. Most of the time you will be fine surfing in board shorts, but a shorty may be needed for early, windy sessions.

WEATHER – Calais	J/F	M/A	M/J	J/A	S/O	N/D
Total Rainfall (mm)	65	75	132	137	150	127
Consistency (d/m)	13	10	13	16	15	16
Temperature min. (°C)	21	22	23	24	24	22
Temperature max. (°C)	28	29	31	31	31	30

NATURE AND CULTURE – Very American colonial feel to it, like Hawai'i. Great windsurfing and diving. On land there's the El Faro maritime museum or the Arecibo Observatory. San Juan is the second oldest city in the Americas - El Morro is the place to go if you want to check the historic old town. There's good hiking in the El Yunque rainforest national park. The nightlife is very lively.

HAZARDS AND HASSLES – Shallow reefs, urchins and some very crowded spots. Localism can be extreme. Car theft is a definite concern. Sewage can be serious around the major cities. There is a high crime rate and lots of guns.

HANDY HINTS – There are plenty of surf shops selling quality equipment cheaply. Try Ramey Surfzone, West Coast and Hot Wavz in Rincon. Wear sunblock in the water and mosquito repellent in the evenings.

SWELL AND WIND

Cold fronts coming off the US East Coast send N swells down towards Puerto Rico. These give waves from 2-15ft (0.5-5m) on the N and NW shores of the island, occasionally reaching 15-20ft (5-6m). The swells wrap onto the W coast giving clean, offshore conditions. E wind swells and occasional hurricanes in the Caribbean will produce waves in other parts of the island, but the NW tip is by far the most consistent. The wind blows predominantly from the E, varying from 46% of the time in Dec to 71% in July. A NE wind is the winter standard, and SE is most common in the summer. The NE wind easily blows out the island's north shore, although not the west coast. Tidal ranges are minimal, but will affect many of the shallowest reefs. Tide charts are available in surf shops. ●

SURF STATS	J	F	M	A	M	J	J	A	S	O	N	D
SWELL Dominant swell												
Size (m)	4-5		3-4		2		1-2		4		4-5	
Consistency (%)	80		65		40		30		70		80	
WIND Dominant wind												
Average force	F4		F4		F4		F4		F4		F4	
Consistency	79		76		83		96		90		78	
TEMP. Wetsuit												
Water temp.	25		26		27		28		28		27	

BRITISH VIRGIN ISLANDS

+ WORLD-CLASS CANE GARDEN BAY
+ CONSISTENT BEACHBREAKS
+ SAFE TROPICAL DESTINATION

– SHORT SWELL SEASON
– LACK OF CONSISTENT REEFS
– BOAT ACCESS ONLY BREAKS
– EXPENSIVE

Tortola is the largest of these islands and the BVI capital, thanks to an important yacht harbour in Road Town. The north shore of the island is dotted with a series of bays and beaches offering a good diversity of surfing locations. The western end is trade protected and cradles one the Caribbean's sparkling gems, namely Cane Garden Bay.

CAPOON'S BAY, aka Little Apple Bay, holds a perfectly symmetrical A-frame reef that should provide a buzz, as does the mushroom tea sometimes served at Bomba Shack, just in front of the break. While getting high is not everyone's cup of tea, a user-friendly, walling wave that can handle big swells and remain unaffected by the trades, most definitely is! Assorted reef and beach peaks can be found on either side of main peak and around the corner at Long Bay, which caters for all abilities. As good as Capoon's Reef may be, the title of 'world-class wave' in this area goes to CANE GARDEN BAY. The west-facing, right pointbreak will only fire on the biggest swells of the year, but when it's on, tubular walls will peel against the hill for rides reaching several hundred metres. It would have been hard to keep such a wave a secret, especially knowing that the beach facing the break is one of the most popular on Tortola. A surf magazine cover shot a few years back drew international

surfers to the place and many US East Coasters and Puerto Ricans now have the place dialled and will plan short hops to Tortola as soon as they see a major swell on the way. It will occasionally get big, and some sections break in just a couple of feet of water over

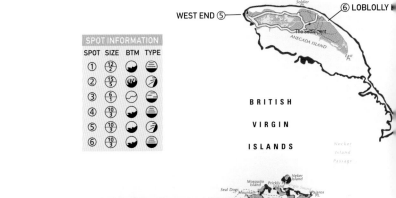

CANE GARDEN BAY

LAT: 18.432199°   LONG: -64.664546°

Picture-perfect Caribbean dream wave that peels alluringly into the sunset-facing bay that is usually a haunt for charter yachts. Appearances can be deceptive as the throaty barrels at the tip of the point hit the numerous coral heads, then race down the line to the inside bowl section, before shouldering off into deep water. There are no easy ones and since it only breaks maybe 20-30 days a year, the locals are as hungry as the Gillette coral. Any NE-E wind is offshore (SE messes it up) and tide isn't a problem, rather it's timing a NW-NE swell that is big enough to make the hairpin journey around the island to the bay. Due E swell has its power sapped by Anegada. Threat of wave-killing breakwall to protect ill-conceived fuel dock ongoing.

CAPOON'S BAY

ALEX DICK-READ

a particularly hungry reef. **JOSIAH'S BAY** is the most consistent beachbreak and unlike Cane Garden, this beach is slightly off the beaten track, attracting more cows than sunbathers. The quality of the wave depends on the shape of the sandbanks, but there's always something to ride on a small day, including a long right, ideally suited for longboarding. Another advantage is that it can hold loads of surfers but unfortunately it stinks when the swell gets overhead. There are more waves on the island, including powerful beachies in remote, roadless locations. Finding them would require boating along the coast or making friends in the small, local surfing community. There are a couple of surf spots on mountainous Virgin Gorda, the island known for its massive boulders. **YACHT HARBORS** reef is worth checking on a large NW swell, it's a tubular A-frame with longer rides to be had on the rights. Other islands and islets have surfing potential, but just aren't reliable enough to be considered proper spots. The east-facing shores of the islands SW of Virgin Gorda are known to receive rideable waves from the occasional summer hurricane swells. Anegada is completely different from all the other British Virgin Islands in that this coral island's highest point is only 10m (30ft) above sea level, in fact the whole island looks just like a giant beach. The surrounding reef is a popular diving area and wide exposure to the wind probably makes it better for sailboarding. **WEST END** is actually a great windsurf spot, but if the wind drops or goes south, a long righthand pointbreak will reveal itself. It can either be a mellow, cruisey wave or turn heavy with huge rips. Another option on the island is **LOBLOLLY BAY**, which is usually onshore since it faces east, but it picks up a maximum of swell. This spot is very remote and it's a long paddle to the peak. On a windless day, there will be a long, relaxed left and a much more intense and hollow right.

SWELL AND WIND

Surf season in the British Virgin Islands is roughly between November and March when winter lows leave the US East Coast before tracking NE towards Europe. They send 2-10ft (0.6-3m) surf on the exposed shores with occasional 12ft+ (4m+) faces at Cane Garden. The season

SURF STATS		J	F	M	A	M	J	J	A	S	O	N	D
SWELL	Dominant swell												
	Size (m)	4		3		1-2		2		3-4		4	
	Consistency (%)	80		60		30		30		60		70	
WIND	Dominant wind												
	Average force	F4		F4		F4		F4		F4		F4	
	Consistency	80		77		85		97		89		76	
TEMP.	Wetsuit												
	Water temp.	25		25		26		27		28		26	

TRAVEL INFORMATION

LOCAL POPULATION:	COASTLINE: 80km (50mi)
Tortola – 23,908	TIME ZONE: GMT -4h

GETTING THERE – Most nationals do not require a visa. There are no direct flights from either North America or Europe. Cape Air and Seabourne fly through Puerto Rico (SJU), but can't carry boards. Leat fly from Antigua (ANU) and St Martin (SXM). Best route is AA or Jet Blue from US to the US Virgin Islands (STT). From there don't take an inter-island flight to Tortola (EIS); instead use the ferry service from St Thomas USVI (1h, $60 r/t). There's a $20 air tax and $5/7 sea dep tax.

GETTING AROUND – Tortola's bus service is unpredictable and taxis are expensive. Rent a little 4x4 (fr. $50/d). Dede's car rental is a favourite among surfers. Fly BVI has flights to Virgin Gorda & Anegada ($60r/t). Ferries island hop to Virgin Gorda ($20) and Jost Van Dyke. If it's within budget, the best way to get around remains a chartered sailboat.

LODGING AND FOOD – The BVI are not a cheap getaway destination; food is pricey and accommodation's in short supply. Most visitors sleep on their chartered yachts. On land the only budget option is Brewer's Bay campground at $15/night. Starting at $110/dble in season, Sebastian's is a middle price hotel and is right on the beach in Little Apple Bay. Sites like Airbnb can hook you into cheaper local rooms for rent.

WEATHER – Because of their position within the trade wind belt, the islands have a balmy, tropical climate. The blazing sun is usually tempered by the constant ocean breezes. Summer is humid with temperatures over 30°C (86°F), winter is slightly cooler. The temperatures drop by 5°C (9°F) at night. Average water temperatures remain around 26°C (79°F) year-round. The total rainfall is quite low and even in the rainy season, starting in late summer and ending just before Christmas, the islands receive less than 5 rainy days a month. Like most semi-tropical and tropical locations, the BVI is in a hurricane zone; watch out between June and November. For all these reasons, the surf season is also the ideal time to visit, especially after Christmas.

WEATHER	J/F	M/A	M/J	J/A	S/O	N/D
Total Rainfall (mm)	40	60	85	85	110	100
Consistency (d/m)	4	3	4	5	5	6
Temperature min. (°C)	22	23	25	25	24	23
Temperature max. (°C)	28	29	30	31	30	29

NATURE AND CULTURE – Cruise the islands on a yacht or on a kayak depending on your budget. Top diving spots include the sunken RMS Rhone, off Salt Island and Horseshoe Reef (Anegada). Good snorkeling in Smugglers Cove. Check out the Baths on Virgin Gorda, a network of giant granite boulders located along the seashore.

HAZARDS AND HASSLES – Skin threats include sunburn, fire coral, urchins and jellyfish. Sharks abound but risks are low. Locals are friendly, but should be respected. Weird things happen during the (in)famous Bomba Shack "full moon parties" in Apple Bay.

HANDY HINTS – Take usual shortboard or longboard plus a semi-gun for big Cane days. Cane Garden Bay Surfboards has a hard core surf shop in Road Town, with boards made by veteran Huntington Beach/Cocoa Beach shaper and BVI resident, Bob Carson. Rental boards and lessons from Jamaican legend Icah Wilmot available at Surf School BVI, Josiah's Bay.

may go on till May but the frequency of swells is then considerably reduced. The E windswell and the occasional hurricane swells will provide summertime surf on the SE exposed shores, but long flat spells are way too common to plan a surf trip at this time of the year. The wind dominance is E year-round with more NE winds between November and March. Surf early or right after storms. The tidal range is minimal, hovering around 30cm. ●

GUADELOUPE

+ CONSISTENT WINDSWELLS   – SLOPPY ONSHORE WAVES
+ LONG WEST COAST RIGHTS   – SCHOOL CROWDS
+ SMALL, EASY WAVES   – TOURIST DEVELOPMENT
+ LAID BACK ATMOSPHERE   – PRICEY

Together with Barbados, Guadeloupe is one of the east Caribbean's most consistent surf destinations. As well as regular trade wind swell it also receives N swell produced by cold fronts moving off the US East Coast in winter. Like Barbados the waves are often windy and rarely get bigger than 8ft (2.5m). French-governed Guadeloupe consists of two main islands, Grande Terre and Basse Terre, joined in the middle, which viewed from above, reveals a butterfly shape. Guadeloupe feels very French, although it has its own unique 'Creole' style. Locals are generally proud to be both French and Guadeloupian. Grande Terre has the majority of the surf spots while Basse Terre only gets surf from S and W hurricane swells. There are also the exposed islands of Marie Galante and La Désirade offshore, which have good potential for explorers.

Facing NE on the crescent-shaped coastline of Grande Terre, LE MOULE is the main surfers' hangout. Good exposure to N-E swells, it's the most consistent and crowded wave around. Normally this reef works as a 2-4ft (0.6-1.2m) onshore left with a juicy take-off right in front of the car park plus there is a rideable beachbreak nearby. Watch out for rocks and urchins when getting in and out of the water at Le Moule. Heading east is a set of dangerous, expert only outside reefs that include LA STATION and CAILLE DEHORS, while ALIZÉ is an easy, fun, protected cove nearby. ANSE SALABOUELLE (a la Bouelle) is a quality stretch of reef where snappy lefts and walled rights pick up all E swells and the locals are always on it. A keyhole leads to ANSE À LA GOURDE'S structured rights off a protruding rock, that are fun when small, challenging when the swell gets big. The tip of the peninsula at POINTE DES CHATEAUX has messy onshore lefts that are suited to improvers. Summer SE swells will light up LA CHAISE, a fast left with a bit of E wind protection. The developed southern shore surf spots are inconsistent, crowded and often onshore in the SE swell/wind pattern. PORT ST-FRANÇOIS is generally sloppy beach/reefbreak and the lagoon is popular with kiters. There are more reefs on the way to LA CARAVELLE in St Anne, where consistent, shallow lefts need more tide to avoid the coral and urchins next to Club Med. The left at PETIT HAVRE is quality, attracting plenty of surfers from the capital, looking for ledgy barrels and some NE-E wind protection. There's plenty of wind and swell protection for beginners and kids at HOTEL NOVOTEL, while experts can search for some juice on Gosier island. The northwest coast is almost always offshore, but a moderate-sized N-NE groundswell is essential. PORT-LOUIS boasts the best wave on the island – a peak with long, playful, tapering right walls and a shorter left. Further up the reef is Pointe Antigues, which needs even more size, but they can link up into a super-long right. ANSE BERTRAND has a choice of walled-up, easy peaks, plus an excellent outside reef called Plombier. Anse Laborde is worth a check, but heading back to Le Moule from Pointe de la Grande Vigie, high cliffs make the few spots boat access only.

LE MOULE

PORT-LOUIS

ALL PHOTOS PIERRE DE CHAMPS

ANSE SALABOUELLE

SWELL AND WIND

The main swell season is from late October to March, with 2-10ft (0.6-3m) N-NE groundswells and consistent 2-5ft (0.6-1.5m) E windswells. Onshore trade wind swell occurs year-round, but it will usually be small. Dominant E trades vary from 44% of the time in November to 70% in July. It tends to have a slightly more frequent NE pattern than SE, except during May-June and Sept-Oct. This is unfortunate as SE winds produce more offshores at the north-facing spots. The hurricane season (June-Oct) offers a better chance to surf spots exposed to the Caribbean Sea, but at this time of year there is no regular groundswell. There is little tidal variation. ●

SURF STATS		J F	M A	M J	J A S	O N D
SWELL	Dominant swell	◐	◐	◑	◐	◐	◐
	Size (m)	4	3	1-2	2	3-4	4
	Consistency (%)	70	60	40	40	60	70
WIND	Dominant wind	◔	◖	◗	◑	◔	◔
	Average force	F4	F4	F4	F4	F4	F4
	Consistency	80	77	85	97	89	76
TEMP.	Wetsuit	🩳	🩳	🩳	🩳	🩳	🩳
	Water temp.	25	25	27	28	28	26

TRAVEL INFORMATION

LOCAL POPULATION: Pointe-à-Pitre – 405,500	COASTLINE: 260km (162mi) TIME ZONE: GMT -4h

GETTING THERE – Visa: Same as France. Europeans can take Air France or a cheap charter flight from France. There are also flights from several American cities, Puerto Rico and nearby islands (Antigua - LIAT; boardbag $80 o/w). Ferry service from Dominica (2h) and Martinique (4h).

GETTING AROUND – There's a good public transport system, but most spots require an expensive rental car ($50/d). The road system is well maintained but the east coast lacks paved roads. Driving can be a bit crazy - use the horn! Le Moule is the best place to base yourself.

LODGING AND FOOD – Most of the hotels are on the south shore. If you can't stay in Le Moule, try St. François (Allamanda fr $260/p/7n; Sunset Surf Camp fr $470/7n) or Sainte-Anne (tropicalsurfcamp.com $520/7n). Creole cuisine is very tasty - try ti-punch, the local drink. A meal will cost around $25.

WEATHER – Like most tropical islands, the climate varies according to exposure to the trades. Grande Terre is the windward side of Guadeloupe, but being mainly flat it doesn't attract many rain squalls from out at sea. Most of the rain falls over the higher side, Basse Terre. The wettest season starts in June and sometimes lasts until December, with heaviest rains possible during the hurricane season of June-October. Temperatures remain around 26°C (79°F) all year with little variation.

WEATHER	J/F	M/A	M/J	J/A	S/O	N/D
Total Rainfall (mm)	75	95	152	197	245	175
Consistency (d/m)	13	11	14	17	18	17
Temperature min. (°C)	19	20	22	23	22	20
Temperature max. (°C)	28	29	30	31	31	30

NATURE AND CULTURE – Apart from visiting spice markets or sailing, Basse Terre offers enjoyable trekking around La Soufrière volcano. Diving is best at Îlets Pigeon, on the Caribbean side. There are mangrove swamps between the two islands.

HAZARDS AND HASSLES – Many of the spots break on limestone or coral, often in shallow water, so watch out for reef cuts. Some spots have many urchins. Avoid hurricane season because Guadeloupe is right in their path and the surf is usually small at this time of year.

HANDY HINTS – Gear is expensive but available at Tong. Lookasurf (Sainte-Anne) and other wind/kite crossover shops. There is a surf school in Le Moule and all the camps do lessons. There are lots of bodyboarders. The population is made up of local Guadeloupe and French expats. French is the official language though most locals speak Creole.

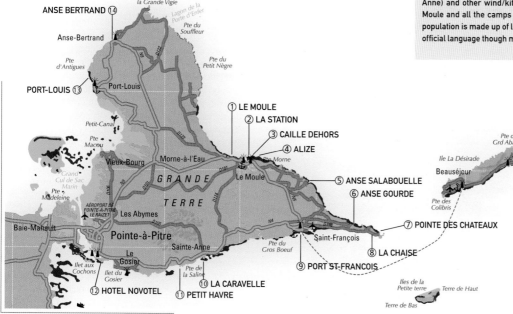

SPOT INFORMATION			
SPOT	SIZE	BTM	TYPE
①	8/3	◕	⬲
②	10/4	◕	⬲
③	15/4	◕	⬲
④	8/3	◕	⬲
⑤	8/3	◕	⬲
⑥	10/4	◕	⬲
⑦	8/3	◕	⬲
⑧	8/3	◕	⬲
⑨	8/3	◕	⬲
⑩	8/3	◕	⬲
⑪	8/3	◕	⬲
⑫	4/1	◕	⬲
⑬	10/3	◕	⬲
⑭	8/3	◕	⬲

Map labels:

ANSE BERTRAND ⑭
Anse-Bertrand
Pte de la Grande Vigie
Lagon de la Porte d'Enfer
Pte du Souffleur
Pte d'Antigues
Pte du Petit Nègre
PORT-LOUIS ⑬   Port-Louis
Petit-Canal
Pte Macou
① LE MOULE
② LA STATION
③ CAILLE DEHORS
④ ALIZE
Pte Morne
Vieux-Bourg
Morne-à-l'Eau
Le Moule
GRANDE TERRE
⑤ ANSE SALABOUELLE
⑥ ANSE GOURDE
Pte du Grd Abaque
Ile La Désirade
Beauséjour
Pte des Colibris
⑦ POINTE DES CHATEAUX
Grand Cul de Sac Marin
Pte Madeleine
AÉROPORT DE POINTE-À-PITRE LE RAIZET
Les Abymes
Baie-Mahault
Pointe-à-Pitre
N4
Saint-François
⑧ LA CHAISE
⑨ PORT ST-FRANCOIS
Sainte-Anne
Pte du Gros Boeuf
Le Gosier
Ilet aux Cochons
Ilet du Gosier
Pte de la Saline
⑩ LA CARAVELLE
⑫ HOTEL NOVOTEL
⑪ PETIT HAVRE
Iles de la Petite terre
Terre de Haut
Terre de Bas

MARTINIQUE

+ GOOD RIGHT REEF SET-UPS   − SEASONAL NORTH SWELLS
+ CONSISTENT TARTANE BREAKS   − ONSHORE TRADE WINDS
+ SAFE TOURIST HAVEN   − SOME CROWDED SPOTS

PLAGE DES SURFEURS

BLISS/SURF-MARTINIQUE.COM

Martinique lies in the heart of the Caribbean Archipelago as one of the many islands making up the group of Lesser Antilles, or "Windward Islands." The land rises gradually from the coast towards the centre and northern parts of the island, where the peaks of the Carbet and the Mont Pelée dormant volcanoes can be found. The southern shores are highly regarded by tourists seeking picture perfect beaches, leaving surfers to focus on the northern and eastern coastline, ideally exposed to winter's North Atlantic swell. Volcanic and coral reefs pepper the island plus the southern beaches provide a summer swell bodyboard option.

Close to the fishing village of Le Prêcheur, **TOMATE** is a long and easy right that breaks over sand and reef, predominantly during the winter northerly swells. **CÉRON** also needs a sizeable N swell, is a bit shorter but packs more punch as it ends in a shorebreak on a beautiful black sand beach. Whilst being good waves, they are but mere shadows of neighboring **ANSE COULEUVRE**, possibly the best

wave on the island. These long, tubular rights start with an easy take-off, but the walls are fast and powerful, before the wave ends over coral and urchins. Skills are required to ride this inconsistent, wind-protected beauty. Located at the northern tip of the island, Grand-Rivière hosts two quality breaks. **BAGASSE**'s powerful, barrelling rights and lefts will attract tube seekers while **CHARLOT** reefbreaks will cater to those looking for longer rides. The rights of **BASSE-POINTE** break directly into the port and getting in is tricky. The lefts across the channel are seriously hollow and usually unmakeable. **LE LORRAIN** is more advisable for beginners; it's a mellow beachbreak away from any crowds. **CHARPENCAYE** is Anse Charpentier's right reefbreak. The take-off is straight into a tube section, followed by a fast, peeling wall that ends on a reef ledge. Be warned that getting in and out requires a bit of reef dancing and that the strong currents have led to a complete ban on swimming here. There's also a beachbreak on the other side of the wild bay. The best concentration of consistent spots is then found on the Caravelle peninsula, a 10km (6mi) long arm of land jutting into the Atlantic near the town of La Trinité. Anse l'Etang Bay has a number of spots including easy rights at VVF (camping), the fast-peeling Entre-deux lefts in the middle, plus **COCOA**, a technically challenging fast and powerful big swell left. Anse Bonneville hosts the **PLAGE DES SURFEURS**, the most consistent (although often messy) and best known spot on the island. After paddling around a large coral patch, mellow rights and lefts can be surfed, with some longer rides possible on the rights. A surf school takes advantage of the smaller inside wave. Out on the point, Roukoukou is a sucky, barreling left and right that handles swell, but not wind. **PELLE À TARTE** is a short walk or a 15min paddle from there. This wave is much more shallow and powerful with a hollow but makeable right and a death defying left that only a few bodyboarders dare tackling. On the south shore of the island, the reefbreaks give way to a string of beachbreaks that tend to close-out quickly and therefore only attract bodyboarders looking for launch ramps. The road to **ANSE TRABAUD** crosses private property and the owner charges $2.50 for the privilege. The wave is a shorebreak on the left side of the beach. There's also a reef outside, but it's an exhausting paddle and rarely worth it. Around Le Diamant a few regulars take on violent shorebreaks such as **DIAMS** or Banzaï. **ANSE CAFARD** is just more of the same stuff and should only appeal to bodyboarders.

MATT CARDINAL

LE LORRAIN

PELLE À TARTE

BLISS/SURF-MARTINIQUE.COM

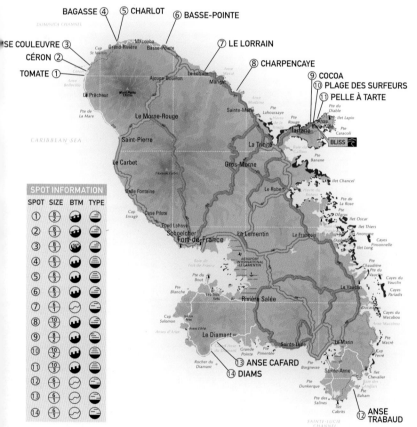

BAGASSE ④　⑤ CHARLOT　⑥ BASSE-POINTE
SE COULEUVRE ③　　　　　⑦ LE LORRAIN
CÉRON ②　　　　　⑧ CHARPENCAYE
TOMATE ①　　　　　　⑨ COCOA
　　　　　　⑩ PLAGE DES SURFEURS
　　　　　　⑪ PELLE À TARTE

BLISS

⑬ ANSE CAFARD
⑭ DIAMS
⑫ ANSE TRABAUD

SPOT INFORMATION

SPOT	SIZE	BTM	TYPE
①	8/2		
②	8/3		
③	8/3		
④	8/3		
⑤	8/3		
⑥	8/3		
⑦	6/1		
⑧	10/3		
⑨	8/2		
⑩	10/2		
⑪	10/3		
⑫	6/2		
⑬	6/1		
⑭	6/1		

SWELL AND WIND

The main swell season is from November to March, with 3-10ft (1-3m) N-NE ground-swells, sent down the North Atlantic by storms and cold fronts off the east coast of North America. Constant 2-5ft (0.6-1.6m) E windswells occurs year-round, so surfing small sloppy waves is always an option around the Caravelle peninsula. The hurricane season can bring some of the largest swell of the year between July and September, but they're highly unpredictable and may well wreak havoc on the island if they get too close. Dominant E trade winds vary from 44% (Nov) to 70% (Jul). It blows NE more than SE except May-June and Sept-Oct. Spots located on the northwest tip of the island will see perfect glassy days with a straight North swell and SE winds. Don't worry about tides. ●

TRAVEL INFORMATION

LOCAL POPULATION: 409,000　　　TIME ZONE: GMT -4h
COASTLINE: 350km (220mi)

GETTING THERE – This is French territory; visas are required for Japanese, Brazilians and South-African citizens. Lamentin Airport (FDF) has regular flights from the US, Europe and other Caribbean islands. Expensive board charges. Martinique to Guadeloupe by catamaran ($130r/t, 3.5h). Tartane is 30min away from Fort de France, 20min from the airport.

GETTING AROUND – Rent a car in Fort-de-France, rates begin at $62/d, including taxes, insurance and unlimited mileage. While public buses are inexpensive, much public transport is by collective taxis, 8-passenger limousines bearing the sign TC. Traffic jams are common and can happen any time of the day.

LODGING AND FOOD – Scattered all over the island accommodation options range from large hotel to family-run establishments called "Relais Créoles," to "Gîtes de France", usually studios in private homes. Around Tartane, try Résidence Océane ($140/dble), L'hôtel La Caravelle ($90/dble) or Bliss from $325/wk. Sample Martinique's culinary magic, a marriage of French and Creole cuisines.

WEATHER – Martinique has a tropical climate with relative humidity ranging from 77-85% all year. The two main seasons are 'carême' with cooler and drier months from January to June, and a wet season called 'hivernage' from July to December. The southern area of the island tends to be drier. The island is warm year-round, with temperatures reaching 30°C (86°F) in the daytime. There is only about a 5°C (9°F) difference between summer and winter temperatures. Two regular, alternating wind directions from NE and ESE.

WEATHER	J/F	M/A	M/J	J/A	S/O	N/D
Total Rainfall (mm)	95	80	160	240	240	170
Consistency (d/m)	15	13	17	22	19	18
Temperature min. (°C)	21	22	23	24	24	23
Temperature max. (°C)	27	28	29	29	30	29

NATURE AND CULTURE – While keeping a Caribbean cachet, Martinique exudes a distinctly French feeling. Hiking, diving and mountain biking are great. There's a wealth of sightseeing: white sand beaches, tropical rainforest, floral gardens and the majestic Mount Pelee. Visit rum distilleries for a sampling of their product before dancing to Biguine and Zouk.

HAZARDS AND HASSLES – Spots around Tartane can get crowded, but it's easy to move to less popular spots. Stay clear of the poisonous manchineel trees that border some beaches; they are sometimes marked with red paint. Martinique has the best medical care in the Eastern Caribbean.

HANDY HINTS – Surfing equipment at Itacaré Surfshop. Take a regular shortboard. Reef boots are advisable. Bliss surf school located on "Plage des Surfeurs" offers surf lessons (group $38/1.5h) and board rentals ($35/d; $130/w).

SURF STATS		J F	M A	M J J	J A	S O	N D
SWELL	Dominant swell						
	Size (m)	4	3	1-2	2	3-4	4
	Consistency (%)	70	60	40	40	60	70
WIND	Dominant wind						
	Average force	F4	F4	F4	F4	F4	F4
	Consistency	80	77	85	97	89	76
TEMP.	Wetsuit						
	Water temp.	25	25	27	28	28	26

BARBADOS

+ CONSISTENT SWELLS
+ FUN, PUNCHY WAVES
+ VARIETY OF SPOTS   – CONSTANT TRADE WINDS
+ PERFECT CLIMATE   – RARITY OF BIG SWELLS
+ CHILLED OUT ATMOSPHERE   – RELATIVELY EXPENSIVE

Barbados belongs to the Windward Islands, sitting east of the main Caribbean chain, and about 350km (220m) northwest of Venezuela. Famous for its holiday resorts, clear blue water and white sand beaches, it also has the eastern Caribbean's most consistent surf. Strong, constant trade winds whip up year-round swell on the windward coast, while in winter, regular N-NE groundswells will bring challenging waves to the iconic east coast break Soup Bowls as well as lighting up the north and west coasts. The south coast also has a cluster of breaks working on multi-directional swells, as they sweep around the tear-drop shaped island. Barbados offers some heavy waves and fun waves in equal measure, depending on the season and most of the spots break onto flat coral reefs or on beautiful sandy beaches. All abilities are catered for on this friendly, laid-back rock and there is enough scope to escape the weekend crowds at the main spots and grab a slice of paradise for yourself.

A 10 minute walk north of Bathsheba, **SANDBANK** or Cattlewash as it is also known, looks like an ideal open beachbreak for beginners. However this stretch is strafed by rips and currents and the line-up is usually messy, unless the right near the rocks is working, so it's better suited to experienced surfers who will get the best from the dumpy close-outs and onshore slop. SOUP BOWL is the island's most consistent and regularly ridden spot. It almost always has at least head-high surf, albeit often onshore. However, even onshore it is a powerful, hollow wave with a couple of different take-off spots, helping spread the weekend crowds, but the first peak is tightly controlled by the locals, who rip it up with consummate ease. Clever observers may spot the peak just south at High Rock, offering

an empty alternative with chambered rights and walled lefts heading down to **PARLOURS**. It's only a 300m paddle down to Parlours, an expanse of peaking right and left runners that seem to improve as the swell builds. Less power and intensity than Soup Bowls on any given day and a scatter gun line-up keeps crowds low and paddling high, especially at double-overhead. Almost as reliable as Soup Bowls, just without the hassling for set waves. **TENT BAY**, a powerful left, walls up and spins down the reef on a straight N swell. Never crowded because somewhere else is usually better. Breaks outside the deep water anchorage in front of the rebuilt Atlantis Hotel. Beneath the lighthouse at **RAGGED POINT**, a powerful, mid to high tide shorey hits the sand when the swell is E-SE. Any N in the swell will mean plenty

TOM CAREY/A-FRAME

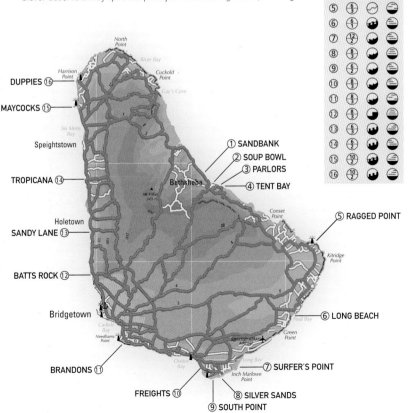

SPOT INFORMATION			
SPOT	SIZE	BTM	TYPE
①	6/2	〰	⊜
②	15/2	〰	⊜
③	15/3	●	⊜
④	8/3	●	⊜
⑤	6/2	〰	⊜
⑥	6/1	●	⊜
⑦	12/2	●	⊜
⑧	8/3	●	⊜
⑨	6/2	●	⊜
⑩	8/3	●	⊜
⑪	8/3	●	⊜
⑫	8/3	●	⊜
⑬	6/3	●	⊜
⑭	8/3	●	⊜
⑮	10/2	●	⊜
⑯	6/2	●	⊜

DUPPIES ⑯
MAYCOCKS ⑮
Speightstown
TROPICANA ⑭
Holetown
SANDY LANE ⑬
BATTS ROCK ⑫
Bridgetown
BRANDONS ⑪
FREIGHTS ⑩

North Point
River Bay
Harrison Point
Cuckold Point
Gay's Cove
Six Mens Bay
Bathsheba
Conset Point
Kitridge Point
① SANDBANK
② SOUP BOWL
③ PARLORS
④ TENT BAY
⑤ RAGGED POINT
⑥ LONG BEACH
⑦ SURFER'S POINT
⑧ SILVER SANDS
⑨ SOUTH POINT
Carlisle Bay
Needhams Point
Oistins Bay
Long Bay
Inch Marlowe Point
Foul Bay
Green Point

SOUP BOWL

LAT: 13.215318°   LONG: -59.521318°

Famous east coast right, full of power and intensity. Vertical drops, thick bowls and big shut down sections that even work in the regular onshore trade winds. Kelly Slater puts Soup Bowl in his "top 3 waves in the world" thanks to its "really good curve that allows all sorts of maneuvers and airs". Winter N swells bring the heavy "Bowls", while a hurricane S direction may provide the fun "Soup" part of the name, while still holding excellent shape. No matter what direction, this is a wave of consequence as it shifts up the size scale. Some days you do need to be Slater to get a set off the dialed-in local crew, but there's rarely a flat day and average midweek crowds will often be mellow. Another unavoidable constant is the army of urchins on the inside along with the omnipresent NE-E trade-winds.

of close-outs, but the cliffy headlands help with the wind and it consistently picks up all available energy. Dangerous cliff path access and lots of rocks around. **LONG BEACH** is a dumpy, erratic beachbreak facing SE that is a favourite with bodyboarders as it sometimes holds banging barrels close to shore. Early mornings on a clean, small to moderate SE swell will look good from the cliffs. Access is free and easy from the Foul Bay parking, while exclusive Crane Bay to the north requires payment and is usually smaller. **SURFERS POINT** can be a fun left set-up with cruisey shoulders bending into the bay and providing a bit of protection from the nor'easters. There are some rights too, with the emphasis on fun, easy rides, making it the ideal home for Zed's surf hire/school. **SILVER SANDS** holds peaks over a beach/reef

PARLOURS

JS CALLAHAN/SURFEXPLORE

WEST COAST

backwash. Lots of urchins and local surfers who have the place wired. **FREIGHTS** probably has the best lefts on the south coast, but it rarely lines-up, since a big S swell is required. Long, fast and hollow when on, there are 3 defined sections starting at the cliffs on the point, where feathered walls flow into the central reef barrels and if you are lucky, more bowls through the inside. Has many moods when small with plenty of shorter rights and lazy, longboard shoulders that make this a useful beginner spot. Access down the cliffs is sketchy and if it is working properly, everyone will be on it. Close to Bridgetown is **BRANDONS**, a sandy reef peak that only works on big hurricane or SE windswells and is offshore in NE trades. Mainly groomed, speedy lefts with the odd tuck section, or fleeting, rounder rights. It gets crowded in winter and is dominated by town locals who love the place. Sloppy and beginner-friendly in summer. The west coast only breaks on the biggest N swells so it's the least consistent part of the island, but the E trade winds will provide the cleanest conditions. The most consistent spot is **BATTS ROCK**, a perfect A-frame peak that is well-known among Bridgetown locals and like most west coast spots, 5 guys is a crowd. Powerful, hollow fast lefts are common. **SANDY LANE**, mid-way down the island, is a short, perfect left, but it's either fantastic, or totally flat. Lowest consistency around, meaning the locals will be out in force when it finally breaks. Backwash airs are all the rage. Sharp, shallow reef. Speedy left barrels over urchin-covered, fire coral reef makes **TROPICANA** a treacherous left for experts only, who usually choose high tide for their tube time. There are more challenging reefs up towards Speightstown like Fort and Sandridge. The long, tapering shoulders of **MAYCOCKS** are a fun alternative to Duppies and will always be smaller and more manageable on a wrapping N swell. Low to mid tide is preferred and the trades are always offshore. Handles the biggest swells on an outside section that keeps the chargers happy. Set in beautiful scenery, but difficult to find without directions.

combo that sucks in SE swell and produces some hollow rights. NE wind is cross-shore so the wind and kite crew will be around, along with some protective locals. At the bottom tip of the island, **SOUTH POINT** offers long lefts over a live coral reef in front of the lighthouse. Breaks up into sections that may link up when big enough, the theme is long, fast left walls with cover-ups or shorter, bowly rights that catch the wind a bit more. Prefers mid to high tide, when it gets a bad

SOUTH POINT

ROGER SHARP

FORT

BERNARD TESTEMALE

On the NW tip of the island is **DUPPIES**, a consistent, powerful right that suffers from strong currents. Probably the best wave on the island after Soupbowls, it is not for the faint hearted. It breaks some distance offshore, is reputed to be sharky, and the name refers to malevolent spirits and ghosts, so the vibe is heavy. Cliffs mean getting caught in the north to south current is a scary proposition.

SWELL AND WIND

The best season for groundswells is from late October to March, when 2-12ft (0.6-4m) N-NE swells wrap around the northern tip of the island to produce clean 1-10ft (0.3-3m) waves on the W coast and bigger onshore waves on the east coast. The other main swell source is the E wind, which consistently kicks up 2-5ft swells. Sometimes they get big enough to wrap onto the S coast where they clean up dramatically. This wind occurs year-round so you're likely to find a rideable wave most days. Barbados is situated too far south to get hit by hurricanes, but their swell often reaches the east coast and when they're big can light up the southern tip as well. From June to October, it's mainly flat on the south coast. The prevailing wind comes from between the NE-SE for 50-70% of the time. NE is more common than SE, except in the summer months. Throughout the year the mornings will often be glassy with residual wind swell offering superb conditions. Despite small tidal variations, most of the best surf occurs at low tide, especially on the south coast. ●

SURF STATS		J	F	M	A	M	J	J	A	S	O	N	D
SWELL	Dominant swell												
	Size (m)	4-5		3-4		2-3		2-3		4		4-5	
	Consistency (%)	80		70		50		50		70		80	
WIND	Dominant wind												
	Average force	F4		F4		F4		F4		F3-F4		F4	
	Consistency	93		91		92		86		92		86	
TEMP.	Wetsuit												
	Water temp.	25		26		27		28		27		26	

TRAVEL INFORMATION

POPULATION: 287,733
COASTLINE: 97km (60mi)
TIME ZONE: GMT -4h

GETTING THERE – Visas are not necessary. From the United Kingdom, direct flights are offered by British Airways (no boards over 6'3") and Virgin Atlantic. AA, Caribbean Airlines, Jet Blue and US Airways from the USA. Caribbean Airlines and LIAT have connections between most of the Caribbean islands. Departure tax is $27.50, usually included in your ticket.

GETTING AROUND – The bus service is very good and a much cheaper alternative to car rental. The big blue buses can carry boards, but the smaller vans can't. Rental cars start at $39/d, try the new Mokes. Drive on the left after getting a local driving license from the rental company for $5.

LODGING AND FOOD – Peak tourist season is from December-March, and the price of decent accommodation can shoot up in these months. You should pay no more than $50/dble in a local guest-house. Stay on the south coast if you need some entertaining and proximity to all-around surf. Try Zed's Surfer's Point Guesthouse at $100-180/n per studio. From South Point, it's 30min to Bathsheba. Near Soup Bowl, stay at Edgewater inn (fr $94) or Crystal water at $120. You can find guest-house rooms around $50. The food is great, with lots spice, and plenty of fish. A meal usually costs around $12 including beer or rum.

WEATHER – Known as "Little England", Barbados is blessed with a near perfect climate. The island receives 3000hrs of sunshine a year and 1500mm (60in) of rain, and the constant trade winds help to keep the humidity and heat at bearable levels. The wettest season is from July-November when tropical fronts pass over the region. The wind is lightest at this time of year. February-May is the driest and windiest period. Hurricanes tend to pass further to the north. In the water, boardshorts and a rash vest suffice for most of the year, although early morning sessions in the winter may call for a shorty.

WEATHER	J/F	M/A	M/J	J/A	S/O	N/D
Total Rainfall (mm)	47	34	85	147	174	150
Consistency (d/m)	10	8	12	17	15	15
Temperature min. (°C)	21	21	23	23	23	22
Temperature max. (°C)	28	30	31	31	31	29

NATURE AND CULTURE – Cruising around the island soaking up the scenery is an enjoyable way of filling a day. Stopping at small rum shops and village stores is the best way to meet the warm, friendly local people. There is good diving and snorkeling on the west coast and wind/kite surfing on the SE tip of the island. More organised excursions like the Jolly Roger pirate ship or Sam Lord's coral castle can be fun but are usually packed out with US and Euro holidaymakers. For a good night out try either the Harbour Lights or Boatyards in town. In some night spots a $15 cover charge includes free drinks.

HAZARDS AND HASSLES – The onshore winds on the E coast are the biggest nightmare and there can be intense rips north of Bathsheba. Take precautions against the strong sun, mosquitoes and reef cuts. The popular surf spots get busy, but usually the atmosphere is cool as long as you're respectful. Drugs are frowned upon by the general community despite extensive use. Police will not hesitate to lock up tourists. Crack problems contradict the generally safe, easy-going reputation of the island, leading to robberies and occasionally violence.

HANDY HINTS – It's very easy to rent gear at Zed's (Inch Marlowe) or Dead or Dread Surf Shop in Bridgetown. Many surf schools and tours available like Melanie's operation. Barbados line-ups are full of U.K. and East Coast American surfers. Take a semi-gun for the bigger days in winter. Immigration will be particularly slow unless you have the name of a guest house or hotel where you are intending to stay.

TRINIDAD AND TOBAGO

+ MAGIC MOUNT IRVINE
+ SPOT DENSITY ON TOBAGO
+ CHEAP, EXCELLENT FOOD
+ CRAZIEST CARNIVAL
+ GOOD FLIGHT LINKS

– INCONSISTENT LARGER SWELLS
– STRONG LOCALISM
– LONG DRIVES TO TRINIDAD SURF
– OLD OAK RUM HANGOVERS
– THIEVERY & POLICE ROADBLOCKS

Located at the very southern end of the Windward Island chain and only 7km from Venezuela on the South American continent, Trinidad and Tobago were populated by indigenous Amerindian tribes (the Arawaks and the Caribs) long before the arrival of Columbus in 1498. The main surfing areas are situated in the north and north-east of the island near Toco, which is too far for a day-trip from Port-Of-Spain, but there is still a huge amount of coastline unexplored by surfers. Two thirds of Tobago is volcanic and mountainous, rising sharply in the east under a dense cloak of tropical rainforest, while the flatter, drier western side offers the nicest beaches. This southwest coast is where all the surf spots are located with the exception of Crazy's. The Buccoo Reef National Park is the main coastal feature, offering not only great surf but also fantastic snorkelling and diving.

The crescent bay of **LAS CUEVAS** holds hollow, fast beachbreak peaks in N to E swells up to 6ft (2m). Always better at mid to high tide and bigger at the western end, a good walk from the fishing village and car park. Fairly consistent in winter, but flat in the summer months, unless there is a hurricane swell. **BLANCHISSEUSE** is a nice sandy beach with some rocks on its eastern side and the best peaks usually at the western end, but there can be some very

strong rips requiring strength and endurance. The protected bay and rivermouth of **GRANDE RIVIÈRE** is the place to head in huge swells when the rest of the north coast is maxed-out. Breaks over rocks on the eastern side by the cement jetty, in 2m+ (6ft+) NE to E swells, but mostly breaks during the hurricane season. **SANS SOUCI** is 15 minutes down the road from the Toco fishing depot where a big rock in the middle of the bay dominates the beautiful scenery. The sandbars develop on either side of the rock depending on the currents and when the left is working, it is usually the best. Takes N round to E swells at 0.5m-5m (2-15ft) and is excellent during hurricane season

SPOT INFORMATION			
SPOT	SIZE	BTM	TYPE
①	6/2	◔	▤
②	6/2	◔	▤
③	10/4	●	▤
④	15/2	◔	▤
⑤	10/2	●	▤
⑥	12/2	●	▤
⑦	10/2	◔	▤
⑧	12/2	◔	▤
⑨	6/2	◔	▤
⑩	6/3	●	▤
⑪	6/1	◔	▤
⑫	4/1	◔	▤

MOUNT IRVINE

BABY MARMOTTE

TOBAGO

BABY MARMOTTE

TRAVEL INFORMATION

POPULATION: 1.34M	COASTLINE: Trinidad 362km
TIME ZONE: GMT -4h	(224mi): Tobago 115km (71mi)

GETTING THERE – No visa. Direct flights to Trinidad (POS) on Caribbean Airlines, Monarch, BA, AA and United. All charge extra for surfboards. Tobago is 2h away from Port-of-Spain by fast ferry, or 15 minutes by air.

GETTING AROUND – Rent a car (Autocenter), because the main surf area is a 2.5h drive from Port of Spain and taxi rides can turn out to be quite expensive. Costs are about $40/d and fuel is cheap. Public transport is possible but not with surfboards. In Tobago you can walk to surf spots.

LODGING AND FOOD – Guest houses in Toco (Patrice Bravo), space is limited, but not in great demand. Staying in hotels entails very long drives. Most hotels in Tobago are scattered around Mt Irvine and Pigeon Point. Inexpensive tasty food like curry and rotis. Shark n' Bakes is a local delicacy.

WEATHER – The climate of both islands is warm and humid, with the dry season running from November to April, and the wet season from May until October. The wet season, also coincides with the June to October hurricane season, with storms most likely to hit in the August and September months. Hurricanes generally track to the north of Trinidad, but usually close enough to generate a significant increase in swell. The dry season is also the windy season, where Tobago in particular can see 37kmh averages for weeks on end. Fortunately, the best breaks in Tobago are on the west coast, and the trade winds are easterly.

WEATHER	J/F	M/A	M/J	J/A	S/O	N/D
Total Rainfall (mm)	55	50	147	232	181	154
Consistency (d/m)	12	9	15	22	18	17
Temperature min. (°C)	20	20	22	22	22	21
Temperature max. (°C)	31	32	32	31	32	32

NATURE AND CULTURE – World famous for flora & fauna. Bird or turtle watching and diving (Speyside) are popular. There are excellent mountain biking tours around the islands. Birth place of Soca music and a surf trip in February will coincide with the famous Trinidad Carnival, 2nd only to Rio's in size, where the focus is on dancing, partying and drinking.

HAZARDS AND HASSLES – Fights in the water are common, with violence directed to those who don't respect the locals or who try to paddle straight to the peak at breaks like Mount Irvine. Banditos are a concern; car jacking and theft of personal possessions is a possibility. Be watchful for poisonous snakes and giant centipedes.

HANDY HINTS – Don't forget mosquito repellent. Take a long-sleeve rash vest and a light-weight springsuit for dawn patrols. There are four surf shops in Trinidad, most famous is "Beach Break" located in the West Mall of Port of Spain. Alan Davis fixes dings and is the only shaper. Rent boards from the locals like Cool Runnings at Mount Irvine beach.

when it gets huge, clean and hollow. To the right of the main jetty in front of the fishing depot, **TOCO** is a super hollow right that breaks only in a N swell. It's very inconsistent and the locals are all over it when it does break – surf elsewhere. **SALIBYA** is the only real barrier reefbreak on the island a short distance from the Toco lighthouse. It's a bit of a paddle to the outer reef where hollow, sectioning lefts and rights break best at low to mid tide on N–NE swells in the winter months. Down the beach from **BALANDRA** fishing depot is an exposed, powerful, all tides beachbreak. Handles N–NE–E swells ranging from 2-10ft (0.5-3m) and is ultra consistent. On Tobago, **MOUNT IRVINE** is generally considered one of the best waves in the Caribbean region. It's a hollow, high-performance right with a lot of barrelling sections over the dead coral reef in N–NE swells up to 12ft (4m). The heavy local crew jump of the rocks but it's safer to paddle out from the middle of the bay. It never breaks in summer, but is fairly consistent during the winter months. Walk about a mile up the beach from Store Bay to access **SUNSET LEFT**, a reef that's a short paddle off the private Pigeon Point area. It gets nice and hollow, and works well with a N–NE swell, from 3-6ft (1–2m). It is a good alternative when Mount Irvine is packed and breaks in similar conditions. Half way along the beach towards Sunset Left is **SUNSET RIGHTS**, a very shallow, hollow righthander, especially at low tide. It rarely get above headhigh and only works when Mount Irvine and Sunset Left are breaking huge. Very inconsistent, but very good. Predictably located right at the end of the runway, **AIRPORT'S** is a hollow, punchy righthander. It works during wintertime, from 4–6ft (1.5 –2m) and is best at low tide. Big swell spot that's not as rare as Sunset Right, but not as consistent as Mount Irvine. **CRAZY'S** is the only break on the east coast of the island, located north of Scarborough, in Goldsborough Bay. Very poor quality, desperation wave working in junky E windswells only. Never reaches headhigh, consistently bad.

SWELL AND WIND

In the dry/windy season months from Dec to April, E trades drive windswell in the 4–8ft (1.2-2.5m) range. During this time, cold fronts pushing off South Carolina and sometimes Florida will set up long period (12–15sec), 4 to 6ft (1.2m–2m) N–NW groundswells. These N swells wrap around the west coast of Tobago where

perfect offshore conditions are generally the rule. The wet/hurricane season relies on trade wind NE–SE swells from June to October, is more fickle and generally smaller. However, westerly tracking tropical storms and hurricanes can not only create very light and variable wind conditions but also large, long period swells, sometimes as much as 30ft (10m). The more common hurricane swell is in the region of 12ft (4m) with a 15sec period, creating the best surfing conditions of the year. Winds are generally easterly, especially in the dry and windy season, ranging from 15 to 25 knots. Winds in the wet season are often lighter, with more variable directions, sometimes even W. The tidal range is 1–4ft (0.3-1.2m) and a rising tide can increase the size of the surf at some spots. ●

SURF STATS		J	F	M	A	M	J	J	A	S	O	N	D
SWELL	Dominant swell		🌀		🌀		🌀		🌀		🌀		🌀
	Size (m)	3-4		2-3		1		1-2		3		3-4	
	Consistency (%)	60		50		30		30		50		60	
WIND	Dominant wind	◔		◔		◔		◔		◔		◔	
	Average force	F4		F4		F4		F3-F4		F3-F4		F3-F4	
	Consistency	88		86		95		91		89		83	
TEMP.	Wetsuit	🏄		🏄		🏄		🏄		🏄		🏄	
	Water temp.	26		26		27		28		28		27	

OTHER ATLANTIC ISLANDS

Unlike the Pacific or the Indian Oceans, the tropical zone of the Atlantic beyond the Caribbean is conspicuously devoid of islands. Despite the mighty Mid-Atlantic Ridge bisecting Cancer and Capricorn, very few mountain tops break the surface and some of the ones that do are either too steep or under-exposed to the prevailing swell. Nevertheless, a few chains prove the quality not quantity theory, welcoming far-travelled swells from colder climes to their equatorial shores and turning on a seasonal wave feast for surprisingly few surfers.

SAO TOMÉ

JS CALLAHAN/SURFEXPLORE

Many African islands are in their infancy when it comes to surf culture.

SOUTH AMERICA AND BEYOND

The only southern hemisphere island group that grabs surfer's attention in the Atlantic is the cluster of 21 islands and islets, 354 km (220 mi) off the NE coast of Brazil. FERNANDO DE NORONHA is also the main island in this volcanic chain and is the home of heavy barreling beachbreaks and a few reefs, earning it Hawaii comparisons in the power department. A long way south near the Tropic of Capricorn, another chain of submarine volcanoes march out from Brazil's continental shelf and break the surface at **Trindade and Martim Vaz**. The Brazilian navy have a tiny station there and although a couple of *Trip* surf mag journalists accompanied a supply mission, they weren't allowed to surf "the perfect waves" on the north coast of Trinidade near the shipwreck and at Turtle Beach. Other Brazillian administered ocean specks include the World Heritage site of Rocas Atoll, solely for scientific research and the ragged rocks of the exposed abyssal mantle that constitute the St Peter and St Paul Archipelago, which barely hold the lighthouse, let alone surfable waves. Being exactly halfway between South America and Africa has made **Ascension Island** a military hangout for centuries and servicemen have been surfing there for quite some time. A couple of adjacent breaks, Deadmans and POL provide lefts and rights depending on whether the swell is coming from the N or the S and both are pretty short, can be heavy and involve getting comfortable around gnarly volcanic rocks. Sitting 1,300km (800 mi) to the SE, **St Helena** has plenty of S swell exposure, but the worst bathymetry possible as the cliffs thrust vertically from the sea, making it a "no surf island".

WEST AFRICA

Heading north of the equator to SÃO TOMÉ & Príncipe will uncover some small, unpredictable waves in a crowdless zone where the surf season luckily coincides with the dry season, making it possible to explore some of the less travelled islands. Annobón is too steep, while Príncipe is a bit shadowed by São Tomé, but if there is a due S swell then south coast beaches like Praia Infante will hold some headhigh waves, albeit onshore. Deeper into the Gulf of Guinea, following the Cameroon line of volcanoes, **Bioko** is so sheltered, only booming SSW will angle into the south coast left called Nacho or the east coast righthand point of Caracas, just north of Riaba. Beyond the armpit of Africa, the 88 Bissagos Islands form a silted up maze of waterways and sit on the most extensive section of continental shelf in West Africa, draining any swells of much power. There may be an epic, long sandy rivermouth among the Unesco Biosphere Reserve, but the shark and hippopotamus infested waters are likely to hold their secrets for years to come.

CAPE VERDE

The archipelago of Cape Verde presents an unusual version on the tropical island theme, particularly SAL, which is so arid many of its landscapes would not look out of place on the moon. Dry, hot Saharan winds scour the rocky earth, making it a world-class wind and kiteboarding spot, as well as holding some excellent righthand reefs and points for the sail-less. **Boa Vista** and **Maio** look similar to Sal and both have N and S swell exposure if the angles are just right. On Boa Vista, check the sandy Praia de Santa Mónica and Praia Varandinha on the SW coast for offshore conditions, plus around Sal Rei at Cabral, the offshore English Reef (mainly kiting) and the bays to the north. There's even a tasty wrapping left on the windward east side at Ervatao. Over on **Santiago**, deep inside the capital's port Praia, there are clean, tidy lefts peeling over cobbles beside a shipwreck at Praia Negra and waves on both sides of Ilha de Santa Maria. More S swell city reefs to the west like the rocky lefts at Coragi. Ponta do Lobo is the area to search on the choppy east coast, but most surfers will end up in Tarrafal on the NW tip.

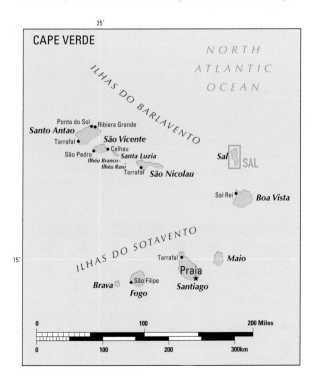

CAPE VERDE

NORTH ATLANTIC OCEAN

ILHAS DO BARLAVENTO

Ponta do Sol • Ribiera Grande
Santo Antao
Tarrafal • **São Vicente**
• Calhau
São Pedro • **Santa Luzia**
Ilhéu Branco
Ilhéu Raso
Tarrafal • **São Nicolau**

Sal SAL

Sal Rei • **Boa Vista**

ILHAS DO SOTAVENTO

Tarrafal • **Maio**

Praia ★
Brava • São Filipe
Fogo **Santiago**

0   100   200 Miles
0   100   200   300km

A string of west-facing, boulder-strewn reefs convert winter W-NW (NW-N is blocked by the other islands) into rights at Punta Brava, Shira and Chao Bom with good lefts at the town break of Caju. There are few beaches on the island and the super craggy coastline is steep and waveless for long stretches, a problem that re-occurs on the neighboring volcano dominated **Fogo**, where the black sand beaches of São Filipe on the west coast are uninspiring and the soaring 80m cliffs make any of the rocky points unapproachable. The tiny island of **Brava** has similarly inhospitable geology and while there may be some waves on rocky beaches beneath the steep cliffs, it is not worth the considerable effort to get there. More crazy rock formations characterize the deeply wind and wave etched coastline of **São Nicolau**, which suffers from filtering by the other islands in S swells, but picks up plenty of NW-N lines. On the sheltered west coast at Tarrafal de São Nicolau, the righthand point at Sabi Sabi is usually offshore and there are rocky black sand beaches, especially at the dried-up rivermouths. Plenty of coastal angles to explore and if the wind drops, north coast beaches like Praia da Areia Branca in small swells. **São Vicente** is shielded from winter NW swells, but there is still north coast action at the two due N exposed beaches of Salamansa or Praia Grande, near Calhau. Popular with surf and wind/kite schools, it's often big and messy, with potential for some righthanders off the eastern headlands. Baia das Gatas is the scene of a big music festival and some occasional lefthanders sweeping round the breakwall in low or W winds. South coast spots are limited to the big sweep of sand at São Pedro, which is usually shoredump, but the wind/kite crew like the strong trade winds whistling down the airport runway. Finally, the last and most exposed island in the *barlovento* (windward) chain is **Santo Antão**, which is unaffected by any swell shadow other than from the E-SE. The young volcanic landscape throws up towers of basalt along much of its littoral extent, so there are less surf spots than might be expected. The northwest coast is fierce and foreboding, with little access to the angry, windblown waves hitting slabs of rock most people would prefer to avoid. From

SANTO ANTÃO

First in the swell firing line from the north, Santo Antão's stark, ragged coastline trips up some large, heavy waves.

Arid, mountainous terrain pervades the *sotavento* or leeward islands in the Cape Verde.

the scary big-wave reef of Ponta do Sol through Ribeira Grande and on to Janela there are miles of boulder-backed black sand beach with some rideable peaks, including the lined-up lefthanders at Vila das Pombas, for confident surfers when the wind drops and the coast road makes access easier. Porto Novo nestles in the SE, missing the bulk of the swell, but can have a wave occasionally. Tarrafal de Monte Trigo is the go to spot for the combination of good N and S swell exposure plus it's dead offshore in the NE winds that usually rip across the mountainous interior.

SANTIAGO

FERNANDO DE NORONHA

+ POWERFUL TUBING
  REEFBREAKS AND BEACHBREAKS
+ CONSISTENTLY OFFSHORE
+ UNTOUCHED, WILD ENVIRONMENT
+ PEACEFUL ISLAND VIBE

– SHORT SURF SEASON
– DIFFICULT ACCESS
– ISOLATED ISLAND LOCATION
– VERY EXPENSIVE LIVING COSTS

Surprisingly, Fernando de Noronha's main source of swell is not from the S like most of Brazil, but from the North Atlantic lows that provide Europe with its surf. These swells have to march thousands of miles south, helped along by favourable winds and ocean currents. The island has had a colourful recent history, having been used as a battlefield, jail, air base and weather station, but has now become a tourist heaven for divers and surfers. It is never under 2ft during Dec-Feb, and swells last for 5-6 days. Like Hawaii, the island is the summit of a huge underwater volcano, rising 4.3km (2.7mi) from the ocean floor. The surrounding deep water and lack of continental shelf allows the swells to hit with unimpeded speed and power, jacking up wave heights in the process. The SE-facing side of the island is too steep and mountainous for any surf, whereas the NW oriented coastline has perfect topography and offshore winds. The steeply sloping beaches make for some fast barrels, which sometimes tend toward the straighthander category, but are perfectly suited to bodyboarders and tube junkies.

Italcabe, in **CONCEIÇÃO**, which is a fast beachbreak and is the centre of the island's beach scene. Closes out quite a bit at the extremes of tide, but can have a right off the eastern corner or some lefts beneath the towering monolith of the Pico do Morro. **BOLDRÓ** is a hazardous reef with some very good lefts and rights that barrel when it's small, but it gets a little crazy when the swell is over 6ft. Lower tides are needed to pull the waves off the rock shelf and swell direction will decide which side fires. Fast and wedgy at the peak, coupled with sharp rocks and some protective locals make this an experienced surfers spot. The northeastern end of the main Cacimba beach surf spot is called **BODE** and it catches some nice peaks in smaller broken-up swells at mid tides. If the swell arrives from the NE then a righthand tunnel will grind off the slab of reef for a longer, pedal to the metal ride. Looking down from the *mirantes* (viewpoints), **CACIMBA DO PADRE** appears as a picturesque tropical beach with perfect clean waves in crystal clear water, against the backdrop of the gnarled volcanic rock brothers known as the *Dois Irmãoes*. This is the most consistent spot on the island and the swell can be doubled in size here, reaching heights of up to 15ft (5m) offering huge, cavernous barrels, before shutting down hard on the fine-sand beach. With enough NW-N swell, it starts breaking on an outside shelf and rolls left through to the inside, getting meaner all the way. There are rights as well, but most of the action is concentrated on the longer, more makeable lefts. Smaller, peakier swells can see a high tide left, wedge off the base of the rocks, but no matter what the size, Cacimba is always hollow and powerful. During the pro contest, crowds explode, but midweek mornings will see a handful of tube-hunters. Beginners should stay closer to town and experienced surfers should take a couple of fast, strong boards, just in case. There are a few more spots dotted around the island, but with a maximum tourist capacity of 450 people at any one time, there's little need to explore.

CELSO/A-FRAME

CACIMBA DO PADRE

When a moderate to big NW swell slams into the northern-most point of Noronha, the classic righthander at **BAIA DA RATA** offers powerful righthand walls for experts with a boat. If the swell is big enough and the tide low enough, then you may get to surf fickle **ABRAS**, the best left reef on the island. It starts off as an open barrel before turning into a carvable wall that in turn becomes a fast hollow, close-out section on the gnarled reef shelf. Nasty rocks pop up everywhere, making entry and exit a real pain. On the other side of Isla **SAN JOSÉ** from Abras, a groomed righthander sometimes breaks into the bay that is usually full of moored up boats awaiting passengers for island and dive tours. Needs W in the swell and lower tides as the island gets cut off by high water. Just down from the harbour, **BOBOCA** will rip across the reef in NW swell and is perfectly offshore in the SE winds. Handles some size and mid tide attracting the locals on the good days. **PRAIA DO MEIO** holds various decent peaks that usually work best on mid tides. The northern end of the beach is Cachorro, below the famous vista from the Fort Remedios, where it is much rockier. More good waves are to be found at Praia do

SPOT INFORMATION			
SPOT	SIZE	BTM	TYPE
①	10/4	◖	〰
②	10/5	◖	▭
③	10/5	◖	〰
④	12/3	◖	▭
⑤	8/3	◑	▭
⑥	8/3	◷	▭
⑦	8/3	◖	▭
⑧	10/2	◷	▭
⑨	15/3	◕	▭

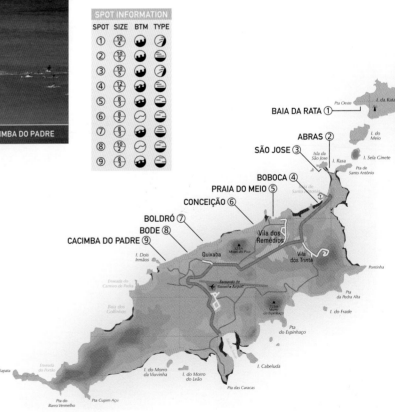

BAIA DA RATA ①
ABRAS ②
SÃO JOSE ③
BOBOCA ④
PRAIA DO MEIO ⑤
CONCEIÇÃO ⑥
BOLDRÓ ⑦
BODE ⑧
CACIMBA DO PADRE ⑨

Pta Oeste · I. da Rata
I. do Meio
Isla da São Jose · I. Rasa · I. Sela Ginete
Pta de Santo António
Vila dos Remédios
Quixaba · Morro do Pico
Vila dos Trinta
I. Dois Irmãos
Fernando de Noronha Airport
Pontinha
Pta da Pedra Alta
Ensenada do Carreiro de Pedra
I. do Frade
Baia dos Golfinhos
Pta do Espinhaço
Pta da Sapata
Ensenada do Purão
I. Cabeluda
I. do Morro da Viuvinha · I. do Morro do Leão
Pta do Barro Vermelho · Pta Cupim Açu · Pta das Caracas

CONCEIÇÃO

LAURENT MASUREL

SWELL AND WIND

Low pressures sitting off the North American east coast generate plenty of 2-12ft NW-N swells between Nov and March. As these systems move towards the Azores, the swell arrives from a more NE direction, helped by the prevailing NE trades and Canaries Current, but slightly hindered by the Cape Verde islands shadow. Fernando de Noronha is also exposed to tropical depressions as they head from Africa to the Americas and will send an off-season swell if they develop into hurricanes quickly enough. South swells hit between April-Oct, but due to onshore winds and steeply rising beaches, they don't produce good quality waves, however, it will always be 1-2ft at this time. Wind patterns are extremely stable, SE is the predominant

SURF STATS		J F	M A M	J	J A S	O N	D
SWELL	Dominant swell	🌀	🌀	🌀	🌀	🌀	🌀
	Size (m)	3-4	2-3	1	1-2	3	3-4
	Consistency (%)	60	50	30	30	50	60
WIND	Dominant wind	🌬	🌬	🌬	🌬	🌬	🌬
	Average force	F4	F4	F4	F3-F4	F3-F4	F3-F4
	Consistency	88	86	95	91	89	83
TEMP.	Wetsuit	🏄	🏄	🏄	🏄	🏄	🏄
	Water temp.	26	26	27	28	28	27

MEIO

LAURENT MASUREL

LOCAL POPULATION: 3,012   TIME: GMT -3h
COASTLINE: 32km (20mi)

GETTING THERE – Many nationalities (Aus, USA, Can, India) need a 90 day Brazilian Tourist Visa before travelling (approx $160), while EU citizens can get it on arrival. There are three flights daily out to Fernando de Noronha (FEN) from Natal (350km/220mi; $245) and Recife (540km/335mi; $340rt) on the Brazilian mainland. Book well in advance with either GOL, TAM Linhas Aéreas or Azul Airlines, as the busy tourist season corresponds with the surf season. GOL take boards as part of your baggage allowance.

GETTING AROUND – Fernando de Noronha is only 8km (5mi) long and 3km (2mi) wide, with lots of rough off-roading so a beach buggy (fr $100/d) or a motorbike is the way to go. Fuel is expensive. Ask at the harbour about renting boats to get to the more remote spots. There is a bus service which drives along BR-363, with detours to some villages. Bicycles can be rented from the Locadora Solimar, Vila dos Remédios and some *pousadas*.

LODGING AND FOOD – There are over 70 pousadas (guesthouses) and most have full-board prices from $80/n/dbl to $500/n/dbl for Pousada Triboju. Food and drink wise you have a choice of either expensive imported items, (like beer), and cheap repetitive seafood served in the *launchonetes*.

WEATHER – Being located just south of the Equator, Fernando do Noronha enjoys a hot and humid climate split between a dry and wet season. SE trades bring the heaviest rain, (nearly every day), from March to July and even into Aug. Temps are very stable, with the air and water being around 26°-27°C, (80-82°F). In the dry season everything turns very brown and burnt, the wet season is much greener. For the best surf and weather come earlier in the season (Nov).

WEATHER	J/F	M/A	M/J	J/A	S/O	N/D
Total Rainfall (mm)	70	190	270	203	45	26
Consistency (d/m)	11	15	22	20	10	6
Temperature min. (°C)	25	24	23	22	23	24
Temperature max. (°C)	30	29	28	27	28	29

NATURE AND CULTURE – An appreciation of nature and hiking will greatly enhance your enjoyment of the island. Aquatic life is very rich with fish, shark, dolphins, (swimming with them is not allowed, nor is spear fishing), and turtles as well as birds and big lizards. There is no nightlife on the island or urban entertainment (except during the competition), if there's no surf then occupy yourself by hiking, snorkeling, fishing or diving.

HAZARDS AND HASSLES – There are plenty of sharks, stingrays and moray eels around but they don't pose much threat. In the wet season there are lots of mosquitoes and bugs. Be careful of sunburn and reef cuts.

HANDY HINTS – The island is a national park with a Nature Tax that favours shorter visits ($140/7d, $375/14d). In addition, there is a Ecological Tax or entrance ticket to the park that costs 65R$ ($32) for Brazilians and 130R$ ($65) for foreigners and is valid for ten days. There are few real locals, but Brazilians from the mainland stay here for weeks on end. Bring absolutely everything you need with you. Equipment is available, but like most goods on the island, it's expensive.

direction varying from 41% in April to 70% in Sept, when it's not blowing SE it will almost certainly be due E. In fact for 94% of the time it blows from one of these two directions. This means perfect offshore conditions on the NW-facing surf coastline. There are some slight variations at the end of the dry season, (Feb-April), when there may be NE and S winds. The semi-diurnal tidal range maximum is 2.34m (7.7ft) and affects the waves a lot, with low tide required for some reefs, while the beachbreaks are usually happiest at mid. ●

SAL, CAPE VERDE

+ GENERALLY UNCROWDED
+ SHAPELY REEF WAVES
+ FURTHER EXPLORATION POSSIBILITIES
+ WINDSURFING HEAVEN
+ GUARANTEED SUNSHINE

– INCONSISTENT, SEASONAL SWELLS
– WINDY
– FLAT DESERT LANDSCAPE
– FAIRLY EXPENSIVE

JODY MACDONALD

ALIBABA

The Cape Verde islands are the southernmost group in the boomerang shaped archipelago of Macaronesia. Made up of 10 major islands, the Cape Verde were used as a stopping off point for the slave ships heading over to the Americas and descendants of these slaves have mixed with the Portuguese settlers. Previously known as Lhana, Sal is the flattest island and the main tourist entry point with various European flight connections. The surf potential was first discovered in the late '80s, by windsurfers in Santa Maria on Sal's southern tip and the island has become synonymous with wind and kitesurfing. The dominant NE trades, powered by the heat of the Sahara are ever-present throughout the year and provide cross or offshore conditions on the west-facing lava reefs that benefit from the Atlantic winter NW swell train. Ponta Preta has emerged as a world-class wind, kite and surf spot, which is quite an achievement to be able to keep all 3 disciplines happy and sometimes sees large waves that tower above the average mast.

Just south of the harbour at **PALMEIRA** sees a short, zippy left break into a clear channel on small to moderate swells and is worth the 35min drive if it is too small in Santa Maria. Quite consistent and rarely crowded, plus there are a couple more reefs out on the southern headland of the bay. **FONTANA** is a pretty place, located in a small bay that produces a mysto right when the swell is big. Needs E or SE winds so not very consistent. **CURRAL JOUL** sits out on the tip of the exposed headland on the north side of the Baía de Joaquim Petinha and will handle as big as it gets. The continuous line of rocks make the line-up difficult to read and it sections off badly in places, so experts only. Rarely ridden and getting in and out is a nightmare unless surfing it off a boat. Deeper in the bay and a much better bet is **ALIBABA**, a superb walled-up righthander that motors down the rocky point, close to the cliffs, so it is less affected by the cross-shore NE'ers. Once again, getting through the rocks can be brutal on board and feet. **MONTE LEÃO** can produce perfect, long rights and has the advantage of being quite sheltered from the wind, as it sits directly below the Sleeping Lion mountain on the leeward side. This SW-facing aspect means it needs a big NW swell to wrap around the headland or a moderate WSW to sneak in between the other islands to begin breaking. The most consistent section is like a pointbreak off a knuckle of reef, 500m from the beach and there are a number of sand/reef options further in, then all the way around the bay to Murdeira. Good place for intermediates to go to escape some size in big N swells. The cluster of rocks at **RIFE** is better suited to wave-sailing since the rights break lazily down towards the channel inside the protected bay, but longboarders may get some rides. The best wave, 30 minutes walk from Santa Maria, is **PONTA PRETA**, which has long rights peeling for up to 300m over sharp, black boulders. Barrel sections, speed walls and wind whipped copings are shared out between the surf and wind crews. It's best with a decent NW swell, low tide and when the usual sideshore wind is light. There's also an awesome, even hollower left off the outside peak, but it's exposed to

MONTE LEÃO

STUART BUTLER

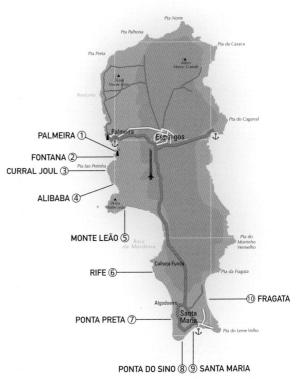

PALMEIRA ①
FONTANA ②
CURRAL JOUL ③
ALIBABA ④
MONTE LEÃO ⑤
RIFE ⑥
PONTA PRETA ⑦
PONTA DO SINO ⑧   ⑨ SANTA MARIA
⑩ FRAGATA

PONTA PRETA

BERNARD TESTEMALE

TRAVEL INFORMATION

LOCAL POPULATION: Sal – 11,000	COASTLINE: 87km (55mi) TIME: GMT-1h

GETTING THERE – Major airlines fly from European cities to Amílcar Cabral International Airport (SID) with national airline TACV and TAP (cheapest from Lisbon). You can also fly from Las Palmas, Fortaleza and Boston. Air tickets to Cape Verde are usually expensive. Domestic flights link Sal with Boa Vista, São Nicolau, São Vicente and the capital Santiago on TACV. Irregular inter-island ferries link to Santo Antao and Brava which have no functioning airport.

GETTING AROUND – It's a small island and almost everything lies within walking distance of Santa Maria. Car rentals (Suzuki Jimny 4WD) are very expensive (fr $520/w), a Quadbike is even more at ($90/d) or a bike. To rent a taxi for a return trip to one of the west coast spots further north will cost $50/rt.

LODGING AND FOOD – There's a wide variety of international hotels (RIU, Melia Tortuga, Morabeza fr $93/p/n/dble). Cheap "pensãoes" (Hotel Santa Maria Beach fr $24/p/n/dble). The cheapest meal you will find is cachupa, at about $5, western orientated food costs more like $25 a meal.

WEATHER – Being the closest islands (620km/387mi) to Africa, Sal and Boa Vista are flat and extremely dry due to the strong trade winds blowing off the desert. This has made the land lightly vegetated, except in the semi-dry riverbeds. Much of the year is reasonably warm (25°C/77°F), although when the dust-loaded, E winds blow from the Sahara (sirocco) they bring intense heat. July to September is the so-called "wet" season, at this time it's very warm (30°C/86°F) and humid and you may encounter the occasional SW gale and rain on the coast but it's rare. The cold Canary Current requires a springsuit in the winter to counter the wind chill factor.

WEATHER	J/F	M/A	M/J	J/A	S/O	N/D
Total Rainfall (mm)	3	0	0	10	30	16
Consistency (d/m)	2	0	0	2	3	2
Temperature min. (°C)	19	19	20	22	23	21
Temperature max. (°C)	23	24	25	27	26	25

NATURE AND CULTURE – Sal is the place to learn to windsurf or kitesurf with one of the many schools. The diving is some of the best in the West Africa area, such as the Buracona hole. Visit the former salt fields of Pedra Lume. The villages on Sal are quiet, but there are a couple of discos at the weekend in Santa Maria.

HAZARDS AND HASSLES – Sharp lava rocks and urchins are a common danger. Most visiting surfers are actually windsurfers, while the locals tend to ride bodyboards and some have reached a high standard. There's little localism to worry about, but show respect. The flying windsurfers at Punta Preta can be dangerous. Take plenty of sunscreen. Tiger sharks are often seen, but there has only been 1 fatality in 2001 on a diver off Raso.

HANDY HINTS – Bring everything including booties. There are a few surf shops (Surf 'n Soul, Tout'sab) and basic rental boards are available through the windsurf schools (Soultripping). Waves don't often get big and heavy enough to need a gun, although the wind can keep you trapped in the lip of the wave, so a slightly bigger board may be useful.

the wind and closes-out suddenly on the barely submerged rocks so experts only. This is a world-class wave so be sure your ability matches up. Not making a section will usually put you and your board on the rocks. Paddle from the beach, timing the shorebreak or sprint from the point on small days. **PONTA DO SINO** is a mixture of sand and reef that's usually bigger than Santa Maria, but often blown out. Swells can wrap around the island and break parallel to the sand making for longer rides and an easy walk back up the beach. Quite consistent as it does work in any swell, anytime of year. Can be some currents sweeping the point. **SANTA MARIA** is an 8km (5mi) sandy beach on the southern tip of Sal that catches the all too rare SW swells and summer NE swells, along with big winter NW on the wrap. Mainly mellow, small beachbreaks, breaking around the wooden pier (Ponton) plus there are some lefts breaking on a reef close to the big hotel and old harbour. Nice, easy, beginner-friendly stretch at high tide over the sand and the left is used as an indicator to the west coast swell size. This is really wind and kitesurf territory and is popular with the locals for a sunset session. Further out on the eastern tip of the bay is Lembje Point which occasionally hosts some seriously nice lefts for all types of surfer. If you're lucky, and the persistent NE trade winds stop blowing, then the regulation 1-5ft (0.3-1.5m) NE windswell might clean up, meaning a check for rare long lefts, at the far end of **FRAGATA BEACH** aka Kitebeach. There may be some good discoveries on the east coast in such conditions, but it's sharky. Don't forget about the other islands, with good waves to be found on Boa Vista, Santiago and Sao Vicente in both winter N and summer S swells.

SWELL AND WIND

The Cabo Verde archipelago is advantageously situated within the Atlantic tropics and catches due S and N swells from both hemispheres. The positioning of the islands means they interfere with each other for any given swell direction, and only the biggest ground swells will travel this far. This means that Cape Verde is a relatively inconsistent island destination. Sal is blocked by Boa Vista island from the S-SE swells, and is only able to pick up NW swells, rare WSW and the omnipresent NE windswells. The best swell generators are the lows that come off Nova Scotia and track over the Azores, between

November and February. Early season is the better time as there are more E winds blowing offshore. NE winds blowing from the Sahara desert are the standard, year round trades. The later in the winter you visit, the more N-NE winds you can expect, inconvenient for most surf spots. During the summer, you may encounter a rare SW gale. NE trades can create mushy windswell on the E coast, which can get up to a decent size. Tidal ranges are minimal (<1m), but they still effect the shallow reefs, causing most waves to break too close to the rocks at high tide. ●

SPOT INFORMATION

SPOT	SIZE	BTM	TYPE
①	6/2		
②	10/4		
③	18/3		
④	12/2		
⑤	6/3		
⑥	6/2		
⑦	15/3		
⑧	6/1		
⑨	6/1		
⑩	6/1		

SURF STATS		J	F	M	A	M	J	J	A	S	O	N	D
SWELL	Dominant swell												
	Size (m)	4		3		2		0-1		2-3		4	
	Consistency (%)	50		40		20		10		40		50	
WIND	Dominant wind												
	Average force	F4		F4		F4		F4		F4		F4	
	Consistency	65		61		94		79		82		67	
TEMP.	Wetsuit												
	Water temp.	21		21		24		26		27		25	

SÃO TOMÉ

+ QUALITY, EMPTY POINTBREAKS
+ CONSISTENT SUMMER SWELLS
+ NO RAIN DURING SURF SEASON
+ UNTOUCHED EQUATORIAL ISLAND
+ BEAUTIFUL SCENERY & WILDLIFE

– MOSTLY SMALL WAVES
– NO ACCESS TO WEST COAST
– EXPENSIVE LOCAL PRICES
– COSTLY FLIGHTS
– MALARIA

Approximately 270km from the western shores of Africa, São Tomé and Príncipe Archipelago are composed of 3 islands: São Tomé is the largest, followed by Príncipe which is 30min away by plane, and finally the tiny islet of Rolas (3km²). São Tomé and Príncipe is a developing country, with an economy based on coffee, cocoa, small-scale agriculture and fishing. Príncipe was the first island where cocoa trees were planted in 1822 by the Portuguese, hence the nickname of the "Chocolate Islands". Many plantations were abandoned after independence in 1975, which wreaked havoc with the economy of the country for decades. The islands are still in reconstruction, but war is history and oil and tourism have taken over as the new way to give a better future for this secluded paradise. Australian and American surfers visited as early as the '70s, and the odd French surfer from Gabon or the Ivory Coast, but travelling surfers remain rare. The first media surf trip to this area was in August 2000, when Callahan, Rarick, George, et al found many promising set-ups along the east coast plus the equator straddling Point Zero Left.

RADIATION POINT

The quickest check from the capitol is **FORTE DE SÃO TOMÉ**, but the historical scenery is usually better than the short, dribbly, boulder rights that are often flat. **LAVADURO** could be a great right slab if it was not facing northeast, meaning the tubes are rarely big enough to clear the rocks. The other end of the beach is the rivermouth at Praia Melão, where righthanders can run down the rock and sand bank, provided there is enough swell. Rivermouth pollution after rain. **RADIATION POINT** is at the easternmost point of the island. This wave is located in the grounds of the giant Voice of America transmitting station - look for the huge antennas. Before driving out to the point, ask permission at the gate (usually refused), otherwise paddle around. Radiation Point is fairly consistent, because even local SE windswell will wrap with enough size to ride, and the SW wind is cross-offshore on the biggest outside section. Beware of shallow rocks and when the tide gets too high, waves will get fat and inconsistent. From there to Porto Alegre is an interesting set of right pointbreaks, which need a decent swell to start rolling. **BATISMO** in Praia das Pombas is a great set up with long walls down the rocky point when a bigger S swell swings up the east coast. Lower tides and any W wind will do. There might be some lefts on the other side of the headland reef on windless days. The same conditions will see

hollower waves at **DIQUE**, a shallow, urchin covered reef/point north of Santana village. Faces SE so quite consistent as it picks up most swells. **AGUA IZÉ** bay looks really nice and the right pointbreak set-up is obvious, but once again needs a strong pulse to fire. Interesting rock formations further round the headland. Large river empties into the sheltered Praia Rei behind the break. Ribeira Afonso has a large curving beach with average beachbreak waves. The cluster of rocks at the southern end of **BAIA COQUEIRO** hold the rivermouth sandbars nicely for some long, relaxing righthand shoulders into the bay. There's another good point/rivermouth named after the **LO GRANDE** river which flows from the mountainous interior. This right picks up a bit more swell and the river flow decides how many holes are blown in the 300m line-up. Water can be murky and rippy. **PORTO ALEGRE**, the African Nias, is the best wave on the island. It's a 200m long boulder/cobble right point that needs a big S swell and W quadrant winds to produce walls that are generally steeper and peel faster than the other pointbreaks on the island. This is the locals preferred spot, but there are usually plenty of waves to go round. Ilheu das Rolas is a small islet sitting on the equator off the southern tip of São Tome. It's an amazingly beautiful island, home to a very upscale dive resort called Pestana Equador, better suited to divers and big game fishermen. To reach the island catch the Cariouco boat from São João dos Angolares or Porto Alegre and cheaper accommodation is available at a "Roça." **PRAIA PESTANA**, or Fishermen's Bay, is a Waikiki-style reform, ideal to have fun on a longboard. Local kids on wooden boards can sometimes be found surfing here. The more serious wave is called **POINT ZERO LEFTS** because surfers take off in the Southern Hemisphere, cross the Equator riding, and kick out in the northern hemisphere. Unfortunately this wave is usually sideshore and when big can suffer from strong currents. Exposed to the west so more consistent than most spots, as long as the wind is from the SE. There is now a decent new road providing access to Praia Jale **ECOLODGE**, beach bungalows directly in front of a rocky lefthander that pulls in the swell, but it's often onshore. The west coast shows potential for long lefts, but the difficult access prevents many from exploring the multiple rivermouths and rocky coves. In the middle of the west coast is **FIM DO CAMINHO** (end of the trail) near Santa Catarina. It's a long wrapping left pointbreak over a bunch of rocks, but it's a 2h drive from São Tomé.

SWELL AND WIND

At this equatorial latitude, only solid S-SW groundswells produce surf. It's usually flat from October to March. The Austral winter brings several main swells a month, producing 2-8ft (0.6-2.5m) waves. Rolas is the most exposed island but it can't handle much size. Radiation

ECOLODGE

POINT ZERO LEFTS

JSCALLAHAN/SURF EXPLORE

TRAVEL INFORMATION

POPULATION: 183,176   TIMEZONE: GMT
COASTLINE: 209km (136mi)

GETTING THERE – 30 day visa necessary ($65) before you go. Vaccination against yellow fever is mandatory. São Tomé (TMS) flights can be very expensive, although it's cheaper for flights from Lisbon. Weekly direct connections via TAP, STP Airways, Air Angola and Africas Connection from $767. Connections to Angola (Luanda), Ghana (Accra), Cape Verde (Sal) and Gabon (Libreville). Departure tax: $20USD in cash.

GETTING AROUND – Rental cars are very expensive. A basic car such as a Suzuki Jimny costs $70/d, or hire a private yellow taxi (no meter), close the deal first and be prepared to pay for 5 persons plus the journey back. Roads are getting better but remain slow and winding. Locals use motorbikes. Rolas is 20 minutes by boat. Island Tours are available: from $1050 with Club Maxel boat.

LODGING AND FOOD – There are pricey luxury hotels, and some cheaper options. On Rolas, Pestana Equador Resort is a diving & fishing resort that costs $145/n/dbl; Jalé Beach Ecolodge bungalow for 2 from $45/day and the much newer Praia Inhame Ecolodge ($58/n/dbl/b&b). Allow $15 per meal. "Roça" are ex-plantation houses. Roça de São João dos Angolares: $55 for dble. Pensão Turismo in ST is $70 for an A/C room.

WEATHER – São Tomé is fully equatorial but because of abrupt topography and oceanic SW winds, there is a great diversity of climates as well as rainfall, going from 2000mm (80in) in the coastal NW to 7000mm (280in) in the SW highlands. Northern and western zones are drier than the rest of the island. The eastern coast is semi-humid, cloaked with rainforest down to the sheltered beaches. The south is generally the most humid and rainy. The main rainy season is from February to May and again from October to November, when an almost constant southerly breeze blows at 10-25 knots. When it rains, the sea becomes muddy. Despite the moisture it is often sunny, and the rains are mostly thunderstorms. During 'Gravana', from June to September, the sea becomes choppy, which makes it difficult to go out by boat. Divers prefer the rainy season for visibility. 'Gravanita' is the name given to Dec-Feb, which is a lighter version of Gravana. Warm water year-round, with a vest in July-August.

WEATHER	J/F	M/A	M/J	J/A	S/O	N/D
Total Rainfall (mm)	94	140	81	0	66	103
Consistency (d/m)	7	9	5	0	6	8
Temperature min. (°C)	23	23	21	21	21	21
Temperature max. (°C)	30	30	28	28	29	29

NATURE AND CULTURE – A paradise for bird watchers, hikers and biodiversity lovers. São Tomé Pico is a volcanic cone at 2024m. Don't miss Obo National Park. Check out Tchiloli, a weird form of theatre where men roam around Cao Grande, a mountain on São Tomé. Visit coffee or cocoa plantations. Sea turtles can be seen at Mikolo Beach.

HAZARDS AND HASSLES – As well as yellow fever shots, full protection against chloroquine-resistant malaria with appropriate drugs and mosquito repellent is essential. To surf the SW coast means going prepared. Radiation Point can be quite shallow but rocks are ok. Rolas can be out of control with strong rips. Friendly locals on local wooden boards are becoming more common.

HANDY HINTS – Bring a longboard for the smaller days. Dollars and Euros are accepted for main payments - no cash machines. Dobras are used for local markets, taxis etc. Santomean cuisine is very rich! Refuse to eat dishes made of sea turtles (meat or egg), or other protected species (shark, earth snails, forest pigeons etc). Eat Calulu, Blabla, Cachupa and Feijoada.

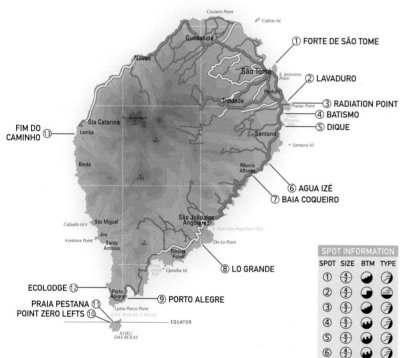

Cruzero Point
Cabras Isl.
Guadalupe
Neves
São Tomé
S. Jeronimo Point
① FORTE DE SÃO TOME
② LAVADURO
Pantufo
Trindade
Praiao Point
③ RADIATION POINT
④ BATISMO
Praia Pompas Bay
⑤ DIQUE
Santana
FIM DO CAMINHO ⑬
Sta Catarina
Lemba
Santana Isl.
Binda
Ribeira Alfonso
⑥ AGUA IZÉ
⑦ BAIA COQUEIRO
São João dos Angolares
Gabado Isl.
São Miguel
Jou
Azeitona Point
Santo Antonio
S. Joan dos Angolares Bay
Do Lo Point
Ribeira Peixe
⑧ LO GRANDE
Quixiba Isl.
ECOLODGE ⑫
Porto Alegre
⑨ PORTO ALEGRE
PRAIA PESTANA ⑪
POINT ZERO LEFTS ⑩
Lama Porco Point
DAS ROLAS CANAL
EQUATOR
ILHEU DAS ROLAS

SPOT INFORMATION			
SPOT	SIZE	BTM	TYPE
①			
②			
③			
④			
⑤			
⑥			
⑦			
⑧			
⑨			
⑩			
⑪			
⑫			
⑬			

Point also boasts consistency and will break on windswell. The SW wind is dominant throughout the year, but it is stronger from June-Sept, blowing 50% of the time as opposed to 35% from Oct-May. Porto Alegre rights need a good swell to break, and rarely reaches 6ft (2m). Access is a problem for west coast spots and other potential locations between Porto Alegre and São João dos Angolares. Check Buoyweather Gabon virtual buoys for forecasts. It takes 3-4 days for South African swells off Cape Town to reach São Tomé. Salinity might be lower in the Guinea Gulf during heavy rainy seasons. Tides are semi-diurnal with 4ft max of tidal range. This affects Radiation Point, which does not work at high tide when small. ●

SURF STATS		J	F	M	A	M	J	J	A	S	O	N	D
SWELL	Dominant swell												
	Size (m)	1-2		2-3		3-4		3-4		2-3		1-2	
	Consistency (%)	30		50		60		70		50		30	
WIND	Dominant wind												
	Average force	F3-F3		F3		F3		F3-F4		F3		F3	
	Consistency	76		74		75		92		85		78	
TEMP.	Wetsuit												
	Water temp.	28		28		27		25		26		27	

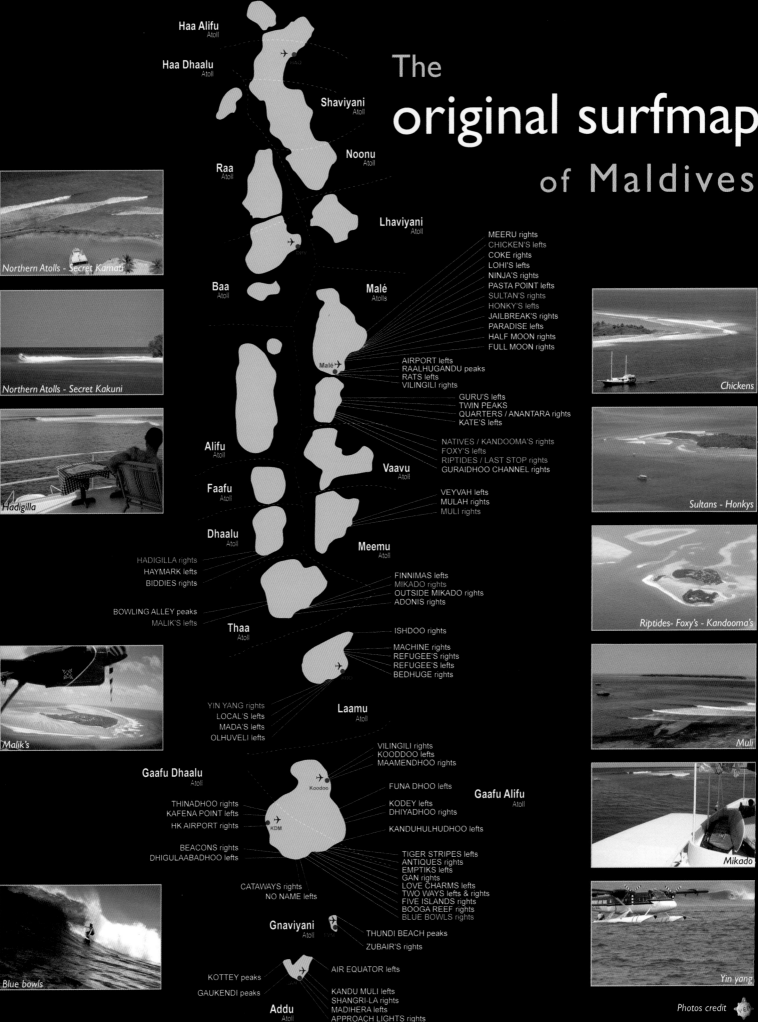

The
original surfmap
of Maldives

Haa Alifu Atoll

Haa Dhaalu Atoll

Shaviyani Atoll

Noonu Atoll

Raa Atoll

Lhaviyani Atoll

Baa Atoll

Malé Atolls

MEERU rights
CHICKEN'S lefts
COKE rights
LOHI'S lefts
NINJA'S rights
PASTA POINT lefts
SULTAN'S rights
HONKY'S lefts
JAILBREAK'S rights
PARADISE lefts
HALF MOON rights
FULL MOON rights

AIRPORT lefts
RAALHUGANDU peaks
RATS lefts
VILINGILI rights

GURU'S lefts
TWIN PEAKS
QUARTERS / ANANTARA rights
KATE'S lefts

Alifu Atoll

NATIVES / KANDOOMA'S rights
FOXY'S lefts
RIPTIDES / LAST STOP rights
GURAIDHOO CHANNEL rights

Vaavu Atoll

Faafu Atoll

VEYVAH lefts
MULAH rights
MULI rights

Dhaalu Atoll

Meemu Atoll

HADIGILLA rights
HAYMARK lefts
BIDDIES rights

FINNIMAS lefts
MIKADO rights
OUTSIDE MIKADO rights
ADONIS rights

BOWLING ALLEY peaks
MALIK'S lefts

Thaa Atoll

ISHDOO rights

MACHINE rights
REFUGEE'S rights
REFUGEE'S lefts
BEDHUGE rights

YIN YANG rights
LOCAL'S lefts
MADA'S lefts
OLHUVELI lefts

Laamu Atoll

VILINGILI rights
KOODDOO lefts
MAAMENDHOO rights

FUNA DHOO lefts

Gaafu Dhaalu Atoll

Gaafu Alifu Atoll

KODEY lefts
DHIYADHOO rights

THINADHOO rights
KAFENA POINT lefts
HK AIRPORT rights

KANDUHULHUDHOO lefts

BEACONS rights
DHIGULAABADHOO lefts

TIGER STRIPES lefts
ANTIQUES rights
EMPTIKS lefts
GAN rights
LOVE CHARMS lefts
TWO WAYS lefts & rights
FIVE ISLANDS rights
BOOGA REEF rights
BLUE BOWLS rights

CATAWAYS rights
NO NAME lefts

Gnaviyani Atoll

THUNDI BEACH peaks
ZUBAIR'S rights

AIR EQUATOR lefts

KOTTEY peaks
GAUKENDI peaks

KANDU MULI lefts
SHANGRI-LA rights
MADIHERA rights
APPROACH LIGHTS rights

Addu Atoll

Northern Atolls - Secret Kamati

Northern Atolls - Secret Kakuni

Hadigilla

Malik's

Blue bowls

Chickens

Sultans - Honkys

Riptides- Foxy's - Kandooma's

Muli

Mikado

Yin yang

Photos credit

HARIYANA I

HARIYANA

DHONI KAKUNI

Zone : Gaafu Dhaalu atoll
Period : March - November
Construction : 2004, refurbished 2012
Length : 26 m (85 ft)
Width : 8 m (26 ft)
Cruising speed : 8-9 knots
Engine : *Daewoo 360 hp*
Electricity : 2 soundproof generators
Cabins : 7 (6 down, 1up) with *Aircon*, large bathroom, 14 beds
Dingy : 6 m (18 ft) – 15 hp outboard
Dhoni : 18 m (55 ft) x 5 m (16 ft) - 4T engine (9 knots), surf rack
Decks : 3, back shaded area for boardbags / Chill out
Crew : 5 people

Zone : Northern atolls
Period : May - August
Construction : 2001, refurbished 2012
Length : 23 m (75 ft)
Width : 6.1 m (20 ft)
Cruising speed : 8-9 knots
Engine : *Quad Seba 120 hp*
Electricity : *Onan 9.5 kw and Yanmar 2.5 kw Generators*
Cabins : 6 with *Aircon*, bathroom, 12 beds
Dingy : 6 m (18 ft) - 15 hp outboard
Dhoni : Kakuni
Decks : 2, shaded top area for boardbags
Crew : 4 people

Zone : All atolls
Period : May - September
Construction : 2001, refurbished 2012
Length : 16 m (52 ft)
Width : 5 m (16 ft)
Cruising speed : 8.5 knots
Engine : 3T 35 hp engine
Electricity : Solar panel, no plugs
Cabins : None, 4 hammocks
Dingy : None
Decks : 2, top floor for boardbags
Crew : 2 people

Maldive**surf fleet**

ATOLL CHALLENGER

EQUATOR

Zone : Central atolls
Period : May - Sept
Construction : 2009
Length : 33 m (108 ft)
Width : 9 m (29.5 ft)
Cruising speed : 10-12 knots
Engine : *Mitsubishi 360 hp*
Electricity : 2 soundproof generators
Cabins : 8 with *Aircon*, large bathroom, 16 beds
Dingy : 2 with 15 hp
Dhoni : on demand
Decks : 3, shaded sundeck for boardbags / Chill out
Crew : 5-6 people

Zone : North Malé
Period : May - June
Construction : 2004
Length : 30 m (99 ft)
Width : 8.5 m (28 ft)
Cruising speed : 11 knots
Engine : *Scania 420 hp*
Electricity : 2 soundproof generators
Cabins : 9 (7 down, 2 up) with *Aircon*, large bathroom, 18 beds
Dingy : 2 with 15 hp outboard engine for 8 surfers
Dhoni : on demand
Decks : 3, shaded sundeck for boardbags / Chill out
Crew : 6 people

Since 2004

MALDIVESURF
CRUISE THE ATOLLS

Guided boat trips all around the atolls
Operated by Antony "yep" Colas, author of the *World Stormrider Guides*

Check our website **www.maldivesurf.com**

INDIAN

OCEAN

INTRODUCTION

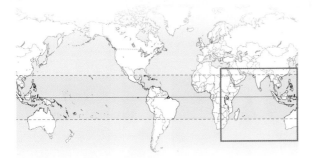

It is surprising that the Indian Ocean is home to the best waves in the world, considering the Pacific is the largest ocean and the Atlantic is the stormiest. What makes it so good is actually the one ingredient that it is so obviously missing – land! When a storm crosses any other ocean, it eventually crashes into a continent, but not in the empty, marine kingdom between the Roaring Forties and the Great Southern Ocean, where low pressure systems have a clear path of circumnavigation, squirting the planet with all strains of south swell. Indonesia and a sprinkling of Indian Ocean islands have proved themselves the most able catchers of this reliable swell, transforming it into a glut of world-class spots in balmy, tropical latitudes, fanned by trustworthy trades and monsoons. Indonesia has fast become the centre of the surfing holiday universe, while a flotilla of charter boats troll the islands of this incredible archipelago for a never-ending "catch of the day". Furthermore, out in the deep blue, sparkling atolls and islands beckon from the Maldives to Madagascar, challenging the traveller to plug into some Indian Ocean power lines.

SWELL

The Indian Ocean sits primarily in the southern Hemisphere, where most of the swells are generated between the Roaring Forties and the Great Southern Ocean located at 60° latitude. These low pressure systems make the journey from the Cape of Good Hope to the SW tip of Australia with year-round regularity, spraying out consistent, quality swell, the bulk of which heads towards Indonesia and Western Australia. Wave size deteriorates as the swells propagate north of the equator towards the Maldives and Sri Lanka, where the swell often swings to arrive from the SE and mixes in with the constant windswell from the monsoon winds. Réunion, and Mauritius are much closer to the Roaring Forties lows and maintain some sizeable waves throughout winter, before it's time to watch out for cyclones/tropical depressions forming in the 15°-25°S latitudes. These systems often travel west towards the Mascarene Islands and Madagascar, providing powerful swell for the east coasts of all the islands when the southern low pressures are at their weakest (Jan-Mar). Unfortunately, they are few and far between, averaging 9 per annum and are accompanied by the NE to SE trade winds of the region (see map). Major cyclones also affect the Arabian Sea (Oct-Nov) and the Bay of Bengal (May-June)

The Mentawai Islands have the elusive 'Goldilocks' factor when it comes to the combinations of swell, wind and reef bathymetry, which always seem "just right".

BANKVAULTS

ROGER SHARP

meaning there are some waves going unridden in frontier surfing destinations such as Lakshadweep, India, Bangladesh, Myanmar and Thailand. Indonesia is the modern surf traveller's Mecca, because the Indian Ocean serves up virtually constant, long distance lines of organised swell to equatorial latitudes. There's the added bonus of occasional cyclone swells arriving from The Bay of Bengal above Sumatra or even rarer still, from the Timor Sea below Nusa Tenggara.

WIND

The Indian Ocean's weather systems are surprisingly complex and the whole of the tropical basin goes through an annual reversal of winds known as the monsoon. The lower latitudes around Mauritius and Reunion see less clocking with SE to S trade winds dominating the winter surf season and reaching maximum intensity from June to Oct, before a friendlier NE sets in for summer (Nov-Mar). The equatorial latitudes of the Maldives and Sri Lanka are influenced by monsoonal periods with NE winds coming down the Bay of Bengal in Dec-March before the switch flicks to the SW pattern that usually covers April-Oct. Shoulder season can be light and variable as the monsoon tries to make up its mind, so expect anything from Mar-May and Sep-Dec. The bulk of the Indonesian archipelago is blessed with far more predictable winds from the E-SE that groom the lefts on the western

SEASONAL SWELL AND WIND PATTERNS

coasts from April to Oct, while the NW wet season winds leave south and east-facing coasts clean from Dec to March. In the doldrums close to the equator, W-NW predominates, but the winds are generally shifty, even non-committal and glassy days are common.

TIDES, CURRENTS AND TEMPERATURES

Tides in the region follow a basic pattern of semi-diurnal odd if the coast faces west and predominantly semi-diurnal even for the east coasts of Madagascar and the Bay of Bengal. Ranges are generally small (mostly under 2m/6ft) apart from Nusa Tenggara which reaches 2.4m/8ft. Currents are most notable in the North Indian Ocean because unlike the Pacific and Atlantic, a seasonal current reversal takes place. This coincides with the monsoon, flowing from the NE towards Africa in winter (Nov-Mar) and then in the opposite direction toward India in the summer months (June-Oct). Called the Somali Current, it follows the wind, but changes little in temperature. Further south, the anti-clockwise rotation of the Agulhas Current (world's fastest at 9km/h) keeps Madagascar and the Mascarenes fed with warm water, before heading east along with the Roaring Forties storms until it swings up past the West Australian coast and finishes

HUVADHOO ATOLL

JODY MACDONALD

Tidal variation is often decided by which way the coast faces and the currents switch with the seasonal monsoon reversal.

its massive circuit as the South Equatorial Current, which flows westward back to Africa and the Agulhas. The Indian Ocean also feeds the warmest sea (the Persian Gulf) and the saltiest sea (the Red Sea) and regularly exceeds 30°C (86°F) in many places including The Maldives, Bay of Bengal and NW Indonesia.

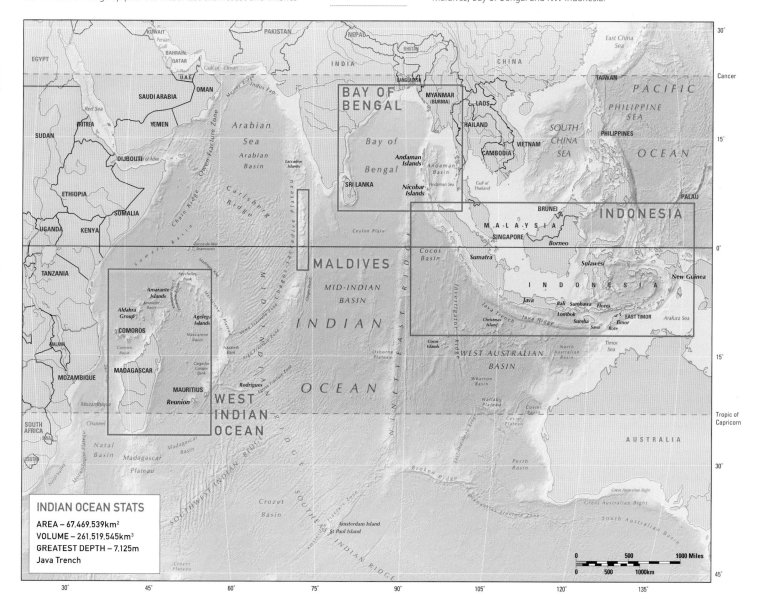

INDIAN OCEAN STATS
AREA – 67,469,539km²
VOLUME – 261,519,545km³
GREATEST DEPTH – 7,125m
Java Trench

WESTERN INDIAN OCEAN

This corner of the Indian Ocean warms its hands closest to the fiery Roaring Forties low pressure systems that blast out a constant procession of quality swell events across the bottom of the basin. Just to the east of Madagascar the Mascarene Islands peep above the ocean parapet, copping a volley of SW swell and are peppered with famous, classy line-ups, hunkered down on the west coast out of the ever-present E trades. Further north, the obscure archipelagos of the Comoros and the swanky Seychelles both have a few draw cards, away from the masses, in a tranquil, tropical setting.

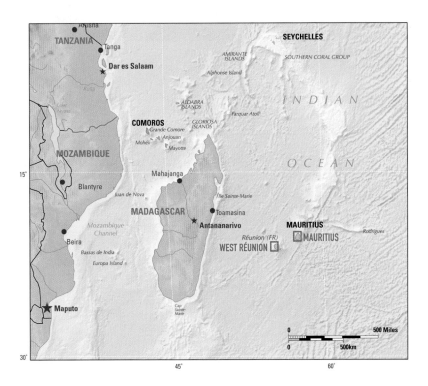

THE MASCARENES

Réunion is oft considered a one-wave island, rarely mentioned unless the boomerang bending lefts of St Leu are the topic of conversation. WEST RÉUNION is more like three separate wave zones, as the circular shape of the island offers variation on wind and swell direction. East of Saint-Pierre's jetty rights and the short lefts of Grande-Anse and Manapany, sees the south coast start, named 'La cote du Sud Sauvage', mainly due to the constant swell and wind action, but also because of a major shift in the island's geology. The coral reefs give way to lava flows and basalt rocks, backed by steep ravines leading up to the volcanic peaks that dominate the east coast, where rainfall is way higher than the west, and dense tropical vegetation cloaks the lower slopes. High precipitation inevitably creates murky water at the many rivermouths, which are the preferred restaurants of the large Réunion shark population. The NE coast from Sainte-Rose to Saint-Denis offers very little opportunity, despite being directly in the summer cyclone firing line and most locals will head to the NW coast for these rare swells.

Some places become intrinsically linked with how they are portrayed in a movie and none more so than MAURITIUS, which became affectionately known by its screen name, *The Forgotten Island Of Santosha*. Like many things on film, the perfect pipes of Tamarin

Bay were shown in their best possible light and many returned disillusioned, saying the camera always lies! Mauritius shares a good few features with Réunion, being a bit more teardrop shaped, with a west side that is mainly NW-facing and therefore set up to work far better in the big S-SW swell convoys, which explains the consistency problems at Tamarin Bay. Consistency is never a problem on the lashed S coast, but the SE winter trades are, so summer NE winds are the Christmas present for this coast. Unlike Réunion, the west coast has an extensive coral reef formation with multiple passes and cuts in the platform. Unfortunately, the curse of the Mascarene east coasts is the permanent, pesky E trades that exceed 32kmh (20mph) for half the time in July and don't drop by too much through Jan.

There's a palpably relaxed outer-island Creole feel to **Rodrigues**, a bit somnolent too, distanced from the mainland bustle of Mauritius. A kite-surfing Mecca, windswept little Rodrigues could be to today's kiters what Tamarin was to yesteryear's surfers - an exotic Mascarene isle unspoiled by tourism, malls, junk food, high-speed motorways, luxury hotels hogging the best beaches and all that kind of stuff. Kiters could make a special Santosha-esque film and still viewers would be mystified by the locale, much like they were before Tamarin Fever infected the entire surf world. The roar of onshore wind and trashed surf is constant, the swell-exposed south coast constantly unsurfable and if your time is limited, you will want to avoid Rodrigues because there is essentially one spot. Passe Jimmy, a narrow hole in the island's western barrier reef that is only surfable on small WSW swells and high tide. Fronted by tiny Île aux Sables, a nature reserve, Passe Jimmy has a right and a left, the left being longer and more high-performance orientated than the right, which tends to be abrupt and hollower. Both are fast and very shallow, breaking over healthy live coral, and are only accessible during high tide, requiring a minimum one-hour boat ride over the shallow lagoon from Baie du Nord or Port Mathurin. The pass closes out with any swell bigger than two metres, and the wind is often blowing too hard offshore, making the waves choppy and unrideable. Occasionally Passe Jimmy can offer fun, clean waves, but Rodrigues is not a place for a designated surf trip. The same can be said of the other Mauritian administered outer island dependencies including the atolls of Cargados Carajos shoals, the immense undersea (scientists have tried to grow an artificial island here) Saya de Malha Bank and the tiny Agalega Islands. Tromelin has an airstrip, a cyclone-warning weather station and a wave-lashed, teardrop reef in the middle of nowhere, but no real surf.

OUTER ISLANDS

There are some surf spots on Grande Comoros, Moheli and even the reef-encircled French Territory of Mayotte, where mostly French mainlanders access by boat, one or two decent waves near the airport on slack wind days. The bulk of the known facts about the **Comoros Islands** are included in Anjouan. The Glorioso Islands are French, while Astove, Cosmoledo, Assumption and Aldabra Islands are one of the five groups of the Seychelles Outer Islands, forming a cluster of barely inhabited nature reserves, weather stations and marginal surfing opportunities for oceanic wanderers. Other far-flung clusters of coralline origin include the Amirante Islands, Alphonse Group, Farquar Group and the Southern Coral Group. The only way these islands will ever get surfed is by private yacht and even if you have money to burn at a resort like Desroches, the small planes mean you won't have a board to ride. The Seychelles look like they should be a surf paradise, but as with the Outer Islands, not all is as it seems and the Honeymooners will always outnumber visiting surfers by a healthy margin.

The **Seychelles** look like they should be a surf paradise, but as with the Outer Islands, not all is as it seems and the Honeymooners will always outnumber visiting surfers by a healthy margin.

OTHER ISLANDS TO CONSIDER

MOYA LEFT

JS CALLAHAN/SURFEXPLORE

INDONESIA
AND THE INDIAN OCEAN

Madagascar and
the Mascarenes

For more information,
check these other
Stormrider Surf Guides
and/or eBooks.

ANJOUAN, COMOROS

+ EMPTY LINE-UPS
+ UNDISCOVERED WAVES
+ BEAUTIFUL LANDSCAPES
+ VARIETY OF SPOTS

– ONSHORE WINDS
– POLITICAL INSTABILITY
– DISEASES AND POVERTY
– INTER-ISLAND TRANSPORT

Located in the north of the Mozambique Channel, between Africa and Madagascar, the Comoros have hidden their surf potential for a long time, until a recent expedition found waves on Anjouan. The volcanic archipelago is made up of four islands; Grande Comoros, Anjouan and Mohéli form the independent Comoros Union, while Mayotte remains a French territory. Tourism is undeveloped thanks to political instability (18 coups in 24yrs, often led by the well-known mercenary Bob Dénard), a lack of infrastructure, extreme poverty and health problems like malaria and cholera. Grande Comoros, the biggest island of the archipelago and overshadowed by the 2361m (7746ft) peak of the Karthala volcano, holds a couple of low tide beachbreaks north of Moroni (Itzandra) sprinkled with a few coral heads. Also check the east coast beaches around Chomoni and the northern reefs near the salt lake. The little reef-fringed island of Mohéli has waves off Fomboni beach, but Anjouan has the best potential for surf with a variety of spots on the SW-facing coast and good exposure to winter S-SW swells ploughing up the Mozambique channel. Hollow ledging rights tour the coral at Dead Fishermen reef or longer, walled lefts start from a shallow peak at Five Pappas. On the windy east coast there are beachbreaks and boulder points plus miles of coastline to explore during the summer cyclone season.

SEYCHELLES

+ USER-FRIENDLY WAVES
+ FEW CROWDS
+ WARM WATER
+ BEAUTIFUL SCENERY

– RARELY SURFABLE
– VERY EXPENSIVE
– WINDY
– LACK OF GOOD SURF SPOTS

After an article appeared in Surfer magazine in 1967, the Seychelles isle of Mahé was put on the world surfing map. Aussie photographer Ron Perrott described it as a paradise, influencing many surfers to make the trip, but they came back disappointed. Small, clean, relatively uncrowded surf does exist, but Mahé suffers from a long, shallow shelf, bad location, and extremely inconsistent swells that struggle to produce more than a dozen good days annually. Sitting too far W for the normal groundswell angles in the Indian Ocean, Mahé is usually bypassed, instead relying on a major S swell to hit, or for consistent onshore winds to create surf on the few exposed reefs like La Passe . When it is big enough to wrap around to the W coast for offshore conditions, rare gems like Anse aux Poules Bleues will break a few times a year, while Anse Gaulette is far more reliable. It's an island of outstanding natural beauty, where lush granite rock mountains, meet gorgeous white-sand beaches, attracting well-off tourists and honeymooners to Mahé and Victoria, which is Africa's smallest capital city.

DAVID PU'U

LA PASSE

WEST RÉUNION

+ CONSISTENT   – EXPENSIVE
+ SPOT DIVERSITY   – CROWDED/LOCALISM
+ SCENERY   – SHARKY
+ SAFE TOURISM   – CRAZY TRAFFIC

A volcanic dot of tropical French idyll, flavored with Creole, Indian, African, and Chinese culture, endowed with some of Earth's finest natural beauty, Réunion is also ideally placed to receive powerful and consistent Roaring Forties swells. It's a volcanic isle with black sand beaches and high peaks, including Piton de la Fournaise, an active volcano known locally as le Volcan. Its last eruption occurred on 2 January 2010 and lasted 10 days. The mountainous geography has a big influence on weather patterns and, consequently, coral reefs have only developed on the leeward W coast because the rainfall there is minimal. The rain has shaped canyons that funnel water into the sea and then through coral passes. Most of the 32 reported spots on the W coast break on fragmented barrier reefs, quite a distance from the beach. There's also normal lava rock bottoms, but they are less numerous and usually have murky water—good habitat for sharks. For the less adventurous, there's a few average black sand beachbreaks along with the popular white sand beaches of Roches Noires and Boucan Canot.

Just north of the unsightly Possession Harbour entrance is a big wave peak called **LE PORT**. Rarely ridden and hard to find, it has a nasty shark factor. St-Gilles is the area's main centre with bars, shops, hotels, good nightlife, and at least 17 breaks scattered around 12kms (7.5mi) of coastline. **CAP REQUIN** swings left round a coral sweep in moderate swells, needing high tides for depth and SE winds for groomed, lip bashing walls. The name is a clue to its sharkiness, like La Cimetiere beachbreak just north, scene of two recent attacks. Crowded **BOUCAN** has a fun, reliable left reef in swell up to 10ft, while the gnarly right only jacks up and barrels in solid size. Down the beach is another small swell left. **AIGRETTES** is mainly a friendly left wall for improvers to hone their cutties, unlike the peak beyond which is a harsh barrel over the urchin covered reef, that is hard to cross. Follow a local. **ROCHES NOIRES** has a string of rights that cover most abilities from the rare, N-swell-loving slabs of Cachera and L'Escalier down to Banc de Sable where even beginners can surf in big swells. The three sections of **LA DIGUE** lefts occasionally link up into one extremely long left ride, offering intermediates a fast wall through the mid-section and shredders a tricky barrel on the inside. Jump off the jetty wall at St Gilles. The fabulous natural lagoon reserve at **L'HERMITAGE PASS** offers surfers the choice between an epic tubing left and a short, intense barrelling right. A 5 knot current makes paddling out easy

JS CALLAHAN/SURFEXPLORE

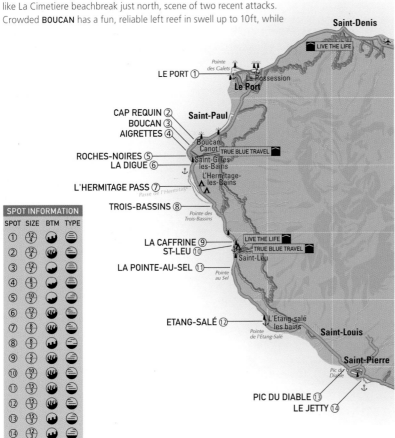

Saint-Denis

LIVE THE LIFE

Pointe des Galets
LE PORT ①
La Possession
Le Port

CAP REQUIN ②
Saint-Paul
BOUCAN ③
AIGRETTES ④
Boucan Canot
TRUE BLUE TRAVEL
ROCHES-NOIRES ⑤
Saint-Gilles-les-Bains
LA DIGUE ⑥
L'Hermitage-les-Bains
L'HERMITAGE PASS ⑦
Passe de l'Hermitage
TROIS-BASSINS ⑧
Pointe des Trois-Bassins

LA CAFFRINE ⑨
LIVE THE LIFE
ST-LEU ⑩
TRUE BLUE TRAVEL
Saint-Leu
LA POINTE-AU-SEL ⑪
Pointe au Sel

ETANG-SALÉ ⑫
L'Etang-salé les bains
Pointe de l'Etang-Salé
Saint-Louis

Saint-Pierre
Pic du Diable
PIC DU DIABLE ⑬
LE JETTY ⑭

SPOT INFORMATION

SPOT	SIZE	BTM	TYPE
①	12/4		
②	12/4		
③	12/2		
④	10/3		
⑤	10/2		
⑥	12/2		
⑦	8/2		
⑧	8/2		
⑨	8/2		
⑩	10/2		
⑪	8/2		
⑫	15/2		
⑬	15/2		
⑭	15/2		

SAINT-LEU

⑩/2

LAT. -21.165254°   LONG. 55.283213°

Famous Indian Ocean reef pass where long, loping lefts bend into a picturesque lagoon. Undoubtedly in the over-used, world-class category, it was chosen as the venue for the original Rip Curl Search competition and can be a handful, even for the world's best. When big enough, a rapido take-off and workable wall on the outside conveys the experienced rider into two filthy bowl sections, bending noticeably and throwing roomy tubes on the inside. Coral heads surface at low and the line-up breaks into sections when small.

L'HERMITAGE PASS

and coming in a nightmare. Both are sharky, work on small swells, and need rare NE winds. The 3 waves at **TROIS-BASSINS** are swell and crowd magnets, having waves when everywhere else is flat. La Barriere is the fast shallow right and odd left that works in any N or S swell. Most people ride The Peak closer to shore in the mouth of the river that has cut a deep pass in the reef. It's a nice little A-frame with feathering lips and tapered shoulders over lava rocks, accessible to most surfers. South of the cut is a fairly fat left wall that occasionally connects up on a due S swell. **LA CAFRINE** is tucked in behind the St-Leu reef offering beginners a nursery right over a deep, urchin-covered, coral slab. The famous lefts of **ST-LEU** provide a truly world-class wave when stronger SW swells hit, usually in winter. It starts with a quick drop and open face wall, ideal for carving big

turns, before bending sharply round the reef into a couple of bowly, hollow sections that throw out a shallow tube. Needs to be overhead to start linking up for the full 300m ride, but will work in sections when it is smaller. Experienced surfers only, despite the easy paddle-out and be respectful of the local pecking order. **LA POINT-AU-SEL** is a voyeurs dream as massive caverns hit a straight section of reef that looks perfect, but is unmakeable. **ETANG-SALÉ** is the windsurfers equivalent of St-Leu, as the SE wind blows cross-shore, but if the winds are calm or NE, then barrels will appear out on the fringing reef. Handles the biggest swells, but the current is so severe it also affects the thumping close-out beachbreaks further up the black sand beach near the bridge. The S coast around St-Pierre is very consistent, with the majority of waves being rights, such as the scary **PIC DU DIABLE** where a powerful wall runs into a small bay that offers a bit of SE wind protection. Aptly named, the Devils Peak has seen multiple attacks in the murky water and a surfer fatality in 2006. Right in front of the harbour wall, **LE JETTY** is another spot that handles plenty of swell and gets busy in summer when everywhere else is flat. A hairy take-off leads into a speed-pump wall that will tube if the wind is N quadrant or light enough. Long ride over the coral shelf that is home to zillions of urchins and of course sharks. There are more waves on the S and E coasts, but there have been shark attacks in these areas and surfing is not advised.

SWELL AND WIND

The main swell is generated by the Roaring Forties around South Africa. During the Southern Hemisphere winter, there are frequent SW swells varying in size from 3-15ft. Although these swells can occur

SURF STATS		J F	M A	M J	J A	S O	N D
SWELL	Dominant swell	🌑	🌑	🌑	🌑	🌑	🌑
	Size (m)	4-5	5-6	6-7	7-8	6	3-4
	Consistency (%)	70	80	90	90	80	60
WIND	Dominant wind	🌀	🌀	🌀	🌀	🌀	🌀
	Average force	F4	F4	F4	F5	F4	F3
	Consistency (%)	65	64	60	76	69	58
TEMP	Wetsuit	🏄	🏄	🏄	🏄	🏄	🏄
	Water temp.	28	27	26	24	25	26

LE JETTY

BERNARD TESTEMALE

TRAVEL INFORMATION

LOCAL POPULATION:	COASTLINE: 207km (129mi)
Reunion – 839,500	TIME ZONE: GMT +4h

GETTING THERE – South Africans need visas. Roland Garros International Airport (RUN) receives direct flights from Mauritius, Seychelles, Madagascar, South Africa, and France. April-July is Réunion's peak tourist season, but you'll save cash if you book a discount ticket to London or Paris, then a separate ticket to Réunion on Air France, Air Austral, Air Mauritius, Corsair, or Air Madagascar. Air France charge from $55-150 per boardbag e/w.

GETTING AROUND – The mountainous interior means driving mainly on the N1 coastal road, which is very busy at rush hours, especially around St-Denis. Basing yourself in St-Leu will save time and money. The "Cars Jaunes" bus service is reliable (you clap your hands to stop the bus). A rental car costs around $400/week and are available at the airport.

LODGING AND FOOD – St-Leu's 3-star Paladien Apolonia is plush but a double room starts at $208/night. Directly across the street from the wave is DodoSpot; a double room there starts at $38/night. They also offer cabins. The Campix campground is open March to November. For cheap deals, stay in guesthouses ($40/$60) slightly out of town or go to St-Pierre or St-Gilles. Spicy Creole cuisine or imported French food is the standard, costing around $15 or even less from "camion" bars.

WEATHER – The tropical climate is very much influenced by the high mountains. The windward coast is very wet, with humidity levels amongst the highest in the world, while the W coast is rather dry. The mountains are often overcast and the coast enjoys clear skies swept by the trade winds. The cyclone season lasts from December to March with major destructive cyclones hitting the island every three years or so. This period is the warmest and wettest, whilst mid-winter can feel cool. May-June and Sept-Oct are usually the best weather months. Springsuits help with windchill when water bottoms out at 24°C (75°F) around August.

WEATHER	J/F	M/A	M/J	J/A	S/O	N/D
Total Rainfall (mm)	82	28	14	6	10	51
Consistency (d/m)	7	4	2	2	2	5
Temperature min. (°C)	22	18	16	14	16	20
Temperature max. (°C)	32	31	28	27	29	31

NATURE AND CULTURE – The interior of the island is beautiful. Maïdo is a 2000m peak that has a breathtaking view over the W coast. Cirques like Mafate, Cilaos, and Salazie are great places for trekking and admiring the view. On the E side, Piton de la Fournaise is the second-most active volcano in the world.

HAZARDS AND HASSLES – In total four people have been killed in eight different shark attacks on surfers in Reunion since January 2011. Don't surf in murky water, on your own, before dark, or after heavy rains. Fire coral, spiny urchins, and shallow reefs are also real threats. With only about 30 spots and hundreds of surfers, the line-ups are competitive. St-Leu is localised and has experienced bouts of violence.

HANDY HINTS – It's a French island with white "Zoreils" (the name of people from mainland France) raising the standard of living. Mixed-race locals speak Creole. The bars are lively and play local sega and maloya music. There are good surf shops, but gear is very expensive.

year-round, the summer season is characterised more by NE tropical storms, but with only about 10 depressions in six months, it can hardly be called consistent. SE trades blow constantly with a more E-NE direction during the summer (Dec-Mar) and more S-SE during winter (June-Sept). The wind can also produce 2-6ft onshore windswell on the windward coast, and side/offshore on the SW coast. Tides are only significant at shallow spots. Tide charts are easily found online. ●

MAURITIUS

+ TAMARINS FLAWLESS LEFT
+ QUALITY REEFBREAKS
+ EXOTIC CULTURE
+ BEAUTIFUL SCENERY
+ MODERATE PRICES

- CROWDS
- TAMARIN'S INCONSISTENCY
- LACK OF SHELTERED WAVES
- EXPENSIVE FLIGHTS

Mauritius has gained an exotic image in the heart of surfers thanks to 1974's *Forgotten Island of Santosha*. The film focused largely on Tamarin Bay, a perfect wave that became a symbol of escapism. The spot had been surfed since the early 1960s, but the epic 8-10ft swell featured in the film captured the attention of the surfing world. Unfortunately Tamarin turned out to be inconsistent, leaving many travelling surfers disappointed. Since then, the focus has shifted to the more consistent, neighbouring island of Réunion. Mauritius has a lack of optimum southwest-facing shores, while the south-facing coast is frequently blown-out by SE trade winds. The local surfing tradition goes back years, but it developed in a sad way, leading to a reputation for localism. Throughout the '80s and '90s, white Mauritians called "White Shorts" regulated the wave at Tamarin, but they have since mellowed considerably and generally is no longer an issue.

PASSE DE L'AMBULANTE

On the NE coast of Mauritius is the town of Grand Gaube; the barrier reef offshore has a couple of righthanders during the off-season, notably the right in front of **ÎLE BERNACHE**, fun and juicy when it breaks, which isn't very often. There is a kitesurfing/ surf school nearby. Near **GRAND BAIE** is the island's second-best left, called "Tagore" by some, rivalling Tamarin when it's on, with localism and a nasty reef. Just south is the **MONT CHOISY** beach area, where there are some shapely reefs offshore (two rights and two lefts), but require a long paddle or hiring a boat from shore. On the NW coast at Trou aux Biches there is a fairly gutless reef wave that is usually quite small, so good for novices. At **BALACLAVA** there is a pass in front of the Oberoi Hotel that has a fun left and a right when small and clean. At the south end of the bay (Baie de l'Arsenal) **LE GOULET** is a good but rare left that only breaks on the biggest of SW swells, having to wrap nearly 180°. At Baie de la Petite Rivière, there is a NW-facing pass in front of La Plantation d'Albion **CLUB MED** that has a left and a right, but both need a big winter swell or summer conditions to break. When the swell is small and clean, sometimes there are a few rideable spots on the barrier reef offshore of **FLIC EN FLAC**. **BLACK ROCKS** is a fast, powerful, folding wall that needs higher tides and more NE than SE wind to hold up the sections, situated across the deep bay from the famous reef at **TAMARIN** (see next page). Just down the coast, **LA PRENEUSE** is a barrelling left along a corner of the barrier reef offshore of the Martello Tower museum. Yet another perfect, but inconsistent left exists at the entrance to **BAIE DE LA PETITE RIVIÉRE NOIRE** that requires a boat ride. Moving down to the consistent Le Morne Peninsula, there is **PASSE DE L'AMBULANTE**, a decent high tide left and right (the right is better) directly in front of Les Pavillons Hotel; it's almost a 1km offshore so find a boat. The small pass in front of Berjaya Resort is called **ONE EYES**, a consistent and crowded weekend spot where shapely lefts spin down a straight reef that gets quite heavy and hollow when overhead. Low tide makes the line-up and the 20min lagoon paddle sketchy. When the swell is small and clean or the wind is NE, **MORNE RIGHTS** can be ridden out on the north side of Passe de la Prairie. Across the channel is the Manawa left and both are very consistent, long and hollow, but you need slack wind, incoming tide, and a boat to reach it. Horrendous out-going currents

on the dropping tide. At Baie du Cap, **MACONDÉ** is a short hollow left that can handle any size, but requires some N or E in the wind and a 10-minute paddle. All the spots further east only work in the morning or with summer NE winds. Facing the cemetery, **GRAVEYARDS** is another left that's rarely good, but usually rideable over the scary reef. Requires a long paddle-out, and needs N wind. One of the most

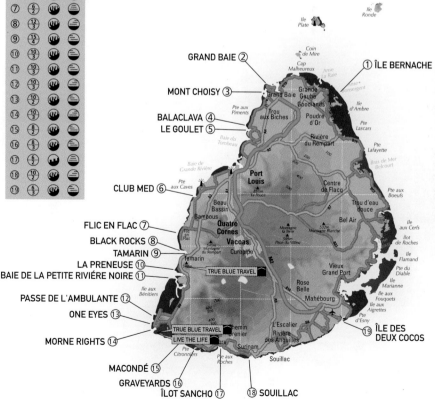

SOUILLAC

MICHEAL KEW

consistent summer spots on the S coast is **ÎLOT SANCHO**, which gets weird rights and lefts on the edge of the reef in the little cove. The right in **SOUILLAC** breaks on a small swell and a N wind on the last bit of fringing reef before the coast gets cliffy. On huge south swells there is a psycho death righthand slab at Gris Gris—it would be a prime tow spot if jet skis were legal on Mauritius! Down at Blue Bay, there is a very good left behind **ÎLE DES DEUX COCOS**, but it is always blown out during winter, hard to access and creates strong currents. The eastern reef of Mauritius has dozens of small passes and possible surf spots, but they are almost always flat and/or blown out.

TAMARIN BAY

LAT. -20.326852° LONG. 57.372085°

A moderate to big SW swell has to wrap heavily to break along the famous reef at Tamarin Bay. Hypnotic, cultured barrels tour the NW-facing reef when a moderate to large SW swell tacks in and long tube time is logged by the mix of locals and lucky holidaymakers. This long, perfectly formed, barrelling left becomes ultra-shallow at low tide, so higher tides are safer. Tuck-ins and speed slashes are the order of the day so lesser surfers should stick to the inside reform or beachbreak. Humourless crowds, urchins, sharp reef, currents and sharks. Tamarin Bay's reputation was built by a '70s movie, The Forgotten Island of Santosha, then destroyed by rampant localism shortly thereafter. It has been forgotten to an extent, since Indonesian consistency and price have deflected the hordes, but it is still a beauty to behold. The blind aggression has gone, but behave and avoid the coral crusted limestone that shows at low.

DAMIEN POULLENOT

TRAVEL INFORMATION

LOCAL POPULATION: 1.3M   TIME ZONE: GMT +4h
COASTLINE: 177km (110mi)

GETTING THERE – Depending on where you are from, a visa may be required – check with the embassy. Flying to Mauritius is expensive; most flights arrive at Sir Seewoosagur Ramgoolam International Airport (MRU) from London, Paris, Réunion, Dubai, and South Africa. Air Mauritius usually charges $25 for surfboards. It's a scenic 90min drive from the airport to Le Morne or Tamarin.

GETTING AROUND – Tamarin is the northern limit of the surf zone and you'll need a rental car to roam the SW. A basic small car at the airport is $40/d. Hiring a taxi costs around $40/half-day. Local buses are usually packed. Driving is done on the left side of the road.

LODGING AND FOOD – At Chez Jacques, doubles start at $70/night. A double in Tamarin Hotel starts at $140/night. Le Morne has several luxury resorts facing the surf (Le Paradis, Dinarobin, Indian Resort, Berjaya, Les Pavillons); all expensive. Package deals are your best bet. Food is good around Tamarin and spicy ($15/meal).

WEATHER – Mauritius differs from the classic monsoon pattern, and its year-round moderate rain generally falls at the end of the day. It's usually hotter and wetter, but with less cyclone risk during the summer (Dec-April). Winter begins in May, but temperatures remain warm enough for most visitors, and this period is considered the most pleasant time. The E coast is drier than the W coast. The water can get a little chilly in winter, requiring a springsuit as opposed to the usual boardies.

WEATHER STATS	J/F	M/A	M/J	J/A	S/O	N/D
Total Rainfall (mm)	205	174	81	61	38	82
Consistency (d/m)	11	10	7	6	4	6
Temperature min. (°C)	23	21	17	17	17	19
Temperature max. (°C)	30	29	26	24	26	29

NATURE AND CULTURE – Unlike Reunion, Mauritius is hilly rather than mountainous, and only the Trou aux Cerfs crater testifies to the ancient volcanic activity. The beaches are some of the most beautiful in the world. Port-Louis spice markets, Pamplemousse Gardens, and Moka Town are all worth a visit. Shellorama Museum next to Tamarin is interesting.

HAZARDS AND HASSLES – Tamarin locals can be surly, but other spots are cool and usually uncrowded. Coral heads are a worry at low tide Tamarin. Most coral reefs are dangerous and involve long paddles from shore. The island is generally safe for tourists.

HANDY HINTS – There are good shapers in Tamarin, and having a locally made board can make you feel safer in the Tamarin line-up! Mauritius is a peaceful blend of Catholics, Protestants, Hindus and Muslims. The Indian population is large. Go with an open mind and see what the melting pot of exotic culture is like. If the surf is flat, there are many things to do. Phoenix, the local beer, is the best in the Indian Ocean.

WIND AND SWELL

During the Southern Hemisphere winter (May-Oct) there are frequent SW swells varying in size from 2-20ft (0.5-6m). Although these SW swells can appear year-round, the summer season is characterised by NE tropical storms, but with only about 10 depressions in six months, it's hardly consistent. Of these, 1-2 will be strong cyclones that can be dangerous and destructive. Winter SE-S trades blow constantly and with a greater strength and frequency July-Sept. Summer winds veer more NE-E, which can also bring 2-6ft (0.5-2m) onshore windswell to the windward coast and side/offshore conditions on the surf-blessed SW corner. Tides only significant at shallow spots. ●

	SURF STATS	J	F	M	A	M	J	J	A	S	O	N	D
SWELL	Dominant swell												
	Size (m)	4		5		6		6-7		5-6		4	
	Consistency (%)	50		70		80		80		70		50	
WIND	Dominant wind												
	Average force	F4		F4		F4		F5		F4		F3-F4	
	Consistency (%)	82		64		61		76		69		77	
TEMP.	Wetsuit												
	Water temp.	27		26		24		22		23		25	

THE MALDIVES

It's strange to think that the lowest, flattest country in the world is in fact perched atop one of the most impressive mountain ranges on the planet and that these lofty peaks are flecked with sand instead of snow. From the Lakshadweep Islands off India's west coast all the way to the British Indian Ocean Territories of Chagos, the 2000m high Deccan Plateau is a result of two tectonic plates meeting. The magma spewed out, massive volcanoes were formed, before sinking back into the sea, leaving behind the rings of limestone and coral we now call atolls. Circular reefs and their passes have turned out to be a pretty good shape for wave creation and this chain just happens to have 26 atolls slung across 2200km (1370mi) of ocean that receives plenty of pulses from the Great Southern Ocean.

The eight atolls north of Malé remain unknown by foreign surfers, however, a fair share of local surfers based in Malé originate from Rasmadhoo in Raa Atoll or Kudafari in Noonu atoll. A growing number of resorts are opening, but none are promoting surfing – yet. Access is still the main key while there is only one airport way up north at Hanimadhoo and Maldivian started flights to Dharavandhoo Airport, Baa Atoll in late 2012. Over the last 10 years, there has been a handful of exploration boat trips up to Haa Alifu atoll that led to the discovery of the sweet righthander called Kakuni, which the Oakley Juniors (De Souza, Melling, Bryson) charged in April 2005. The potential for more discoveries still remains massive, despite slightly less generous exposure to southern swells. As crowd pressure increases in other parts of the Maldives, there will be more perfect waves found in the North, the only question being, will they be consistent enough for travelling surfers? Some boats have been heading to Baa and Lhaviyani atolls as they are the closest to North Malé. While the Maldives surf scene revolves around the popular breaks of NORTH MALÉ atoll, there is also a number of breaks in the **South Malé Atoll** area, including Quarters (Gulhi), Kate's (near Veligandu Huraa/Palm Tree Island Resort), Natives (Kandooma Resort, who claim exclusivity over the rights) and Riptides/Foxy's (near Guraidhoo Island), a chunky mid channel right, facing a racy, shallow left. **Vaavu** misses out on east coast surf due to its extended south coast, but **Meemu** has a little cluster of waves accessed by the Medhufushi resort and an increasing number of safari boats. Veyvah holds fun, zippy lefts with great length of ride. Tucked in a bit, Mulah needs more swell to serve up user-friendly rolling rights for improvers plus. Muli Inside is a full wrap right, that needs big swell, but is SE

YEP

FOXY'S, SOUTH MALÉ

Maldives

For more information, check these other Stormrider Surf Guides and/or eBooks.

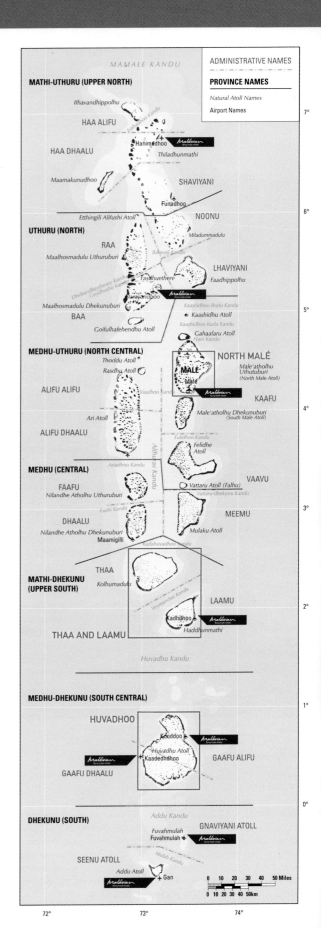

OTHER ISLANDS TO CONSIDER

LAKSHADWEEP ISLANDS

+ VIRGIN REGION
+ DISCOVERY POTENTIAL
+ NO CROWDS
+ LAND-BASED SURF ACCESS
+ AWESOME MINICOY PIER

− LACK OF MELLOW WAVES
− SLOW BOAT FROM MAINLAND
− ONE BREAK ISLAND
− EXPENSIVE CONTROLLED TOURISM

ALAN VAN GYSEN

Lakshadweep is a Union Territory of India, (formerly known as the Laccadive Islands), but these atolls share far more in common with the Maldives than they do with the Subcontinent. Across the 12 atolls, containing 36 islands, only 10 are inhabited, where the population of 60,000 is squeezed onto less terra firma than the 32km2 (12mi2) total area of the country. Kavaratti is the capital, where a new desalination plant uses cold water from the depths to provide drinking water and power. A growing number of tourists arrive by ship from Kochi, India and the destination island rotates. Surfers have been out there, and scored, keeping it quiet until *Castles in the Sky* showcased the super tubes that break either side of the big concrete pier at Minicoy. Minicoy sits in isolation a long way south, putting it closer to the swell source and a more likely candidate for regular waves. The best place to look for surf is on the bigger islands like Androth, Amini, and Agatti, where the airport and main accommodation is. The reefs are often straight without any gaps so the tips of the islands will need investigation. It is a long way for the southern hemi swells to travel so June to September should offer the best chance of scoring a SE or wrapping SW swell onto the east coasts, avoiding the W winds. The NE monsoon period will be too small to justify the time and expense it takes to get to this remote chain, which also sees the occasional NW swell from the Arabian Sea.

ADDU

Directly below the Equator is the southernmost Addu Atoll where Gan island was used as a British Royal Air Force base until 1976. When tourism started to boom in the '80s, many people from Gan and neighbouring Foammulah were recruited in the resorts because they could speak good English. The result now is a thriving population of 20,000, living in some of the biggest villages in the Maldives, connected by the second longest system of roads and causeways, linking the western shores of Addu. Best known for diving wrecks like *British Loyalty*, torpedoed by the Japanese in 1942, this part of the Maldives is slowly unveiling it's potential for surfing. First scoped by Tony Hussein in 1996, very few people have surfed Addu until recently. The roads allow land access to a range of breaks like Kottey and Approach Lights, a long heavy right at the end of the new international airport that feels safer at high tide. The reality is that Addu Atoll doesn't have Maldivian standard, perfectly shaped, soft-breaking waves. Beginner/improvers will struggle with the technical breaks that require speedy riding techniques and the sharky, shallow reefs can be intimidating.

+ EMPTY BREAKS
+ SWELL CONSISTENCY
+ OVERLAND SURF ACCESS
+ SOME DIRECT FLIGHTS
+ EQUATOR VILLAGE DEALS

− LACK OF MELLOW WAVES
− EXTRA DOMESTIC FLIGHT
− ONLY ONE EXPOSED PASS
− EXPENSIVE DHONI ACCESS
− PRICEY

LAURENT MASUREL

SHANGRI LA

wind protected, while the long walls of Outside work from tiny and are offshore in SW winds. From Meemu south, swell becomes more consistent and both THAA AND LAAMU atolls are nicely placed at the bottom of the central chain to pick off the swell and some of the spots work in surprising swell and wind conditions. The western atolls of **Alifu**, **Faafu** and **Dhaalu** are wind exposed and cut off from the SE-S swell supply, although there are a few waves at southern and western passes in certain conditions, but few charters are bothering to look carefully enough. HUVADHOO atoll has seen crowds increasing as a number of land based resorts open, adding to the fleet of long range charters that now ply the wave-rich waters from Beacons to Tiger Stripes. Crowds should never be a problem when travelling down to **Addu** atoll, where the waves get heavier and the remote islands give the feeling of real seclusion, almost 500km from Malé.

NORTH MALÉ

+ WORLD-CLASS RIGHTS AND LEFTS
+ RARELY FLAT   – CONSISTENTLY SMALL
+ NO WIND BEFORE SW MONSOON   – OFTEN CROWDED
+ UNIQUE BOATING LIFESTYLE   – BOAT ACCESS RESTRICTIONS
+ LUXURY RESORT OPTION FOR   – TOP PRICES
  NON-SURFERS   – NO BUDGET LAND TRIPS

HONKY'S
SULTAN'S

LAT. 4.312117°   LONG. 73.586281°

Over the last decade, Maldives has gained a solid reputation for clean, almost beginner-friendly waves that break on the most exposed parts of the atoll reefs. Comprised of 26 atolls, surfing in the Maldives has remained focused on North Malé, which claims the best density of lefts and rights within a 2hr cruise. Combined with an appealing proximity to Hulhumalé international airport, it's an especially convenient, fun-wave playground for time-restricted, wealthy travellers. The Maldives surf has been one of the longest kept secrets, because Australian Tony Hinde managed to keep it quiet among his close friends between 1974 and 1988. These days, the 4 passes gathering the bulk of the swell are often crowded with all types and abilities of recreational surfers, from the resorts, guest-houses or charter boats, but the vibe is always laid-back and friendly.

Honky's and Sultan's stand as the ultimate dream combination of rights and lefts breaking on both sides of Thamburudhoo island, which still belongs to the army, so dhoni access only. Honky's works in the typical NE winter winds enticing swell onto a nicely walled outside section that gets bigger and faster as it hits "Fred's Ledge" section on the inside. Offers short barrels and a bit more punch than most when the tide drains out. Sultan's is North Malé atoll's most surfed spot and handles plenty of size, which helps spread the big crowd of mixed abilities, down the 300m line-up. Starts with a regulation drop and walls up for a while before rounding out through the inside sections. Both waves suffer from strong currents.

S urprisingly, the surf in Malé is very uncrowded despite the capital having the highest population density in the world. It's mainly locals who surf **RAALHUGANDU,** the main break in town, yet it is one of the most consistent and powerful waves in Maldives. On big SE swells, a few travellers manage to surf Rats treacherous lefts on the SW corner of Malé, or across the channel on Vilingili where shallow rights spin across a bumpy reef. There's a left beside the runway on Hulhumalé that is rarely surfed, because the tail section is deadly and access is not easy. On nearby **FURANA,** the Sheraton Full Moon resort has started surfing programs for guests.

The rights are fairly fickle, until a 2m+ SE swell hits with a 12 sec+ period, transforming it into one of the best rides in the country. Kanduoiygiri, or just **KADU** for short, can also be good with similar big swell conditions, but will be smaller than everywhere else. Across the wide channel, Paradise Island tried to sell itself as a surf resort, but the lefts are little more than a closeout. The next reef pass north stands at the heart of the Maldivian surf scene, with no less than 4 epic breaks. First up is **JAILBREAKS,** a right that becomes everyone's favourite for it's length and soft-breaking sections. The jail is gone now, but those staying at Himmafushi guest-house should remember that the area facing the wave is off-limits because of the Drug Rehabilitation Centre. **HONKY'S** and **SULTAN'S** are the most famous and crowded line-ups in the region, so the resorts work on rotating 2hr access slots. **PASTA POINT** is exclusive for the max. thirty surfing guests booked into the

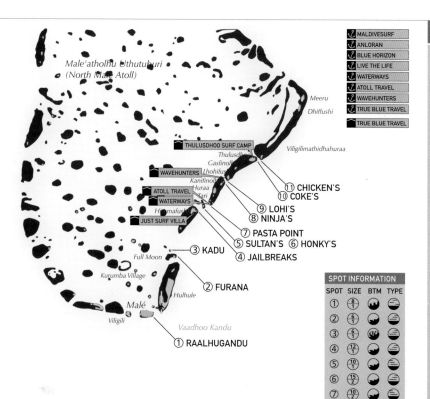

MALDIVESURF
ANLORAN
BLUE HORIZON
LIVE THE LIFE
WATERWAYS
ATOLL TRAVEL
WAVEHUNTERS
TRUE BLUE TRAVEL
TRUE BLUE TRAVEL

Male'atholhu Uthutuburi
(North Malé Atoll)

Meeru
Dhiffushi
Viligilimathidhahuraaa

THULUSDHOO SURF CAMP
Thulusdhoo
Gasfinolu
WAVEHUNTERS
Lhohifushi
Kanifinolhu
ATOLL TRAVEL
WATERWAYS
Himmafushi
JUST SURF VILLA
Huraa

⑪ CHICKEN'S
⑩ COKE'S
⑨ LOHI'S
⑧ NINJA'S
⑦ PASTA POINT
⑤ SULTAN'S ⑥ HONKY'S
④ JAILBREAKS
③ KADU
② FURANA
① RAALHUGANDU

Full Moon
Kurumba Village
Malé
Viligili
Hulhule
Vaadhoo Kandu

SPOT INFORMATION

SPOT	SIZE	BTM	TYPE
①			
②			
③			
④	12		
⑤	10		
⑥	15		
⑦	10		
⑧			
⑨			
⑩	12		
⑪	10		

Chaaya Dhonveli Resort. Thirty mins north by boat, in front of Club Med on Kanifinolhu, **NINJA'S** rights appeal to improvers and cruisers on small, clean swells, as they tend to close-out over shoulder-high and lack shape. **LOHI'S** keeps its old Lohifushi name, despite becoming Hudhuranfushi resort. Being host to 5 WQS events (Deep Blue Open 2001-2005), Lohi's is a longer wave than Pasta, but not as perfect. The outside section holds the monsoon wind better, while the inside can be a dramatic freight train. Again, if you don't stay here, you don't surf here. Another 30mins sail north, the last pass is the safari boat favourite because it catches more S swell (and wind unfortunately!). **COKE'S** (see next page). **CHICKEN'S** left is home to long, playful lefts that can sometimes produce 10 second barrels, but not if the SW wind is up. Varies greatly in quality and crowds. On major SE swells and strong S winds, it might be worth checking the rights of Meerufenfushi Corner, but expect more than fast zipping lines!

PASTA POINT

JS CALLAHAN/SURFEXPLORE

TRAVEL INFORMATION

LOCAL POPULATION:
Malé – 103,693
TIME ZONE: GMT +5h

COASTLINE:
Maldives – 644km (402mi)

GETTING THERE – Free 30d visa on arrival. Europeans make up 60% of the guests coming to Malé (MLE) with Emirates (Dubai), Qatar Airways (Doha) or Sri Lankan (free stop over in Colombo, Sri Lanka), which all take 30kg check-in luggage with no boardbag tax. Arrivals from the east will probably fly surfer-friendly Malaysian or Singapore. Dhonis or speedboats will do the transfers to surf safari boats or resorts.

GETTING AROUND – It's all about navigation. Safari boats and dhonis cruise 6-8 knots, while speedboats go 25-30 knots, but you will mainly use dhonis to go surfing, running on fixed time schedules from the resorts. Navigation is strictly controlled, leaving no space for improvisation with local fishermen.

LODGING AND FOOD – Stay in one of the few surf resorts, unless you can find/afford boat transport (dhoni $250/d; speedboat $2000/d). North Malé atoll resorts are expensive, best prices (based on double occupancy) are Chaaya Dhonveli at $338/n with surf transfers and Hduranfushi around $180/n + $55/d dhoni ride. Guest-house (Himmafushi, Huraa, Thulusdhoo) offer $100/d pricing, but don't serve any alcohol. Surf safari boat deals vary a lot depending on boat status, group size and the season (higher priced Oct-April): expect to pay between $100-300/d. Extras: beer ($5). Pricing will increase rapdily over the years because of the impact of a growing VAT on tourism goods (T-GST at 8% in 2013, possibly 12% in 2014).

WEATHER – Typical, tropical, monsoon climate with plenty of rainfall. The NE monsoon (*Iruvai*) is the driest period with lighter winds from NE. During this period (Dec-Mar) temps soar and sunshine is plentiful. During May-Oct the monsoon comes from the SW (*Hulhangu*), bringing thunderstorms, gusty winds, overcast skies and regular rainfall to the atolls. June-July is the worst and usually when boats go to dry dock for repair. Most of the year averages around 27°C (80°F), night and day, because there is no cooling land factor.

WEATHER STATS	J/F	M/A	M/J	J/A	S/O	N/D
Total Rainfall (mm)	32	40	240	212	172	113
Consistency (d/m)	2	2	13	13	10	6
Temperature min. (°C)	23	25	25	24	24	23
Temperature max. (°C)	29	31	31	29	29	29

NATURE AND CULTURE – Scuba-diving and snorkeling is among the world's top 10 because of huge species variety, quantity of fish (no nets allowed in the country) and perfect water temperatures (27-28°C/80-82°F), while coral gardens are really growing back since the intense 1998 El Nino bleaching. Hand-line fishing (spearguns prohibited), either trawling or at anchor is just intense: Spanish mackerel, yellow-fin tuna, barracuda, wahoo, rainbow fish, trevally, batfish, jobfish and triggerfish. Visiting villages will only take 1hr since most islands are tiny.

HAZARDS AND HASSLES – Despite loads of marine life it's safe. Although having a gentle slope and being quite smooth, pay attention to shallow reefs. Tidal rips and intense sunburn can be more of a threat. Crowds in North Malé are now a reality and boat wakes at some spots (Sultans) can be a hassle. Regimented group timetables may get on some people's nerves; talk with the captain/surf guide for optimum surf schedules.

HANDY HINTS – Bring 2 boards with spare fins, leash and at least 1 tropical wax bar for every 3 days. No need for a gun - take a fish instead. Boats don't necessarily have snorkeling and fishing stuff, bring your own. A surf hat and good sunblock may help you to wait for the right set waves! Don't bring alcohol or pork products.

JAILBREAKS

ROGER SHARP

SWELL AND WIND

The Indian Ocean is the most active ocean in the world with southern latitude swells remaining quite frequent, even during the austral summer. Lows tend to radiate a strong SW push of long 12-18sec period swell, that often arrives from a more S direction plus some shorter period (9-15) SE pulses. This groundswell is matched half of the time by windswells from various directions depending on the position of the high pressure systems. The full surfing season starts in March and ends in November, but generally speaking May-October is when the bulk of the swells arrive and most of the resorts and boats enter the high season. The SW monsoon tends to blow more W early and

COKE'S

LAT. 4.370845°   LONG. 73.656653°

Heading North the last major pass is a safari boat favourite because it catches the maximum S swell, even though it also catches the wind badly. Coke's (or Cola's, depending on your taste) has often been rated as the hardest breaking wave in North Malé with a vert take-off, high barrel factor and nice shape over the shallow reef. Two new guesthouses and local crew add to the often crowded vibe and there's strong currents on the tide drop – experienced, fit surfers only.

ANDREW SHIELD

late season, with the dominant WSW averaging 10-20mph. December to February is the heart of the tourist season (NE monsoon) with countless honeymooners, cruisers, divers and small 2-3ft choppy windswells from the NE. March-April as well as November are transition months of weaker winds, sunny weather, less crowds but significantly less consistency with 3-5ft swells. Period is often more significant for wave size than wave height. Tides are unpredictable but create intense rips between islands, making it sketchy to paddle across channels. Depending on tide, you have either incoming or outgoing currents, so check with the dhoni captain. High tides are safer at most spots. ●

SURF STATS		J F	M A	M J	J A	S O	N D
SWELL	Dominant swell						
	Size (m)	2	3-4	4-5	5-6	4	2
	Consistency (%)	40	60	80	80	60	40
WIND	Dominant wind						
	Average force	F3	F2-F3	F3	F3	F3	F3
	Consistency (%)	74	71	70	53	83	73
TEMP.	Wetsuit						
	Water temp.	27	28	27	26	27	25

THAA AND LAAMU

+ CONSISTENT IN SW MONSOON
+ LONG, WRAPPING REEF WAVES
+ NEWLY DISCOVERED, UNCROWDED
+ WORLD-CLASS YINYANG, MIKADO
+ COMFORTABLE SAFARI BOATS

– LACK OF CONSISTENT LEFTS
– MORE CRUISING BETWEEN SPOTS
– HARDLY EVER BIG
– EXPENSIVE DOMESTIC FLIGHT
– NO RESORTS, NO CHEAP BEER

With an Indian Ocean swell window from direct E through S to W, Laamu atoll and Thaa atoll are newly discovered central atoll surf zones with many high-quality reef pass setups. These two atolls alone present 150 islands and almost 650km (400mi) of coastline to the frequent swell. The central atolls of the Maldives enjoy an abundance of medium-sized, perfect reefbreaks, the majority of which are righthanders. A settled and peaceful area of sparse population, access to the majority of these waves is by charter boat alone, despite planned resorts. Unlike other island chains, the expense and low number of boats in this area of the Maldives keeps crowds low. With waves such as Mikado and Yin Yang known for their pristine barrels, under the right conditions the central atolls are tropical perfection.

On the west coast of Thaa atoll, **BOWLING ALLEY** is a scenic deep-water peak that closes out onto a reef inside the atoll. When the wind blows from the SE, head to Hirilandhoo where a long, speedy, but inconsistent left called **MALIK'S** can offer high quality barrels. To the east lies **ADONIS**, a sectiony right that favours N winds and breaks off the eastern tip of Veymandhoo pass. SE-SW swell first hits **OUTSIDE MIKADO** before refracting onto the inside reef. Favouring high tide, Outside Mikado is a fast right with a dodgy end section over uneven reef. The inside section is suited to performance surfing, but due to the inconsistency of the reforms it cannot handle a crowd. Just to the west lies a swell magnet left with long walls and barrel sections, ideal under light N, NW or calm conditions. Moving east, **INSIDE MIKADO** is a perfect wraparound righthander that's inconsistent at low tide, but mid tide through high can deliver perfect peeling waves with short barrel sections. Inside Mikado is offshore in a SW wind, and receives protection from Kanimeedhoo Island, but a W or NW wind will spoil this flawless line-up. **FINNIMAS** is an exposed lefthander that needs NE, N or light NW winds to break well and across the pass a right sometimes breaks.

To the south of Thaa atoll is the smaller and more exposed Laamu atoll. **YIN YANG** is the most consistent wave in the area, working best under strong SE swell when thick barrels and a powerful inside section can be punishing. The outside section breaks in deep water, and can be an option in NW winds that blow out the inside, but watch out for the bowl. In SW winds, the outside becomes choppy and the inside turns on. If the swell is big and the wind from the NW, it may be worth heading inside the pass to **MADA'S**, a short and shallow left. If Yin Yang hits 4ft (1.2m), two other passes on the east-facing coast of the atoll will start breaking. **BEDHUGE** is a remote, perfect right that breaks on big SE swells and any W wind. Across the pass **REFUGEE'S LEFTS** are short and shifty requiring specific SE swell direction to line up while **REFUGEE'S RIGHTS** are only for speed demons that can race the close-out sections. **MACHINE** is usually the best option; a winding, tubular right best on an incoming tide and is rideable even in small swells. On the northeast tip of the atoll is **ISDHOO BANK**, a rarely surfed righthander that comes alive in big S-SE swells with S-SW winds. Surf charters stop here in transit to the Southern Atolls.

MIKADO

ALAN VAN GYSEN

YIN YANG

YEP

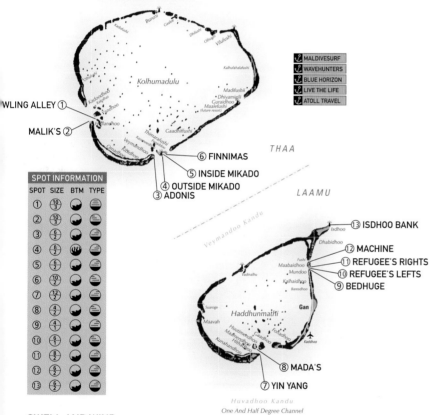

Kudahuvadhoo Kandu

MALDIVESURF
WAVEHUNTERS
BLUE HORIZON
LIVE THE LIFE
ATOLL TRAVEL

WLING ALLEY ①
MALIK'S ②

Kolhumadulu

THAA

LAAMU

⑥ FINNIMAS
⑤ INSIDE MIKADO
④ OUTSIDE MIKADO
③ ADONIS

Veymandoo Kandu

⑬ ISDHOO BANK
⑫ MACHINE
⑪ REFUGEE'S RIGHTS
⑩ REFUGEE'S LEFTS
⑨ BEDHUGE

Haddhunmathi

Gan

⑧ MADA'S
⑦ YIN YANG

Huvadhoo Kandu
One And Half Degree Channel

SPOT INFORMATION

SPOT	SIZE	BTM	TYPE
①			
②			
③			
④			
⑤			
⑥			
⑦			
⑧			
⑨			
⑩			
⑪			
⑫			
⑬			

SWELL AND WIND

The Maldives host consistent medium-sized surf, and are rarely flat between March and November. The predominant swell throughout the year comes from the SE-SW. Waves are fed by consistent lows tracking through the Roaring Forties, as well as the odd cyclone. Spring tides are just over a metre, and during neaps the range is small, but tidal rips can be a problem as water drains or floods the atolls. December-March is sunny and dry (*Iruvai* season, NE monsoon) while May-October is more windy and humid (*Hulhangu* season, SW monsoon); April and November are the transition months. Late March through to mid May are generally clean and calm, ideal conditions for boat cruising. As the SW monsoon approaches, the weather will begin to alternate between thunderstorms and sunshine, with heavy rain likely. The wind doesn't get too strong, and even in the heart of the monsoon season clean days are common. Wind conditions can be divided into three clear periods. The prevailing wind from April to August is SW-W, from September to November it swings SW-NW, changing again from December to March, when it predominately blows NW-NE. ●

TRAVEL INFORMATION

LOCAL POPULATION:
Thaa - 13,846 ; Laamu - 14,313
TIME ZONE: GMT +5h

COASTLINE:
Maldives – 644 km (400mi)

GETTING THERE – See Malé. From Malé fly to Kadhdhoo airport (KDO), using Maldivian (not be mistaken with Kaadedhdhoo - KDM). The flight takes 40 minutes, costs approximately $360 rtn and is very scenic. Laamu atoll is 220km (136mi) from Malé, and takes approximately 24 hours by sea. Boats in the Maldives don't cruise at night, so this will take two days. The easiest option is to fly in.

GETTING AROUND – There are planned resorts in the Thaa atoll, and the possibility of a guesthouse opening at Mikado, but the majority of waves in this area are surfed using live aboard boats. Blue Horizon and Wavehunters boats currently operate in this area – the Maldivesurf Atoll Challenger boat ($210/day) and the Tropicsurf Blue Lagoon ($380/day.)

LODGING AND FOOD – Cabins with air-conditioning are a luxury in the heat. Boats provide decent quality food and fresh fish is a certainty. Ask for Roshi Mashuni!

WEATHER – The "Iruvai" is the NE monsoon (Dec-March), typified by dry weather and light N winds. The WSW monsoon, "Hulhangu" lasts from mid May through to mid November, and is likely to feature overcast weather and storms. Rainfall averages 1924mm (77in) per year, mostly clearing quickly after strong thunderstorms. The Maldives receive around 2704 hours of sunshine per year, helping to keep water temperature between 28-30°C (82-86°F). Neoprene for sun and reef protection only.

WEATHER STATS	J/F	M/A	M/J	J/A	S/O	N/D
Total Rainfall (mm)	32	40	240	212	172	113
Consistency (d/m)	2	2	13	13	10	6
Temperature min. (°C)	25	25	25	25	24	24
Temperature max. (°C)	30	31	31	31	30	30

NATURE AND CULTURE – The Maldives are teeming with ocean life, so take advantage with fins, mask and snorkel. Tuna, Maori wrasse, swordfish, sailfish and marlin are common, plus whale shark visit frequently. The fishing is excellent quality. Expect friendly village culture.

HAZARDS AND HASSLES – On the whole the reef is flat and smooth, but it can be shallow so bring reef boots. Sharks are usually small and benign, sea lice and urchins are rare. There are few diseases and hardly any mosquitoes. The islands are peaceful and settled, the local people mellow. Travellers should be aware of sunburn and sunstroke, take high-factor sunscreen. Remember: no alcohol, pornography or spear guns allowed through customs.

HANDY HINTS – Factor in some time in Malé to relax, surf the good waves in town, and soak up the unique island vibe. There is very little surfing equipment available and it is expensive, so take everything. Also take entertainment for time off from the surf, such as books or DVDs. If money isn't an issue hire a seaplane and go search as new discoveries await.

SURF STATS		J	F	M	A	M	J	J	A	S	O	N	D
SWELL	Dominant swell												
	Size (m)	2-3		4		5		6		4-5		2-3	
	Consistency (%)	60		80		90		90		80		60	
WIND	Dominant wind												
	Average force	F3		F2-F3		F3		F3		F3-F4		F3	
	Consistency (%)	76		48		71		68		83		47	
TEMP.	Wetsuit												
	Water temp.	28		29		29		28		28		28	

HUVADHOO

+ ATOLL PASS PERFECTION
+ RELATIVELY LOW CROWDS
+ CALM WATER CRUISING
+ AWESOME FISHING AND SCENERY

– STORMY WINTER SEAS
– NEW LAND CAMPS
– LONG TRANSFERS
– EXPENSIVE CHARTERS & CAMPS

TIGER STRIPES

Gaafu Dhaalu (South Huvadhoo) has an exposed south-facing coast, boasting a dozen good passes, in a 2 hr cruising zone. Charter boats are still the most popular form of access despite new resorts opening, making this an expensive, luxury type surf trip, but unlike the Mentawai's, only a few boats operate in the area. Three southern atolls tried to break away from the Maldivian government as recently as 1962, keeping this area well outside the "Tourist Zone" and until recently government permits were required to travel here. Maldivian pioneer, Tony Hussein, discovered the areas potential in 1973, keeping it to himself until the first charters began in 1993, but it remains a secluded destination on the world surf atlas.

The two options are to fly to Gaafu Dhaalu (silent 'u') and meet the charter or "Safari Boat", avoiding the two days motoring (in good weather) that it takes to cruise from Malé to the surf zone. Lucky punters will score good lefts at AIRPORT'S with a strong S-SW

swell and NE wind, but the boat usually heads direct to BEACONS, 2hrs away, at the first southern reef pass. Touted as the Maldives gutsiest wave, Beacons' powerful rights tube onto a shallow, unforgiving reef. SW swells will break down the reef, but a SE swell will create peaks slamming straight onto closeout sections of coral. Less intense is CASTAWAYS, exposed on an outside reef that is predictable, but shallow on the end section, especially at low tide. Anything N is offshore and the deserted island backdrop is idyllic. Un-named lefts flank both Beacons and Castaways across the channels, which have their days in big swells, but tend to go unridden. BLUE BOWLS is the most flexible right, tucked inside the pass and protected from SW-W winds. More of a point style wave, it has good length of ride and nice bowly sections for performance moves. All swells, all tides and all sizes. 30 minutes motoring east, FIVE ISLANDS is another righthander that breaks hard and hollow on the shallow inside reef. The outside section encourages deep take-offs into racy walls and handles the biggest swells at all tides. TWO WAYS does just that and the right is generally better, but it needs a big swell to hit its protected position, making it a favourite with intermediates. Fun peeling, long walls with a bit of depth to the water. Directly next-door are the reliable lefts of LOVE CHARMS, which can handle E winds and any size swell. Low tide is best when it is small, soft and broken into two distinct sections. Bigger swells morph it into a long, hollow wall, with powerful pockets. The next pass to the east is a narrow inlet between the islands of Gan and Gadhdhoo, where the first local surfers are starting to ride the lefts and reforms at TIGER STRIPES. ANTIQUES are the rights, which are always a couple of feet smaller and way more forgiving than the lefts. Named after the narrow gouges in the reef that give a striped effect, Tigers has some real growling lefts in a strong swell. Tricky take-offs into a long speed wall before committing to an inside tube section that wraps and peters out in the channel. Unimpressive when small, it always seems to be bigger than everywhere else. All tides, all variations of S swells and any N wind. KH'S is almost east coast and the two distinct take-off spots link together in bigger swell and tide conditions. There's scattered, quality surf like KOODOO and VILIGILI, located in Gaafu Alifu (North Huvadhoo Atoll), surfed by boats on their way to/ from Malé. Despite its idyllic location in the doldrums, the sea can be pretty rough, especially crossing the one and half degree channel.

BLUE BOWLS

FIVE ISLANDS

LAURENT MASUREL

TRAVEL INFORMATION

LOCAL POPULATION: Huvadhoo – 20,000

TIME ZONE: GMT +5h

COASTLINE: 644km (400mi)

GETTING THERE – Connect at Malé airport for inter-atoll flights or board vessel for long voyage south. Maldivian fly from Malé to Kaadedhdhoo, five times per week (1h10min, $390 r/t), no charge for boards but 25kg total baggage weight, 8-9ft length limit applies, pack light! Superb, scenic flight!

GETTING AROUND – From Kaadedhdhoo airport, the charter boats (and resorts) will pick you up. Having a dhoni and a dingy will allow groups to split up and surf different breaks with ease.

LODGING AND FOOD – All mod cons aboard a handful of safari boats including the original Horizon II and the latest modern gin palace the Anloran, booked through all the big agents (Atoll Travel, Maldivesurf, LTL, True Blue, Waterways, Wavehunters, etc). New resorts are open on Vatavarehaa (Blue Bowls), Maguhdhuvaa (Two Ways) and Lonudhu, (Tiger Stripes). Prices improve going in a larger group. Food is varied as long as it is fish! Go snorkeling for lobster.

WEATHER – It's a typical tropical monsoon climate with 2 definite seasons and high yearly rainfall. NE monsoon is the driest period with lighter winds from NW to E. During that period (Dec-March), temps get very hot and sunshine is plentiful, accompanied by high humidity. The SW monsoon brings many storms, so May-Oct is characterised by gusty SW winds and regular rainfall. Consider these points when booking a non-AC boat. A shorty is rarely required as water temps remain around 28-30°C (82-86°F), meaning boardies, long sleeved lycra and sunhat!

WEATHER STATS	J/F	M/A	M/J	J/A	S/O	N/D
Total Rainfall (mm)	205	174	81	61	38	82
Consistency (d/m)	11	10	7	6	4	6
Temperature min. (°C)	23	21	17	17	17	19
Temperature max. (°C)	30	29	26	24	26	29

NATURE AND CULTURE – Nature and Culture – Typical boat trip culture of insane fishing, great snorkeling (no tanks available), surf vids and board games. Vaadhoo and Gadhdhoo offer telecom services and village scenery while Vaadhoo is renowned for its kunaa (fine hand-woven mats).

HAZARDS AND HASSLES – At 0° latitude, your worst enemy is the sun. Serious high factor sunscreen is crucial. Keep well hydrated and treat coral cuts carefully. Horrendous tidal rips rip through the passes. No alcohol, pornography, drugs or spear guns are allowed at customs. Few mosquitoes, even on islands, where there is some dengue fever and isolated cases of leprosy.

HANDY HINTS – Bring two shortboards and reef equipment. Surf shops in Malé are expensive with little gear. Rental boards available on maldivesurf website. Names are confusing - Gaafu Dhaalu is South Huvadhoo or Suvadiva and many atolls and faros share identical names, but slightly different spellings.

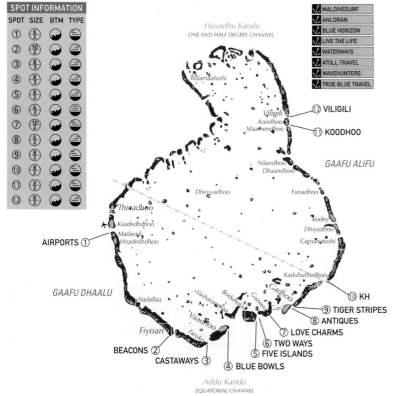

SPOT INFORMATION

SPOT	SIZE	BTM	TYPE
①			
②	10		
③			
④			
⑤			
⑥			
⑦	10		
⑧			
⑨			
⑩			
⑪			
⑫			

- ✓ MALDIVESURF
- ✓ ANLORAN
- ✓ BLUE HORIZON
- ✓ LIVE THE LIFE
- ✓ WATERWAYS
- ✓ ATOLL TRAVEL
- ✓ WAVEHUNTERS
- ✓ TRUE BLUE TRAVEL

Huvadhu Kandu
ONE AND HALF DEGREE CHANNEL

Kolamaafushi

Vifigili — ⑫ VILIGILI
Koodhoo
Maamendhoo — ⑪ KOODHOO

Nilandhoo
Dhaandhoo — *GAAFU ALIFU*

Dheyvadhoo
Funadhoo

Thinadhoo
Kodey
Kaadedhdhoo — Dhiyadhoo
Madaveli — Gemanafushi
AIRPORTS ① — Hoadedhdhoo

Kaduhulhudhoo

GAAFU DHAALU
Nadallaa — Gadhoo — ⑩ KH
Vashavarulhaa — Boduhuraa
Cazeera — ⑨ TIGER STRIPES
Vaadhoo — Gan — ⑧ ANTIQUES
Fiyoari — Faruko — ⑦ LOVE CHARMS
BEACONS ② — ⑥ TWO WAYS
CASTAWAYS ③ — ⑤ FIVE ISLANDS
— ④ BLUE BOWLS

Addu Kandu
EQUATORIAL CHANNEL

SWELL AND WIND

Swell comes from the usual Indian Ocean culprits of the Roaring Forties storms, the occasional cyclone, and localised windswells. Due its size and location, Gaafu Dhaalu is the only atoll with SW-SE exposure. March-Oct is the most consistent swell season with usual 2-6ft (0.6-2m) waves on the most exposed breaks, plus some 6-10ft (2-3m) swells in the depths of the southern hemisphere winter. However, this coincides with the SW monsoon (*Hulhangu*) and the

boats don't operate during the stormy, windy conditions from May-August. The best period is the NE monsoon (*Iruvai*) for clean and sunny conditions during Feb to April and Sept-Oct. Winds will generally have a NW - NE direction but the monsoon can be early or late, bringing unwelcome SW winds to the transition periods. Any wind from the S to E quadrant kills off all the breaks, especially when it's small. Dec-Jan suffers flat spells, but exposure is better than Malé Atolls. This time of year the charter boats are fully booked by the diving operators around Malé, who have yet to start diving trips in the south. Semi-diurnal odd tides bring an unpredictability to the reef passes, where intense rips drain in and out of the atoll, so check with the boat captain before jumping over the side! ●

	SURF STATS	J	F	M	A	M	J	J	A	S	O	N	D
SWELL	Dominant swell	◕		◕		◕		◕		◕		◕	
	Size (m)	2-3		4		5		6		4		2-3	
	Consistency (%)	50		80		40		40		80		60	
WIND	Dominant wind	◔		◔		◑		◑		◑		◔	
	Average force	F3		F2-F3		F3		F3		F3-F4		F3	
	Consistency (%)	76		48		71		68		83		47	
TEMP.	Wetsuit	🩱		🩱		🩱		🩱		🩱		🩱	
	Water temp.	28		29		29		28		28		28	

BAY OF BENGAL

The countries surrounding the Bay of Bengal are usually not considered to be true surf destinations, yet the fact that Sri Lanka and the Andaman Islands are stacked with waves should come as no surprise. They are close neighbours to the Maldives and Mentawais, two heavyweight surf destinations and cover all the bases from crowded, fun beachbreaks along the cheap tourist strips of Sri Lanka to empty, intense reefs in the adventurous wilds of Little Andaman. Add the exotic draw of Myanmar and Thailand, where perceptions may be altered and 2ft monsoonal wind slop gives way to waves of surprising height, power and shape during their on season.

SRI LANKA

Sri Lanka's surf scene has always centered on either Hikkaduwa or Arugam Bay, depending on the season. There is plenty more empty, soft beach and reefbreak along the west coast, both north and south of Colombo, but the problem is size during the offshore period of the NE monsoon. Wave size doubles by mid July, but the westerly winds usually put paid to any decent shape. Towns like Bentota and Wadduwa have shifting peaks in calm wind conditions, while other stretches of coast are armoured with breakwalls and jetties. That explains why the crowds are concentrated in **SOUTHWEST SRI LANKA**, leaving a lot of south-facing spots in seasonal limbo, some working in big swell and W-N winds, while others need the NE winds of winter. Much of the beachbreak is shoredump most of the time, but there are a lot of rocky coves that can transform unruly swells into something

As Myanmar opens up to tourists, the 800 mainly uninhabited, Mergui islands, present a tantalizingly large Andaman Sea exploratory into the unknown.

MERGUI ARCHIPELAGO

JS CALLAHAN/SURFEXPLORE

OTHER ISLANDS TO CONSIDER

PHUKET, THAILAND

Thailand's western shoreline has enough decent waves to attract surfers looking for cheap local costs and the famously warm Thai smile and hospitality. Apparently, a Kiwi guy was responsible for introducing surfing to Phuket back in the '70s and the younger Thais have embraced the sport as it fits their laid-back lifestyle. Da was probably the first Thai surfer in the late '70s. Regulars in the water are now a mixture of local Thais and foreigners from the sizeable expat community. Phuket now holds annual surf contests and supports a growing and enthusiastic surfing fraternity. The "Land Of Smiles" should not be rated as a mainstream surfing destination, but a fun surf in uncrowded and friendly conditions is on the cards for those passing through. Well-known tourist spots like Patong Beach and Kata Beach can deliver some decent rides, but undoubtedly, the most famous wave in Thailand was the 26th December, 2004 tsunami that took 5500 victims, mostly along the 865km (537mi) of coastline facing the Andaman Sea. Two-thirds of Thailand's huge coastline is in the Gulf of Thailand with occasional waves during the NE monsoon at Koh Samui or near Songkhla.

+ UNCROWDED, MELLOW WAVES
+ WARM, TROPICAL WATER
+ OCCASIONAL POINTBREAKS
+ CHEAP, PARTY DESTINATION
+ EASY, SAFE TOURISM

– SHORT SWELL SEASON
– MUSHY, ONSHORE CONDITIONS
– INCONSISTENT AND RAINY
– MASS TOURISM

CHRIS BURKARD

worth searching for. Check out Dickwella, Nilwella, Tangalla and the extensive sands leading to Hambantota, before the main road heads inland to skirt the massive wilderness of the Yala National Park and onto the sandy right points of SOUTHEAST SRI LANKA. It is not recommended to travel too far into the NE, not because the recently ended civil war has ravaged this region for decades, but because it's basically one featureless and continuous beachbreak. It is also size deficient most of the time and aside from a few scallops holding up the odd right and onshore slop in the NE monsoon, there is little reason to go up the coast, other than to escape the large groups of foreign surfers who regularly descend on Arugam Bay, often to hold their own national surfing contests.

THE ANDAMAN SEA

Although they are a territory of India, The ANDAMAN ISLANDS and **Nicobar Islands** are a long way from home, acting as the dividing line between the Bay of Bengal and the Andaman Sea. Of the 550 islands, only a handful of them have been surfed and there are undoubtedly more spots to be discovered, especially in the north of the chain where swell regularity is much lower. Plenty of problems revolve around access, which is heavily restricted to most indigenous tribal regions and in fact a blanket ban exists for foreigners to travel to the Nicobar Islands, ostensibly for the protection of the indigenous tribal groups, unique flora and fauna. Even tsunami relief aid workers were denied entry, leading some to believe the protection is for the strategic air and naval bases on Car and Great Nicobar. Apparently, no permit is required for Indian nationals to visit the Nicobars, but you do need a written permit from the Assistants Commissioner's office and the Forestry Department to access parts of the island inhabited by tribal groups, particularly around Indira Point, which is India's southernmost point. Recently, some Indian surfers explored this area and found some amazing world-class surf on the southwest coast of Great Nicobar, plus some tasty reefs and righthand pointbreaks along the SE coast up to the main area of habitation at Campbell Bay, where a fun peak hits the breakwall in a strong S swell. Car Nicobar, Teressa and Katchal Island all have ample swell exposure from the S-W, along with the promising reef bathymetry and Teressa and Katchal Island have been surfed by passing yachts (without permits).

Over on the eastern perimeter of the Andaman Sea, the Tanintharyi division of **Myanmar** is home to the jumble of 800 Mergui islands,

For more information, check these other Stormrider Surf Guides and/or eBooks.

which come in all shapes and sizes. The new government is slowly opening the archipelago for tourism, yet the only hotel on Khayin Khwa (Macleod Island) closes down for the 6 months of the SW monsoon as waves of up to 3m batter the tranquil beaches. Many dive boats operate live-aboards in this area and it would take a lot of searching to find the beach and reefbreaks that undoubtedly exist in this largely unexplored area. Steep granite and limestone also hinders any good surf in places, so often it is just average mellow beachbreak like Koh Phayam, a Thai island at the bottom of the archipelago. Further south in **Thailand**, Phuket is where most surf tourists congregate, hoping for some headhigh monsoonal swell without the onshore wind destroying it. Heading south and east, the coastline breaks up into a jigsaw of islands, that invariably sees less and less of the WSW swell as Aceh shuts the window and the plunging granite cliffs encourage diving rather than surfing. This is particularly true of the Similan Islands, which offer awesome scenery above and below the waterline, but very little in the wave department.

Government restrictions and red tape have kept the Nicobar islands off limits and only a few spots have been surfed by passing surf charter raids.

RANMOHAN PARANJAPE
NICOBAR ISLANDS

SOUTHWEST SRI LANKA

+ QUALITY MELLOW WAVES
+ OFFSHORE NE MONSOON
+ BEAUTIFUL SCENERY
+ FRIENDLY LOCALS
+ CHEAP

– WINDS & SWELLS CONFLICT
– SMALL WAVES
– NO WORLD-CLASS SPOTS
– LOCALISM AT HIKKADUWA SPOTS

The south coast of this extraordinarily beautiful country is open to the same regular, long distance SW swells that pepper Indonesia. However, unlike Indonesia, unfavourable, local, monsoonal wind patterns arrive during the prime May-Oct swell season, bringing onshore winds. This means that most surf travellers, wanting to score glassy conditions, venture here during the much quieter swell period of Dec-March, but even at this time of year waist to headhigh waves are common and the conditions are perfect. The centre of the south coast surf scene are the handful of reefs in the resort town of Hikkaduwa.

LAZY LEFTS

Thanks to plenty of local colour, stunning beaches, ease of access and cheap living costs the southwest coast of Sri Lanka has long been a popular hangout for surfers, hippies and beach tourists. The variety of mellow reefs at Hikkaduwa, perfectly groom the small, clean SE-SW swells that tend to favour the lefts. On a big swell, **NORTH JETTY** will catch some long lefts over a rugged reef bang in front of the harbour wall. The outside reef of **BENNY'S** is a 5 min paddle and offers a pretty radical and fairly long left that can hold

big swells. Shallow at low and suited to intermediates plus riders. The most consistent spot is **MAIN REEF**, which has fun, but generally slow lefts and rights on a flat coral reef facing the A-Frame Guest House. Often warbled with wind and seriously crowded, it has seen some outrageous localism over the years, so go easy. Better at low to mid or somewhere quieter? South of Main Reef is **INSIDE REEF**, which is another, left-leaning peak that deals out some power, without as many takers. Get it early before the wind and kiteboarders descend. Beyond here is a long stretch simply called **BEACHBREAK**, which varies from a fat wave, ideal for the many beginners taking advantage of the warm water and cheap rentals, to an occasionally fun wedgy shorebreak, good for bodyboarders. If it ever gets big, the closed-up **RIVERMOUTH** will have a rideable wave, although the water can be very dirty at this fishing beach. **GALLÉ** is southeast from Hikkaduwa, and is the most interesting colonial town in the area. A left breaks near the jetty just outside of town, but it doesn't work very often. In the town itself the shallow reefs in front of the old city walls always seem on the verge of working but never quite do it. Just beyond Gallé is idyllic **UNAWATUNA**. The magnificent curl of beach here is largely sheltered from surf by fringing reefs, but a playful little right breaks off the point at the western end of the bay. A bit further east is **KOGALLA**, where two expensive hotels are located. The reefs here don't pick up as much swell, but when it's on, the left has a bit more push and is not for beginners. Beyond these is the super-consistent reef/beachbreak at Kabalana beach aka **THE ROCK**. It's a wedgy beast, breaking in front of a huge offshore rock in all tides and NE winds. If it's flat here go and do something else for the day! Midigama, the next village along, is less consistent than Hikkaduwa and the two spots are more exposed to S winds. **RAMS RIGHT** is a short, powerful right that breaks over a shallow reef and offers frequent tubes. The aptly named **LAZY LEFTS** is an old coral shelf found a little further east, where a slow, fat left trundles along for 100m. Can get a bit of backwash. Chilled out place, nice, basic accommodation and far less crowded than Hikkaduwa. The beachbreak in **WELIGAMA** can be surfed even when small and is ideal for beginners. It's also worth a peek when the rest of the south coast is blown-out. **MIRISSA** has possibly the most beautiful beach in the country as well as a very fickle right point at the western end of the bay. Needs heaving due S swell to swing into the SE-facing bay and get the little rights spinning,

HIKKADUWA

LAURENT NEVAREZ

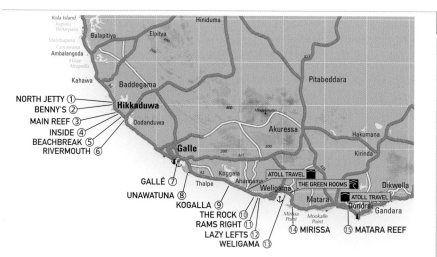

NORTH JETTY ①
BENNY'S ②
MAIN REEF ③
INSIDE ④
BEACHBREAK ⑤
RIVERMOUTH ⑥
GALLÉ ⑦
UNAWATUNA ⑧
KOGALLA ⑨
THE ROCK ⑩
RAMS RIGHT ⑪
LAZY LEFTS ⑫
WELIGAMA ⑬
⑭ MIRISSA   ⑮ MATARA REEF

close to the basalt rocks. There are also a couple of lefts in the vicinity. **MATARA BEACH** gathers in plenty of swell to a wide, open strand that is replete with Buddhist temple on an islet. The eastern bays towards Meddawatta are best, where there are some good guesthouses and a range of decent peaks to choose from at all but high tides. Back over to the west of the town there's a couple of mysto reefs including a fairly hollow left. The area between Dondra and Tangalla contains a number of beachies and occasional reefbreaks, but they need a lot of swell to get going and north quadrant winds.

SWELL AND WIND

The same swells that turn Indonesia on, deliver the goods to Sri Lanka, although the higher latitude causes some swell decay. The main problem is that the most consistent SW swell season (April-Oct) will be accompanied by frequent SW to WNW onshores. It's still possible to surf in the morning but expect rain, dirty water and strong winds (10-20mph) with the 3-8ft (1-2.5m) swells. The best time for the S coast is at the start and end of the dry season (November to April), when NE winds are most likely to coincide with the bigger SW groundswells. During the dry season, waves are typically 2-6ft (0.5-2m) and clean, so it's rare to see it totally flat in Hikkaduwa, at any time of year. Even during the NE monsoon, the afternoons tend to go onshore. The wind affects the spots east of Gallé far more than the Hikkaduwa breaks. Tidal ranges are minimal, and the A-Frame surf shop in Hikkaduwa provides tide tables. Most shallow reefs will change significantly with the tides. ●

SPOT INFORMATION

SPOT	SIZE	BTM	TYPE
①	6/3		
②	10/3		
③	10/2		
④	8/2		
⑤	6/1		
⑥	6/3		
⑦	6/2		
⑧	8/2		
⑨	8/2		
⑩	8/2		
⑪	6/2		
⑫	6/2		
⑬	4/2		
⑭	6/2		
⑮	6/1		

TRAVEL INFORMATION

LOCAL POPULATION: Hikkaduwa – 101,382	COASTLINE: 1340km (837mi) TIME ZONE: GMT +5h30

GETTING THERE – No visa for stays of up to one month. It's fairly cheap to fly to Colombo (CMB) with the Middle Eastern airlines generally offering the best deals. There are no domestic flights. Hikkaduwa is 3h from the airport.

GETTING AROUND – A taxi to the airport is ± $100e/w. If you're on a budget trip take a train for $1-1.50. Renting a car and driver is easily arranged from $25-40 per day, but not really needed unless you're planning on exploring a lot. Self-drive is not easy to arrange and not recommended.

LODGING AND FOOD – Sri Lanka can be done on a real shoestring budget - always bargain down prices. Basic room in Hikkaduwa fr $12/d (Why Not Guest House), or $53 for more comfort (A Frame or Hotel Moon Beam). The food in Sri Lanka is phenomenal. There's an endless variety of healthy curries, plenty of seafood and the fruit is simply out of this world. Expect to pay $5 for a meal.

WEATHER – It's a typical tropical monsoon climate with two definite seasons. *Maha* means NE monsoon (Nov - Mar) and this is the driest and sunniest period for the SW. The transition periods have very hot temperatures (March-April), but relief can be found in the mountains. The rainy monsoon lasts from April to Oct and the winds blow strong onshore (SW - *Yala*), bringing lots of rain. This rainy period lasts until Nov, which is the coolest, most pleasant time to travel. Most of the year the water temperature remains a perfect 27°C (80°F), so you can ride rubberless.

WEATHER STATS	J/F	M/A	M/J	J/A	S/O	N/D
Total Rainfall (mm)	92	190	282	132	255	250
Consistency (d/m)	8	15	22	15	19	15
Temperature min. (°C)	22	23	25	25	24	22
Temperature max. (°C)	31	31	31	29	29	30

NATURE AND CULTURE – The island where Jonah was spat out of the whale and Adam and Eve walked in paradise has much more to offer than average surf or snorkeling on the coral reefs. Visit colonial Gallé, climb Adam's peak for the spectacular sunrise and see the Buddhist temples in Kandy. Wildlife (elephants and leopards) is plentiful in the national parks. Hikkaduwa has surprisingly good nightlife.

HAZARDS AND HASSLES – In past years there have been some serious cases of violent localism towards visiting waveriders from the local Hikkaduwa surfers although things appear to have calmed down a little now. Bring a good attitude, be mellow in the line-up and instead of aggression, you'll be treated well. Sewage pollution and coral cuts mix badly. Hikkaduwa itself is starting to look pretty shabby (although a new road by-pass should improve things) and the beach is suffering from serious erosion meaning that in places there's almost no sand left to sit on.

HANDY HINTS – The A-Frame surf shop is the base for Mambo Surf Tours, who can arrange trips to waves in other areas of the country. Reef End do lessons. Very battered boards can be rented for $3/h. A gun is not needed. Learn a few words of Sinhala and you'll be greeted with smiles.

MIRISSA

PAUL KENNEDY

SURF STATS		J	F	M	A	M	J	J	A	S	O	N	D
SWELL	Dominant swell	◉		◉		◉		◉		◉		◉	
	Size (m)	3		3-4		5		6		4-5		3	
	Consistency (%)	50		50		30		30		40		50	
WIND	Dominant wind	◉		◉		◉		◉		◉		◉	
	Average force	F3-F4		F3		F4		F4		F4		F3	
	Consistency	85		59		89		89		80		60	
TEMP.	Wetsuit	🩳		🩳		🩳		🩳		🩳		🩳	
	Water temp.	27		28		28		27		27		27	

SOUTHEAST SRI LANKA

+ CONSISTENTLY CLEAN & RIDEABLE
+ VARIOUS SANDY RIGHT POINTS
+ LAID-BACK FRIENDLY VIBE
+ AMAZING SIGHTS AND WILDLIFE
+ CHEAP

– CONSISTENTLY SMALL
– CROWDED ARUGAM BAY
– MIXED ABILITY LINE-UP
– SLOW TRANSPORT
– INTENSE HEAT AND INSECTS

First surfed in 1964, Arugam Bay is no surf secret. Despite the 2004 Boxing Day tsunami disaster, the waves are still breaking better than ever, with consistently small, perfect righthand peelers that make Arugam Bay an intermediates heaven. A-Bay (the 7 villages) is often compared to an undeveloped Kuta, Bali in the late '70s since the civil war kept the village in its most basic form. Things are looking up now with new roads and bridges improving the access, no more checkpoints and more accommodation options for the growing stream of foreign surfers searching for the long, sheltered sand-bottom pointbreaks along this southeastern coast.

Wave quality varies depending on sand build-up from point to point, which is heavily affected by river flows. **SANGAKAMANDA** rivermouth is hardly ever surfed since access is difficult and wave quality not really worth it. **KOMARI** is a 20min walk from the end of the road to a small lighthouse on a rocky headland. Aka Green Point, it's hard to find and gets blown out in the afternoon sea breezes. The best northern spot is **POTTUVIL POINT**, which can have 800m (875yd) long rides from the tip to the beach, with a barrel in the middle in front of the huge granite rocks. Waves hug the shoreline and although small in size, can be big on fun. A-Bay needs to be 4-6ft for Pottuvil to break, making it a low consistency break. Walk 700m north to ride a similar but shorter point away from the crowds. **POTTUVIL BEACH** has a scalloped cove with point-style rights pushing wide and deep, making it a perfect beginners zone only 20mins tuk-tuk ride from Arugam Bay. The **MAIN BEACH** is usually a close-out, but near the bridge, there can be a wedgy A-frame over the offshore rocks. The reform in front of **MAMBO'S** guesthouse can be a beginner's heaven, because it is always offshore, grooming tiny perfect walls, close to shore, making it simple to walk back up the beach. The southern point of **ARUGAM BAY** is a top-class wave breaking over an old coral reef, which can be dangerously shallow and sectiony at low tide. It's very consistent and often crowded with occasional barrels in front of the corner, but the afternoon SE sea breeze messes it up. South of the landmark **CROCODILE ROCK** is a sandy point with mushy rights, requiring a 20 min walk to get to, including crossing two rivermouths where the potential to bump into some wildlife is high. Less well known **PEANUT FARM** is the best quality option within easy travel of Arugam, despite the 20min walk from Panama. Sucky rights break close to the rocks, while the beachbreak is perfect for beginners. **PANAMA RIGHTS** only works when the rivermouth is closed, offering rocky rights and a tiny reform by the boats. **OKANDA**, is about 1h by tuk-tuk from A-Bay and picks up as

POTTUVIL POINT

STUART BUTLER

OKANDA

ANDREW SHIELD

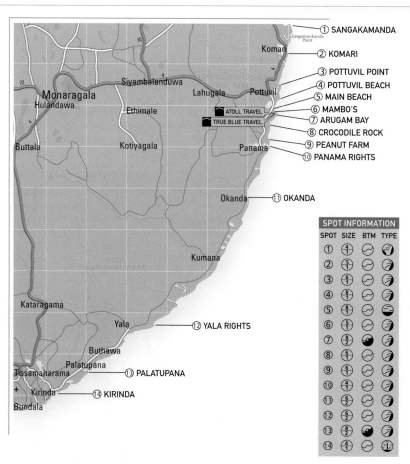

①	SANGAKAMANDA
②	KOMARI
③	POTTUVIL POINT
④	POTTUVIL BEACH
⑤	MAIN BEACH
⑥	MAMBO'S
⑦	ARUGAM BAY
⑧	CROCODILE ROCK
⑨	PEANUT FARM
⑩	PANAMA RIGHTS
⑪	OKANDA
⑫	YALA RIGHTS
⑬	PALATUPANA
⑭	KIRINDA

SPOT INFORMATION

SPOT	SIZE	BTM	TYPE

much swell onto a sucky outside sandbar below a whale-shaped rock. The super-fun walls inside the cove are always offshore. Yala National Park offers a huge unexplored surf area that's consistent until the midday sea breeze sets in, but access should only be attempted by boat from Kumana. Ask the Rangers about surfing **YALA RIGHTS**, but expect to pay entry fee and jeep hire. On the east side of Yala National Park, the most popular and expensive Block 1 entrance leads to **PALATUPANA** village, where there is a guest-house, beautiful reddish sand dunes and a decent little right point off a rocky shore. Treasures have been found off the Great Basses reef shipwrecks in **KIRINDA**, where jetties hold some easy, small, but clean peeling waves.

ANDREW SHIELD

TRAVEL INFORMATION

| LOCAL POPULATION: | COASTLINE: 1,340km (832mi) |
| Ampara District – 648,057 | TIME ZONE: GMT +5h30 |

GETTING THERE – 30-day visa upon arrival. Fly Sri Lankan to Colombo (CMB) from Europe. Daily flights with Singapore or Malaysian from SE Asia or USA. Airport is in coastal Negombo 45min north of crazy Colombo traffic. A-Bay is 9h drive away ($125 o/w by private van). Bus is 12-20hrs, twice daily ($3) Break up the scenic journey with an overnight stop in the "Hill Country", Kandy, or Ella/Haputale.

GETTING AROUND – A-Bay is only 300km (186mi) away from Colombo so 40km/h is a good speed. Road network is light, potholed and there are multiple army checks. No traffic around A-Bay except Pottuvil. Hire a van ($50/day with driver) or use tuk-tuk (local ride $1) or walk. Boat rides are tempting but 4x cost and 2x time; A-Bay to Okanda is 2h by boat but 1h by tuk-tuk.

LODGING AND FOOD – Cheap beach guest-houses like Arugam Bay Surf Resort cost $20/d for room with fan. Medium priced Hideaway is $50/d/ dbl and great food ($66B&B). A/C places include Siam Hotel ($45/n/tw), Tri-Star ($40-60). Book Stardust Hotel with Atoll Travel. Food is tasty, sometimes spicy, around $5 for a full meal.

WEATHER – Arugam Bay area is ideally located to avoid the ravages of the two annual monsoons that hit the island from opposite directions - the SW (May-September) and NE (Nov-Feb). This southeastern corner is the driest part of the country and it's stifling hot in the summer before the SSE sea breeze kicks in. The desert-like weather cools nights off, making sleep without A/C possible after 11pm. Average annual precipitation hits 1,900mm (75in) from thunderstorms and proper rainy days are rare apart from occasional NE storms, mostly during the off-season time of the year. Our TrincoMalée weather stats from 200km north are wetter than A-Bay area. Weather records show an average of 330 sunshine days/year!

WEATHER STATS	J/F	M/A	M/J	J/A	S/O	N/D
Total Rainfall (mm)	115	53	49	79	164	361
Consistency (d/m)	7	5	4	5	9	17
Temperature min. (°C)	24	25	26	25	24	24
Temperature max. (°C)	28	31	33	33	32	28

NATURE AND CULTURE – Yala National Park is the main wildlife sanctuary; enter from Okanda (cheaper than Tissama), but you need to rent a vehicle ($50-80/day). Check Kumana Bird Sanctuary. Many Hindu shrines close by like Katara-gama. Sri Lanka is a paradise: Sigiriya citadel, Kandy Perahera Festival, Ayurvedic massages, Full moon parties!

HAZARDS AND HASSLES – Now the war is over, crowding is becoming an issue, especially July-Sept. Some countries have been holding national pro contests at A-Bay, shutting down an already aggressive line-up. Because the wave is forgiving, many improvers enter the mix and bad etiquette or drop-ins are a fact. The local surfers are skilled and will take many waves, regardless. The roads are slow, there's very little shade at most spots, so take enough water and make sure your tuk-tuk driver will pick you up after surfing.

HANDY HINTS – Bring cash, because the Bank of Ceylon in Pottuvil is a nightmare. You can rent NSP boards at Aloha and SurfNSun. Bring a fish type of board.

WIND AND SWELL

The main swell producer is the SW monsoon pushing constant 4-10ft (1.2-3m) SW windswell from May-August, along with long-distance S swells from the 20°-50° latitudes, mainly between March and November. Swell direction matters for those long distance swells and S-SE is obviously better than S-SW. Because of distance and angle, waves mostly break in the 2-6ft (0.6-2m) range and 3-4ft (1-1.2m) is the perfect size for A-Bay. Above this size, A-Bay becomes sectiony, so it's best to ride other spots like Pottuvil, Peanut Farm or Okanda.

ARUGAM BAY

LAT. 6.838210° LONG. 81.840700°

A-Bay has been a stepping-stone on the Indian Ocean trail for a long time, thanks to its reputation for being a class act in an exotic, laid-back zone. Long, lazy rights peel down the sand and rock point for hundreds of meters, bending to parallel the beach and slowly diminishing in size along the way. It starts off with a bit of a hollow section, then walls and shoulders in inviting sections that are more playful as opposed to powerful. This means all abilities are found in the extremely crowded line-up and drop-ins, snaking and bad vibes are commonplace during the peak season of May - August.

Bengal Bay does produce some rare NE swells in the 2-4ft (0.6-1.2m) range, but it's mostly onshore with overcast skies, rainy weather and running rivermouths. During the SW monsoon, the day starts with a bit of early morning sickness, then light offshore up to 11-ish, before the low to moderate S-SE sea breeze starts messing up the outside sections. Tidal range is only 2ft (0.6m) max, but A-Bay's sand-covered reef gets shallow and getting in and out at low tide is a bit tricky. Only slight changes for the neighbouring spots. ●

STATS		J F	M A	M J	J A	S O	N D
SWELL	Dominant swell	🌀	◗	◗	◗	◗	🌀
	Size (m)	1-2	2	4	4	3	1-2
	Consistency (%)	30	40	80	80	60	20
WIND	Dominant wind	◴	◔	◕	◔	◕	◔
	Average force	F3-F4	F3	F4	F4	F4	F3
	Consistency	85	40	88	89	79	52
TEMP.	Wetsuit	🏄	🏄	🏄	🏄	🏄	🏄
	Water temp.	27	28	28	27	27	27

ANDAMAN ISLANDS, INDIA

+ VIRGIN CORAL REEFBREAKS
+ KUMARI POINT
+ LIMITED SURF CHARTER OPTIONS
+ UNTOUCHED, WILD TRIBES

– UNFAVORABLE WINTER SEASON
– SHORT IDEAL SEASON WINDOW
– EXPENSIVE BOAT OR CAMPING
– OPPRESIVE HUMIDITY

Dubbed "The land of the head-hunters" by Marco Polo, who was the first Western visitor to this chain of 572 islands, islets and rocks, now commonly referred to as the Andaman and Nicobar Islands. With only 36 of the 239 Andaman Islands inhabited, the dense tropical forests support an exotic, fragile ecosystem of unique flora and fauna, preserved and protected in 96 sanctuaries and nine national parks. Geographic isolation, heavily restricted travel, mysterious Stone Age culture and totally uncharted waters characterise this zone. Geologically akin to the Sumatran island chains, the Andaman's have been on many surfers' travel wish list since being unveiled in the late '90s by wandering photographer, John Callahan.

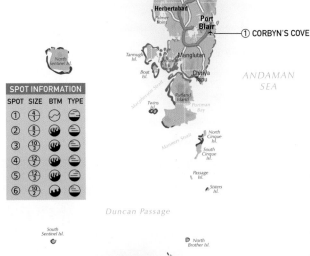

JARAWA POINT

Port Blair only merits a short stay for surfers. Havelock is a popular island with resorts and swell can sneak in from the south, but it will usually be flat and only fit for a bodybash. Close to Port Blair is the main tourist beach of **CORBYN'S COVE**, just east of Ramshackle airport, where the palm-fringed beachbreak is generally flat or a tiny closeout, unless there is windswell from the E-SE or booming S filtering through. There are no reliable breaks on the tiny Twin Islands off Rutland or the Cinque Islands, which are dive, snorkelling and tourist day trip destinations. An exposed, wide reef pass on North Sentinel Island has been surfed, but these areas are off limits and the Sentinelese locals have a habit of attacking any strangers with spears and arrows! Tiny, uninhabited South Sentinel may hold a hollow left wall on its eastern side in certain conditions. Little Andaman offers the best swell exposure from the S-W, as it isn't blocked by the Nicobars, sitting a little to the SE. **JACKSON CREEK** offers a safe anchorage inside a large shielding headland fringed by a wind and swell exposed reef. It is an excellent left, but needs E-S winds to be offshore and a decent swell to wrap so it's quite inconsistent. No crowds unless you include illegal fishing boats and unbelievable mosquitoes. Past the two stretches of beachbreak on the west coast is another left called **TOTEM REEF** that needs the same SE wind to be perfectly offshore, but can still be rideable during the NE monsoon. The SW tip of the island should show the most swell, especially at **MUDDY'S**, a solid, wedgy lefthander that

works in NE winds and barrels hard in sections. Around Sandy Point is the main event, namely **KUMARI POINT**, which was the fastest and longest right pointbreak/reef in the country. Unfortunately, due to the recent spate of earthquakes in the region, this most photogenic of reefs has been lifted out of the water and now only breaks for about a quarter of it's former glory. Instead of a pin wheeling right point, the line-up has broken up into a more peaky, sectiony affair, but still shows some above average form when there's enough S-SW swell and winds from the N quadrant. The inside section has got even

KUMARI POINT

JARAWA POINT

SWOP SURFBOARDS

hollower as it spins down to the creek mouth channel in the reef. Most surfers concentrate on the reliable left reef up the east coast on the northern headland at Butler's Bay known as **JARAWA POINT**, named after one of the indigenous tribes. It's positioning leaves W swells out of the equation, but anything S will hit a rocky, limestone shelf that curves into the bay, turning any N winds offshore. When it's on, a fast jetting left sucks up and peels from start to finish. Even when it's smaller, it still offers fun park walls that tumble down the reef in sections, offering hits and shoulders, with the chance of a few cover-ups at bigger sizes. Most Andaman waves are fairly easy with good shape and fantastic colours on the reef below. Further south across the 10° Channel, the Nicobar Islands are off limits, protecting their surf potential and their unique indigenous population from outside interference.

SWELL AND WIND

The same SW monsoon swells hitting Sumatra travel as far as the Andaman's, 10° or so above the Equator, albeit arriving with less power and consistency. Unfortunately, most of the breaks are directly onshore in the SW winds, so therefore, the season is a short spell from Mid-March to Mid-May. Some have scored in the Dec-Feb slot, but flat spells are guaranteed, especially at Butlers Bay on the east coast. The best conditions occur when there is an early season swell with perfect NE winds, before it switches when the SW monsoon arrives, sometimes as early as April. Choose your time very carefully; April seems to be the most reliable month. Once the SW monsoon is on, the sea gets rough with constant 15-25 knot winds, blowing out spots, but creating a small windswell for Phuket beaches. Semi-diurnal tidal phases are smallish, but affect some spots heavily. ●

SURF STATS		J F	M A	M J	J A	S O	N D
SWELL	Dominant swell	🌀	🌀	🌀	🌀	🌀	🌀
	Size (m)	2	3-4	4-5	5	4-5	1-2
	Consistency (%)	40	70	10	10	20	30
WIND	Dominant wind	🧭	🧭	🧭	🧭	🧭	🧭
	Average force	F3	F2-F3	F3-F4	F4-F5	F3-F4	F3-F4
	Consistency	76	60	73	83	51	66
TEMP.	Wetsuit	🏄	🏄	🏄	🏄	🏄	🏄
	Water temp.	27	28	29	28	27	27

TRAVEL INFORMATION

LOCAL POPULATION:	**COASTLINE:** 2,000km (1,250mi)
Andaman & Nicobar	**TIME ZONE:** GMT +5h30
Islands – 360,000	

GETTING THERE – Foreigners need an Indian tourist visa, plus a 30-day tourist permit must be obtained on arrival at Port Blair from the immigration authorities. Plan to lose one day in PB to get entry permits and paperwork in order. Port Blair is served by Alliance Air/Indian Airlines flights from Kolkata and Chennai (fr $250 e/w). Jet Airways have daily Chennai flights from $100 to 400 e/w. Book very early. 3 to 4 ferries per month depart Kolkata and Chennai, taking 60h and costing $30 e/w for a bunk or $125 for deluxe cabin.

GETTING AROUND – Get around Port Blair by moped, on hire for $5/day. Boats from the mainland moor at Haddo Jetty, 1km north of Phoenix Jetty, the arrival point for inter-island ferries and surfing charters (Phuket is 65h sail away). Ferry to Hutbay every day – 6-8h crossing (dep Port Blair 6.30am and arr 2.30pm). Return can be a real hassle as black market, corruption and bribery are involved in securing tickets to the only ferry. The rich can avoid this headache with a 25min helicopter ride! On Little Andaman there's limited auto, taxi and jeeps available to tour the dam, but cars are useless except between Hut and Jarawa. Proposed construction of new jetty at Butler's Bay may affect surf.

LODGING AND FOOD – Butlers Bay now has tourist huts available on the shore. Surfers have camped on the point, but prepare to be eaten alive by mosquitoes and sand flies. There's guesthouse and government accommodation in Hut Bay. Boat charters are the only way to get to the best spots, but few operate – The family run, 72ft (21.6m) sailing yacht Scame does min 12d tours at $190/p/d collecting guests in Port Blair after the 3 day crossing from Phuket (www.surf-sail.com). The 51ft (15.3m) Gaea is a wooden, ketch-rigged trimaran, taking scuba and surfing tours around the Andaman Sea.

WEATHER – The climate remains tropical throughout the year with temperatures varying between 24°c (78°f) and 35°c (94°f). Due to the incessant sea breeze, the Andaman's has very humid weather. The SW monsoon first touches Indian soil in the Andaman's and then proceeds towards the mainland. From mid-May to October, heavy rains flush the islands, often bringing violent cyclones that leave the west coast beaches strewn with fallen trees. In November and December, less severe rains arrive with the NE monsoon. The best time to visit these islands is between mid November and April. Annual rainfall can reach 3180mm (127"in)! Water temps remain warm year round; take 2 pairs of boardies at least!

WEATHER	J/F	M/A	M/J	J/A	S/O	N/D
Total Rainfall (mm)	30	40	420	400	380	190
Consistency (d/m)	1	4	18	21	20	12
Temperature min. (°C)	23	25	26	25	25	25
Temperature max. (°C)	28	30	29	27	27	28

NATURE AND CULTURE – Home to stone-age tribes (Onge, Jarawa, Sentinelese) these reclusive aboriginal people live in impenetrable jungles, and still practise age old rituals including some cannibalism. In the Nicobars, the people of Chowra are believed to have some occult powers over winds, waves, tides, current, etc., and to manipulate them to their advantage. In Port Blair, the Cellular Jail is worth a visit and Ross Island will give a lasting impression of British imperial rule. Little Andaman has elephant safaris through the rainforest and they train them to carry logs. Trek to the White Surf and Whisper Wave waterfalls. This is a world-class diving zone with large pelagics and amazing visibility. Great fishing.

HAZARDS AND HASSLES – Due to its remoteness, any emergency would take days to repatriate; take a well-stocked first aid kit. If camping, take a water purifying kit - fresh drinking water is hard to find. Sand flies on the beach are bloodthirsty and merciless and impossible to avoid in many areas. The bites really linger and like coral cuts, are easily infected – keep all wounds/bites clean and covered. These islands are wild; mind the sea crocs and potentially hostile tribes.

HANDY HINTS – Take everything including two regular shortboards, reef boots and repair kit, plus snorkelling equipment for the many flat/windy days.

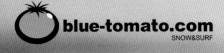
blue-tomato.com
SNOW&SURF

RE -USE
-FILL
-DUCE
-CYCLE

THE BALICAMP & SAMA SAMA

FOLLOW YOUR PASSION

Customized Surf Guiding & Coaching and Trailblazing Surf Boat Trips.
Benefit from our knowhow and let us make the most out of your time.
East Nusa Tenggara: Lombok – Sumbawa – Komodo – Sumba – Savu – Rote – Timor
Sumatra: Panaitan – Enggano – Mentawai – Telo – Nias – Banyak – Simeulue
Maluku Islands: Ternate – Halmahera – Morotai
Bali & Java

www.thebalicamp.com
www.samasamaboattrips.com

INDONESIA

Bali is where it all started, first in the 1930s at Kuta, then reignited with interest by the discovery of Uluwatu in the early '70s. The Bukit peninsula soon became synonymous with perfect barrels as more world-class waves were introduced to an insatiable surf world. Surfers flocked to the region, crowds grew and so started the eternal search for perfection in every corner of the huge Indonesian archipelago. Yet the discovery of G-Land, Panaitan, Nias, the Hinakos, the Banyaks and the Telos all paled in significance compared to the Mentawai Islands, which quickly ascended the throne and ruled the world as the most sought after surf on the planet. This embarrassment of riches doesn't only apply to the western islands and it wasn't long before the southeastern islands of Nusa Tenggara formed stepping stones from Bali, with each major island hosting at least one world-class wave including probably the world's best wave, Desert Point on Lombok. This area should attract surfers by the thousands, but in true Indo style, it is not so simple. While surf camps draw in visitors to a few prime spots, the rugged terrain and sparse infrastructure have left many coasts wild and undeveloped, offering the sort of vibe and exploration potential that existed on Bali 30 years ago.

mystery, emanating from the mountainous interior. This largest island in the Mentawai chain has only been lightly surfed by long-range charter crews grabbing an opportunistic wave on the way to the Nias area. That means spots on the backside are more often seen from the northern tip at Tanjung Sigep, down to the impossibly sheltered Teluk Tabekat and out to the headland at Sikabaluan, but most will pass by like ships in the night. A good deal of the SW-facing coast is straight line reefs, exposed and messed up by wind and swell, but a few obvious jinks in the coast could produce a left or two at Tanjungs Sakaladat, Sataerataera and Simasuket. Many captains will have a few spots sussed for certain conditions and there are some mellow breaks in the playgrounds area that get ridden like Taileleo, a fun mal slide facing south, Pearlers peak nestled behind Masokut and a righthander round the backside near the Muara harbour. Due to sheer spot density, we have split the **MENTAWAI ISLANDS** into **Playgrounds, Pulau Sipura**, and both the **Pagai islands**. It is important to recognise that while there are 40-60 named breaks, many more are out there, being surfed by experienced captains who know the deal.

PHOTOGERSON

DARK CRYSTAL

The islands of Sumatra have proven to host the greatest concentration of high quality waves on the planet and new contenders like Dark Crystal continue to appear, even in the Mentawai charter boat commuter belt.

SUMATRAN ISLANDS

In the North **SIMEULUE AND BANYAK** still maintain a frontier status, avoiding the charter boat congestion of the Ments through a combination of lower consistency and spot density, treating smaller groups to some lively waves, including one of Indo's best rights. **NIAS AND THE HINAKO ISLANDS** need no introduction, as Lagundri Bay is the original tropical paradise found. Once again, seismic activity has had a direct effect on the waves here, with the scorecard well in the black since Lagundri Bay has raised its reef and its game after the last 'quake. If you get stuck in the unlovely port of Sibolga, the offshore islands around Musala have some waves and are a beautiful place to hang out.

The hulking mass of Siberut presents a primal vista, with the hardwood forest shrouded in mist and it exudes an air of power and

PANAITAN ISLAND

Once G-Land hit the surf press, it wasn't long before the other extremity of this densely populated island was explored and the challenging reefs of West Java were mapped. However, in the busy Sunda Strait splitting Sumatra and Java, the horseshoe-shaped Panaitan Island has proven to be a lucky charm for tube hunters of all persuasions. One Palm Point puts the "ow" in shallow while Apocalypse defines the "awe" part of awesome and each wave throws down a serious gauntlet to both goofies and regulars looking for a challenge. Deeper in the strait a cluster of islands attract big crowds of boats, but not to surf, rather they are there to observe the most famous volcano in the world, Krakatoa and the recently risen Anak Krakatau (Child of Krakatoa). The Dutch called Pulau Sertung the 'Forsaken' island, which tripled in size from ash and pumice fallout after the 1883 eruption and being a low island, it has some waves off the southern point, but the rest of the islands are steep, volcanic or too deep and sheltered in the strait for any consistency. While the bay inside Panaitan is where all the surfers hang out, there are a few spots to check on the SE coast around the rangers station.

GETTING TO INDONESIA

GETTING THERE – There are 3 main international airports, the biggest being Soekarno-Hatta Airport (CGK) at Tangerang, Banten, near Jakarta, which is also the domestic hub (a shuttle ride away) for national airline Garuda Indonesia flights. Garuda is a surfer friendly airline and boards are part of your luggage allowance then a special sporting goods excess baggage tariff of $5/kg applies. Bali has many International flights on dozens of carriers to all corners of the world or else connect to Jakarta for more choice. Garuda flies from 24 countries, mainly in Asia, but has plans for massive expansion to include EU and US routes direct to Bali. A number of international airlines also fly direct to the third major airport of Medan in Sumatra, as well as Padang, Bandung, Surabaya, Solo, and Manado from Singapore or Kuala Lumpur, often on Low Cost Carriers like Air Asia.

VISAS – 9 SE Asian countries plus Chile and Peru enjoy free 30 day visas, while 52 nationalities are eligible for a visa on arrival when using the 15 airport and 21 seaport 'international gateways'. $25 for 30 days non-extendable - you must leave and return for another tourist visa. Pay at fee counter, then go to visa counter before immigration. All other visas must be applied for at an embassy prior to leaving. 60 day visas are longest available. International departure tax as of February 2010 is 150,000 in rupiah cash (approx $15) in Jakarta and varies at other international airports; the domestic departure tax in Jakarta is 30,000 rupiah ($3) and also varies elsewhere.

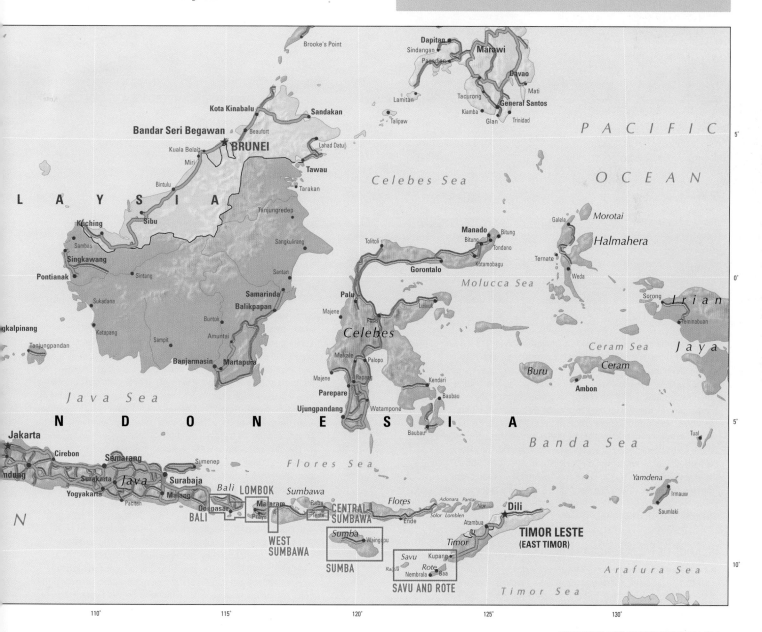

OTHER ISLANDS TO CONSIDER

DAVID SPARKES

For more information, check these other Stormrider Surf Guides and/or eBooks.

BATU ISLANDS

Often referred to as the Telos, the 51 Batu Islands have dodged the bulk of the Nias and Mentawai crowds for much the same reason as the Banyaks. There are fewer big name spots and the best set-ups often require stronger swells, usually from the rarer W direction. However, consistent, year-round, headhigh surf can always be found with plenty of fun, easier line-ups that cater to most tastes and abilities. A few surf camps have opened, but for independent travellers, this place is a mission without a boat to get around and it has a reputation for malaria and other diseases. There are flights from Medan and Padang to the small strip at Lasondre on Tanahmasa, plus ferries from Nias, but most of the waves are found on the smaller islands to the NW. Check around and in between the larger islands of Telo, Sipika and the more exposed reefs of Pulau Sigata. Like the Mentawais, refraction brings swell in at unusual angles so don't discount either end of Pulau Pini during big pulses. Down south on Tanahbala, there are some less frequented breaks with longer travelling times between them especially if going all the way to Bojo. The camps all have their own names for the spots, so it depends on who you travel with, but there is no doubt this group holds some excellent waves and since the equator runs through here, winds are rarely a problem with plenty of glass and a spot for all wind/swell combos.

BALI

The transformation of Bali from sleepy tropical island idyll to bustling global surf super-power has been swift and merciless, with massive tourism development taking place on the cliffs of the Bukit Peninsula above the revered waves of Uluwatu, Padang Padang and beyond. Kuta Beach is now a writhing centre of commercialism and the vibe is expanding all the way up the coastline of West Bali to Canggu. The waves over in East Bali are just as perfect and there are more reefs than ever being charged, led by the latest trendiest righthander on the island, Keramas. Looking for waves further north of Padang Bai harbour along the miles of black sands and coral reefs below the majestic peaks of Agung, Batur and Abang is unlikely to bear fruit unless rare conditions like a pumping S is doing a big wrap. The proper north coast of Bali attracts divers and snorkelers to placid waters rarely stirred by NE-E windswell.

ISLANDS OF NUSA TENGGARA

A mere stone's throw away from Bali across the deeply cut channel is LOMBOK, a different, drier world that is like an exploded version of the Bukit Peninsula on Bali, just without the 5 star hotels. The real touristy feel is reserved for the Gili's way up the north of the Lombok Strait, which feed off huge swells and NW winds, but there are further possibilities for surf along this west coast north of Sengigi and amongst the serene islands nestling behind Bangko Bangko. The south coast is cliffy and rocky, with lots of little islets and punctuated by a few really deep bays, which give Lombok way more flexibility in regards to swell size and beginners waves. It's hard to suss the waves from the charter boats, who have their usual stops, but rarely find the time to explore, so there are quiet corners along this coast for sure.

The next surf zone of WEST SUMBAWA has been surfed for decades, but due to lack of good transport links, it has remained a boat itinerary for most. Scar, Supers and Yoyo's are firm favourites, but cruise around the corner and a wave wilderness opens up along the south coast for 180km (110mi). Once again the charters are in a hurry to get to the name breaks and safe anchorages so few spots are regularly surfed. The predominant coastal angle would favour NW wet season winds, but there are many deep bays backed by high coastal ranges that funnel winds down valleys to meet the sea at rivermouths and reef passes that are going to work during the dry season. Remoteness, rough seas and no roads are going to keep this coast off the maps for years to come. After the brief interruption of the surf ghetto at Lakey Peak in **CENTRAL SUMBAWA**, normal service is resumed to the east of Wara Point out to Tanjung Langundu and the huge natural estuary that signals the end of the surf zone. What swell that does get through to Komodo and Flores is dashed against sea cliffs, proving this area is for divers and dragon hunters.

SUMBA is a large zone that is only lightly covered, with dozens of scarily high quality waves interspersed between the major breaks on the map. Between Nihiwatu and Tarimbang a contorted playground of reefs, bays and rivermouths beckons the longer range boat charters, who are the only ones that are going to be able to access these waves that work in a range of different wind/swell combos, taking experienced captains quite a while to work out and extra diesel to keep commuting between safe anchorages and the empty line-ups.

The same can be said of **SAVU AND ROTE** a region that cops stronger wind than most places in Indonesia, which often brings cross-chop to line-ups that look like they should be offshore. Like Sumba, there are more breaks to be sniffed out, but wind direction and strength will be critical, as will the direction that the swell arrives through the narrow SSW to W window. West Timor's far southern coast is SW swell exposed at a couple of obvious reef set-ups, but it soon transforms into long sandy beaches and large rivermouths bringing sediment from the mountainous interior. Over the border into East Timor there's a few pockets of reef platform around Suai, Betano, south of Beacu and the Lore area, but all in all it is uninspiring, wind blown and far too much hassle when Rote is hardly crowded. Consistency has to be the biggest worry, along with the appearance of large saltwater crocs using the many muddy river estuaries as a gateway to their feeding grounds. Far to the SW, a series of tiny, uninhabited atolls and shoals cling to the Australian continental shelf like Hibernia, Ashmore and Cartier, which are traditional Rote fishing grounds referred to as Sand Island. Used by asylum seekers to enter Australia, you couldn't

Bringing a bit of rock'n'roll to stone age Sumba.

The required combination of big swell and NW wind means the Gili Isles remain a rare treat.

find a more remote, wind-blown, flat reef that probably has a few corners on rare days, but isn't worth the mission and best left to the 14 species of endemic sea snake. Timor translates as "east" and surfers should take note. To head further towards Irian Jaya is counter productive as Australia shuts the window, the continental shelf cuts the power and weather systems get funky. There is of course plenty of E wind swell generated and in fact the north coasts of the islands strung between Flores and Pulau Wetar can get the odd sloppy wave, but what wind chop there is, usually heads straight to Sulawesi.

SIMEULUE & BANYAKS

+ QUALITY REEF BREAKS
+ CONSISTENT HI-SEASON SWELLS
+ MOSTLY UNCROWDED
+ UNTOUCHED SCENERY

– NO BUDGET OPTIONS
– LACK OF INFORMATION
– DANGEROUS NAVIGATION
– MALARIA

The remote island of Simeulue is located 120km (75mi) from the Sumatran west coast, where the surprisingly busy town of Sinabang thrives on trading cloves. To the east, and closer to the mainland by 50kms, the Banyak Island group is in the South Aceh Regency, supporting small populations on seven of the bigger islands, while the majority of the others remain uninhabited. Not surprisingly, these "many" islands have kept off the radar as Aceh's civil unrest made getting permits difficult until recently. Many spots remain nameless, or have multiple names from the different boat operators that ply these waters, but there's a wide choice of lefts and rights, ranging from shallow barrels to deeper, long, cruisey waves as well as some good off-season beachbreaks.

AURASURFRESORT.COM

green, hawksbill and leatherback turtles. At the southern end of the island is **COBRAS**, a real swell magnet left that lines up a superlative long barrel on the right swell direction and is a go to spot when the swell is small. There's also a right named Warrens across the deep channel. The **TREASURE ISLAND** righthander is long and sweet, serving up multiple barrel sections with relatively easy take-offs in a pristine environment. It needs a medium S-SW swell to get going and NW winds and is one of the best waves in the region when it fires. The outside indicator reefs are for barrel-crazy experts only and further inside the bay is Minis, a playful right with a short barrel and workable face on large swells. A wide bay on the SW shore of Pulau Tuangku, the largest island in the Banyak group, is known as Bay of Plenty since it's very consistent and hosts several breaks. The left at **LOLOK POINT** is an excellent wave for those with sufficient tube-riding skills and lust for speed. Too shallow when small, a medium to heavy swell will produce majestic speed walls that head into shacking sections over the inside reef. If it looks too heavy, head deeper into the bay and try the intermediate-friendly lefts of **DINDOS/TOY TOWN** that peel predictably and playfully down the coral. Both work in E quadrant winds and higher tides, but are surfable on low tide depending on the swell direction. On the other side of the bay is **GUNTURS/JOYSTICK** a shorter right that's comparatively playful when small, but morphs into a seriously challenging, take-off barrel, linking into a hollow, shallow end section when overhead swells hit. This is one of the most consistent waves in the area, working on all swells and tides and improves with the push. Bay of Plenty is versatile in NW-SE winds, so if the lefts are wind-affected, the right will usually be clean. The entire bay needs SW swells to get between Nias and Bangkaru – Treasure Island can have 6ft of South swell when the Bay is flat. South of Pulau Pinang, the mythical Lizard's Nest is worth looking for. A long righthander that's sensitive to swell direction, it produces a magical 10-second barrel when it's pumping from the SSW.

SWELL AND WIND

Equatorial shores generally suffer from a lack of exposure to swells, but the Southern Indian Ocean is the most efficient swell machine on the planet. Expect numerous 6-10ft (2-3m) SW swells (225°) per month between April and October, as well as occasional 3-6ft (1-2m) swells during off-season, with various 2-6ft (0.6-2m) cyclonic swells and some 1-2ft (0.3-0.6m) underlying wind swell. This area receives the same swells as the Mentawai between April and October, the

Just off the southern coast of Simeulue on Pulau Tapah, **TEA BAGS** is a challenging right that freight trains down a fringing reef when the swell is up. Other waves in the Busung village area include a sculpted right at the entrance to a deep bay, a fast left wall that hugs the corner of reef on the southern headland and an offshore bombie in the middle. Powerful beachbreaks hit the next bay south in small swells. There's also an easier left reefbreak on the SE tip of Simeulue called **THAILAND** with a steep drop and plenty of shoulder for cutbacks, plus a heavy, shallow, fast right to the east. The potential for good surf extends for miles up the coast with indented bays, scraggy reefs and miles of volcanic sand beachbreaks; however weather conditions are treacherous and the lack of safe anchorages makes it a navigational nightmare. **PULAU BABI** (Pig Island) is wide open to all swells, offering big drops into banking, full rail turns when it is pumping. Further inside peels a shorter, hollower right into the beach. The Banyak Islands' spots are usually shallow and fast, especially when it is smaller and all are sensitive to swell direction, switching between carvable walls and gut wrenching barrels. Pulau Bangkaru is well endowed with quality, consistent waves starting on the west coast with **TURTLES**, a fun, walling left and occasional slot beside the picturesque Pelanggaran Beach, popular with egg-laying

COBRAS

SURFBANYAK.COM

TREASURE ISLAND

JEREMY WILMOTTE

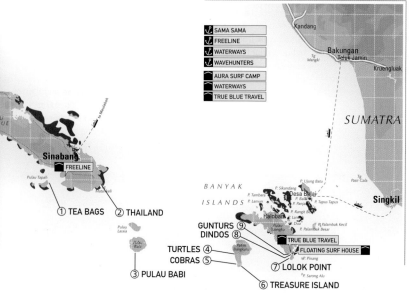

SAMA SAMA
FREELINE
WATERWAYS
WAVEHUNTERS
AURA SURF CAMP
WATERWAYS
TRUE BLUE TRAVEL

Kandang

Tg Mangki

Bakungan
Teluk Jamin
Kruengluak

SUMATRA

to Meulaboh

Sinabang
FREELINE
Pulau Tapah
Matakeli

BANYAK
ISLANDS

P. Ujung Batu
P. Sikandang
P. Tambara
P. Balik
P. Lamun
P. Panjat
P. Rangit B.
P. Dua
P. Palambak Kecil
P. Palambak Besar

Desa Balai

P. Tapus Tapus

Tg Pasir Gala

Singkil

① TEA BAGS   ② THAILAND

Pulau Lassia

Pulau Babi

GUNTURS ⑨
DINDOS ⑧
Halobari
Pulau Tuangku
Pulau Bangkaru

TURTLES ④
COBRAS ⑤

TRUE BLUE TRAVEL
FLOATING SURF HOUSE

③ PULAU BABI

⑦ LOLOK POINT
P. Pinang
P. Sarong Alu

⑥ TREASURE ISLAND

SPOT INFORMATION

SPOT	SIZE	BTM	TYPE
①	15/6		
②	10/2		
③	15/2		
④	10/3		
⑤	12/3		
⑥	12/4		
⑦	15/2		
⑧	10/2		
⑨	12/2		

TRAVEL INFORMATION

LOCAL POPULATION: Simeulue – 80,279
COASTLINE: Simeulue – 382km (239mi)
TIME ZONE: GMT +7h

GETTING THERE – Int. flights to Medan from Singapore (Silk Air, ValuAir), KL and Penang (Air Asia, Malaysia Airlines, Lion Air). Domestic flights include Garuda, Lion Air, Air Asia, Batavia Air, Merpati and more. Merpati, Buana Air and Susi Air service Sibolga and/or Singkili. The dreary, smelly port town of Sibolga is a slow, twisting 8h bus ride from Medan. For Simeulue, flights from Medan to Sinabang on Merpati & Susi Air, plus ferries from Meulaboh & Singkili. There is no airport on Banyak. Ferries cross from Tapaktuan (12h), Bakongan (6h) or Singkil (3h) to Desa Balai on Pulau Balai.

GETTING AROUND – The lack of regular transportation makes it difficult to visit the Banyak Islands and the good waves are only accessible by boat. Boat owners on Pulau Palambak take people to snorkel, but many are scared of the west coast of Tuangku. Booking a trip with a reliable surf trip operator is the only way to go, unless you have your own boat and plenty of cruising experience in the region.

LODGING AND FOOD – SurfBanyak.com do an 11-night charter aboard Surf Banyak II from $2695/p. 11 nights onboard The Dream are from $2,495/p. Local surfer owned Floating Surf House ($1500/10d) is moored behind the reef in Bay of Plenty. On Simeulue, Aura Surf Resort (fr $165/n) including surf transfers. The Baneng Beach retreat on Simeulue island resort is $115/p/n + transfers.

WEATHER – The climate in these islands is typically equatorial with very high temperatures interspersed by a few months of rain. Temperatures vary little across the year. Western Indonesia's dry season is May-Sept but 1-2h late afternoon showers can still be expected. During the October to April rainy season, it's rare to see more than half a day pass without any precipitation. Water is as warm as it gets, neoprene would only serve as reef protection. Lack of winds is good for glassy surf but does not help to dry clothes or feel cool – it takes a few days to adapt.

WEATHER	J/F	M/A	M/J	J/A	S/O	N/D
Total Rainfall (mm)	120	110	130	130	200	220
Consistency (d/m)	6	8	7	7	10	10
Temperature min. (°C)	23	23	23	24	23	23
Temperature max. (°C)	30	31	31	31	30	29

NATURE AND CULTURE – This is one of the remotest areas on earth, forget about raging nightlife and think eco-activities: trek and dive on Pulau Palambak or Pulau Balai. See the turtles laying eggs at night on Pulau Bangkaru. The untouched jungles offer unique flora and fauna and are best explored by boat.

HAZARDS AND HASSLES – With few surf-related charters making it this far up and only two camps, crowds should not be a problem. Chloroquine-resistant malaria cases have been reported – use prophylaxis. Earthquakes and tsunamis are real threats. These shallow and treacherous reefs are far from medical attention: take a helmet, boots and serious medical equipment.

HANDY HINTS – Take everything, there are no exchange facilities and surfing equipment is unheard of. Pulau Balai (Banyak) is one of the only places with electricity in the evening. The Banyak Islands are getting increasingly popular with travelers and may not remain off the beaten path for long.

optimal season being June-August. It still receives less swell than Nias, which can block some due S, so swells from 190° round to west (270°) are best, with 190°-220° being the most consistent. Bawa and Asu are relatively close if it's really too small and you have a fast speedboat or a day's travel time. Due to the doldrums latitude, wind patterns are pretty calm, producing glassy to 8kmh (5mph) wind conditions for 70% of the time, and there are no real dominant winds. Seasonal trends usually cite NW for January to May yet it tends to be more ENE, while instead of a SE trend from June to Sept,

it's often more W-NW. Historical figures show stronger NW for October to Dec, but in fact E-SE are more likely. The bottom line is winds are really variable and local knowledge goes a long way. Tide ranges are only 2-3ft (0.6-1m) but matter plenty at shallow spots, where sharp reefs pose a real threat. ●

SURF STATS

		J	F	M A M	J J A	S O N	D
SWELL	Dominant swell						
	Size (m)	3	4	4-5	5-6	5	3-4
	Consistency (%)	55		65	75	85	70	60
WIND	Dominant wind						
	Average force	F2	F2	F2	F2	F3	F3
	Consistency (%)	55		56	45	56	63	59
TEMP.	Wetsuit						
	Water temp.	29		28	28	27	27	28

NIAS & HINAKOS

+ WORLD-CLASS RIGHTS
+ CALM WINDS
+ OFF THE BEATEN TRACK FEEL
+ INEXPENSIVE

– LONG, HARD ACCESS
– MALARIA
– CROWDS
– SUFFOCATING HEAT, HEAVY RAINS

The perfect righthander at Lagundri Bay on the island of Nias was the first world-class wave discovered in the Sumatra region. Nias was first surfed in 1975, by Aussie surf pioneers Peter Troy, Kevin Lovett and John Giesel. They put up with swarms of malarial mosquitoes and the most primitive of living conditions to ride absolute perfection in the jungle. These days, it's much easier to get to Nias Island and a slew of losmens fringe the deep bay, competing to accommodate the constant stream of surfers. The massive 2005 earthquake tipped the island, lifting reefs in the south with some waves improving and others disappearing. Just offshore in the Hinako Islands, the two super-consistent, crowd-spreading spots have also been affected; Bawa's bowly rights have suffered while Asu's lengthy lefts have got even hollower over the lifted reefs.

The swell sucking Hinako Islands sit a mere 8km (5mi) off Nias, but it's a good 65kms (43mi) and 5hrs boat ride from Teluk Dalam in the south. Long, sweeping lefthand lines refract around the northern tip of tiny **ASU** island, stand up and pitch down the impressively long and shallow reef. Speed is essential to make some of the pinching sections and it gets heavy at size, which it handles with ease. Perfect barrels on its day. Reef uplift (1-2m) has lowered wave quality, intensified the ridiculously shallow end "Nuclear Zone" reef and made getting in and out from the five land camps a

real coral scramble requiring boots. If the wind swings onshore NW, then everyone will think about heading south to the remote and fickle right of **BAWA**, a growling beast that shifts around nastily as it unfolds over a gnarled slab reef. Consistently picks up more swell than anywhere and transforms a solid SW swell into round, cavernous pits through the sketchy inside bowl section. It's a challenging, powerful wave for chargers and tube junkies and a regular escape from the Lagundri circus. There are more lefts and rights to be sniffed out on the other tiny islands of Hamutala, Imana and Heruanga. Furthest north on Nias is **AFULU**, where pretty left lines used to swing down the reef that unfortunately rose up to 2.5m in the '05 quake. It needs plenty of swell to break, and will be shallow over the uncompromising coral. It's a 15min walk from the nearest village, a short boat ride from the Hinako Islands, or long overland drive from Lagundri. Round the headland from Lagundri is **SHARK HOLE** (aka Secret or Hualohilho), an average left reef that is protected from any E wind and offers a barrel at take-off, a few racy sections and easier shoulders into deeper water. Improves with size and rarely crowded since it is a 2-hour walk from Sorake beach. The adjacent beachbreak peaks can get good right around the curve of Pantai Walohiu. Since the 2005 earthquake, all the waves in Lagundri Bay have been affected (uplift min 0.3m), including **INDICATORS**, a very shallow, hairy right with pinching barrels, where it's critical to wait for the right wave and then kick out before the disastrous end section. Only attracts a handful of locals and hellmen, on the few days a season it works. It's been called many things including Nias, Lagundri, Sorake and most often just **THE POINT**, but whatever name is used, it always ends up in the

ASU

INDICATORS

PAUL KENNEDY

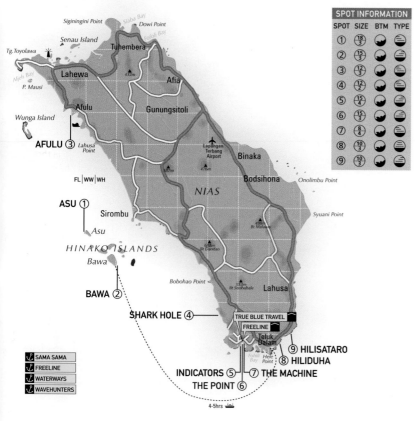

SPOT	SIZE	BTM	TYPE
①	18/3		
②	15/3		
③	12/3		
④	12/2		
⑤	6/4		
⑥	15/3		
⑦	8/4		
⑧	10/3		
⑨	10/3		

SAMA SAMA
FREELINE
WATERWAYS
WAVEHUNTERS

TRAVEL INFORMATION

LOCAL POPULATION: Nias & Hinako's – 756,762
COASTLINE: Nias – 380km (236mi)
TIME: GMT +7h

GETTING THERE – Most int. flights come through KL, Singapore or Penang on Air Asia, Singapore, Malaysian, Garuda and Lion Air. Internal connections to Jakarta, Bali, Banda Aceh and Padang with assorted Indo carriers. 1hr flight from Medan to Gunungsitoli (Nias) is serviced by Merpati, Riau Air and new, larger Wings Air planes (cheapest). Weekly flights leave from Padang to Gunung Sitoli, but are always heavily booked. Board charges apply (usually over 15kg total luggage) and all Sumatran airports charge dep tax (15,000Rp to 30,000Rp). Ferries run from Jakarta and Penang (Malaysia) to Medan. The ferry route from Sibolga (see Simeulue) to Gunung Sitoli (3hrs fast; 12hrs overnight) is very cheap but spartan! It takes about 2.5-3 hours from Gunung Sitoli to Lagundri by minibus. To get to Asu, the camp boats pick up guests from Sirombu.

GETTING AROUND – Once in Lagundri everything lies within walking distance. Teluk Dalam is a short bemo ride away. Most roads are poorly surfaced. To go exploring, renting a motorbike ($20/d) is easier than using trucks and bemos. Car hire with driver from $50/day.

LODGING AND FOOD – The Sorake Beach Resort has closed so no 3 star options and intermittent electricity supply means a/c is often pointless and lamps/candles are the norm. There are at least 30 losmens (from 2-12 rm) built on stilts overlooking the point, which have cheap accommodation (from $5/n), plus you are expected to eat your meals in them. There is a surf camp at Asu (Asucamp fr $45/n). Typical Indonesian meals based on fish and rice.

WEATHER – Nias has a typical equatorial climate with very high temperatures and humidity, which vary little year-round. Western Indo dry season is from May-Sept. but frequent 1-2 hour showers can still be expected, usually at night. The rainy season is from October-April. The water is some of the warmest in the surf world, getting close to 30°C/86°F around post Christmas.

WEATHER	J/F	M/A	M/J	J/A	S/O	N/D
Total Rainfall (mm)	115	117	150	160	235	237
Consistency (d/m)	7	8	9	9	14	15
Temperature min. (°C)	22	22	23	23	22	22
Temperature max. (°C)	30	32	32	32	31	29

NATURE AND CULTURE – 1hr from Lagundri, Bawomataluo village has an impressive temple, shown on the 1000Rp note. Obstacle jumping and war dances are cultural showpieces.

HAZARDS AND HASSLES – Several surfers have contracted malaria in Lagundri but recent draining of swamps have greatly reduced the threat. It's more prevalent inland along with dengue fever. In the Hinako Islands chloroquine-resistant strains of malaria are present – take precautions! Lagundri is a deep-water spot, but most reefs around here are shallow so be prepared to hit the bottom. Lagundri attracts some petty criminals – keep your gear locked down. Theft has reduced, replaced by high pressure memento selling. Young local surfers make up a third of the crowd and are slim, fit, fast and have it wired, but are friendly and relaxed in the water although they take plenty of waves. Show respect as the Nias people are proud and capable of getting angry.

HANDY HINTS – It's easy to buy, rent or repair boards. Bring boots, helmet and 7-8ft guns for the Hinakos. There is a small clinic and a police station in Lagundri. Best money exchange rate is back on the Sumatran mainland or in Gunungsitoli. There are new ATM facilities and internet in Teluk Dalam.

world's top 10 waves. Here's why; the paddle out through the keyhole is dry hair simplicity, the take-off is predictable, the barrel is a flawless almond shape that peels with precision at the perfect speed for up to 9 seconds, the reef is well covered, even though the recent up-thrust has made it barrel harder from waist high up to double overhead and beyond, plus the light seaward current from the channel deposits you nicely back at the peak, ironing out any shoulder bump on the way. It's all tides, all (light) winds, all year (with luck) and all too easy to stay encamped in one of the many losmens or hotels that line Sorake Beach. Negatives include the crowd, some localism, flying boards, sea-lice, the crowd.... Losers in the new reef levels include Kiddieland, which has been replaced by a softer inside section of The Point and **THE MACHINE**, an ultra hollow left barrel, deep in the bay, that now needs huge spring high tides and a macking swell. It has a new kink in it mid wave so making the channel is unlikely. There are also a variety of other lesser waves in the neighbourhood, within walking

PAUL KENNEDY

HILIDUHA

JS CALLAHAN/SURFEXPLORE

distance to the west (Sobatu) or back towards Teluk Dalam harbour (Rivermouth). **HILIDUHA** aka Dipi, is a sheltered reef peak that turns on sucky, committed tubes when the swell is up. 10km north of Teluk Dalam harbour, in front of the village **HILISATARO** is a swift, sucky right at the south end of the bay that will be working when The Point is bigger, i.e. strong S-SW swell and light N-NW winds. Aka Rock Star, it attracts a few boats.

SWELL AND WIND

Nias is only 60kms north of the equator, receiving plenty of organised swell from the Southern Ocean lows. Expect numerous 6-10ft (2-3m) SW swells from April-Oct and some occasional 3-6ft (1-2m) swells during the off-season along with various 2-6ft (0.6-2m) cyclone swells that can have lots of W in them. Historical data shows a 100% swell consistency from April to September, averaging out at 7ft with a 14sec period and peaking at 12ft/21sec. The first half of the year shows mainly light NW for half the time plus oiled glass, zero winds for a whopping 20% of the time. Winds get a bit stronger through July to November with a more E-SE dominant direction, but it is still variable and early/late glass-offs are a given. October seems to be the windiest month with a combo of SE and NW at 10-20mph. Tidal ranges are only 2-3ft (1m), but it has an effect on the super-shallow reefbreaks, especially since the earthquake, which saw some reefs rise by up to 2.5m (8ft) while an island just 20km (13mi) north subsided by 1.7m (5.5ft). ●

	SURF STATS	J	F	M	A	M	J	J	A	S	O	N	D
SWELL	Dominant swell	◑		◑		◑		◑		◑		◑	
	Size (m)	3-4		4-5		5		6		5-6		4	
	Consistency (%)	60		70		80		90		70		60	
WIND	Dominant wind	◔		◕		◔		◔		◑		◔	
	Average force	F2		F2		F2		F2		F3		F3	
	Consistency (%)	55		56		47		56		63		59	
TEMP.	Wetsuit	🩳		🩳		🩳		🩳		🩳		🩳	
	Water temp.	29		28		28		27		27		28	

THE POINT, LAGUNDRI BAY

LAT. 0.569781°   LONG. 97.7346°

Legendary righthander with many names, but just one trick – to produce flawless, precision barrels. Answers to Nias, Lagundri, Sorake or simply The Point and is always high up all natural-footers dream-wave list. Recent earthquakes have improved length, hollowness and consistency, attracting ever-growing crowds to what was already a popular pilgrimage since the wave came to prominence in the '70s. It now works from tiny to tow-in, producing a more powerful, rounder barrel that can stay open for double digits, without feeling like the flat reef will gobble you up for falling. Easiest paddle-out in the world, helpful current, wind resilient and a postcard location with plenty of cheap accommodation just add to the positive vibe. Ride it at least once in your life, but you will never ride alone.

MENTAWAI ISLANDS

+ TOP SWELL CONSISTENCY
+ LIGHT, VARIABLE WINDS
+ VARIETY OF WORLD-CLASS SPOTS
+ YEAR-ROUND WAVES
+ WARM, CLEAR WATER
+ EXOTIC ISLANDS, UNIQUE CULTURE

– VERY EXPENSIVE CHARTERS/CAMPS
– CROWDED LINE-UPS
– MALARIA
– DANGEROUS NAVIGATION
– LONG TRANSIT TIMES

In a very short period of time, this wild and remote chain of islands, lying about 90k's (55mi) off the Sumatran mainland, have become the most sought after destination for surfers looking to ride "the best waves in the world". This bold claim is rarely disputed, as those who score a solid SW swell will testify and few return from the Mentawais disappointed with the wave quality and quantity. The key to this rapid ascension to the pinnacle of world surfing lies in the sheer concentration of truly world-class breaks and an unmatched flexibility when it comes to handling different swell and wind combinations. Being a degree or three below the equator helps massively, as the light, flukey winds provide a variety of directions unseen in other parts of Indonesia and it often transpires that proper glassy conditions bookend the day. Furthermore, the geomorphology of this seismically active region seems to cause unusual swell refraction and diffraction, creating unexpected waves round the back of islands and islets where none should normally exist. These coral encrusted lava reefs fringe a still relatively untouched rainforest and many of the tribal inhabitants of the remoter regions, still cling to a traditional subsistence lifestyle, maintaining little contact with the outside world. Progress is unavoidable though and whereas 15 years ago, yacht charters were the only way to go, now a half dozen land camps have been established at the banner waves and many more are planned.

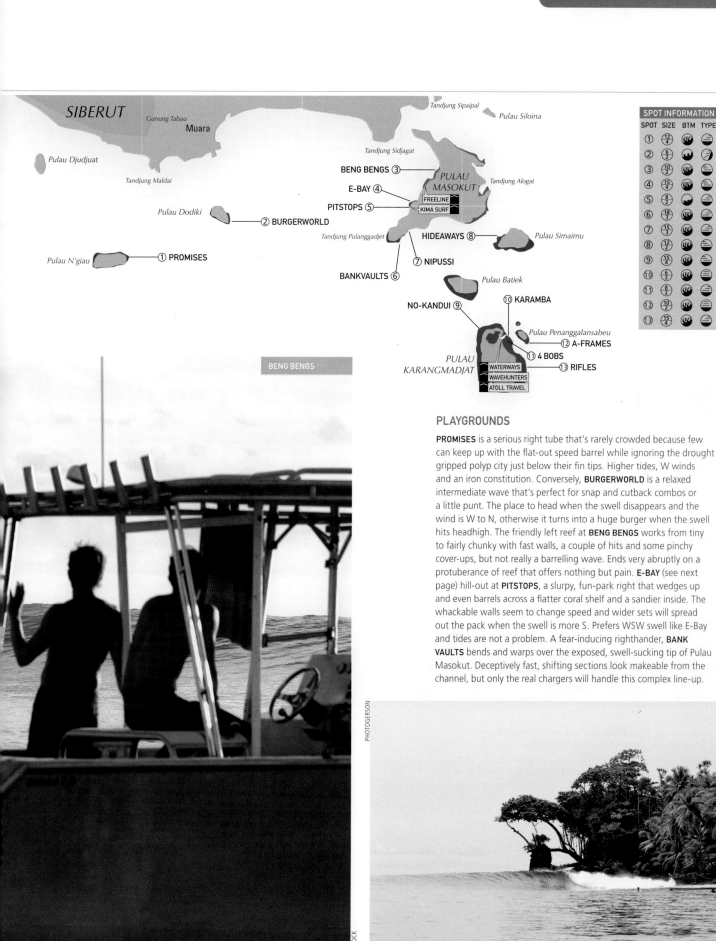

SIBERUT
Gunung Tabau
Muara

Pulau Djudjuat

Tandjung Maldai

Pulau Dodiki

Tandjung Sipaipal
Pulau Siloina

Tandjung Sidjagat

BENG BENGS ③

PULAU MASOKUT

Tandjung Alogat

E-BAY ④
PITSTOPS ⑤
FREELINE
KIMA SURF

② BURGERWORLD

Tandjung Pulanggadjet
HIDEAWAYS ⑧   *Pulau Simaimu*

① PROMISES
Pulau N'giau

⑦ NIPUSSI

BANKVAULTS ⑥

Pulau Batiek

⑩ KARAMBA

NO-KANDUI ⑨

Pulau Penanggalansabeu
⑫ A-FRAMES

PULAU KARANGMADJAT
⑪ 4 BOBS
WATERWAYS
WAVEHUNTERS   ⑬ RIFLES
ATOLL TRAVEL

SPOT INFORMATION			
SPOT	SIZE	BTM	TYPE
①	12/4		
②	9/2		
③	10/2		
④	15/4		
⑤	8/2		
⑥	18/3		
⑦	15/4		
⑧	12/4		
⑨	15/4		
⑩	9/2		
⑪	8/2		
⑫	10/2		
⑬	15/4		

BENG BENGS

PLAYGROUNDS

PROMISES is a serious right tube that's rarely crowded because few can keep up with the flat-out speed barrel while ignoring the drought gripped polyp city just below their fin tips. Higher tides, W winds and an iron constitution. Conversely, **BURGERWORLD** is a relaxed intermediate wave that's perfect for snap and cutback combos or a little punt. The place to head when the swell disappears and the wind is W to N, otherwise it turns into a huge burger when the swell hits headhigh. The friendly left reef at **BENG BENGS** works from tiny to fairly chunky with fast walls, a couple of hits and some pinchy cover-ups, but not really a barrelling wave. Ends very abruptly on a protuberance of reef that offers nothing but pain. **E-BAY** (see next page) hill-out at **PITSTOPS**, a slurpy, fun-park right that wedges up and even barrels across a flatter coral shelf and a sandier inside. The whackable walls seem to change speed and wider sets will spread out the pack when the swell is more S. Prefers WSW swell like E-Bay and tides are not a problem. A fear-inducing righthander, **BANK VAULTS** bends and warps over the exposed, swell-sucking tip of Pulau Masokut. Deceptively fast, shifting sections look makeable from the channel, but only the real chargers will handle this complex line-up.

PHOTOGERSON

DAN HAYLOCK

BURGERWORLD

E-BAY

LAT. -1.899910°   LONG. 99.291532°

DAN HAYLOCK

A lush, lefthand smoker with perfect form, especially when there's more W in the swell and E in the wind. Tight take-off zone, vert drop, quick turns then a race to the safety of the channel under the curtain, avoiding the two big rocks at high tide. Handles all size swells, but it's really fickle so dont expect to score it on a two week tour.

A-FRAMES

Gets better when it's double overhead or bigger, but expect to get pinned on the inside reef as the sets refract from wide, cutting off the escape to the channel. Tucked into a corner close to shore, **NIPUSSI** gives lesser mortals a chance to work the consistent walls that are effectively the end of the Bank Vaults swell train. Longer drops can be had across a couple of sections of reef and the inside zippers can offer a short tube ride, before it goes dry at the sign-posted shut down. **HIDEAWAYS** produces a deceptively heavy left chamber that beckons chargers into a bendy bowl section as perfect as any in the Ment's. When it's on, the drop is sharp and speed through the next section is required, ending in a shouldered wall. So much better in a W swell with decent period and it's not fazed too much by the S devil wind. Suicidally shallow at low tide – advanced surfers only. **NO KANDUI** is the perfect name for the most difficult and technically demanding left in the Mentawai. A seemingly endless fringing reef stretches down the west coast of Karangmajat Island causing cylindrical, lefthand barrels to wink at viewers anchored on the NW corner. The featureless line-up makes it hard to know if you are in position and only an

air-drop to full tilt, in the barrel, speed pump will be good enough to get into the wave and have a chance of weaving through some of the cavernous sections that spin off down the 500m reef. Rarely backs off enough to allow turns, this is a tube-fest of the highest order. Perfect conditions are SW swell, light E wind, mid to high tide and at least 8ft faces as the reef is bloodthirsty when small. Not too consistent, not too crowded and not for everyone .

Slap bang in the middle of Playgrounds anchorage, **KARAMBA** offers something for the longboard crew to check their speed and trim on predictable ruler-edged walls. Lefts offer surprisingly long rides around mid tide and it's usually uncrowded, as full refraction of S swell keeps size down. Across the channel **4 BOBS** is an enjoyable, warm-up right for the less intrepid. Take-off behind the peak for a whackable wall before a cutback section tapers off into deep water. Watch out for stunning, but shallow coral heads on the inside. **A-FRAMES**, aka Kandies Left, welcomes S swell onto a large, peaky, playing field. The wedges may offer a short right, but it's the left that attracts the boat crews sheltering in the safe anchorage. Drop, snap, tuck and play around with this less daunting line-up that needs N quarter winds and a lower tide to spread the punters. Not too shallow, but getting caught inside can result in a long and arduous paddle-out at size. Gun barrel, straight shooting, take no prisoners, righthand super-sprint. **RIFLES** riders have to maintain faster than a speeding bullet mentality to keep abreast of the constantly peeling sections and ahead of the foamball. It's not always perfect, often shutting down unmakeable sections, but when it aligns, it's one of the best waves on the planet. Slack or light NW wind, due S swell, not low tide and head to double over provide the opposite conditions to No-Kandui and a regular footers dream wave. Turbo charged advanced surfers only.

SIPORA

SILABOK ISLAND needs some W in the swell to be half the size of exposed breaks and is clean in the dreaded S winds. Manageable lefts hit the north coast at Muka Ikan (Fish Face) and Tikus (Rat) offering walls, shoulders and the occasional stress-free cover up for improvers and cruisers. **ICELAND** is a brooding leviathan that ramps up swell size thanks to an abrupt transition from deep to reef. Powerful and moody, it's a cavernous barrel ride when a medium to large SW-W swell hits, making it a good training ground for big-wave junkies on longer boards. **OMBAK TIDUR** translates as Sleeping Wave peeling down a long, straight, fatally-flawed reef south of Iceland. Likes more S in the swell to focus in on the reef, serving up racy walls and the odd heaving curtain call, hopefully groomed by the rare NE'er. Tucked away at the end of Ombak Tidur, **ARIKS** needs a big SW-W swell to penetrate the channel and throw up a barrel on take-off before backing off and throwing again. Some days it's just a fun, smackable wall, but it's always littered with coral heads at low tide. **SUICIDES** shallow and square lefts spew down a coral shelf over the channel from Ariks in SW-W swells and SE winds. Higher tides and wave heights aid make-ability, but this is a hard-core experts only spot. Yet another world-class left, **TELESCOPES** offers more flexibility than most waves in the area. The take-off is steep but not ridiculous and allows entry to a flawless, steady tube section then a whacking wall to a bend in the coral shelf where the next slot beckons. It's predictable and rarely pinches, is deeper than other reefs, can peel for 200m and handles the constant traffic of intermediates and experts alike. When it's big (up to triple overhead) the outer reef sets rumble in to the entry point with power and purpose - beware of the wide sets

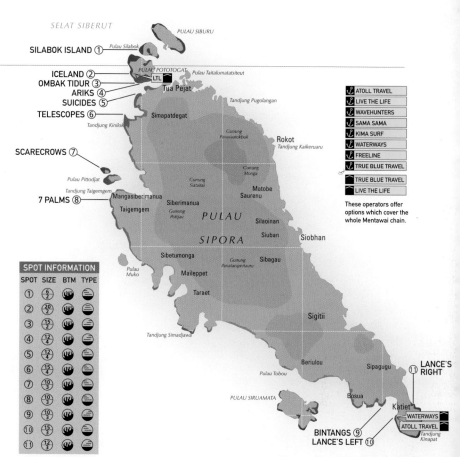

ICELAND

LANCE'S RIGHT

LAT. -2.37525° LONG. 99.8601°

Lance's Right (or HT's) is the pin-up centrefold for the Mentawai islands, bringing a new machine-like level to the word perfection. At the top of the coral platform. The Office section breathes in sharply, scooping up the next lucky expert who is hoping to be there when it exhales deeply, then launches through the Main Peak and into the inside where the shallowness of the Surgeons Table awaits. Size determines whether these 3 link and if any turns can be attempted. Perfection arrives with 6-8ft of S-SW swell, light W or no wind and at least 2hrs of tide. It's surprisingly consistent considering the swell refraction required and the afternoon land breezes can clean it up quickly. Dangers are coral heads appearing, trying to duck dive when caught inside and being pushed too deep by the entrenched crowd.

pinning you on the reef with its swirling currents. Prefers some W in the swell and mid tide will usually produce the epic sesh. Shifty, swell-sucking left reef, SCARECROWS takes all swell directions, is always bigger than Telescopes, has plenty of water depth and is a crowd spreader on account of the wide clean-ups that roam towards the channel. Can be messy and very average at high, but always sneaks in a few good ones at some stage of the tide. Good for intermediates when small to medium size and experts will crack out the guns at size. Broken sections of reef at 7 PALMS hold small to medium swell lefts perfect for wall racing and cruising on a longboard. Consistent swell puller, but often sections and shuts down a bit. BINTANGS equates to a surprisingly fun, frothing righthander that offers a great escape from the crowds at the left across the bay. Wont handle too much size, but when it's on, a slabby, take-off barrel section recedes into a bendy

bashing wall that's always better with more water over it. Like yin is to yang, **LANCE'S LEFT** is the perfect foil to its more famous righthanded brother. When the wind is in the E and there's a sniff of S swell, up to 3 defined sections will wrap into the bay at the bottom of Sipura Island, delivering anything from small lumpy walls to warp speed barrels at the top, centre and tail of the reef. Shifts mischievously in overhead swells and suckers the greedy into a corrugated end section that's both beautifully hollow and unmakeable in equal measure – get out while the going is good! Mid tide is best and it will handle beyond double-overhead for the hellmen. Super-consistent so often crowded these days, although the shifting line-up looks after those who wait wider for the guaranteed sneaker sets. Getting caught inside on a big day is terrifying - use the keyhole if you end up on the reef. **LANCES RIGHT** (see above).

MACARONIS

LAT. -2.78525°   LONG. 99.9703°

Machine-like, fun park left with all the rides. Barrel-riding, lip-smacking, air-popping and wall-gouging are religiously practiced by the hordes who come to ride the "world's funnest wave". The coral platform curves alluringly into the deep bay and the speed at which Macca's peels is fairly predictable, starting with a perfect pipe section and often ending with a ruler-edge quarter pipe wall. Jostling at the take-off is a given and it is easy to get pushed too deep when it's smaller. Looking further up the reef it sometimes looks doable and unlikely stories of pros making it right down the reef exist. The reef is sharp and shallow, but somehow less threatening than comparable depth spots. Getting caught inside will usually result in being flushed to the end if the sets are pouring through. Best at head and a half of SW swell, mid tide and E wind, it maxes out at double overhead, when the tubes go square. Remains surprisingly fun even if there is a direct onshore SW wind. There's a land camp, good anchorage, viewing tower and a constant supply of hungry surfers wanting their own plate of carbs!

THE PAGAIS

Macaronis Rights are usually ignored by the constant charter traffic that enters the beautiful deep-water anchorage of Teluk Pasangan. Flips between long carvable walls and some throwing tube sections. N-NE wind, a decent S swell and plenty of tide required to smooth out the juts in the reef. **MACARONIS** (see above). Extremely hollow uber-tube, **GREENBUSH** flourishes when the rare conditions of spring high tides and moderate S-SW swell meets a N quadrant wind. Vert drop, stall for the barrel then get on the gas as it coils and accelerates over ever shallower reef. May spit you out in the channel or slam the door, but it's safer in the barrel than straightening out. Finicky

and fickle for tube-masters only. **ROXIES** is forgiving without being soft due to a deeper, flat reef and easy paddling channel return to the peak. Fun from small to headhigh with whackable walls, turning into proper open barrels from take-off when overhead. **RAGS LEFT** was one of the losers in the reef-rising earthquakes of recent times. It used to reel off perfectly down the front of the reef, but now it is prone to hideous boils and churning shallow fingers of coral. Up the top of the reef, perfection and ugly shut-downs happily co-exist and experts will need an air-drop, trusty pintail and a gung ho attitude to handle the big days. Toothy right with a bite to match its intimidating bark, **RAGS RIGHT** is close to the gnarliest wave in the Ments. Starts with a beyond vert, no mistakes, quick-as-you-can take-off followed by undulating, sometimes square barrels, vortexing down a featureless reef where eventually the coral heads are going

GREENBUSH

BERNARD TESTEMALE

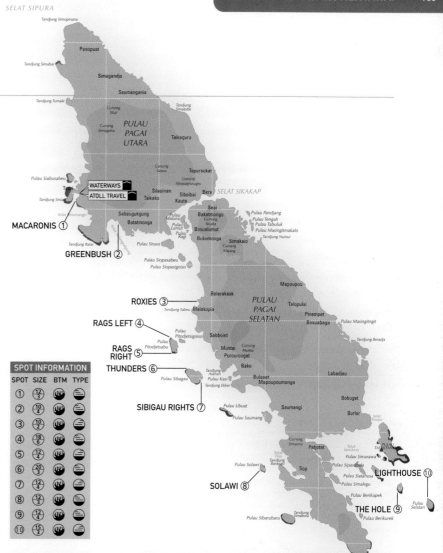

to appear in the exit. Even experienced surfers will struggle with the endless tube-time over barely damp, beautifully sharp coral, plus the need for constant speed and readjustment behind the curtain. **THUNDERS** rumbles in from deep water, exuding more power and heavy water characteristics than most Mentawai spots. Thick peaks pop up in a range of spots, requiring a bigger board to negotiate the long drop leading to either shoulder hook or inside drainer barrel sections. Refracts heavily, focusing powerful whitewash on anyone caught inside, a situation guaranteed for most surfers. Works from tiny to huge and speed barrel sections can appear up the reef in a moderate S swell, but this is the go-to spot when it's flat elsewhere. **SIBIGAU RIGHTS** provide a north wind escape spot that rarely lines up needing more W in the swell to wrap in stop start walls along an ill-defined reef. Higher tides will be relaxed shoulders at half the size and regularity of Thunders around the corner, but offers an option for intermediates and crowd-free waves. **SOLAWI LEFTS**, aka Turuns is another well-formed fringing reef around a tiny tropical idyll, offering up chunky left walls and tubes in SE winds and more westerly swells. There's a right off the south of the island if the wind switches N and there's also more waves to scope on Pagai Selatan. Scary left mincing machine that churns out lifetime best barrels and reef rash floggings in equal measure. **THE HOLE** needs very specific conditions to make it safe enough to surf. Swell needs to be very S just to get in and winds need to be NE-E or non-existent, while high tide moves the take-off to a shallower section up the reef. The inside bowl is the real danger and sets turn inside-out over this coral slab, entombing all but the best. Big wrap is required to hit **LIGHTHOUSE** and regularly does as S-SW swells coil around the island in pointbreak fashion. Down the line speed walls and the odd cover-up become heaving power pockets at 10ft +, but since it faces the same direction as Lances Right, a W quadrant wind is required. Climb the 46ft lighthouse for a unique photo perspective.

LIGHTHOUSE

JSCALLAHAN/SURF EXPLORE

TRAVEL INFORMATION

LOCAL POPULATION:	COASTLINE: 960km (597mi)
Mentawais – 70,000	TIME: GMT +7h

GETTING THERE – Connections to Padang Minangkabau Int. Airport from Kuala Lumpur on Air Asia and Singapore on Tiger Airways. Domestic flights arrive from Jakarta, Medan, Batam, Bandung and Subang on Garuda, Batavia Air, Lion Airlines, Mandala Airlines, Air Asia, Sriwijaya Air & SMA (Sabang Merauke Air). SMA operates a Padang to Rokot (Sipura); Surf Air amphibians go direct to Macaronis resort. Susi Air have 12 seat Cessna charters. Board charges vary wildly across the airlines and small planes have a 2 board limit & length restrictions. It's a 3-4 hour ride by speedboat to Tua Pejat, but most charters take twice that. Overnight ferries from Padang to Siberut, Tua Pejat/Sioban (Sipura) and Sikakap (North Pagai.) are slow (up to 14hrs) and subject to timetable change (different vessels to different ports on different days!). Ambu Ambu prices start from around $15 e/w for V.I.P lounge chair to $35 e/w for a cabin. Mentawai Express fast ferry takes 4hrs and carries 170 passengers. Most charter guests will be whisked from Padang airport to either of the harbours at Teluk Bayur or Pelabuhan Bungus and set off without having to stay overnight in Padang.

GETTING AROUND – Most surfers are likely to be aboard one of 50-60 charter boats operating in the Mentawai's. Many boats boast superior top-end speeds, but most will be cruising in the low teens, knots-wise. Long-distance travelling is often done at night and weighing anchor when the wind shifts often becomes a race to get to the next spot. Staying in one of the 8 land-based surf camps (soon to increase with many more planned) means using the hi-speed dingies if the local breaks aren't working and can be a bouncy ride on the longer inter area strikes. Independent travellers have been discouraged by difficulties like getting from the lee-side ports across to the surf and finding accommodation in the local villages. Roads are rare and there's only a few motorbike/walking paths to major spots like Macca's, so most villages are best accessed by boat.

LODGING AND FOOD – Yacht charters offer unrivalled flexibility to be in the right place at the right time and are still the preferred option for a Mentawai surfari. Vessels carry from as few as 5 to as many as 14, so factor in the instant crowd. Levels of luxury vary from pimped-up, gleaming white sports cruisers and catamarans to local sailing ketches. Land camps are now firmly established in the Playgrounds area (Ebay, Pitstop Hill, Wavepark, Kandui), Sipora (Aloita, Awera, Kingfisher, Katiet) and Nth Pagai (Macaronis). Trips are usually for 10-12 days and cost anything from $150-$400/d depending on the luxury of your boat/resort. Check out Atoll Travel, Freeline, Waterways, Wavehunters and True Blue Travel for prices and options. Many boats/camps are booked out at least a year in advance, especially for peak season. Some villagers do put surfers up – be generous in return.

WEATHER – Temperature variations are minimal year-round with a night/day range of 21-32°C (70-90°F). Equatorial Indo "dry" season is Jan-Aug, but frequent 1-2 hour showers can be expected, usually falling at night. Rainy season is Sept-Dec, which requires an umbrella or poncho as it rains frequently (Sumatra means storms!). The water is some of the warmest to be found in any surf region averaging 27°C (80°F) and sometimes creeping up to 30°C (86°F)! Old hands often wear white cotton tee-shirts instead of lycra to aid evaporative cooling. Night time humidity remains high so modern metal-hulled cruisers need air-con below decks.

WEATHER	J/F	M/A	M/J	J/A	S/O	N/D
Total Rainfall (mm)	112	117	155	155	235	238
Consistency (d/m)	9	9	10	11	16	16
Temp min. (°C)	22	22	22	22	22	22
Temp max. (°C)	30	32	32	32	30	30

NATURE AND CULTURE – The virgin forest, rugged topography, rare flora and fauna and a unique tribal society make the Mentawai's an ideal spot for trekking. Neolithic material culture has evolved for 2-3000 years on Siberut, which is the place to experience daily life in an authentic Mentawai village. Eco-friendly tours offered by various surf and trekking companies are now doing more to benefit the local populations and the land-based camps are increasingly sourcing food and labour from local villages. A local government tax on every visiting surfer (land or sea) is earmarked to help create infrastructure. Surfaid International has already vastly improved health care by fighting preventable diseases like malaria, through education and mosquito net distribution.

BANKVAULTS

HAZARDS AND HASSLES – The surf is intense. Be prepared for long hold-downs and nasty reef cuts; take a well-stocked first aid kit. Boat operators can provide basic first aid assistance like suturing, but any major injury this far from expert medical attention can be fatal. Only choice is one of Padang's 3 hospitals, which were all damaged in the '09 quake. Staph infections are commonplace. Strong rips are a hassle and the sea-lice can be extreme. Heat exhaustion can occur after super-long sessions - stay well hydrated and screened from the midday sun. Sea sickness can strike anyone - take prevention measures (pills, bands, etc). Rampant and very dangerous strains of malaria are a serious threat and many anchorages are close enough to shore for mozzies to attack.

HANDY HINTS – Bring lots of spare surf equipment like wax and leg-ropes. In the prime season, bigger boards can help at spots like Thunders and Iceland, but not too long to fit and turn in the perfect barrels. Try to charter with a group of surfers all at the same level of ability. Avoid paddling out en masse when other boat guests are already out. A bit of patience will help the ambience as will avoiding the thought that "we were here first, this is our wave!" Sharing what is obviously a huge resource by surfing some of the less crowded waves will often be more rewarding than hassling for bombs at Lance's and Maccas everyday.

PHOTOGERSON

SWELL AND WIND

Sumatra's angle is square on to the predominant SW swells and the latitude is just the right balance between receiving long-distance orderly swell and avoiding too much swell decay. During March-Nov, regular 6-12ft (2-4m) groundswells arrive from the S to SW and occasionally WSW to due W, translating to a maximum triple-overhead at the most exposed, big wave spots, but more likely averaging around headhigh to double overhead wave face heights. The peak months of May to August show the highest average size around 7ft (2.3m), with July and August offering the biggest days, longest periods and a very high percentage of forecasted 5 star rated days. This is also the time when the SE winds dominate and pick up in speed. Early and late season often gets almost as good with less consistent, but equally lined-up 5-6ft (1.5-2m) swells, an average 11-12 second period and a NW wind regime that rarely exceeds 10mph (16kph). Glassy conditions prevail for a whopping 15% of the time and the dominant winds run parallel to the islands, so most consistent spots are offshore either on a NW or a SE wind, although there can be sudden squalls with strong, variable winds. Keeping an eye on the weather and being able to move with the wind shifts is key to maximising wave count and is another reason the Mentawais are so suited to charters rather than 1 break land camps. There's also a chance of some 2-6ft (0.6-2m) cyclone swells coming from the western quadrant, plus locally generated SE wind swells may provide some waves in flat spells. Tidal ranges are only 2-3ft (0.5-1m) and the spring/neap factor is less pronounced here, but this will affect the many shallow spots where coral heads break the surface at low tide. ●

SURF STATS		J F	M A	M J	J A	S O	N D
SWELL	Dominant swell	◔	◔	◔	◔	◔	◔
	Size (m)	5	6	7	8	6-7	5
	Consistency (%)	70	85	90	90	90	70
WIND	Dominant wind	◕	◔	◔	◕	◕	◕
	Average force	F3	F3	F3	F3	F3	F3
	Consistency (%)	42	37	41	53	60	46
TEMP.	Wetsuit	🩳	🩳	🩳	🩳	🩳	🩳
	Water temp.	29	28	28	27	27	28

PANAITAN ISLAND

+ HIGH CONSISTENCY
+ WORLD-CLASS LEFTS & RIGHTS
+ BARRELS GALORE
+ MOSTLY UNCROWDED
+ CLOSE TO JAKARTA

- SHARP SHALLOW SPOTS
- NOT FOR BEGINNERS
- SEA URCHINS AND CORAL
- BOAT ACCESS ONLY
- MALARIA

Close to the sprawling cities of Jakarta and Bandung, West Java is the most densely populated region in Indonesia with around 42m inhabitants. Despite the huge population, this SW tip of Java is a wild, unspoiled land in places, with large National Parks and World Heritage sites preserving the largest area of lowland rainforest in Java. One of the countries most daunting yet rewarding barrels pinwheels down the coral crusted lava of Panaitan Island, which forms a part of the Ujung Kulon National Park.

Multi-peak, ripable rights that break on the extensive outside reef of **PANAITAN BOMBIE**, beyond the confines of the bay. Great when the swell is small and it is an easier wave than most on the island, despite the currents. Needs early/late glass or rare N winds to be good. Have no **ILLUSIONS**, it's rare to see perfect right peelers spin down the reef section tucked inside Sabini Point. Shallow and fast, Illusions needs more S in the swell to line up properly and will barrel nicely, but any SE wind will chop it up badly so early, late or off-season. **APOCALYPSE** - there's a clue in the name of this gnarly beast of a wave that sits deep in the bay and pretty well describes the end shutdown section. Air drops, a very square looking barrel and increasing speed to sudden close-out make this another experts wave, despite having better coral coverage than the left. Appeals to the experienced natural footers sick of getting out-run at One Palm.

Quite consistent and often better on the drop (if you make the drop!). **INSIDE RIGHTS** are where average surfers will revel in the lack of death defying pits and have fun on a mix of lip-smacking walls and little hooks. A regular performer in off-season W winds and any SE-SW swell. Across the deep inner bay, **INSIDE LEFTS** provide a reliable pressure valve and let-your-hair-down performance wall that intermediates will love and experts will shred. Long rides, low tides and good vibes prevail, as it usually has a wave when the banner waves don't thanks to its excellent wind protection. Aka Pussy's, it's sometimes crowded when the bay is blown-out. **NAPALMS** is a barrel machine further in the bay from One Palm and a little easier to master than its big brother. Lets you into a fast wall before sucking hard on the sharp inside coral heads. Low tide is risky and the SE winds give it a cross-shore chop you could do without, but the bay and little headland help to keep it clean. Fairly consistent so other boaters will be on it and the adjacent short left further in towards Inside Lefts. There are more waves around the SE coast near the Rangers station.

ONE PALM POINT

LAT. -6.655053°   LONG. 105.171153°

World-renowned left holding some of the longest barrels on earth in a pristine wilderness setting. It is super-shallow, very dangerous and hard to get to. Low tide equals suicide for all but the pros and mere journeymen have to wait for mid tide and/or smaller swells to make it from the air drop to deeper water in the channel. Requires a fairly high line to stay out of trouble, making it a real backhand challenge. Can be incredibly long when aligned on S-SW swells and any E wind. It's not always perfect by any stretch, but has rideable waves in the highly consistent bracket (7/10). Smart pig-doggers wear rubber!

INSIDE RIGHTS

ANDREW SHIELD

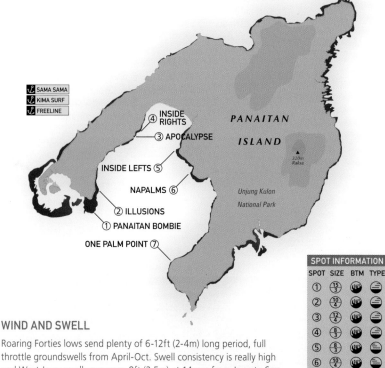

SAMA SAMA
KIMA SURF
FREELINE

④ INSIDE RIGHTS
③ APOCALYPSE
INSIDE LEFTS ⑤
NAPALMS ⑥
② ILLUSIONS
① PANAITAN BOMBIE
ONE PALM POINT ⑦

PANAITAN
ISLAND

320m
Raksa

Unjung Kulon
National Park

SPOT INFORMATION

SPOT	SIZE	BTM	TYPE
①	15/3		
②	10/4		
③	12/4		
④	8/3		
⑤	8/3		
⑥	10/4		
⑦	15/3		

WIND AND SWELL

Roaring Forties lows send plenty of 6-12ft (2-4m) long period, full
throttle groundswells from April-Oct. Swell consistency is really high
and West Java usually averages 8ft (2.5m) at 14secs from June to Sep.
The SSW direction is perfect for penetrating the prominent SW-facing
bays on Panaitan Island. Even the off-season is rarely flat, because of
the Southern Ocean's constant swells in the 2-6ft (0.6-2m) range, plus
the depths of the Java Trench help focus wave energy on the coast.
SE trade winds start in April blowing offshore for the lefts until Oct/
Nov. November and December are transitional months with oscillating
winds predominately from the SE around to the W-NW. Through the
wet season (Dec-Mar), it shifts to W-NW with W first and then NW,
grooming the rights on Panaitan. Tides can be weird so get a tide
chart off the web. There's a big tide and a small tide every day that
affects most breaks.

SURF STATS

		J	F	M	A	M	J	J	A	S	O	N	D
SWELL	Dominant swell												
	Size (m)	3-4		4		4-5		5-6		4-5		4	
	Consistency (%)	60		80		90		90		80		70	
WIND	Dominant wind												
	Average force	F3		F3		F4		F4		F4		F3	
	Consistency (%)	55		62		62		73		66		76	
TEMP.	Wetsuit												
	Water temp.	29		28		28		27		27		28	

TRAVEL INFORMATION

LOCAL POPULATION:	COASTLINE: 2,885km (1,793mi)
Jakarta – 8.8M	TIME ZONE: GMT+7h

GETTING THERE – There are plenty of cheap flights to Soekarno-Hatta
Airport (CGK) at Tangerang, Banten, near Jakarta, which is also the
domestic hub for national airline Garuda Indonesia flights. Garuda is a
surfer friendly airline and boards are part of your luggage allowance then
a special sporting goods excess baggage tariff of $5/kg applies.

GETTING AROUND – To rent a boat to get to Panaitan Island, try the ports
at Samur (2-3hr boat ride), Tanjung Lesung (3-4hr), or Anyer & Merak (7-
8hrs). Many small local boats get into difficulty on the rough Sunda Strait,
so the safer option is a proper surf yacht charter. Make sure boat has safety
equipment, enough food, water and fuel for the trip plus emergencies.

LODGING AND FOOD – Panaitan is a World Heritage site so when a camp
was built in 2005, outcry followed. The camp is now disused and aside
from the odd tribal forager or park ranger, the island remains uninhabited.
Panaitan Island Ecosurf offer a choice of staying on small local craft,
camping on Panaitan beach or staying at neighbouring Peucang Island
Eco Lodge (fr$100/d). Java Rhino Ecosurf offer similar, also out of Tanjung
Lesung. Yacht charters on Just Dreaming out of Anyer (fr $2000/9n) can
be booked with Freeline. Kima Surf also offer a charter option ($1500/d
10 person max).

WEATHER – This is a wet tropical climate and the dry season (May-Oct)
is the best time to visit. SE trades blow in from 11am and often die off
around 4pm so most spots will have a wave at some time of the day and the
weather is reliably good, with only occasional evening thunderstorms. The
rainy season, (Nov-April) on the coast can see morning drizzle, whereas
afternoons have intense rains, usually from Jan-Mar. At this time, it can
rain all day, but you may get lucky and have plenty of sunshine. El Nino
years will see more dry season weather and temps from a night low of
23°C (74°F) to a day high of 33°C (92°F). Humidity levels are high in the
rainy season and it brings out the insects. Water temperatures will hover
around 27-30°C (80-86°F), year-round, but some do wear wetsuits and
booties at One Palm to protect against the inevitable reef floggings.

WEATHER	J/F	M/A	M/J	J/A	S/O	N/D
Total Rainfall (mm)	300	117	105	55	77	172
Consistency (d/m)	18	13	8	5	7	13
Temperature min. (°C)	23	23	23	23	23	23
Temperature max. (°C)	29	31	31	31	30	30

NATURE AND CULTURE – The national parks are home to some very rare
wildlife such as Javan rhinos, leopards (the tigers are gone), wild boar and
deer, endangered primates, multitudes of snakes and plenty of marine life
including tiger sharks. Treking in the National Parks or book a boat trip out
to witness the rapid rise of a new volcano Anak Krakatau (Child of Krakatoa),
which has grown to over 300m since appearing in 1932 and is becoming
increasingly active.

HAZARDS AND HASSLES – Both One Palm Point and Apocalypse are heavy
duty waves and hitting the sharp reef is highly probable. Safety gear from
boots to helmets and even a light wetsuit can reduce the risk of trip-ending
cuts. Sharks are definitely present, but well fed. Malaria is a much higher
risk on Panaitan than the mainland coastal provinces so take precautions
to avoid being bitten.

HANDY HINTS – A specialist board is needed for the heavier waves on
Panaitan, where you must take everything you may need for survival. Be
careful of local boat hire - stories of running out of fuel/food/water are rife
and there is nothing/nobody out there to help.

BALI

+ MANY WORLD-CLASS SPOTS
+ WET & DRY SEASON WAVES
+ BEGINNER AND EXPERT SPOTS
+ UNIQUE BALINESE CULTURE
+ WILD NIGHT-LIFE
+ CHEAP

– VERY CROWDED WAVES
– TRAFFIC JAMS
– DANGEROUS DRIVING CONDITIONS
– TOUTS AND HUSTLERS
– INCREASING POLLUTION

Bali is "The island of 1000 temples" which the locals believe is blessed by the gods. The gods certainly have blessed the local surfers, because they live in a perfect, tropical surf paradise. Although 40 years of booming tourism development has drastically transformed the landscape and the line-ups, Bali remains an essential surfing experience. There is no denying the quality and quantity of its surf, when SW swells wrap consistent lines around the Bukit Peninsula into straight offshore winds, creating a list of world-class lefts, including Uluwatu, Padang Padang, Bingin and Kuta Reef. Add to these the quality beachbreaks of Kuta and Legian, plus the east side rights of Nusa Dua, Sanur and Keramas or Shipwrecks and Lacerations on Nusa Lembongan, then it becomes obvious that Bali has one of the highest concentration of quality waves on the planet. Its geographical position mid-chain with the plunging depths of the Java Trench just offshore plus the island like symmetry of the Bukit peninsula poking into the regular SW swell train, offering offshore flexibility during the predictable trade wind seasons are just two of the defining factors that make Bali's surf so good. There's a huge variety of wave types from sublime, coral-floored caverns to supine, sand bottomed beachies that seem to bring the best out of surfers from complete beginners to budding pros. This microcosm of perfection has bred a couple of generations of supremely talented local surfers, who surf with a grace and ease that sits beautifully alongside the poise and unhurried approach to life that the general Balinese population exudes.

WEST BALI

Slopey, light-lipped left that trundles down a smooth cobblestone and sand point, making **MEDEWI** feel more like So' Cal than Bali. Can be the islands longest ride when it lines up on a S-SW swell, with fast crumbling walls and shoulders for up to half a kilometer. Seems to prefer a bit more water, but wont handle SE or NW trades so it's a typical, west coast, dawn patrol spot. Long, busy 2hr drive from Kuta, so best bet is to stay at the losmens on the point. **BALIAN**'s rivermouth rock shelf peak is a reliable swell magnet, focusing the bulk of its size and power on the long left. Often way bigger than other west coast beaches, shifty, steep peaks arrive unannounced, sweeping up the pack of improver longboarders and experienced shortboarders. Can sometimes barrel on the smaller inside waves over the shallower part of the reef, but it is generally a wall to shoulder ride.

North of Kuta and usually a bit bigger are the intermediate-friendly peaks at **CANGGU**. The black sand moves around the reef a bit and sets do shift around, keeping the inevitable dawn crowd on their toes. The inside reef is tricky at low and high tide cuts off the beach in places so mid tide is often best, especially on the lefts. More peaks down the beach towards Pererenan. **OLD MANS** forms the southern edge of the Canggu stretch and perennial favorite with the longboard and SUP crew as the long, lined-up rights skirt the lava reef. Generally fat and friendly up to headhigh, it can handle some sizable sets that will feather a long way out. There's a small swell left that shoulders through to the rocky outcrop and low tide will be messy and mushy. Easy parking. Beware foot burning black sand. It's mainly slop and shoredump between Canggu and **BRAWA BEACH**, where some rocky reefs anchor the sand and shape up some nice rights and a few lefts at mid to high tide. Good for improvers/intermediates and wont be as crowded as Canggu, but the road in is a long detour if coming from Kuta. In **SEMINYAK**, there's plenty of access roads leading to dozens of shifting sand bars that might be perfect A-framed peaks or surly, thumping close-outs as the swell gets overhead. Exposed to plenty

BALIAN

DAVID PU'U

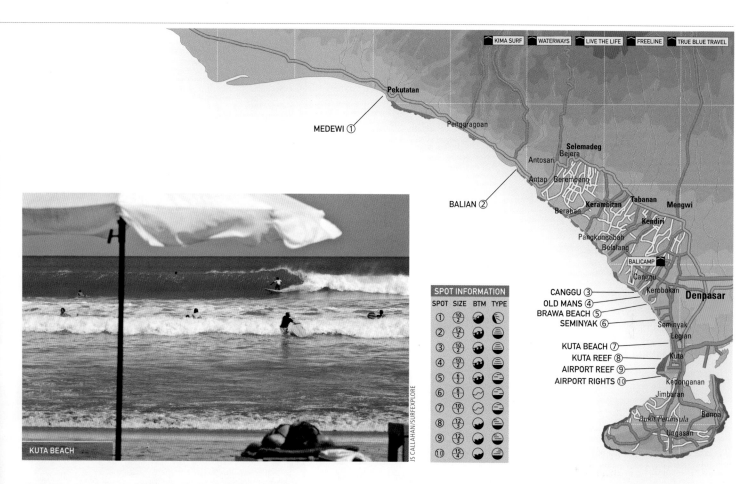

KIMA SURF   WATERWAYS   LIVE THE LIFE   FREELINE   TRUE BLUE TRAVEL

Pekutatan

MEDEWI ①

Penggragoan

Selemadeg
Bejera
Antosari
Antap   Gerembeng
BALIAN ②
Beraban   Kerambitan   Tabanan   Mengwi
Kendiri
Pangkungtibeh
Belalang
BALICAMP
Canggu
CANGGU ③   Kerobokan   Denpasar
OLD MANS ④
BRAWA BEACH ⑤
SEMINYAK ⑥   Seminyak
Legian
KUTA BEACH ⑦
KUTA REEF ⑧   Kuta
AIRPORT REEF ⑨
AIRPORT RIGHTS ⑩   Kedonganan
Jimbaran
Bukit Peninsula   Benoa
Ungasan

SPOT INFORMATION			
SPOT	SIZE	BTM	TYPE
①	10/2		
②	12/2		
③	10/2		
④	10/2		
⑤	6/2		
⑥	6/2		
⑦	10/1		
⑧	12/3		
⑨	12/3		
⑩	12/4		

KUTA BEACH

JS CALLAHAN/SURFEXPLORE

of swell, this stretch can be double the size of Kuta. Tides affect the quality and shape massively and often strong rips make it impossible to stay in position. Check Petitenget, Ku De Ta, and Double Six for the best banks. Famous, fine-grained **KUTA BEACH** has been bringing surfing to the masses since the 1930's. Visually, the tropical idyll has been buried beneath concrete, but it still attracts surfers of all abilities to what can be super-fast tunnels or dribbly, knee-high corners. On any given day, there may be a dozen yellow rash vests, proning on their first ever waves alongside a Balinese local effortlessly punting a 360°. The mayhem continues on the beach where endless streams of hawkers offer paintings, jewelry, tattoos, shells, T-shirts, drinks, ice cream, day-trips, transport, beach loungers, umbrellas and board hire, just to name a few! Usually better from mid to high, the trades are more offshore here, but water quality is very dubious after rain.

KUTA REEF sits a good 700m offshore, waiting for enough swell to swing around the projecting runway and hit a couple of sections of reef. The main reef is a fine left drop, stall, barrel, slash kind of wave and gets ledgy as it hits 8-10ft faces. Further up the reef is a short section of wall that is less hollow and closes out as the reef straightens, but needs mid tides at least. Trades can really rip into the waves by the afternoon and a dawn patrol in no way guarantees a smaller crowd of local rippers who demand respect. Gets way overcrowded with boatloads paying to ride from the southern end of Kuta Beach, avoiding the 20min paddle. **AIRPORT REEF** holds multi-peak ripable lefts that may not be perfect, but sure can be fun for the smaller crowd willing to go the extra mile. The two peaks sometimes link and open up, otherwise it's a performance wall that can give some long rides at higher tides. Picks up more swell than the Rights or Kuta Reef, but is more exposed to cross/off trades. Easier to suss out and get waves off the less aggressive crowd. Book your boat ride back! One of Bali's premier waves, **AIRPORT RIGHTS** is fairly

fickle, needing a chunky SW-W swell and higher tides to show its true colours. On its day, it can produce flawless deep pits, spinning the length of the reef triangle beside the airport runway. Seriously shallow and fast from headhigh up when it's an experts only wave and plenty of them will appear. Often slams shut over the sharp coral base. It's almost a 1km paddle so get a boat from north Jimbaran Bay.

BALICAMP.COM

CANGGU

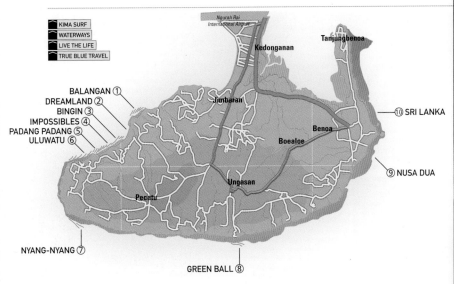

KIMA SURF
WATERWAYS
LIVE THE LIFE
TRUE BLUE TRAVEL

Ngurah Rai
International Airport

Kedonganan
Tanjungbenoa
Jimbaran

BALANGAN ①
DREAMLAND ②
BINGIN ③
IMPOSSIBLES ④
PADANG PADANG ⑤
ULUWATU ⑥

Benoa
Boealoe
⑩ SRI LANKA

Ungasan

⑨ NUSA DUA

Pecatu

NYANG-NYANG ⑦

GREEN BALL ⑧

BUKIT PENINSULA

The mirage-like left spinner at **BALANGAN** is often a sectiony close-out, depending on swell direction and tide height. More south in the swell may make it a bit peaky and parallel the reef more, but the real deal starts at overhead to double on a SW-WSW and 0.4-1.4m tide co-efficient. First peak in front of the huge cave and undercut headland lets you in before having to race the speeding wall/tube down to the middle of the bay where the next pack are dropping into swinger sets and the wave that just outpaced you. Intermediates will deal with small swells, experts will charge the big days. Beneath the shadow of the hulking, metropolis-scale hotel, golf course and condo development that sprawls across the Bukit from Balangan to Bingin, **DREAMLAND**'s once tranquil beach is now a tourist hotspot, with all mod cons, but very little soul. The wave is well suited to the masses, offering a decent left wall and short shouldering right off the peak, over a sandy reef platform that is good and deep. Best at low tides in small swell, otherwise it misses the reef and becomes a fat, uninspiring shoredump. In overhead conditions, it can barrel

SPOT INFORMATION			
SPOT	SIZE	BTM	TYPE
①	15/4		
②	10/2		
③	8/3		
④	12/4		
⑤	12/4		
⑥	15/2		
⑦	8/3		
⑧	8/3		
⑨	20/4		
⑩	12/4		

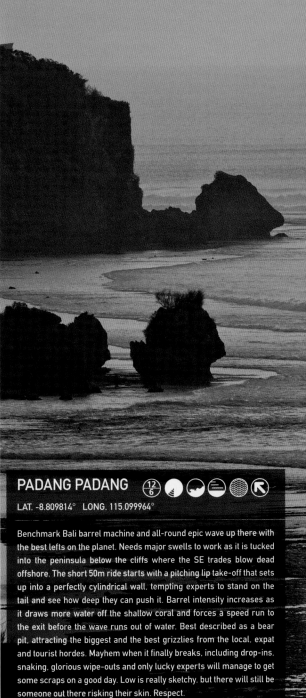

PADANG PADANG

LAT. -8.809814° LONG. 115.099964°

Benchmark Bali barrel machine and all-round epic wave up there with the best lefts on the planet. Needs major swells to work as it is tucked into the peninsula below the cliffs where the SE trades blow dead offshore. The short 50m ride starts with a pitching lip take-off that sets up into a perfectly cylindrical wall, tempting experts to stand on the tail and see how deep they can push it. Barrel intensity increases as it draws more water off the shallow coral and forces a speed run to the exit before the wave runs out of water. Best described as a bear pit, attracting the biggest and the best grizzlies from the local, expat and tourist hordes. Mayhem when it finally breaks, including drop-ins, snaking, glorious wipe-outs and only lucky experts will manage to get some scraps on a good day. Low is really sketchy, but there will still be someone out there risking their skin. Respect.

JASON CHILDS/A-FRAME

BERNARD TESTEMALE

BINGIN

and challenge the constant crowd of mixed ability. **BINGIN** is best described as short, sharp and shallow. The tight take-off zone at the end of the shelf beneath the impressive Bukit cliffs is always packed with goofy's trying to nail the backdoor take-off and kick out before the dry reef shutdown a mere 50m later. All tides are do-able but high is fun and low springs is tempting fate. Just getting a wave is tricky but dialed-in locals will reward patience and punish pushiness. **IMPOSSIBLES** becomes possible when a moderate to large, long period S swell sweeps past Ulu's and Padang onto this long coral reef at low tide. There's usually three sections separated by straight bits of reef, so getting caught behind the curtain is a given. Looks picture perfect from the cliffs, but the reality is it's impossibly fast at some point in the wave. Often gets a cluster at the tip of the wave over the channel from Padang and also down near the shelf at the end, but crowds aren't a problem. Rideable at high when it gets warbly and full – low is the go for making it through the many barrel sections. Same paddle-out as Padang, while getting in over the sharp low tide reef is best done in booties. **PADANG PADANG** (see above). **ULUWATU** (see next page).

NYANG-NYANG is Bali's "if it's flat here, it's flat everywhere" wave, located on the exposed south coast of the Bukit at the bottom of impressive cliffs. The long trail down keeps crowds away, but it's more the fact winter and summer trades are basically onshore so early, late or a flukey N wind is the go. It also maxes out very quickly as the rights get overhead and the barrel sections become shut-down sections. The reef is ragged and always seems closer than it actually is, but higher tides will see more water in the channel and more chance of the lefts showing as well. Strong rips, sneaker sets and plenty of sea life make this an advanced riders and fitness fanatics spot, considering the hellish walk back up. Beautiful, empty beach. GREEN BALL shares much with Nyang Nyang in that it is a swell-magnet right, horribly exposed to the trade winds and is at the bottom of a long, strenuous cliff path. If the wind isn't on it, then a fast, punchy right sucks and spins off the reef, then walls up nicely before pitting on the last bit of reef beside the channel. Home of the strongest current in Bali, which whips out to sea at various angles, making it hard to stay in position. Offshore NUSA DUA is a righthand supermarket with a confusing amount of aisles to go shopping in. All available swell is sucked into the entrance of the deep Lombok Strait and bent onto this 2km curve of coral reef. Unlike other Bukit set-ups, it focuses into a vast array of shifting peaks, hitting different lumps of the reef and drawing up into powerful, heavy-lipped bowls and long sections of speed carve walls. At size, the drops get serious and thick, while unpredictable sections add to the sense of roulette – eventually you will get one on the head. It rarely links up into a super-long ride, but the paddle back out always seems longer against the background drift north and if you try the zippy, open lefts on the far inside section, prepare to be punished paddling back out. Wet season, all-day-staple and dry season sneaky early. Conserve your strength and pay for a return boat ride out there. SRI LANKA is another quality wave that happens to be out the front of a Club Med. Off-season thrill a minute barrel when a big S-SW swell wraps enough to spin down the short, straight coral platform that faces out to the NE. Sucky and round from the take-off to the kick-out shut down section, but it has to to huge at Nusa Dua to be working well. It's only a medium consistency spot so when it finally breaks, the locals descend.

ULUWATU

LAT. -8.816372°   LONG. 115.085626°

Ultra-consistent "Ulu's" is the focal point of Balinese surfing thanks to its ability to handle any size swell from small to large and spread the biggest of crowds across a wide playing field of reef. Its sectioning, hollow walls always produce great waves, starting with faster, high tide, occasional tuck-ins up at Temples that lead down to the muscular, steep drops of The Peak where open face and hollow pockets unfold directly in front of the famous cave. It can sometimes jump the deadspot and barrel through to the start of the Racetrack, which twists and bends the wailing walls in an ever increasing race against the falling curtain. When swells exceed the 8-10ft mark, Outside Corner will rumble into life, with heavy, thick-lipped sections at low tide for experts on sturdy pintails. Main hazard is the crowd, followed by the reef and the constant, higher tide sweep that requires aiming for a spot well south of the cave to come in. Blow it and you'll paddle another 15min circuit.

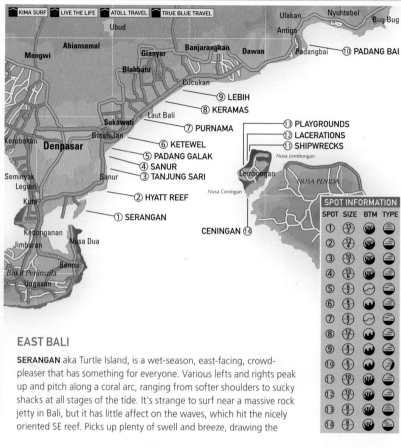

SPOT INFORMATION			
SPOT	SIZE	BTM	TYPE
①			
②			
③			
④			
⑤			
⑥			
⑦			
⑧			
⑨			
⑩			
⑪			
⑫			
⑬			
⑭			

EAST BALI

SERANGAN aka Turtle Island, is a wet-season, east-facing, crowd-pleaser that has something for everyone. Various lefts and rights peak up and pitch along a coral arc, ranging from softer shoulders to sucky shacks at all stages of the tide. It's strange to surf near a massive rock jetty in Bali, but it has little affect on the waves, which hit the nicely oriented SE reef. Picks up plenty of swell and breeze, drawing the crowds when the winds go W. Chilled out warung scene after clearing the security check to get on the island. In front of the upmarket hotel strip, **HYATT REEF** is where tourists play in the calm waters of the lagoon on all sorts of craft and surfers make the long trek by boat out to the barrier reef for energetic righthanders that rumble off the furthest point. There's two sections separated by a big hole in the reef and the outside shares similarities with Nusa Dua, but the hap-hazard, rip torn peaks are even hollower. Further inside, rapid, walled rides guarantee tube-time as they suck over the shallower part of the reef. Nasty when big, it's an advanced break and a constant paddle against the the current, until it backs off at dead high. **TANJUNG SARI**, another hotel namesake line-up, where a big bend in the reef and a shallow channel provide both rights and lefts on either side. The rights can be picture perfect and peel for a good few hundred meters, providing the tide is lower and a good sized S-SW swell has already awoken Sanur. Fast and sectiony is the vibe with scant coral cover, so each wave is a bit of a lottery. The lefts are easier, with a nice cover-up section before a short wall to the channel. Less crowded than Sanur with an easy paddle out. **SANUR** is the east coast super-right that guillotines mercilessly over a sharp slab of coral and pinwheels at mach one for hundreds of meters, before closing out on the inside dry reef. Unfortunately, Sanur Reef needs a serious swell to even begin breaking and wont get classic until it is well overhead, meaning Nusa Dua will be twice as big. These huge swell conditions are rarer in the rainy season window when it's offshore all day, so consistency drops further. On smaller days at lower tides, it breaks up into funnelling walls and long shut-down sections, but with more swell and tide, barrel predictability and length of ride improves dramatically. The inside section is often unmakeable on all but the biggest tides and days of the year and even then it will claim many victims. To say it is crowded is an understatement and some localism is likely.

SERANGAN

KERAMAS

LAT. -8.598839° LONG. 115.339514°

Keramas is the jet-set plaything and new pro contest hang-out as its reputation for barrels and high octane performance ramps grows. Picks up plenty of east coast swell and focuses it on a jagged lava reef that opens up straight from the drop then just asks to be bashed before the wave closes-out on the inside. Surprisingly consistent and increasingly crowded for the dawn glass sessions. Plenty of current when it gets bigger, always crowded and some bad vibes from over-zealous ex-pats and local surf guides.

PADANG GALAK is a foot-burning black sand beachbreak that flips from low tide mushy shoulders to dredging shore-dump at high tide. Mid tide may conjure up something in-between and glassy mornings can be fun for the improvers trying to get some waves away from the crowds. The rivermouth can sculpt bars, but more likely bring river pollution to the better peaks to the south. Won't handle much above headhigh and needs some N in the wet season wind. The east coast reefs switch to a lava base at KETEWEL and are every bit as intimidating as the coral. Spacious, angular pits unfold over an uneven base that demands high tide to be safe enough to challenge. Add in the southerly aspect and it means that morning glass and spring highs are the best option, so it's not too consistent, plus requires real skill to master. PURNAMA sits in a bucolic Bali backdrop of rice paddies and traditional houses, adding to the laid-back persona of this 2.5km

strip of glinting lava particles. The sand will always be hotter than the average beach peaks that prefer mid tides and morning glass, but a scout of the reefs to the south may yield some punchy rights. KERAMAS (see above). LEBIH's lava reef benefits from sand deposition courtesy of the nearby rivermouth. Like many east coast spots, S swell has a direct angle on the coast and early morning land breezes keep it clean. Looks best at mid and offers intermediates a chance compared to the Keramas line-up. Rivermouth not best for water quality or rips and rocks pop out of nowhere. Rare pointbreak at PADANG BAI needs a minor miracle to break well. Big S swells will wrap into the natural harbour around a headland and peel down the rocky reef for up to 150m at mid tides. Problem is it needs W winds so you are unlikely to get the maxing swell in off-season.

Over on Nusa Lembongan island, SHIPWRECKS is non-existent at low tide, but starts breaking on the push to mid and sets start rearing up out of the deep Lombok channel, peeling fast with a high, tight envelope and open shoulder. Gets packed with surfers of all standards so snagging one and avoiding the scratchers is part of the deal. Getting the tide just right is the trick - mid on springs, higher on neaps. Hard core right with excellent, wide open tube time on offer as the tide floods the sharp, shallow reef. LACERATIONS is a pitching, air-drop entry from the peak into a straight barrel section then a further sucky bowl as it approaches the channel marked by floating mooring lines that litter the bay. Not easy, not long and not empty. Nestled below cliffs, PLAYGROUNDS offers good SE trade protection and is the most user-friendly spot on Lembongan. It's an easier paddle, being closer to shore, continues to break at lower tides, is a little bit deeper and offers more wall to work as opposed to the flat out barrels nearby. The lefts are better with a few lip-bashing opportunities along a tapered wall, while the rights may pitch slightly, but fade quickly. Constant current to paddle against and the whole area is surrounded by a flotilla of cruisers, pontoons and leisure craft catering for the daily influx of Bali tourists.

LACERATIONS

FREDERIC VERGER

TRAVEL INFORMATION

POPULATION: 3,891,428   TIME ZONE: GMT+8h
COASTLINE: 437km (271mi)

GETTING THERE – Many flights on dozens of carriers to all corners of the world or else connect to Jakarta for more choice. National airline Garuda has recently had an EU ban lifted and plans massive expansion to include EU and US direct routes direct to Bali. Boards are included in baggage allowance then at $5/kg excess. Ferry links from Java (Ketapang - Gilimanuk) and Lombok (Lembar - Padang Bai or Gili/Teluk Nare - Benoa). There are trains from Jakarta to Surabaya then to the ferry port at Ketapang, where the bus takes over. Noisey, slow, smoke-filled bus service runs from Jakarta (takes 24hrs) or Yogya (16hrs) to Denpasar. Lorena buses have the best reputation.

GETTING AROUND – International license required to drive in Indonesia. Motorbike rentals from $5/d. Board shoulder straps are essential although some bikes have racks. 4WD Suzuki rental is $23/d; air-con is worth it. Driving conditions are sketchy – expect vehicles on wrong side of road, wrong way down one way streets or even on the footpath! Bemos (local unmarked taxis) are everywhere and drivers are always asking tourists "transport?". New bitumen roads have made break access simple, but Kuta traffic has become incredibly congested – allow extra time mid-afternoon. Pay a few thou' rupiah to park everywhere. Cycling works quite well around Kuta/Legian. Boats to Nusa Lembongan leave from Sanur/Benoa and take 1h30 (fr $7.50).

LODGING AND FOOD – A true kaleidoscope of accommodation can be found in Bali starting with sublime beach front or back-alley Kuta losmans (guest houses) that cost from $8-$25/night and finishing with the ridiculous exclusive resorts of Nusa Dua or Jimbaran for anything up to $8000 per night!. There are many surf camps offering all inclusive packages (transfers, accom, board hire, lessons, transport, guiding, etc) for reasonable prices starting around $40/d (Balicamp, Kima) for room/ bungalow to $70+ for self contained family houses. Villa rentals are widely available, especialy around Canggu and the Bukit. Large scale development on the Bukit has all but ended the super-cheap beach warung option and replaced it with rooms for around $10-15/n with basic amenities. Classic Indonesian dishes like nasi goreng (fried rice) and sate ayam (chicken sate) are delicious and as cheap as $2-3. Great seafood available - try the Jimbaran fish restaurants.

WEATHER – The two distinct seasons don't always run like clockwork and El Nino years in the Pacific usually extend the dry season to its' limits of April-Nov when temps range from a night low of 23°C (74°F) to a day high of 33°C (92°F), tempered by sea breezes and the odd rain shower during the night. Conversely, La Nina patterns can bring unseasonal, torrential rains in mid dry season months. Nov-April is hotter, wetter, and more humid. Jan-Feb suffers from heavy afternoon rains and stifling humidity averaging at 85%. The mountains can be quite cold, especially at night. Water temps are usually a tepid 28°C (82°F), but can dip to 25°C (77°F) and always feels a tiny bit cooler at the deepwater spots like Nusa Dua. Surfing in a white T-shirt can aid cooling while a light vest may add a thin veneer of protection against the reef and cold mornings.

WEATHER	J/F	M/A	M/J	J/A	S/O	N/D
Total Rainfall (mm)	300	177	105	55	77	172
Consistency (d/m)	18	13	8	5	7	13
Temperature min. (°C)	23	23	23	23	23	23
Temperature max. (°C)	29	31	31	31	30	30

NATURE AND CULTURE – Unusually for Indonesia, the Balinese practice an unusual form of Hinduism with a dash of Buddhism and Animism, creating a fascinating religious culture centred on ritual ceremonies and offerings. Favourite tourist haunts include the artist village of Ubud, sunrise over Lake Batur and the lofty volcanic peak of Agung mountain, which dominates the landscape. There are also famous temples (Uluwatu, Tanah Lot, Besakih), myriad shopping opportunities and great restaurants serving international and local Indonesian meals. Kuta nightlife is a legendary, hedonistic melting pot of nightclubs and parties fuelled by cheap(ish) alcohol.

HAZARDS AND HASSLES – Mosquitos carry dengue fever, Japanese encephalitis and malaria (officially not present on Bali) - avoid bites. Considering the lack of sewage treatment and general sanitation levels, it's not surprising that cholera, typhoid, hepatitis, Bali-belly and TB are prevalent. Avoid rivermouths. Don't drink local water supply, ice or fruit/veg not freshly peeled/cooked. Dogs can carry rabies. Be careful of thieves, scammers and hustlers - drugs are a big no-no. Motorbike road-rash or shallow reef-rash are biggest threats. If injured seriously, many recommend flying to Singapore or Darwin for hospital treatment as opposed to entering Denpasar Hospital. Private clinics and hospitals have improved treatment facilities but are expensive cash up front deals - get medical insurance!

HANDY HINTS – Kuta has the highest concentration of well-stocked surf shops in the world and prices may compare favourably when looking at high airline board charges. It is possible to sell your gear to local shops and giving kids your spare boards, boots, leg ropes is normal practice. Learn some basic Indonesian, which is easy to pick up. Be courteous to the local surfers who may include surfing legends Made Kasim, Wayan Suwenda, Ketut Menda, Wayan Ganti, Made Switra, Rizal Tandjung, Ismael Dooley and Made Adi Putra to name just a few.

SWELL AND WIND

Like the rest of the south-facing islands in the archipelago, Bali benefits from an almost endless supply of Southern Ocean groundswell arriving form the S to WSW (180°-247°) but by far the most consistent direction is due SW (225°). These swells range from 3-12ft (1-4m), with averages around 5ft @ 11secs from Nov-March, then upping to 7-8ft @ 14secs in the middle of the April to Oct high season. Underlying windswell can mix in from the SE to the W but has little bearing on the surf at most breaks. Sometimes, 6-10ft (2-3m) tropical cyclone swells can arrive from far off disturbances in the western Indian Ocean off the coast of Madagascar and occasionally from storms a lot closer, forming around the Keeling Islands and NW Australia through the southern hemisphere summer. The big Bay of Bengal typhoons are too far north for Bali. Swells are focused onto the Bukit Peninsula because of the deep-water channels on either side of Bali, particularly the east side Lombok channel, which can draw in overhead waves to Nusa Dua when everywhere else seems too small. The ESE trade winds blow reliably from April to Oct, giving west Bukit breaks a 50% chance of being a 5 star day throughout June, July and August. Transition months can have oscillating winds with a bit of everything - Nov blows mainly from the SE to SW. Winds then shift SW-NW for the Dec to March wet-season, with either side of W dominant and a higher percentage of SW than NW, which is not ideal for many east coast spots like Nusa Dua, Serangan and Keramas.

March is more W-SW with 1 day in 5 swinging back to ESE offering the chance of empty Ulu's for the switched on. Wet season wind speeds are on the whole lower, usually staying below 10mph (16kph) compared to the dry season SE trades which regularly hit double that. Tide charts are posted in surf shop windows. There is a big and a small tide each day (semi-diurnal odd) and some spots only work at certain stages of tide especially if it is small. Full and new moons often see a jump in swell size as tidal range increases and these spring high tides occur around the same time of day throughout the year. Charts are widely available in surf shops and on the internet. ●

SURF STATS		J	F	M	A	M	J	J	A	S	O	N	D
SWELL	Dominant swell	◐		◐		◐		◑		◐		◐	
	Size (m)	4-5		5-6		6-7		7-8		6		4-5	
	Consistency (%)	60		80		90		90		80		70	
WIND	Dominant wind	◓		◓		◐		◑		◑		◓	
	Average force	F3		F2		F3		F3		F3		F3	
	Consistency (%)	65		88		74		80		79		72	
TEMP.	Wetsuit	👕		👕		👕		👕		👕		👕	
	Water temp.	29		28		28		27		27		28	

LOMBOK

+ VOTED WORLD'S BEST WAVE
+ CONSISTENT YEAR-ROUND SURF
+ GREAT SCENERY
+ NO MASS TOURISM
+ CHEAP LODGING AND FOOD

– OVERCROWDED DESERT POINT
– ONLY ONE OUTSTANDING BREAK
– HARD ACCESS TO EASTERN SPOTS
– LACK OF ACCOMMODATION
  OUTSIDE KUTA

At its closest point, Lombok sits only 18km (11mi) east of Bali, yet major physical, cultural, linguistic and religious differences exist. The deep strait separating these islands links the Indian and Pacific oceans and is part of the "Wallace Line", an established physical division between Asia and Australia. Bali is green with lush, tropical vegetation, while Lombok is drier, more rugged, with completely different flora and fauna. While the mountainous north rises to 3726m (12,224ft) at the top of Mount Rinjani, the south is a range of low inland hills spread behind the sweeping bays and pure white sands of the southern beaches. In terms of location, most surf breaks are truly breathtaking, but are generally regarded as of lower quality or intensity than Bali's, with the notable exception of Desert Point, elected " Best Wave in the World" by Tracks magazine's readers.

Furthest west of the 3 small Gili islands, **GILI TRAWANGAN** has a shallow fringing reef off the southern tip, serving up fast, hollow, but generally flawed right lines. Tricky wave to ride and plenty of current so experience required. Needs hefty S-SW swells to clear the coral that is usually frequented by snorkeling tourists. More a party, couples, chill out destination so don't expect many waves. **GILI AIR** is over-protected from swell and dead onshore when the SE

JASON REPOSAR

trades blow, meaning this is a very unlikely score. Huge SSW swell, big, dropping, spring high tide and light W-NW wind cook up some short, sharp barrels that peel perfectly down the SE tip. A surprising amount of locals do surf **SENGIGI**, a circular reef that is mainly a left plus a sectiony right, which needs rare N winds. Plenty of SW swell and tide will clear the coral and fire off some cylindrical lefts, but it spends most days below the chest-high minimum required. **DESERT POINT** (see right).

DESERT POINT

LAT. -8.749826°   LONG. 115.824170°

When it is on, Desert Point is indeed one of the longest, makeable lefthand barrels on the planet with over 20 seconds tube time possible on one wave. The take-off area can shift around a little but generally rewards a deep attack. High speed is the key as it quickly winds up and starts peeling mercilessly across the shallow reef, cutting a trench in the coral where the mechanical lips have been slamming for centuries. The caverns get larger and faster as the inside section commits the tube rider to a lock-in that usually ends on dry reef. Only surfers good enough to deal with the tricky exit, the shallow reef, evil out-going currents and plenty of wave-starved rippers should apply. Desert's has a reputation for inconsistency, with only the biggest groundswells igniting it and high tides making it disappear as fast as it came. Surf charters keep flocking from Bali and dedicated hardcore surfers wait for weeks in basic beach shacks, forming a frenzied, barrel-hungry pack on those rare classic days. Boats have access to the sheltered bay of islands behind Bangko Bangko where there are some big swell, high tide options for intermediates around the other Gili islands like Ringgit.

Decent lefts run at **BELONGAS** when the SSW swell hits this isolated reef just right and winds are E or even NE. Racy lip line with some tuck sections that will suit average surfers just fine at mid tide. **MAWI** is a quality, south coast, dry season break that works in all swell sizes, set in a beautiful west-facing bay. Consistent spot that attracts boats and land-based surfers from Kuta and Grupuk losmens when the SE blows strong. Small swells see a fun, peeling peak until the hollower right starts closing out at overhead size. The powerful left then rumbles on down the reef up to double overhead plus, offering a heavy drop/barrel section, hooking wall and final tube before shut down. Very strong currents in the channel and a nasty sharp reef mean intermediates need to be on their toes. Pointbreak style set-up on western fringe of pretty beach, **MAWUN** causes SE-SW pulses to radiate round the reef for some long, high performance walls. Consistently has swell, but glassy or NW winds required, so it's a wet season spot. A short boat ride to the next bay west of Kuta unveils some low tide rights that trip into a fast inside barrel. **AIR GULING** is exposed to swell and wind that needs to be more N than W, so it's rare to score after 9am. If the tide is up, check the short, rippy, hollow lefts at the reef gap, mid-bay. **KUTA** is the surfing hub of Lombok, another wet-season-centric spot as the righthander on the western headland is offshore in NW winds and likes a SE-S swell. Like Mawun and Air Guling, the left across the channel is lower quality and often messy, but both are fun, no consequence waves for all abilities and a lazy session instead of driving off in search of better waves. 2km east of Kuta, out on the reef fringe in front of the Novotel, **SEGAR**

is a small swell, wind sensitive, fun righthander, plus occasional left. More peaks in either direction, but NE is offshore so early mornings or glassy, peaky off-season days will produce easy rides for the odd crowd. A straight shooting S swell will penetrate the bay and unload on **TANJUNG A'AN**, a nasty sharp reef with serious tubing intent. Guaranteed shade-time, this is heavy water, especially below mid tide and not a wave to be attempted by the meek. N winds or early glass make it less consistent than other spots nearby and due to its quality, has a few local "minders". Like the impressive twin peaks on the headland, **OUTSIDE GRUPUK** is more rolling hill than impressive cliff. Orderly drop and plenty of shoulder real estate make it accessible to improvers when small and intermediates when big. Breaks consistently on any S swell, but easily blown out by any southern hemi wind. Mid to high tides and often crowded. **DON-DON** breaks in the middle of the bay, in front of the semi-submerged wooden fishing frames once the tide has moved in a few hours. Non-abrupt glide into predictable, easy walls that are a bit faster on the lefts. Like all the Grupuk spots, can get stupidly crowded with all skill levels in the water, so be wary and give the beginners room. **INSIDE GRUPUK** is mainly rights, unless small and fairly similar to the other waves in the bay, namely rolling, simple drops and slopey walls ideal for improving turn combos and generally cruising. Just as crowded as the other waves; pick up a boat

SPOT INFORMATION			
SPOT	SIZE	BTM	TYPE
⑤	10/3		
⑥	12/3		
⑦	6/3		
⑧	8/3		
⑨	6/2		
⑩	6/2		
⑪	4/2		
⑫	4/3		
⑬	6/2		
⑭	6/2		
⑮	6/2		
⑯	10/2		
⑰	6/3		
⑱	8/2		

OUTSIDE GRUPUK

RUSSEL MCCARTHY

MAWI

KIERAN NASH

in the village for easy access. The road coming from Kuta stops in **AMPANG**, an east facing village, so it requires a rare combination of S-SE swell and W wind. In these conditions, long bowling rights break south of the village at Awang, offering tubes over a shallow coral platform. **INSIDE EKAS** is a generously covered reef peak marooned in another deep bay/estuary that needs a moderate SW swell to wake up. Sucky and swift, the shorter rights feather up nicely and open up occasionally, as the SE trades blow into the barrel. Meanwhile, the longer lefts wall and roll predictably, inviting big hits in a playful, safe and therefore crowded environment. Low to mid tide for the rights, high for the lefts and any flavour E wind. The chaotic, powerful left at **OUTSIDE EKAS** shifts and jumps around the line-up below steep cliffs at the eastern headland. Consistently drags in far more swell than Inside Ekas, the high speed walls and odd tuck section can get really long at size, when it becomes an advanced surfers break. Currents are strong and hold-downs are long, plus there's sea-life and crowds. Out on the exposed SE tip of Lombok, a series of reef cuts and passes offer small swell options, including the lip-smacking performance ramps of **SEREWEH** up the eastern channel. If there's no sign of whitewash on these reefs, then Lombok is officially flat. Really a wet season option as a small SE swell and N winds are needed to make the long boat ride worth it. Hard to access by land, hard to scope by sea.

SWELL AND WIND

Wet season tropical cyclone positions can vary greatly, thus sending short-lived swell from a 180° window, packing as much power as winter depressions. Winds blow like clockwork: the mild E-SE trades start in April, SE being the major direction, up to October with more S winds towards the end of the season. November is a transition month with oscillating winds around SE-SW. Then, it shifts to W-NW with W first and then NW until end of March. Get a tide table online or in Bali and pay attention to the range: there is a big and a small tide every day, with many spots working only at mid to high tide. ●

TRAVEL INFORMATION

LOCAL POPULATION – 3.166,685   **TIME ZONE** – GMT +8h
COASTLINE – 464km (290mi)

GETTING THERE – Direct intl. flights from Singapore with Silk Air and from KL with Garuda and Air Asia to Selaparang Intl. Airport (AMI) near Mataram. Garuda, Lion Air and Merpati have daily flights from Denpasar, Jakarta and Surabaya from $50/rt. Standard ferries run between Padangbai (Bali) and Lembar ($3 o/w, 4h). Many fast boat services (Gili Cat, Blue Water Express, etc), but are more expensive than flying ($30 o/w, 2h; from Benoa). Taxi to Kuta (1h; $23) or ride public bemos from Mandalika terminal in Mataram.

GETTING AROUND – The road network is good although minor roads can be tricky; expect problems during wet season. Typical Indo bus and bemo services across the island – slow, rough but cheap. Rent a Suzuki for $35/d (insurance included) or a motorbike for $5/d. Charter a local fishing boat for around $12/d or get single 2-3hr rides to the waves in Grupuk bay for $2 per person (min 4). Week-long surf charters leave from Benoa Harbour, Bali to Desert Point and West Sumbawa, sometimes stopping in Grupuk and Ekas.

LODGING AND FOOD – Basic rooms in Kuta cost under $5, for more comfort head to the Kuta Indah Hotel (fr $32) or the luxurious Novotel. Very basic hut accommodation is available at Bangko-Bangko (Deserts) and Laut Surga (Ekas), where there are also new, expensive, surf tourist options. Lombok Surf Camp has all inclusive beginner packages from $550/wk in the soft Grupuk waves. For surf charters check Freeline, Surf Travel Online and dozens more offering a range of vessels, duration and price. Be aware only the purpose-built surf charters like Sri Noa Noa will sail the south coast in heavy seas; the local jukungs will go round the north. Lombok food revolves around poultry, meat and fish cooked with tropical veggies in spices and coconut milk sauce.

WEATHER – Lombok lies less than 400km (250mi) south of the Equator in the tropics. Days are almost universally 12hrs long with sunrise at around 6.20 a.m. and sunset at 6.30 p.m. The daytime temperature averages 30°C (86°F) all-year-long, but take warm clothing if planning a trek of Mt. Rinjani. Lombok's tropical monsoon climate has two distinct seasons: dry (May to September) and wet (October to April). Monsoon refers to the wind – even in the wet monsoon the rain tends to be short lived and localised. May, June and July are considered the best, while Jan-Feb suffer heavy rains and stifling hot temps. Water remains around an ideal 28°C (82°F), so a shorty would only be used for protection against the reef.

WEATHER	J/F	M/A	M/J	J/A	S/O	N/D
Total Rainfall (mm)	310	150	70	35	65	220
Consistency (d/m)	19	15	8	3	7	16
Temperature min. (°C)	25	25	25	24	25	25
Temperature max. (°C)	30	30	29	28	29	30

NATURE AND CULTURE – Trekking at least part of the way up Rinjani is the reason many tourists come to Lombok, take a packaged tour to join them. Activities include kite surfing, diving, snorkeling, fishing, cycling along the coastal road to appreciate the breathtaking cliff scenery, or even skateboard the bowl in Grupuk. Witness traditional culture in Relbitan and Sade, north of Kuta.

HAZARDS AND HASSLES – Desert Point is a super-gnarly wave; rips, shallow reef and crowds of frothing surfers all contribute to the danger; wear a helmet. Other spots break softer, but medical attention is more than an hour away in Mataram. Bring some reef boots. Theft stories are common. Tip someone to be a security guard for vehicles and belongings. Nearest bank is Praya (1hr), so take enough cash.

HANDY HINTS – Boards can be fixed or rented from Kuta Reef Surf Shop or Kimen Surf in Kuta. It's common practice to hire a local surfing guide. Bring a regular shortboard and a semi-gun, especially for Desert Point. Unlike in Hindu Bali, Islamic Sasaks make up 90% of Lombok's population.

SURF STATS		J	F	M	A	M	J	J	A	S	O	N	D
SWELL	Dominant swell												
	Size (m)	4-5		5-6		6-7		7-8		6		4-5	
	Consistency (%)	60		80		90		90		80		70	
WIND	Dominant wind												
	Average force	F3		F2		F3		F3		F3		F3	
	Consistency (%)	65		88		74		80		79		72	
TEMP.	Wetsuit												
	Water temp.	29		28		28		27		27		28	

WEST SUMBAWA

+ CONSISTENT SWELLS
+ WORLD-CLASS WAVES
+ SEMI-CROWDED
+ EXPLORATION POTENTIAL

– SE TRADE WIND RESTRICTS CHOICE
– SLOW OVERLAND ACCESS
– LACK OF ALTERNATIVE ACTIVITIES
– NO DIRECT FLIGHTS

Heading east from Lombok, the climate remains dry, supporting a brown, parched landscape of scrub and bush, clinging to lowland hills and a smattering of volcanoes. Sumbawa's Mt Tambora ejected 4 times the magma of Krakatau, killing 72,000 and caused the "year of no summer" in 1816. These days the island remains sparsely populated, infrastructure is rudimentary with few good roads and the bustling tourist towns of Bali and beyond have yet to materialise here. Surfers have however, carved out a couple of epicentres alongside the two best west-facing surfing coasts. Across the Alas Strait from Lombok, a concentrated stretch of sharp, shallow reefs leave little to the imagination with names like Super Suck and Scar Reef, attracting thrill seekers who are usually on one of the many charters cruising between Bali and Rote.

NORTHERN RIGHTS is a treacherous angle of reef that needs the biggest, straightest SW swell, mid tides and a rare N wind to make the journey up the channel worth it. There are other waves around if the swell is pumping, but generally the coves and bays of reef-protected beach hold little more than straighthanders. This theme continues down through Serewah Bay to the harbour and rivermouth at Labuhan Lalar, where once again a massive swell is needed to refract onto the reefy beach at **FLY**, hitting a right triangle and a few easy peaks along its length. Somewhere for improvers to escape the swell, but not the zillions of flies attracted to drying fish and the polluted river. **DOWNTOWNS** becomes the default wave when

Scar is too small or crowded and offers less critical peaks, including a nice right that sucks in swell and peels off the northern extremity of Jelenga Beach. This stretch has better coverage at mid to high tide and is an easy option paddling out through the keyhole if staying in the beach accommodation. **SCAR REEF** is the main attraction in West Sumbawa, offering multiple barrel opportunities for advanced surfers willing to take a risk with possibly the sharpest reef in Indo. It starts off fast with a throwing take-off, then constant tongues

ANDREW SHIELD

SCAR REEF
LAT: -8.854826° LONG: 116.758603°

This walled-up left showcases perfect bowls and racy lines leading into a series of inside backdoor sections. Constantly changing through the tide over this aptly named coral reef, low to mid tide is barrel city, often throwing out a new section before exiting the last, making poise and positioning paramount to drive on down the line. Nice roll-in take-offs at high tide open up the face for carves and creativity as the seriously sharp reef is buffered, but never ignored. High consistency, so it just depends how many charters are around for the crowd level, which should be intermediate plus.

SPOT INFORMATION — SPOT SIZE BTM TYPE (1–9)

LOMBOK · Alas Strait · SUMBAWA

NORTHERN RIGHTS ①
FLY ②
DOWNTOWNS ③
SCAR REEF ④
BENETE ⑤
SUPER SUCK ⑥
YO-YO'S – THE WEDGE ⑦
YO-YO'S – THE HOOK ⑧
SEJORONG ⑨

Pulau Kalong · Pulau Namo · Labuhan Tano · Poto Tano · Spakek · Seteluk · Kertasari · Taliwang · Labuhan Lahat · Jereweh · Maluk · Tg. Amat · Mangkun · Sejorong · Tongo

SAMA SAMA · KIMA SURF · WATERWAYS · FREELINE · TRUE BLUE · TRUE BLUE TRAVEL · ATOLL TRAVEL

of the lip flick out to swallow you as a series of backdoor sections demand high speed and clear positioning to thread the wave to the sketchy inside closeout. Its personality changes constantly as low tide madness becomes perfect mid-tide bowls, before giving way to fast sloping walls and envelopes at high. Can pick up quickly without warning, sometimes bringing cool, deep water from the channel and will handle triple overhead. Only 5km down the coast is **BENETE**, a major containership terminal and port, which gives you a clue as to how protected this deep bay is. Big NW swells have to bend plenty to create another classic left over a shallow shelf beneath cliffs. This one is top to bottom from the peak to the final section where it closes-out and there's nowhere to go if caught inside by the shifting peak. Inconsistent because E trade winds bump it up, while S-SW is offshore and it's only safely surfed at high tide. Maluk Bay is the home of **SUPER SUCK**, which continues the West Sumbawa pattern of a deep, cliff-lined bay, waiting for a bigger SW-W swell to show

YO-YOS – THE HOOK

BRAD MASTERS

TRAVEL INFORMATION

LOCAL POPULATION:
West Sumbawa – 530,117

COASTLINE: Sumbawa – 1309km (813mi)
TIME ZONE: GMT +8h

GETTING THERE – Sumbawa Besar (SWQ) is not on many airlines routes; Lion Air and Merpati link to SWQ from Lombok. Lion, Merpati and Kartika fly from Denpasar to Bima Regency, miles away. Sekongkan airport still has no service. From Bali, most people go overland; first a 4hr ferry to Lombok, then cross Lombok by car, bike or an 8hr bus followed by another 2hr ferry ride to Poto Tano then 1-2hr drive to Taliwang or Maluk; total travel time is 11-13hrs at best. Easiest of course, is to sail by charter boat out of Bali, surfing Lombok on the way. There are also expensive seaplane and fast boat options.

GETTING AROUND – The main road across the island follows the northern coastal route. The road infrastructure down the west coast has been improved since the Batu Hijau mine opened in 2000. From Sumbawa Besar airport, it's a further 3hr journey to Taliwang/Jereweh and the waves. All the waves are close to shore so no need to hire local fishing boats.

LODGING AND FOOD – Charter boats; Sri Noa Noa is an Australian owned 46' twin masted schooner ($1065/6d – Freeline). Kima boat goes as far as Scar ($1000/7d). Cheap, land-based losmen accommodation is available at Jelinggah (Scar), Maluk (Super Suck) and Sekongkang (Yo-Yo's) from $5/n. Supersuck Hotel starts at $25/n. The upscale Tropical Beach Club in Sekongkang caters to the ex-pat mining community, next to the charter airstrip.

WEATHER – Warm to hot temperatures, regular sea breezes and some overnight rains temper the dry season from May-Oct. The average temp is 28°C (82°F). Nov-April is wetter, cloudier and hotter. Jan-Feb suffers from heavy rains and stifling hot temperatures. Warm clothing is needed for forays into the mountains. West Sumbawa is drier than the eastern end of the island and the brown, scrubby hillsides explode with greenery during the wet. Water temps are a stable 28°C (82°F) year-round. Boardies and a rashy plus a shorty and booties for protection against the nasty sharp reefs at Scars and Super Suck.

WEATHER	J/F	M/A	M/J	J/A	S/O	N/D
Total Rainfall (mm)	300	177	105	55	77	172
Consistency (d/m)	18	13	8	5	7	13
Temperature min. (°C)	23	23	23	23	23	23
Temperature max. (°C)	29	31	31	31	30	30

NATURE AND CULTURE – Boat charter flat day options include good fishing and snorkelling, otherwise take a long book. Sumbawa is not as culturally rich as Bali. There are some great buffalo races in the rice paddies, but most of the more interesting sites are a long way inland.

HAZARDS AND HASSLES – Hitting the reef is going to be your major worry. Malaria is also a problem (take a net) and travelling overland will be slow and frustrating.

HANDY HINTS – Take everything you need (no surf shops) including an Indo gun for those frequent 8ft+ conditions. This trip is usually linked in with one to Lombok. Be very careful of cheap offers in Bali, scams happen!

its world-class colours. The name says it all, especially at low tide, which is usually only surfed by bodyboarders or the very best tube technicians and depth is measured in inches. Take-offs are beyond critical and require an angled, straight into the barrel approach, which briefly lets up before increasing speed towards the inevitable straight reef shut-down. A resort and some cheap losmens hold the bulk of the keen, patient crowd, bolstered by boats descending when this fickle wave finally fires. Crowded and intense. Sekongkang Bay is a swell magnet, with a couple of exposed slabs referred to as **YO-YO'S** thanks to the refraction off the cliffs. **THE WEDGE** does just that as smaller S-W swells bounce off the towering cliffs to form a steep but easy drop into a short punchy right that sucks up nicely before it ends abruptly. **THE HOOK** sits further down the reef where it curves into a proper channel and is more likely to hold up and spin off some makeable barrels. Neither spot handles SE trades nor major swells, so small, glassy mornings at mid tide are best. Around the headland the coast begins facing south around **SEJORONG**, which is over-exposed to swell and wind. Off-season NW winds combined with smaller ground and windswells will hit a long reef pass, shaping up some section, speed walls to shoulders that are rarely ridden by passing boats. Bad currents may also bring tailings from the massive Batu Hijau open cut copper and gold mine that reputedly dumps into the ocean and rivers around here. Further west is an even better right reef pass and then miles of wilderness waves waiting for the SE trades to die off.

SWELL AND WIND

Sumbawa receives all the normal Indonesian swell trains and the 6-12ft (2-4m) swells from April-Oct are needed to penetrate the western bays. Statistically, the Western Sumbawa Alas Strait doesn't quite get the same amount of long period, bigger swells that hit Bali and Java and 5 star days are rarer. Slight variations include less swells from a due S direction and W swells are blocked, so only pulses that

are 15° either side of SW will get in. The E-SE trades can be reliable (80% of the time) and very strong, averaging 25km/h (16mph) in July, but mornings can still be offshore as cool mountain air descends to the coast before convection brings the sea breeze. During the off-season the wind shifts to a W-NW direction, starting with W predominance and moving around to a NW direction towards the end of March. This is a good time to check the south coast or head to Lakey Peak. Download the diurnal tide chart so you know when the big tide is going to give the shallow reefs enough cover. ●

SURF STATS		J	F	M	A	M	J	J	A	S	O	N	D
SWELL	Dominant swell												
	Size (m)	4		5		6		7		5-6		4	
	Consistency (%)	60		80		90		90		80		70	
WIND	Dominant wind												
	Average force	F3		F2		F3		F3		F3		F3	
	Consistency (%)	65		88		74		80		79		72	
TEMP.	Wetsuit												
	Water temp.	29		28		28		27		27		28	

CENTRAL SUMBAWA

+ DENSITY OF WORLD-CLASS SPOTS
+ CONSISTENT CONDITIONS
+ LEFTS AND RIGHTS
+ DRY SURF SEASON
+ CHEAP, EXOTIC, LOW TRAFFIC

− SOMETIMES VERY WINDY
− LONG PADDLES
− TRICKY LOW TIDES
− CROWDS
− BAD PUBLIC TRANSPORT ACCESS

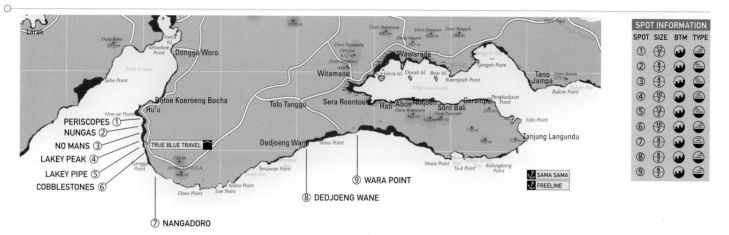

PERISCOPES ①
NUNGAS ②
NO MANS ③
LAKEY PEAK ④
LAKEY PIPE ⑤
COBBLESTONES ⑥
⑦ NANGADORO
⑧ DEDJOENG WANE
⑨ WARA POINT
TRUE BLUE TRAVEL
√ SAMA SAMA
√ FREELINE

While many of the charter boats leaving Bali head east towards Nusa Tenggara, they usually only make it as far as the west coast of Sumbawa, so to get to the fabled waves of Teluk Cempi Bay in Central Sumbawa means a long, tedious journey by plane and taxi from Bali. Just south of Hu'u, Lakey (Lakai) Beach, is a long, wide, palm-lined stretch of ivory sand, fronted by reef. Since its discovery by Australian surfers in the mid '80s, Hu'u has been known to offer a varied selection of waves for every ability & taste. The total number of visiting surfers in the area can hit 150-200, especially when early morning high tides are happening, producing the best waves in glassy conditions. An extensive 500m wide lagoon needs to be negotiated to get out to the reef and at low tide some more rock-hopping is required.

PERISCOPES is a 40 minute walk, but only a short 100m paddle-out. This wave requires a big swell with more S in it and can hold up to double overhead. Hit it early in the morning with a coinciding high tide, as this wave needs plenty of water over the reef to make it out of the barrel onto the shoulder. This is a natural footers tube riding paradise so expect crowds of 'em! NUNGAS can peel off like a mini version of G-land, grooming 200m long lefts with alternating shack and whack sections to play with. Many surfers get diverted on the long walk to Periscopes, opting for long ride, short walk. Nungas bends into a big calm bay, happily accepting more size than the Peak and not too much S in the afternoon trades. 300m right of Lakey Peak is a shut down section of reef called NO MANS that may have a short shallow ride in small, lumpy swells. LAKEY PEAK (see next page). Just 400 meters to the south is LAKEY PIPE, a gnarly reef with a fairly sedate take-off, which then hits the shelf and throws out a solid backdoor barrel that leaves enough space to drive a small

ROGER SHARP

PERISCOPES

LAKEY PEAK
LAT. -8.80479°   LONG. 118.378°

Perfect Lakey Peak peels off short, 30-40m lefts and rights into channels either side. The right will often throw up backdoor tube rides but gets too shallow at low tide, when the left is churning out predictable, ideal speed barrel rides. Mid tide lip-smacking sessions will appeal to intermediates and the flattish reef is user-friendly, except during full or new moon phases. Getting out to the Peak is easy by either paddling the 450m or taking the zodiac for around $2 return. Lakey Peak can hold juicy sized waves, but the optimum time to hit it is when it's in that perfect headhigh plus range.

car through. Optimum at mid to high tide and double overhead, but the Pipe can also take it from tiny to triple. Walk 45mins (or rent a zodiac) to escape the Lakey crowds at a deep reef channel called COBBLESTONES. Nice walled-up rights on one side and lefts barrelling into the channel opposite, pick up more swell and handle some solid size at mid to high tides. Arrange a lift on a motorbike to get to NANGADORO that offers both a spinning left and two right reefs, which pick up more swell than any other spot. Enjoy the hot springs.

On small days with NW winds, venture to the south coast where great rights occasionally hit DEDJOENG WANE during the off-season. In the same conditions, check the outside reefbreaks at WARA POINT, 4km south of Sondo and a very long paddle.

SWELL AND WIND

Winter (May-September) is prime surf season, overloaded with 3-12ft (1-4m) swells, but plagued by sideshore afternoon trades. The SE trade winds start in April and the skies begin to dry. Mornings are often light offshores. The really windy season starts from the end of July until middle of November with 13-25 knots trades and the wind is cross-shore on the beach. Being the wet season, the official Indo off-season, November through February is not the best time of year for surf, but there is the chance of some cyclone swell and south coast spots will be offshore in the W-NW winds. The diurnal tide (one radical change per day) is a factor, so get a tide chart to plan your trip around AM highs. ●

ANDREW SHIELD

ROGER SHARP

LAKEY PEAK

TRAVEL INFORMATION

LOCAL POPULATION:
Dompu/Bima Regencies – 800,000
TIME ZONE: GMT +8h

COASTLINE:
Sumbawa – 1309km (813mi)

GETTING THERE – Don't bring in more than 3 boards – heavy fines. Sumbawa ferries depart from Labuhan, Lombok and reach Poto Sano in 2h, but it's unreliable. Best is by plane using the 5/wk Merpati flight, which wont carry big boardbags. Bima r/t flight costs about $165. Best to get a pick up from your hotel.

GETTING AROUND – Land transport is much more difficult to get than in Bali. Take a taxi-bemo or a bus from Bima (5h from Sumbawa Besar) to Dompu's Ginte Bus Terminal then take a cidomo (horse cart) to the Lepardi Bus Terminal. Or charter a bemo from Bima to Hu'u (2-3h) for about $35 per person, or private transfers $70-80 per vehicle one way.

LODGING AND FOOD – Growing number of places to stay in Lakey, 3km south of Hu'u. Aman Gati Hotel has 40 rooms (fr$49/dbl). 7nt package from Bali; (fr$470). Next door are Lakey Peak Surf Houses and bungalows (fr$35-$130/n). The original 22 room Mona Lisa Bungalows with well-maintained places ($15/nt). Aircon can almost double the room rate. Food is cheap.

WEATHER – Sumbawa is a transitional volcanic island and it has a tropical monsoonal climate. The wet season generally occurs from November through February with heavy monsoon rainfall and clouds. The dry season, from May to October, can still experience rain but is generally fine, clear and hot. Average annual rainfall is 1350mm (53in). Temps are relatively warm, ranging from 23-32°C (74-90°F) all year-round. It can be breezy around August and September, but boardshorts and a rashie should do.

WEATHER	J/F	M/A	M/J	J/A	S/O	N/D
Total Rainfall (mm)	229	177	105	55	77	172
Consistency (d/m)	18	13	8	5	7	13
Temperature min. (°C)	23	23	23	23	23	23
Temperature max. (°C)	29	31	31	31	30	30

NATURE AND CULTURE – Not as lively as Bali. Visit Bima Sultan Palace on 99 old teak stilts, see Raba Dompu weaving village and Doro Bata relics in Dompu. Dompu is used by tourists as a stopover point to Mount Tambora. The trek takes 2 nights camping in a rain forest and 1 night to the 2,851m (9354ft) summit. Check Komodo island for its famous dragons.

HAZARDS AND HASSLES – The reef at Lakey Pipe can be nasty and long walks on low tide reef make booties almost compulsory. Surfing has 30 years of history, so there are now 2nd generation locals. It can be a bit aggro for the best conditions. Walk to the more remote spots – take good shoes and enough water. Low malaria risks.

HANDY HINTS – There are no surf shops around Lakey apart from wax at some of the hotels. A gun could be necessary for the 6-10ft (2-3m) days. There are rarely boat trips to Lakey area as boats go Bali - West Sumbawa or Sumba - Rote.

SURF STATS		J	F	M	A	M	J	J	A	S	O	N	D
SWELL	Dominant swell	◕		◕		◕		◕		◕		◕	
	Size (m)	4		5		6		7		5-6		4	
	Consistency (%)	60		80		90		90		90		70	
WIND	Dominant wind	◑		◔		◔		◔		◔		◑	
	Average force	F3		F2		F3		F3		F3		F3	
	Consistency (%)	65		88		74		80		79		72	
TEMP.	Wetsuit	🏄		🏄		🏄		🏄		🏄		🏄	
	Water temp.	29		28		28		27		27		28	

SUMBA

NIHIWATU

JS CALLAHAN/SURFEXPLORE

East Nusa Tenggara (NTT) is, in many ways, different from the rest of Indonesia. NTT includes 566 islands, of which only 42 are inhabited, and the bulk of the population live on the three main islands of Timor, Flores and Sumba. It is geographically, ethnically and culturally a border area where the transition from Asia to Australia and Micronesia takes places. Deep offshore trenches and inter-island channels allow plenty of swell to hit the southwest-facing coast of Sumba, where waves of consequence get thrown onto the reefs of dead coral, volcanic rock and boulders. Sumba is not for everyone; the food and accommodation are basic and the mixed ethnic population speak 3 different languages. Huge megalithic tombs and thatched, peaked huts dot the landscape, while in the line-up, intrepid travellers are now sampling the oceanic power of this ancient island.

PERO RIGHTS are tricky and unforgiving with a sketchy cliff, dead-end section, requiring wet season NW-N winds. Must be well overhead to start breaking, making it a low consistency, experts only wave. The western tip of the island is generally better during the dry season when E-SE winds blow cross/offshore for the lefts. Across the rivermouth channel, **PERO LEFTS** can be excellent as swell is refracted heavily into big bowl sections with ample tube-time. Highly consistent, this wave holds as big as it gets and there is decent accommodation in Pero at Homestay Story. The fringing reef at **WAINJAPU** consistently holds long makeable lefts, providing there's not too much W in the swell. Potentially good rights on the other side of the bay. Explore eastwards for a few quality, hard to find reefs. **PANTAI MAROSI** is actually a big, shifty, deepwater right with power and long hold-downs in chunky SW swells. The scenic bay is sensitive to wind plus there's an outside left and a small swell, hazard-free beachbreak. The often debated case of **NIHIWATU** is quite unique in Indonesia, since the deluxe resort claims exclusive use of

"Occy's Lefts" for the happy-few who can afford it. Founder Claude Graves says it avoids the usual surf-slum scenario and generates more benefits for the local communities. The famous lefts work on any size, the bigger the better and get really fast and hollow at low tide. Fat righthanders break across the bay from Nihiwatu and there are Sunset style rights and lefts on the next point that can be accessed by boat or car in about one hour. There is also a righthand reef wave at the end of the beach that breaks on small days. The rivermouth at **WAINUKAKA** is better in the wet season and almost only rideable at high tide with quality rights and lefts over a constantly changing sandy bottom. Stay at Homestay Ahong in Rua or Aloha Hotel in Waikabukak. Only 3hrs drive from Waingapu, **MILLER'S RIGHTS** in Tarimbang are probably Sumba's most ridden wave and the line-up is sometimes crowded from May to Sept. Fortunately, the wave is so long it could soak up a big crowd, and fast, hollow sections split the pack into clusters between the softer shoulders that are quite accessible to improver/intermediates. Waves can be a bit funky with SE trades, but they break year-round and are usually clean early morning and during the wet season. It takes a bit of effort to get to the beautiful horseshoe bay and a further 15min walk or 20min paddle from the beach accommodation at Marthens Homestay. Big wave chargers may look at the offshore location known as **MANGKUDU ISLAND**, where the challenging lefts can reach 15ft (5m) plus there is a mellower right on the other side, only offshore during the wet season. Mangkudu made headline news when the army came to occupy the island, supposedly taken over by surfers! There is a surf camp. East Sumba is actually the name of the first surf lodge located in Kallala next to 3 fairly consistent lefts working on different swells and tides. **THE OFFICE** is an all-round wave, suited to most surfers, offering fun, lazy walls, the odd cover-up and a forgiving nature, plus there's empty beachbreak for beginners on the inside. **RACETRACK** is more challenging with a steep drop into a barrel section and fast walls, best tackled at mid tide. **FIVE-0** hits a bend in the reef and throws some serious lips, attracting the skilled surfers willing to take a chance on the highest tides in exchange for some big shacks.

SPOT INFORMATION			
SPOT	SIZE	BTM	TYPE
①	15/6		
②	9/3		
③	10/3		
④	12/3		
⑤	12/3		
⑥	8/3		
⑦	10/3		
⑧	15/4		
⑨	6/2		
⑩	6/2		
⑪	10/3		

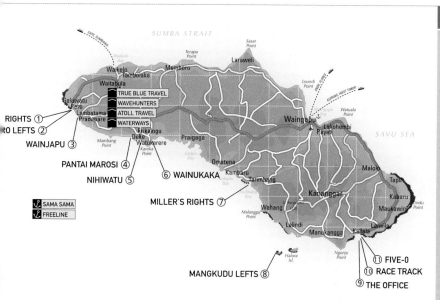

Map labels:

SUMBA STRAIT

Sapé Sumbawa
Waikelo Bay
Terapa Point
Sasar Point
Laraweli
Memboro
Loundi Point
Kupang West Timor
Watuala Point
Waingapu
Lakohembi
Payeti
SAVU SEA
Maiolo
Tapil
Kabaru
Maukawini
Undu Point
Kanangar
Kambaru
Tarimbang
Wahang
Malanggu Point
Lalindi
Laiwila
Manukangga
Kaliala
Halura Isl.
Ngunju Point

Wakelo
Tambolaka
Waitabula
Galuwatu
Pero
Lambatama
Pradapare
Arikalogu
Deke
Watukarere
Karoka Point
Mambang Point
Praigaga
Landipi Bay
Omatena

TRUE BLUE TRAVEL
WAVEHUNTERS
ATOLL TRAVEL
WATERWAYS

RIGHTS ①
RO LEFTS ②
WAINJAPU ③
PANTAI MAROSI ④
NIHIWATU ⑤
⑥ WAINUKAKA
MILLER'S RIGHTS ⑦
MANGKUDU LEFTS ⑧

⑪ FIVE-0
⑩ RACE TRACK
⑨ THE OFFICE

SAMA SAMA
FREELINE

WIND AND SWELL

Dry season (Mar-Oct) Indian Ocean swells can sometimes reach 12-15ft (4-5m) from a SSW- WSW direction. The main trend is the SE trades, which blow-out many exposed spots, especially from June-Sept. Unlike Bali, the trades don't blow consistently during the day, instead there are on and off windy periods. Obviously, trades gets stronger as the day progress, but sometimes thunderstorms can change wind patterns, so early and late glass-offs are common. Expect many 6-12ft (2-4m) days with windy line-ups, better suited for experienced surfers. Because of the deep ocean trench and direct SW swell exposure, Sumba gets big, with less nooks and crannies than western Nusa Tenggara islands. That's why the wet season (Nov -April)

SURF STATS		J F	M A	M J	J A	S O	N D
SWELL	Dominant swell	◉	◉	◉	◉	◉	◉
	Size (m)	3	4	5	5-6	4-5	3
	Consistency (%)	60	80	85	90	85	60
WIND	Dominant wind	◑	◓	◔	◔	◔	◑
	Average force	F3-F4	F2-F3	F3-F4	F3-F4	F3	F2-F3
	Consistency (%)	72	71	74	74	79	56
TEMP.	Wetsuit	🏄	🏄	🏄	🏄	🏄	🏄
	Water temp.	29	29	28	26	27	29

MILLER'S RIGHTS

TRAVEL INFORMATION

POPULATION: 611,954   TIME ZONE: GMT +8h
COASTLINE: 593km (369mi)

GETTING THERE – From Bali, almost daily flights to Waingapu (WGP) served by Trigana Air, Pelita Air, or Merpati Airlines, cost around $97 o/w. Nusantara Airlines (Twin Otters) 3 times a week from Denpasar or Kupang to Tambolaka (TMC), situated between Waikabukak and Waikelo seaport. Ferries link Waingapu with Flores, Savu and Timor.

GETTING AROUND – This dry, mountainous island stretches 210km (130mi) along a NW-SE axis, 40-70km (25-44mi) wide. Waikabubak and Waingapu are 137km (85mi) apart, about 3-5h by bus. Daily trucks trundle 5hrs between Waingapu-Tarimbang\$3. To rent a car with driver will cost $60/day min and go slow through winding roads. 1h drive = $10. 1h boat = $18. Motorbike hire from $8/d. Lots of daily commuting between homestays and spots.

LODGING AND FOOD – Choose between cheap & basic homestays near the surf or hotels as far as 45mins away. East Sumba camps $60/d; Marthens (Tarimbang) $20/d inc. food; Ahong (Wainukaka) or Aloha Hotel are $10/d. Nihiwatu 5 days min. $5k+ (7n/dbl). Le Nautile (Marosi) $90/d. Story (Pero) $10/d. Cheap food at about $5 a meal. Most charters (Sama Sama, Indo, Sri Noa Noa) will sail out of Kupang, West Timor and take in Rote and Savu, before making the long crossing to Sumba.

WEATHER – NTT has a semi-arid climate, with moderately low rainfall during the SE monsoon (Apr-Nov), because it lies in the rain-shadow of the Australian continent. West Sumba is far wetter, turning green and fertile in the wet season, while East Sumba is more dry and mountainous (highest peak is 1,225m/4020ft). Temps vary from hot in coastal areas (30-35°C/86°-95°F) to very cool in mountainous areas (15-17°C/59°-63°F). There is a dry season (May to November), and a rainy season (December to April). In many coastal areas not a drop of rain falls during most of the year. The coastal rainfall varies between 50-200mm (2-8in) a year, up to 1,625mm (65in) in the west Sumba mountains. Boardshorts year-round.

WEATHER	J/F	M/A	M/J	J/A	S/O	N/D
Total Rainfall (mm)	340	140	20	5	10	150
Consistency (d/m)	18	8	1	0	1	13
Temperature min. (°C)	24	24	24	23	24	25
Temperature max. (°C)	28	30	31	30	32	31

NATURE AND CULTURE – Sumba is well known for its sandalwood, horses, impressive megalithic tombs and typical hand woven textile (*ikat*). The most spectacular ceremony is the Pasola, the ritual fight with spears featuring hundreds of horsemen. It is a wild martial event, and although the government now insists on blunted spears, serious injuries are common and occasional deaths.

HAZARDS AND HASSLES – Reef cuts and long hold-downs are guaranteed. Anticipation will be the key as spots work on specific conditions and hopping from one spot to another is slow and tedious by road. Take malaria pills. Be patient.

HANDY HINTS – Most charters (Sama Sama, Indo Odyssey, Sri Noa Noa) will sail out of Kupang, West Timor and take in Rote and Savu, before making the long crossing to Sumba. Take a gun during dry season and as much supplies as you can carry. If you go feral, you need to speak Bahasa Indonesian.

is also a good time to consider for friendlier conditions at the rights of Tarimbang, Wainukaka or Mangkudu with NW winds being offshore. Nusa Tenggara has more extreme tidal range than the rest of Indonesia, with a big tide and small tide everyday, ranging up to 8ft (2.4m). Finding tide charts is difficult and some spots are best on the bigger spring tides. ●

SAVU AND ROTE

+ MELLOW, ACCESSIBLE WAVES
+ CHEAP LOSMEN OPTION
+ FEW CHARTER BOAT CROWDS
+ PERFECT DRY SEASON WEATHER

– SMALL SWELL WINDOW
– STRONG TRADE WINDS AFTER 10AM
– LACK OF NIGHTLIFE
– ISOLATED SPOTS WITH NO LAND ACCESS

Shaped by the chain of powerful volcanoes that stretch right across Sumatra and Java, the 550 islands of East Nusa Tenggara differ greatly from western Indonesia. Hot, dry trade winds blowing from Australia make for an arid landscape in direct contrast to typical Indonesian tropical rainforests. Coupled with geographical isolation from the main Indonesian surf hubs, the islands of Savu (also spelt Sawu, Sabu, Hawu, etc) and Rote have remained a bit of a frontier, with most surfers looking to escape the Bali crowds heading to Nusa Tenggara's more accessible islands of Lombok and Sumbawa. Tucked in above Australia, this region has a narrow swell window with only its SW corner facing the Indian Ocean swells, so can suffer flat spells when the rest of Indo is working on a due S. But in typical Indo fashion, minor islands can hide major surf breaks and Rote, Savu and the surrounding outcrops are no exception, roaring to life in a straight SW swell.

More than a 160kms west of Rote lies tiny **PULAU DANA**, where its long, barrelling left pointbreak and attendant right pick up all available swell and the only locals are turtles. Left is offshore in the trades, the right isn't. **RAIJUA** has a set of classic lefts on the SW tip of this remote, desolate island, including a really long, smoking fast, lower tide left that can barrel top-to-bottom for long sections. There's also a wild, rippy outside bombie at high and an insane, cliff-hugging wedge. The left and wedge work better in W swell and more S in the wind. These waves are only ever surfed by the passing charters, at the halfway mark between Sumba and Rote. Savu is the biggest island (pop. 30,000), but it's definitely off the beaten path and local infrastructure is not geared to western tourists, so once

again, it's boat access only. **SAVU LEFTS** hit a coral fringe near the main town Seba, lining up some heavy walls with hollow sections if the swell is strong enough and the trades are offshore. **SAVU RIGHTS** are extremely fickle, occasionally firing off perfect right drainers down a swell-sheltered reef that gets blown to bits by the trades. Needs a massive swell to wrap around with as much W direction as possible to create some ruler-edged wonders and probably the best barrel in the east. The wind swell combo means most people get skunked waiting for this one. Lying just off the SW tip of Timor, Rote is the southernmost island in Indonesia. Some surf spots are located on offshore islands and require chartering a boat. **NDAO** is only 15km offshore, but the people are very different and have their own language. The western reef tip has good exposure to swell and holds a left in any type of E wind plus there's a right further S in glass or N winds. Both feature fast, steep drops and racy walls. The cross-currents don't help and there's a good chance of seeing some reef

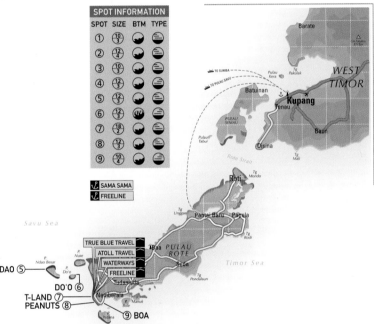

SPOT INFORMATION			
SPOT	SIZE	BTM	TYPE
①	10/2		
②	12/3		
③	10/3		
④	12/3		
⑤	12/3		
⑥	12/3		
⑦	18/2		
⑧	12/3		
⑨	10/4		

SAMA SAMA
FREELINE

NEMBERALA

JS CALLAHAN/SURFEXPLORE

SAVU RIGHTS
JS CALLAHAN/SURFEXPLORE

TRAVEL INFORMATION

LOCAL POPULATION:
Rote – 60,000, Savu – 30,000

COASTLINE: Rote – 291km (180mi)
TIME ZONE: GMT +8h

GETTING THERE – Direct flights to Kupang (KOE) with Merpati, Garuda, Batavia and Mandala from Jakarta, Surabaya, Bali, Sumba and Flores. Airnorth fly from Darwin to Dili, but not Kupang anymore. Daily morning ferries link Bolok, Kupang to Pantai Baru, Rote ($4, 4h), or fast Baharai Express from Tenau, Kupang Bay to Ba'a harbor ($10-14, 2h), then it's a 2h drive to Nemberala. Rough seas can cause cancellations since the slow ferry sank in 2006, killing around 40 people.

GETTING AROUND – To get around the island, rent a bike, a motorbike or go to Busalangga or Ba'a to hire a bemo for a day. Charter a local boat to reach the nearby offshore islands. Take the Savu ferry from Kupang (twice a week, overnight 9 hrs, fr$5), which continues on to Sumba. Some surf charter boats offer the full crossing to Sumba and Sumbawa, others just cruise around Rote.

LODGING AND FOOD – Cheap losmen accommodation close to T-Land usually includes food (Anugurah; Tirosa fr $10/n). Waterways, Atoll Travel and True Blue all book the comfortable Nemberala Beach Resort (fr $190/p/n inc. surf boat transfers). Freeline book Malole Surf House created by '65 World Champ Felipe Pomar (fr $1950/12n inc. transfers + zodiac) plus one of the only late season boats, the Sri Noa Noa (fr$2660/12n inc Bali-Kupang flights). The Sama Sama does early season charters (fr $1800/10n). There are only a few places to stay on Savu. Nightlife is quiet around Nemberala, with only a few little restaurants to try for a change of scene.

WEATHER – Central highlands and closeness to Australia make for irregular seasons in the area, but the long dry season (May-Oct) makes the islands semi-arid. The dry season is warm but rarely too hot, tempered by sea breezes and some overnight rains. Average air temp is 30°C (86°F) and the water around 28°C (82°F). Nov-April is rainier and cloudier, while Jan-Feb suffers heavy rains and is considered a time to avoid.

WEATHER	J/F	M/A	M/J	J/A	S/O	N/D
Total Rainfall (mm)	340	140	20	5	10	150
Consistency (d/m)	18	8	1	0	1	13
Temperature min. (°C)	24	24	24	23	24	25
Temperature max. (°C)	28	30	31	30	32	31

NATURE AND CULTURE – Nemberala's reef supports varied marine life – go snorkelling. Check out the ikats (woven textiles). Rote's unique palm hats and dance to the sound of the sasando, the 20 stringed local guitars made of lontar palm that also supplies boat & housing material plus sweet, nutritious (sometimes alcoholic!) tuak. Animist rituals still take place on Savu.

HAZARDS AND HASSLES – T-Land is a mellow wave, until it gets big and the reef is not so sharp. Most other spots break harder and closer to the reef. A boat trip in this area guaranties less crowds. Chloroquine resistant malaria has been reported; take precautions. East Timor's independence in May 2002 has helped to decrease tensions in the area.

HANDY HINTS – Pick up any surf accessories in Bali. Bring your shortboard and an Indo gun if you want to charge huge T-Land. Learning a little Indonesian will help you get around an area of many obscure dialects. Respect local beliefs in Savu, no matter how strange!

sharks out here. In the land of lefts, a long right like **DO'O** is welcomed, but facing almost north, it mainly works before or after the standard surf season in glassy or NW winds. Higher tides needed to cover the sharp coral reef. Baa is the main city on Rote, but Nemberala Beach, with its reefbreak and white sandy beach, is the place to be for surfers and tourists alike. The local spot, **T-LAND**, is a consistent left with 3-4 sections that can connect for a 300m+ ride. The name may sound like G-Land, but this is a much more accessible wave, that peels at low tide and walls up at high tide if the swell is around the headhigh range. When a moderate to large SW pulse arrives, it transforms into a heavy barrel and speed wall combo at double to triple overhead. Can have a lot of people out, but the long 25min walk from the beach and paddling between the take-off spots spreads the pack. Other waves in the area include the low tide bombie peak over the channel plus the inside reef beginners waves near the fishing boat harbour. North of T-Land there's more quality like Suckie Mama's short, round rights and a choice of slow or fast loping lefts at the openings in the barrier reef. If the swell is breaking up, a 30min bike ride to the exposed outside reef of **PEANUTS** will offer more intense barrels over a shallower reef than the neighbouring T-Land. Not as long and more wind sensitive, but superb reef on its day plus some rights on the correct swell direction. If there's enough push in the swell, **BOA** will wake up and hiss along an east-facing setup that's hollow, challenging and unlikely to be good unless its blowing W or light winds.

WIND AND SWELL

Roaring Forties lows send plenty of 6-12ft (2-4m) swell from April-October but the swell window for the West Timor region is smaller than much of Indonesia. Swell direction is critical and the more W the better, which usually makes September more reliable than the biggest month June. Swell charts often show Bali getting pounded while Rote is much smaller on the fringe of the arriving swell. The E-SE trade winds can be strong, consistently in June, and kicking up an underlying SE windswell. Winds shift to a more southerly direction from September on, which is still offshore for the west-facing lefts, but other spots should be surfed before 10am. The

off-season is dominated by lower strength SW-NW winds, buffing the rare east-facing locations, but combined with inconsistent swell, means the summer season is a gamble that rarely pays out. Early/late season should be the best time for a boat trip, before the trades strengthen, making navigation and anchorage more difficult. There is a big tide and a small tide every day and some spots only work on certain stages. ●

SURF STATS	J	F	M	A	M	J	J	A	S	O	N	D
SWELL Dominant swell	◕		◕		◕		◕		◕		◕	
Size (m)	3		4		5		5-6		4-5		3	
Consistency (%)	60		80		85		90		85		60	
WIND Dominant wind	◗		◔		◔		◔		◖		◑	
Average force	F3-F4		F3		F3-F4		F3-F4		F3		F2-F3	
Consistency (%)	72		71		74		74		79		56	
TEMP. Wetsuit	🩳		🩳		🩳		🩳		🩳		🩳	
Water temp.	29		29		27		26		27		29	

Freeline

Indonesian Surf
Adventures

Since 1992

www.freelinesurf.com.au

www.anloran.com

A SURF CHARTER BY
SURFERS JUST FOR SURFERS

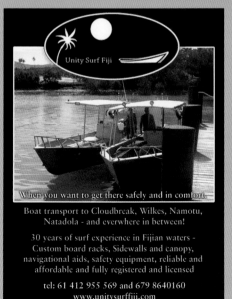
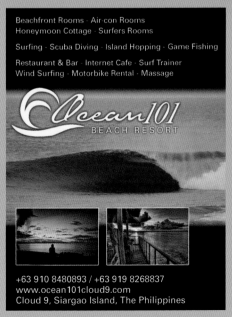

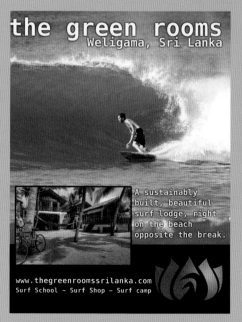
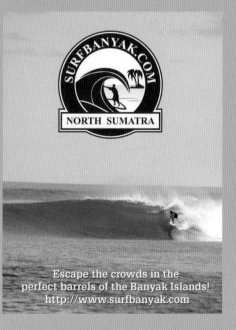
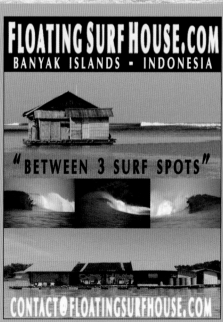

PIPELINE, OAHU NORTH SHORE, HAWAII

INDEX